FILM CRITICISM, THE COLD WAR, AND THE BLACKLIST

The publisher gratefully acknowledges the generous support
of the Humanities Endowment Fund of the University
of California Press Foundation.

Film Criticism, the Cold War, and the Blacklist

Reading the Hollywood Reds

JEFF SMITH

UNIVERSITY OF CALIFORNIA PRESS

Berkeley Los Angeles London

University of California Press, one of the most distinguished university presses in the United States, enriches lives around the world by advancing scholarship in the humanities, social sciences, and natural sciences. Its activities are supported by the UC Press Foundation and by philanthropic contributions from individuals and institutions. For more information, visit www.ucpress.edu.

University of California Press
Berkeley and Los Angeles, California

University of California Press, Ltd.
London, England

A portion of chapter 5, "The Cross and the Sickle: Allegorical Representations of the Blacklist in Historical Films," is derived from the the article titled "Are You Now or Have You Ever Been a Christian?: The Strange History of *The Robe* as Political Allegory," which was published by Manchester University Press in *Film Studies*, no. 7 (winter 2005): 1–31. ISSN 1469–0314. This revised version of chapter 5 is republished by permission. © 2005 Manchester University Press.

Library of Congress Cataloging-in-Publication Data

Smith, Jeff, 1962–.
    Film criticism, the Cold War, and the blacklist : reading the Hollywood Reds / Jeff Smith.
        pages   cm
    Includes bibliographical references and index.
    ISBN 978-0-520-28067-0 (cloth : alk. paper)
    ISBN 978-0-520-28068-7 (pbk. : alk. paper)
    ISBN 978-0-520-95851-7 (e-book)
    1. Motion pictures—Political aspects—United States.   2. Motion pictures—United States—History—20th century.   3. Cold War in motion pictures.   4. Communism and motion pictures—United States.   5. Blacklisting of entertainers—United States—History—20th century.   I. Title.
    PN1995.9.P6S65   2014
    791.43 6582825—dc23   2013037614

Manufactured in the United States of America

23 22 21 20 19 18 17 16 15 14
10 9 8 7 6 5 4 3 2 1

The paper used in this publication meets the minimum requirements of ANSI/NISO Z39.48–1992 (R 2002) (*Permanence of Paper*).

Contents

Illustrations

Tables

Acknowledgments

Any time a book takes as long to write as this one has, one finds that there are many, many people who provided assistance and help along the way. The origins of *Film Criticism, the Cold War, and the Blacklist* date back to my time at Washington University in St. Louis. At the outset I especially want to thank William Paul for his early encouragement. In convincing me to pursue other areas of academic interest beyond that of sound and music, Bill greatly helped me to expand my horizons as a film critic and historian. Many of my other colleagues at Wash U also merit my gratitude, including Richard Chapman, Wayne Fields, Gerald Early, Robert Hegel, Pier Marton, Lori Turner, and Rafia Zafar. I also want to thank the students in the seminar I taught my first semester there, particularly Annie Gilbert, Richie Zevins, Michael Bowley, and Jordan Fischler. I also wish to express my appreciation to the many friends I had in St. Louis, especially Jon Graas, Matthew Shipe, and Matt Nicholas. Our semiregular vinyl record parties helped keep me sane as I forged ahead with the research and writing on this project.

In 2006 I got the extraordinary opportunity to return to my Badger roots and to join a fraternity for which I have always had the utmost respect and admiration: the film faculty at the University of Wisconsin–Madison. It is a great pleasure to have such warm and wonderful colleagues. Vance Kepley deserves special mention for sending me into the archives more than thirty years ago to see what I could find out about Dalton Trumbo. Lea Jacobs, J. J. Murphy, Kelley Conway, Ben Singer, and Masha Belodubrovskaya have all earned my abiding esteem and gratitude. You are simply the best.

I also want to thank Colin Burnett, Heather Heckman, Mark Minett, and the other students in the graduate seminar on the Hollywood blacklist that I taught in 2007. Brad Schauer and Pearl Latteier both helped me gain a better understanding of postwar science fiction and the Hollywood social problem film respectively. And, although the list of UW-Madison graduate students who provided moral support and intellectual inspiration is much too long to include here, I would be remiss if I didn't mention Andrea Comiskey, John Powers, Amanda McQueen, Maureen Rogers, Derek Long, Leo Rubinkowski, and Eric Dienstfrey for their assistance in refining my conception of film allegory and its relation to Hollywood's politics.

I also have sustained many long and rewarding friendships that date back to my brief time as a visiting faculty member at New York University. I especially want to thank Richard Allen, Shawn Shimpach, Nitin Govil, Denise McKenna, Mia Mask, Roger Hallas, and Matthew Fee for their interest and encouragement. My gratitude also goes to many other colleagues in far-flung places around the globe who read and commented on various sections of the manuscript, including Brian Neve, Peter Stanfield, Frank Krutnik, Steve Neale, Murray Smith, Matthew Bernstein, and Dave Pratt. I also wish to thank the anonymous reviewers employed by the University of California Press, who not only saved me from some cringe-inducing errors but also provided extraordinarily useful advice for revisions.

George and Pamela Hamel deserve special thanks for their support of faculty research at the University of Wisconsin. This book quite literally could not have been completed without you. Your generosity is truly, truly amazing.

Several research facilities also provided assistance, including the Wisconsin Center for Film and Theater Research, the Margaret Herrick Library at the Academy of Motion Picture Arts and Sciences, UCLA's Film & Television Archive, and USC's Warner Bros. Archives. I thank the staff at all of these places but especially Maxine Fleckner Ducey and Mary Huelsbeck. The WCFTR is a genuine treasure for both the city of Madison and the state of Wisconsin. I am so blessed to have it in a place that I call home. Thanks also to Mary Francis, Kim Hogeland, Rachel Berchten, and the rest of the staff at the University of California Press. To Mary: most editors probably would have given up on me as I labored mightily to get the manuscript to a point where I felt comfortable sharing it. I am so glad that you were persistent and patient, and I am truly delighted that my book will join so many great books in UC Press's film catalog. Kudos also to Joe Abbott for his careful and thoughtful work copyediting my manuscript. Besides correcting some of my bad writing habits, Joe also saved me from the embarrassment of some additional "howlers." And a shout-out also to Matthew Perkins, who ably tracked down some information for a few fugitive sources.

I've saved my most heartfelt expressions of gratitude for last. My deepest, most sincere thanks go to David Bordwell and Kristin Thompson. When the opportunity to return to Madison arose, I knew it would be a great chance to rekindle our acquaintance. Yet in my wildest dreams I could not have imagined how genuinely fulfilling and gratifying it has been. For years you've been a guiding light to me through your exceptional scholarship and your profound love for cinema. I am only too happy to have such kindred spirits as colleagues and friends.

I also wish to thank my mother, my sister, and all of my family, whose love and support mean the world to me. This leaves me with the one person I could not possibly thank enough, since mere words just won't cut it. Michele, you are the love of my life, my inspiration, and unquestionably my better half. By the time this book comes out, we'll have celebrated our twenty-fifth anniversary together. I look forward to spending the next twenty-five years in the warmth of your embrace.

Introduction

What More Can Be Said about the Hollywood Blacklist?

The notion that many films made between 1948 and 1960 commented on American politics of the period is so commonplace as to be banal. Several books analyze this relationship, ranging from Nora Sayre's pioneering *Running Time: Films of the Cold War*, published in 1982, to J. Hoberman's *An Army of Phantoms: American Movies and the Making of the Cold War*, published in 2011.[1] Aside from these book-length studies by academics and cultural critics, references to politics are found in myriad paratextual materials for films produced during the blacklist period. In the booklet accompanying Criterion's edition of Stanley Kubrick's *Spartacus* (1960), Stephen Farber says of Dalton Trumbo, one of the original Hollywood Ten: "The screenwriter introduced one sly touch tweaking McCarthy-era watchdogs. Near the end of the movie, after the revolt is crushed, the tyrannical general, Crassus, announces ominously, 'In every city and province, lists of the disloyal have been compiled.'"[2] In a documentary about *The Robe* (1953), included as a special feature of the Blu-ray edition of the film, UCLA professor Jonathan Kuntz says: "People often look at certain movies in the 1950s during the blacklisting era and see kind of coded representations of the whole blacklisting experience. Certainly *On the Waterfront* and *High Noon* are classic examples of Hollywood films of that period that can be read as being really or secretly about the blacklisting experience. *The Robe* has to fall into that category also. At the end of *The Robe* we have a tribunal in front of Caligula that is just like the 1947 HUAC hearings."[3] The evidence appears to be all around us. Many important Hollywood films produced between 1948 and 1960 are seen, in one way or another, as responses to the blacklist, McCarthyism, and the Cold War.

Yet this widely shared understanding of the relationship between Hollywood film and its political context did not emerge fully formed in the blacklist period. Rather, it developed over several years as a gradual process of long-term critical engagement with these texts. In examining the ways critics interpret films against the backdrop of the Cold War, one discerns two important tendencies. The first is to view the films as propaganda produced to comply with an implicit directive from HUAC to make more explicitly anti-Communist cinema. The second involves seeing the films as allegories that offer disguised comment on American politics in the 1950s— that is, the threat of domestic Communism, on one hand, or the pernicious effects of the blacklist, on the other.

Combining reception studies with primary document research, *Film Criticism, the Cold War, and the Blacklist* traces the way these two critical lenses produced a consensus regarding the various ways the blacklist shaped the meanings of Cold War cinema. This group of films includes not only canonical titles, like *High Noon* (1952), *On the Waterfront* (1954), and *Invasion of the Body Snatchers* (1956), but also lesser-known titles, such as *Storm Warning* (1950) and *Warlock* (1959). My aim is to show how these films became indices of the postwar period's underlying political tensions.

A BRIEF OVERVIEW OF BLACKLIST FILM SCHOLARSHIP

Over the course of the past five decades the Hollywood blacklist has become one of the most scrutinized topics in the field of film studies. One of the reasons for the blacklist's importance is that it represents one of the darkest periods in Hollywood's long history, a time when members of the industry had their careers damaged or destroyed by the Red-baiting politics that swept through the country as a whole. As the controversy surrounding Elia Kazan's honorary Oscar in 1999 illustrates, many of those affected by the blacklist have neither forgiven nor forgotten those who betrayed them.

When I began working on this project twelve years ago, there was already a fairly voluminous body of literature on the Hollywood blacklist. Indeed, I was aware that any new study risked being a mere footnote appended to a long list of published secondary literature on the topic. Within this existing body of work there already were insightful memoirs by blacklisted writers, such as Lillian Hellman's *Scoundrel Time*, Lester Cole's *Hollywood Red*, and Walter Bernstein's *Inside Out*.[4] Penetrating historical accounts of the labor issues and activism that eventually led to the institution of the blacklist included Larry Ceplair and Steven Englund's *The Inquisition in Hollywood* and Nancy Lynn Schwartz's *The Hollywood Writers' War*.[5] Revisionist accounts of the blacklist's impact on filmmaking practice included Thom Andersen's pathfinding essay, "Red Hollywood."[6] There was a major collection of interviews conducted with formerly blacklisted writers, directors, and actors.[7] There were even early studies of the blacklist's impact on Hollywood's storytelling and representational strategies, including an influential volume by Peter Biskind.[8] And, of course, filmmakers themselves tackled the moral and legal issues of the blacklist in *The Way We Were* (1973), *The Front* (1976), and *Guilty by Suspicion* (1991).[9]

Collectively, these earlier works told a kind of "standard story" about how the blacklist came about. Although each of these historians and critics offers a slightly different variant of this narrative, they almost always include the following historical events as part of the larger context:

Labor activism in Hollywood during the 1930s, particularly of those involved in the formation of the Screen Writers Guild (SWG)

The participation of actors, directors, and screenwriters in Popular Front causes of the 1930s

The establishment of the House Committee on Un-American Activities (HUAC) in 1938

Disaffection within the American Communist Party arising as a result of the Nazi-Soviet Nonaggression Pact of 1939

Hearings on Communist influence in Hollywood conducted by the Dies Committee in 1940

Senate hearings on Motion Picture and Radio Propaganda in 1941

The studios' production of pro-Soviet films during World War II, a time when the United States and USSR were allies

Labor strife associated with the Conference of Studio Unions strike in 1945

Winston Churchill's "Iron Curtain" speech in 1946, in which the former British prime minister expressed concern about the Soviets' establishment of satellite countries in Eastern Europe

The Truman administration's establishment of a loyalty oath program in 1947

HUAC's investigation of Communists in Hollywood in October of 1947 (HUAC questioned both "friendly" and "unfriendly" witnesses during the hearings. "Friendly" witnesses, such as Gary Cooper, Louis B. Mayer, and Ayn Rand, shared their personal observations about the threat of Communist subversion in Hollywood. "Unfriendly" witnesses were called to account for their current or previous Communist Party membership. Nineteen "unfriendly" witnesses were subpoenaed, but only eleven of them ultimately testified.)

The Waldorf Statement announcing in December of 1947 that the studios fired the ten screenwriters, directors, and producers charged with "Contempt of Congress" in the wake of the HUAC hearings

The indictment and prosecution of American Communist Party leaders for Smith Act violations in 1948 (The Smith Act prohibited any individual or group from advocating the overthrow of the U.S. government.)

Alger Hiss's conviction on perjury charges in 1950

Joseph McCarthy's infamous Wheeling, West Virginia, speech on February 9, 1950, in which he announced he had the names of 205 Communists currently employed in the State Department

The publication of *Red Channels: The Report on Communist Influence in Film and Television* in 1950

The renewal of HUAC's investigation of Hollywood in 1951 (Hundreds of people working in the film industry were blacklisted as a result of HUAC's much wider inquiry. These new hearings also established the precedent that individuals could only clear themselves by "naming names" of other Communist Party members known to them.)

Whereas the scholarship on the blacklist was already quite substantial when I began this book, it has grown considerably since that time. In 2007 and 2008 alone three new accounts of the blacklist appeared.[10] New memoirs by blacklisted writers and artists continue to be published.[11] We have also seen a spate of critical biographies of blacklisted screenwriters and production histories of notable left-wing films.[12] Moreover, as was the case with historiography on the blacklist in the 1980s and 1990s, there also have been some revisionist accounts of the blacklist's impact on Hollywood. Jon Lewis, for example, argues that the studios' complicity with HUAC's investigations enabled them to better control their workforce by forestalling future labor activism for several decades after the hearings.[13] Last, building on the work of Sayre and Biskind, several books published since 2000 consider the blacklist's impact on the meanings of Hollywood films produced during the Cold War era.[14]

Of particular note is the trio of works by Paul Buhle and Dave Wagner countering the notion that the Hollywood left's politics did not have a significant impact on the cinema they created.[15] Buhle and Wagner's work has been controversial, partly because of some factual errors contained in the books and partly because of vituperative responses sent to the "letters to the editor" sections of some major film journals.[16] Yet, in the main, Buhle and Wagner make a compelling case that leftist directors and screenwriters left an important legacy in the way that they engaged social and political issues in their work and adapted neorealist storytelling principles to the Hollywood system. Finally, filmmakers themselves also continue to grapple with the blacklist's legacy in documentaries, like *Trumbo* (2007) and *Blacklist: Recovering the Life of Canada Lee* (2008), and in fictional films, like *One of the Hollywood Ten* (2000) and *The Majestic* (2001).

All of these works expand on or revise earlier periods of blacklist historiography. Yet some new strands of blacklist scholarship have emerged since the mid-1990s. Consider the handful of histories of the blacklist written from a conservative perspective, each of them aiming to correct a perceived left-wing bias in earlier accounts that mostly treat HUAC witnesses as victims of political repression.[17] Other new works essentially defy simple categorization. For example, Joseph Litvak's *The Un-Americans* revisits many of the same issues that Victor Navasky explored in his canonical study of informers, *Naming Names*, but puts a completely different spin on them.[18] Described on the book jacket as a "candidate for instant classic of Jewish cultural studies," Litvak's work merges critical and queer theory with poststructuralist analytics to tease out the role of sycophancy and "comic cosmopolitanism" as key nodes of Jewish identity during the blacklist era. Examining the way these discursive threads were interwoven with Red Scare politics, Litvak uncovers both the psychological and cultural roots of Jewish cooperation with McCarthyism, an alliance made more startling by the fact that HUAC's image of the Communist threat seemed to be that of a European Jewish intellectual.

These new directions serve as a useful reminder that the vicissitudes of blacklist scholarship roughly mirror a set of larger changes in Cold War historiography. Historians like John Lewis Gaddis, David Caute, and Ellen Schrecker provided foundational studies of both foreign and domestic policy during the Cold War era.[19] Others, however, have adopted a frankly revisionist approach to this material, much of it informed by the release of the Venona transcripts, the decoded cable messages between the KGB and its American stations.[20] Although this work offers a thorough overview of the period, several other scholars have examined more specific facets of Cold War history and culture, including studies of American Communist Party leaders, of U.S. nuclear policy, of the political alliances of anti-Communists and segregationists, and of the role of the Young Pioneers and radical summer camps in Communist political culture.[21] Several additional studies examine the Cold War's impact on American literature and popular culture.[22]

All this scholarship begs a larger question; namely, is there anything new to be said about the Hollywood blacklist? Clearly, the blacklist's effect on the film industry has been exhaustively researched, as has the role of Popular Front politics in American cinema. That being said, although several scholars examine *how* the blacklist period influenced Hollywood's representational and storytelling techniques, no one, to my knowledge, has undertaken a study of *why* those strategies took the particular shape that they did.

For this reason *Film Criticism, the Cold War, and the Blacklist* adopts a forthrightly metacritical approach to the field of blacklist studies. It is one thing to read a postwar film as an expression of industry anxieties about the Hollywood blacklist. It is quite another to see how film critics have forged connections between the threat of domestic Communism, on one hand, and the cinematic tropes of the femme fatale, the western outlaw, and the alien from outer space, on the other. The notion that filmmakers used the cinematic medium to examine or comment on the political, moral, and cultural implications of the blacklist is well documented. What is less well understood is the way the knowledge of these efforts influenced critics' interpretive strategies, the nudge given to them regarding the meaning and significance of particular cycles of postwar cinema.

PERIODIZING BLACKLIST AND COLD WAR INTERPRETATIONS

The reading formations described above did not emerge fully formed, appearing like Athena out of the heads of critics like Robert Warshow or Bosley Crowther. Rather, they developed quite gradually, their contours only becoming evident more than two decades after the blacklist itself was established. As Thom Andersen argues in "Red Hollywood," historical study of the blacklist developed in phases, each of which is demarcated by the appearance of major studies of HUAC's investigation of Hollywood. Andersen's periodization tracks fairly closely with what I see as the gradual development of a "blacklist" reading formation.

Andersen notes that the first cycle of works dealing with HUAC's investigation of Hollywood were "partisan works, obviously, written in the belief that their arguments could change people's lives."[23] Yet whereas much of this first wave of blacklist scholarship took up clear political positions, the works that highlighted a blacklist subtext in American films of this period were few and far between. There are some possible reasons for the paucity of politically oriented interpretations. If HUAC's investigations dampened the expression of left-wing sentiments in Hollywood films themselves, such a "chill" probably extended to film reviewers at daily newspapers and weekly magazines. Even if reviewers detected an implicit critique of the blacklist in *High Noon* or *Silver Lode* (1954), it seems unlikely that they would risk the wrath of their editors or their readers by explicitly articulating such meanings within the space allotted to them. Generally speaking, mainstream film reviewers of the 1950s had little or nothing to say about these subtexts. Instead, they largely treated these films as the packaged Hollywood entertainments that they ostensibly were intended to be.[24]

For this reason the few references to McCarthyist or Cold War subtexts in American cinema of the 1950s tended to appear in the work of foreign critics and occasionally in the work of the Communist Party press. For example, before becoming a director, Karel Reisz wrote a pioneering essay on Hollywood's postwar cycle of anti-Communist films for Britain's *Sight and Sound*.[25] In 1954 Harry Schein, a Swedish polymath—film critic, chemist, and president of one of Sweden's largest engineering firms—published a critical essay in a leading literary magazine on the American western's mix of symbolic, psychological, and moral elements. Schein called *High Noon* "the most convincing and, likewise, certainly the most honest explanation of American foreign policy."[26] Tellingly, although Schein performed perhaps the first allegorical reading of *High Noon,* he interpreted the film in geopolitical terms as a critique of the United Nations' timidity in the face of Communist aggression. In "The Evolution of the Western," however, legendary French critic Andre Bazin briefly countered Harry Schein's reading, stating that in *High Noon,* "it is also a rampant McCarthyism that is under scrutiny."[27] Finally, in 1957 Ernesto G. Laura published a short essay in the Italian film journal *Bianco e nero* that drew a connection between the "pod people" of *Invasion of the Body Snatchers* and the threat of Communist takeover.[28]

Aside from these observations by foreign critics, one finds occasional references to such allegorical subtexts in the *Daily Worker*.[29] For the most part, though, this attention to subtext was confined to reviews of Hollywood biblical epics. In a review of MGM's *Quo Vadis* (1951) David Platt states that he was "intrigued by the central theme of the film which remarkably parallels events in our own times. This theme—it was completely overlooked by the New York reviewers—concerns the witchhunters of the year 62 A.D. and their attempt to eradicate unpopular ideas by force and violence."[30] Similarly, a review of *Salome* (1953) observed, "There is a marked similarity between the witchhunt against John and the thought-control trials at Foley Square. John the Baptist is accused of sedition and inciting the people to violence. If he were speaking out today he probably would be tried under the Smith Act."[31] Thus, in this first wave of blacklist scholarship, when commentary on a film's political dimensions was offered, it came from places well outside the orbit of Hollywood and its institutions.

The next phase of blacklist-themed interpretation coincides roughly with the appearance of several important memoirs and early studies of the blacklist, such as Alvah Bessie's *Inquisition in Eden* and Walter Goodman's *The Committee.*[32] This period also saw attempts by Hollywood institutions to recognize the contributions of blacklisted writers. Between 1969 and 1976, for example, the Writers Guild of America (WGA) gave its Laurel Award for career achievement to three formerly blacklisted writers: Carl Foreman, Dalton Trumbo, and Michael Wilson. Likewise, in 1975 the Academy of Motion Picture Arts and Sciences officially recognized Trumbo as the winner of the 1956 Oscar for Best Original Story for *The Brave One,* an award that originally went unclaimed when it was bestowed on Trumbo's pseudonym, Robert Rich.[33]

In coming to grips with the Hollywood blacklist's legacy, a more widely shared understanding of blacklist-era subtexts emerged in the mid-1960s and early 1970s. In her influential essay "The Imagination of Disaster" Susan Sontag identified a particular strain of science fiction cinema of the 1950s as one that represented an underlying fear of Communist subversion.[34] Carlos Clarens's *An Illustrated History of Horror and Science Fiction Films* excoriated *Red Planet Mars* (1952) for its "preposterously propagandistic plotline" and its "absurd amalgamation of Nazism and Communism."[35] In 1974 future *Chicago Tribune* critic Michael Wilmington wrote a politically inflected analysis of Nicholas Ray's *Johnny Guitar* (1954) for the *Velvet Light Trap.*[36] By the time Nora Sayre's *Running Time* was published, she was more or less surfing a wave established in a more piecemeal fashion within these journal essays and book chapters.

The third wave of blacklist film interpretations more or less consolidated received opinion. Here again, blacklist film criticism tracks fairly closely with the overall trajectory of blacklist historiography. The early 1980s saw the publication of *The Inquisition in Hollywood, Naming Names,* and *The Hollywood Writers' Wars* as key texts of this period. According to Andersen, much more than their predecessors, these books center more intently on the blacklist's victims: "the Communists of Hollywood, and the ex-Communists who became 'friendly witnesses.'"[37]

This focus on labor, politics, and the blacklist's victims saw counterparts emerging during this phase of blacklist-themed film criticism. This period, for example, saw the publication of important works by Daniel Leab and Thomas Doherty on the postwar cycle of anti-Communist propaganda films.[38] Other scholars built on the insights of previous critics by gradually expanding the canon of blacklist allegories. Just as some critics saw *On the Waterfront* as Kazan's cinematic defense of his decision to cooperate with HUAC, other critics saw similar issues at play in Alfred Hitchcock's *I Confess* (1952) and Edward Dmytryk's *The Caine Mutiny* (1954).[39] Similarly, once critics identified *Invasion of the Body Snatchers* as a film expressing an underlying tension about the threat of Communism, others found similar patterns in *The Thing (From Another World)* (1951), *It Came from Outer Space* (1953), *Invaders from Mars* (1953), and *Them!* (1954).[40] Furthermore, following the lead of Carl Foreman, who suggested that *High Noon* offered disguised commentary on McCarthyism and the Hollywood blacklist, John Lenihan identified a wide range of westerns that contained an implicit critique of Cold War politics, including *The Fabulous Texan* (1947), *Rio Grande* (1950), *The Last Outpost* (1951), *Springfield Rifle* (1952), *The Command* (1954), and *Bad Day at Black Rock* (1955).[41]

Beginning in the late 1970s, capsule reviews and film society notes indicate that these blacklist and Cold War subtexts filtered beyond academia into the public at large. A 1981 item in *Esquire* said of *High Noon:* "The retired marshal attempts to rally the townspeople to meet the imminent threat but finds that they would rather risk lawlessness than risk the dangers of resistance. It is this aspect of the story—the cowardice of decent citizens when confronted with tyranny—that led some liberals to view the 1952 film as a parable of the McCarthy era."[42] Program notes for a *Cinema Texas* screening of *The Thing (From Another World)* stated bluntly, "The film is seen as being symbolic of McCarthyism and the fight against Communism on the home front."[43] Likewise, the program notes for a 1993 American Cinematheque showing of Don Siegel's *Invasion of the Body Snatchers* asserted that the "original film version of Jack Finney's horror classic is a paranoiac's delight. A skillful comment on the Red Scare, this film is also quite subtle on its own terms."[44]

Reviews of film remakes from this period provide another strand in this emerging consensus. In a 1982 review of John Carpenter's *The Thing,* Roger Ebert writes, "The two 1950s versions [of films based on John W. Campbell's story 'Who Goes There?'], especially 'Invasion of the Body Snatchers,' were seen at the time as fables based on McCarthyism; communists, like victims of the Thing, looked, sounded, and acted like your best friend, but they were infected with a deadly secret."[45] Peter Travers's review of Abel Ferrara's *Body Snatchers* (1993) took a similar tack. Comparing Ferrara's treatment of Jack Finney's novel to the 1956 film, Travers writes, "Some saw it as Siegel's attack on Sen. Joseph McCarthy, the head pod behind the House Un-American Activities Committee, who turned citizens into

Commie-hunting mobs during the '50s. Others saw it as Siegel's attack on the Communists themselves as aliens in our midst."[46] The fact that blacklist and Cold War subtexts seeped into the consciousness of film programmers and newspaper critics suggests that, by 1993, such insights had become a critical commonplace.

The current phase of blacklist scholarship, according to Thom Andersen, might be characterized as one of mild revisionism. This revisionist strain is evident both in his video documentary *Red Hollywood* (1995), coproduced by Noël Burch, and in the quartet of works by Buhle and Wagner. These works try to overturn a bit of conventional wisdom about the blacklist's victims, namely that their works were mostly composed of apolitical hackwork, virtually indistinguishable from the vast output of other stuff released by Hollywood. As Andersen says of his collaboration with Burch, "We began to dream about making a film that would prove that the victims of the blacklist had created a distinctive and significant body of film work."[47] In mounting this counterclaim, revisionist historians also sought to show that the work of blacklistees had aesthetic merit, repudiating Billy Wilder's oft-quoted quip about the Hollywood Ten: "Only two of them have talent. The rest are just unfriendly."[48]

Andersen and Burch's *Red Hollywood* appeared in the midst of a major effort by the Screen Writers Guild to reinstate the credits of blacklisted writers. By 1997 the specially appointed Blacklisted Writers Committee within the SWG restored credits that originally had been allocated to fronts or pseudonyms on more than eighty films.[49] Bernard Gordon proved to be the biggest beneficiary of this initiative, having his writing credits restored on thirteen films, including *Hellcats of the Navy* (1957) and the British science fiction classic *The Day of the Triffids* (1962).[50]

Gordon, however, was not alone. Several blacklisted writers discussed herein received belated recognition for their black market work. Albert Maltz, for example, received credit on two films discussed in subsequent chapters: *Broken Arrow* (1950) and *The Robe*. Michael Wilson had his credits restored as the screenwriter for such noted films as *Friendly Persuasion* (1956), *The Bridge on the River Kwai* (1957), and *Lawrence of Arabia* (1963). As recently as 2011, nearly sixty years after *Roman Holiday* (1953) was released, Dalton Trumbo finally received his due for the story he contributed to William Wyler's classic romantic comedy.[51]

The current phase of blacklist film criticism, though, doesn't track as closely with the blacklist histories produced by Andersen and Burch or Buhle and Wagner. Indeed, this period is characterized less by revisionism than by the widespread diffusion of the maxim that Cold War politics shaped the meanings of many films produced during this period. I argue that the current phase of blacklist film criticism began in 1993 with the publication of John Belton's *American Cinema / American Culture*, a book that sums up much of what was established in earlier periods of blacklist scholarship.

Belton devotes a lengthy chapter to Hollywood and the Cold War, analyzing the effect of Red Scare politics on the film industry from the Palmer raids of 1919, which resulted in the deportation of five hundred foreign citizens suspected of political radicalism, to Mikhail Gorbachev's establishment of *glasnost* and *perestroika* policies in the 1980s, which ultimately produced the dissolution of the Soviet Union.[52] Belton's synopsis of this period includes many elements of the blacklist's "standard story" that I listed earlier. What truly distinguishes Belton's coverage of the blacklist period, though, is the attention he gives to the meanings and subtexts of films produced in the Cold War era. Besides discussing the "anti-Commie" cycle made just after HUAC's first round of hearings, Belton also elucidates the allegorical dimensions of various science fiction films, biblical epics, adventure films, and westerns. As a popular and widely read textbook, *American Cinema / American Culture* did much to establish a consensus view of the way Cold War politics were depicted onscreen.

By the late 1990s the critical exegesis of blacklist subtexts began to seem "old hat." After several decades of blacklist-themed criticism, the simple notion that 1950s films reflected a McCarthyist zeitgeist had lost much of its novelty. Thus, when critics revisited canonical blacklist film texts, they adopted a new rhetorical tack. That is, critics often included a quick and dirty acknowledgment of Cold War subtexts before they moved on to their central argument, which usually involved some aspect of identity politics that had been neglected in previous interpretations. In the first paragraph of a 1996 essay on *Johnny Guitar*, for example, Jennifer Peterson notes that director Nicholas Ray challenged convention "by turning the paradigmatic western conflict between individual and community into an anti-McCarthyist allegory."[53] Having disposed of the Cold War dimensions of *Johnny Guitar*, Peterson then goes on to discuss her real subject: the film's treatment of gender mobility, sexual orientation, and hysteria. Katrina Mann's 2004 essay on Siegel's *Invasion of the Body Snatchers* adopts a reading strategy that strongly parallels Peterson's. After conceding in her first sentence that *Invasion* achieved an iconic status for its representation of Cold War anxieties, Mann goes on to analyze the film in terms of other symptomatic subtexts, namely Mexican migrant labor issues and threats to white patriarchal hegemony.[54]

Blog posts and Internet discussion forums provide additional evidence that "Red Scare" subtexts are commonly recognized among certain canonical 1950s titles. A survey of 267 user reviews of *High Noon* linked to the film's Internet Movie Database (IMDb) web page for the film shows that about sixty of them make some passing mention of the blacklist, the Cold War, HUAC, or McCarthyism. Interestingly, several of these references occur in reviews where the author claims not to understand the analogy or where the author gets key details of it wrong (e.g., that Joseph McCarthy led the investigation of Hollywood Communists). This suggests that reviewers' comments recapitulated something they'd heard elsewhere about *High Noon*, further reinforcing the notion that the film's status as anti-HUAC allegory is received wisdom. User reviews of other, lesser-known titles attest to the robustness of this aspect of film culture. Although Allan Dwan's *Silver Lode* generated much less comment than *High Noon*, eleven of its fourteen user reviews describe it as an anti-McCarthyist parable.

I've offered this brief sketch of blacklist film criticism because it indicates a particular pattern in the way these films have been described in both contemporaneous and modern reception contexts. As we will see, most of these films were initially treated as routine Hollywood productions, with reviewers mostly evaluating them in terms of their artistic merit or entertainment value. Some, like *High Noon* and *On the Waterfront*, received very positive notices and went on to earn further accolades in the form of Oscar nominations and other year-end awards. Others, like *Pickup on South Street* (1953), initially garnered negative reviews, an assessment that would be altered considerably in the long view of history. Still others, like *The Red Menace* (1949), were trashed by critics both then and now. In sum, while critical opinion on this body of films diverges widely, initial discussions of them were conducted almost entirely on evaluative grounds.

Over time, however, critics increasingly saw these films as a response to their historical context. Beginning in the 1960s and 1970s, many critics and scholars started to recognize these films as disguised comment both on the Hollywood blacklist and on the U.S. domestic and foreign policy that gave rise to the Red Scare. Because so many of the titles discussed in this book follow this pattern, they provide an apt demonstration of Janet Staiger's claim that such patterned historical variation in reception informs new viewers' horizon of expectations. Staiger cites Pierre Macherey's model of context-activated reception, in which Macherey proposes that meanings build up on a text as "'everything which has been written *about* it, everything which has been collected on it, become[s] attached to it—like shells on a rock by the seashore forming a whole incrustation.'"[55] Following

Macherey's "sedimentary" metaphor, most blacklist criticism occupies the middle layers of a work's "incrustation" of meanings, accumulating neither at its core nor its surface but somewhere in between.

Of course, this historical survey covers only *what* critics and scholars have said in interpreting Cold War cinema as either propaganda or blacklist allegory. To better understand *how* and *why* these analysts forged connections between the meanings of these films and their historical context, one must look not only at interpretation as a particular type of critical practice but also at the way filmmakers themselves "leveraged" Hollywood storytelling technique to provide cinematic commentary on the industry's and nation's politics. *Film Criticism, the Cold War, and the Blacklist* is largely metacritical in its ambit, but I have, on occasion, offered some of my own analysis of films central to the blacklist canon. In doing so, I hope to add something original to the critical excursus I have just described.

THE STRUCTURE OF THE BOOK

Film Criticism, the Cold War, and the Blacklist is divided into two sections. After an introductory chapter that explains my methodology, the next two chapters deal with anti-Communist propaganda films produced between 1947 and 1957. More specifically, these two chapters show how filmmakers' reliance on the conventions of film noir and the social problem film caused them to imbue these anti-Communist propaganda films with scenes that offer a surprising perspective on the Communist Party's perceived appeal to women and racial minorities. The second section consists of four chapters that examine the way that films made during this same period sometimes have been understood as political allegories. Although at first blush it might seem that I am comparing apples and oranges, the rhetorical strategies of propaganda and allegory mirror one another to the extent that they are didactic forms. In propaganda the polemical elements of the work are explicit; indeed, these instructional and agitational aspects are the form's very raison d'être. In allegories the didacticism of the work is implicit. In some cases the moral dimension of the allegory is cued as the text's own preferred interpretation. In other forms, such as fables, the lesson is appended to the story and functions as a succinct summary of its meaning. In the case of blacklist allegories this moral dimension involves the evils of government overreach and political oppression.

The first chapter of *Film Criticism, the Cold War, and the Blacklist* aims to situate the readings of blacklist subtexts within their respective theoretical and historical frameworks. The chapter surveys the major theories of both propaganda and allegory, reviewing the central precepts found in the work of Jacques Ellul, Angus Fletcher, Sayre Greenfield, and Maureen Quilligan. By establishing this theoretical framework, I show how critics engaging with blacklist-era films implicitly rely on these ideas in performing their interpretations. Yet it is also worth noting that blacklist interpretations are simply an aspect of much more general critical practices. Drawing on recent work in cognitive psychology, neuroscience, and behavioral economics, I examine the specific interpretive protocols that have made these readings possible.

In chapter 2 I argue that anti-Communist films noir, such as *I Married a Communist* (1949), frequently transpose topical political material onto genre conventions in a manner that equates Marxist political belief with gangsterism and petty criminality. In doing so, anti-Communist films noir depict the political seduction of red-blooded American males as rooted in an irrationality often associated with noir as a discursive construct. While Hollywood's equation of Communists with gangsters was undoubtedly deceitful and unscrupulous, it proved necessary for two reasons: (1) Communists posed a certain problem for screenwriters and directors owing to the fact that they were defined by their beliefs rather than their actions; and (2) because membership in the Communist party was not illegal in and of itself, Hollywood's propaganda efforts sought to justify the policing efforts directed at Communists by showing them as a quasi-criminal enterprise, one that differed little from more familiar forms of organized crime. Beyond its equation of Communism and gangsterism the anti-Communist film's conversion narratives sometimes problematize the noir convention of the femme fatale by blurring the boundaries between public political life and domesticity. By showing women as active participants in the public sphere, these anti-Communist noirs suggest that the Communist Party does something arguably much worse than promoting class equality and collective ownership of the means of production; it enthusiastically violates the norms for American women regarding femininity and domesticity.

Chapter 3 examines the treatment of race in anti-Communist films made during the late 1940s and early 1950s. Several film historians have already addressed the anti-Semitic tone of anti-Communist discourse, as well as the extent to which HUAC's investigations quelled the political expressions of liberal directors and screenwriters involved in the postwar cycle of social problem films. Other historians also note that the American Communist Party took several steps to try to build grassroots appeal to African Americans in the 1930s. As the cycle of anti-Communist propaganda films demonstrates, appeals to racial minorities played an important role in Communist Party rhetoric in the 1930s and 1940s. In analyses of *The Red Menace, I Was a Communist for the FBI* (1951), and *Big Jim McLain* (1952), I examine the legacy of these recruitment efforts, as well as the contradictory treatment of race evident in the cycle as a whole.

Drawing on Victor Navasky's landmark work on the blacklist, *Naming Names*, chapter 4 explores the particular personal, professional, and legal dilemmas faced by those actors, screenwriters, and directors summoned to testify before HUAC. Building on this previous scholarship, I explore Hollywood's imaginative treatment of these dilemmas in films that deal with the issue of informing. By examining a range of crime dramas and police procedurals that deal with reluctant witnesses, I analyze the political dynamics of cooperation and resistance evident in case studies of four films—Stuart Heisler's *Storm Warning*, Alfred Hitchcock's *I Confess*, Sam Fuller's *Pickup on South Street*, and Elia Kazan's *On the Waterfront*. Although these films share certain plot structures, they nonetheless illustrate the range of responses Hollywood took to allegorizing the dilemmas of HUAC witnesses.

Chapter 5 examines the role of historical allegory in blacklist interpretations. Using the past to represent the present is a common strategy in readings of films that depict historical events. Not surprisingly, a rather diverse group of historical films have been read against the Hollywood blacklist in this way. This interpretive strategy, however, raises several unanswered questions about the nature of allegorical intention and reception. Using *The Robe* and *Spartacus* as case studies, I examine the particular problems of chronology and causation that historians and critics have encountered in treating these films as historical allegories.

Chapter 6 surveys the way particular tropes and themes of the Hollywood western, such as rugged individualism, Manifest Destiny, and the role of violence in society, function as commentary on the era's Cold War politics. Because of the genre's familiar themes, several westerns contain elements that encouraged critics to read them as either allegories of the Hollywood blacklist or as allegories of U.S. foreign policy under Truman and Eisenhower. Three particular tropes of the western prove to be fairly consistent elements of these allegorical readings: the frontier, the lynch mob, and the outsider. Through analyses of films like *Broken Arrow, High Noon, Silver Lode, Johnny Guitar,* and *Warlock,* I show how these tropes inflected, challenged, and problematized the liberal western's critique of McCarthyism.

My final chapter takes up the issue of blacklist and Cold War allegories in 1950s science fiction films. As was the case with westerns, several prototypical conventions of the genre have lent themselves to allegorical treatment.

These include such elements as aliens, monsters, dehumanization, nuclear terror, vegetation, brainwashing, passing, sleep, and plague. One reason Hollywood science fiction cinema has been such fertile territory for allegorical interpretations is the sheer preponderance of tropes that motivate anti-Communist or anti-HUAC readings. More than the other genres included in this study, though, the inherent ambiguity of these science fiction elements allows them to be read in ways diametrically opposed to one another. Many titles, like *Invaders from Mars, Them!*, and *Invasion of the Body Snatchers*, have been read as both anti-Communist and anti-McCarthy allegories, sometimes simultaneously.

By adopting a multiperspectival approach—one that combines narrative and stylistic analysis, archival research, and cognitive theory—*Film Criticism, the Cold War, and the Blacklist* aims to provide a thorough overview of the way that the institutions of the Hollywood blacklist and of U.S. policy influenced the interpretive strategies of critics and scholars. Up until now, I have relied on tacit, commonsensical definitions of *propaganda* and *allegory*. Now I want to sketch out a more precise definition of each of these terms and show how they mesh with other heuristics employed in academic interpretations of films. It comes as no surprise that blacklist film criticism displays both continuities and differences with film interpretation conceived as a specific kind of critical practice. It is to this issue that I now turn my attention.

1 A Bifocal View of Hollywood during the Blacklist Period

Film as Propaganda and Allegory

We have seen that a comparatively small but important group of postwar American films have been interpreted as Hollywood's response to the Red Scare. But what produced this consensus view of postwar American cinema? Along with the appearance of the earliest histories of the blacklist and the memoirs of blacklisted writers, as well as the industry's belated recognition of those writers' contributions, a third aspect of American film culture of this period fostered the impression that Cold War–era cinema was fertile territory for the exploration of political subtexts: the introduction of film criticism into the academy. Although this aspect was not specific to blacklist film scholarship, it was nonetheless a crucial element in establishing a framework within which this reading formation could develop and flourish.

As Dana Polan and others have pointed out, there is a long history of academic interest in film as a particular type of cultural artifact.[1] But it was not until the 1970s that universities began awarding doctorates in film studies as a distinct and autonomous discipline. As the field developed professional organizations dedicated to film studies, academic journals turned away from evaluation and increasingly turned to the study of film theory and criticism. As David Bordwell notes, film criticism was an outgrowth of film reviewing by professional journalists, but the meaning of a work supplanted its aesthetic worth as the chief object of inquiry. "Now the author of a film book," writes Bordwell, "was apt to be an academic, whose professional career required publications bearing a scholarly imprimatur. In sum, the academicization of film publishing created an expanding institutional base for interpretive criticism."[2] Not surprisingly, blacklist interpretations became more common as a result of this change. As film scholars combed through films of the 1950s for their implicit and symptomatic meanings, the field came to accept the premise that certain films, and even entire genres, allegorized the political tensions around the HUAC investigations and U.S. foreign policy.

Rather than trying to answer the question of *what* these Cold War–era films mean, this book asks *how* they came to mean. In this chapter I more closely examine the two particular strategies film critics employed in identifying specific examples of American cinema as commentary on the era's anti-Communist politics. On one hand, some critics, either explicitly or implicitly, describe the cycle of anti-Communist films produced between 1948 and 1958 as a type of propaganda. Although most critics acknowledge that Hollywood made these films to curry favor with investigative bodies like HUAC, the cycle contains an overt, polemical address to viewers that illustrates the potential threat Communist infiltration posed to the American way of life. This cycle of anti-Communist films contained its own ideological contradictions, however, partly because of Hollywood's reliance on established storytelling formulas. On the other hand, many critics also point out that films produced outside this cycle of anti-Communist propaganda sometimes found indirect ways to comment on the politics of the period. Most of these critics implicitly identify allegory as the means by which this commentary is offered. In its simplest dictionary definition, an allegory is "a story in which the characters and events are symbols that stand for ideas about human life or for a political or historical situation."[3] By this logic, blacklist allegories thematize the evils of political repression and the abrogation of civil liberties.

Rather than simply taking these two interpretive strategies at face value, I argue that they should be contextualized within a much broader understanding of propaganda and allegory as specific communicative acts. How, for example, is propaganda defined and how does this definition differentiate it from a more general sense that cinema functions within a structure of social, cultural, and political ideologies? Likewise, how does cinema "code" its representations in such a way that they can be interpreted as blacklist allegory? How do these blacklist allegories fit within a larger conception of allegory as a genre of literary or cinematic texts? This chapter's aim, then, is to situate blacklist criticism within an understanding of propaganda and allegory as rhetorical modes.

A METACRITICAL APPROACH TO FRAMING BLACKLIST FILM INTERPRETATIONS

One of the chief inspirations for this book is David Bordwell's *Making Meaning: Inference and Rhetoric in the Interpretation of Cinema*.

Bordwell's book proved to be quite controversial when it was first published in 1989. Because Bordwell disentangled and diagnosed the rhetorical strategies, reasoning routines, and interpretive protocols used by academic film scholars, some prominent critics believed that he was calling the entire practice of interpretation into question. More than that, Bordwell also identified several institutional pressures that seemed to favor film interpretation over other kinds of intellectual inquiry within the field. These included the pressure to publish felt by junior faculty in tenure-track positions, the "one film = one article" convention that developed among prominent journals in the field, and the conflation of interpretive practice with theorizing about cinema that encouraged critics to use single films as ways of explicating or complicating theoretical premises. These factors, among others, created a kind of "perfect storm" of interpretation across the discipline. With a text in hand and a widely shared set of tools to analyze it, virtually anyone could produce a publishable "reading" of a particular film title.

It would be wrong, though, to suggest that *Making Meaning* rejects film interpretation *tout court*. I say this both because Bordwell takes pains to emphasize he is not offering an outright rejection of interpretation and because Bordwell himself makes interpretive claims in some of his other books. In the last chapter of *Making Meaning* Bordwell acknowledges that innovative schemas for interpretation have played a genuinely salutary function within film studies as a discipline: "Many exemplars deserve our praise because they have introduced conceptual schemes that reorient our understanding. They have activated neglected cues, offered new categories, suggested fresh semantic fields, and widened our rhetorical resources. Innovative frames of reference have heightened our awareness of what can be noticed and appreciated in artworks."[4] Although Bordwell praises certain kinds of interpretation in *Making Meaning*, he also calls attention to the drawbacks of ordinary—rather than innovative—film criticism. One such drawback is the fact that the veridical status of most interpretive claims is indeterminate. Says Bordwell, "Contemporary criticism, in aiming to interpret everything it can find, has usually set itself against theoretical principle by refusing to stipulate when something will *not* count as a valid interpretive move or as an instance of meaning."[5]

By highlighting both the windfalls and pitfalls of film criticism, Bordwell provides a set of criteria for evaluating stronger interpretations over weaker ones. If a reading of a film seems facile or unenlightening, perhaps it is because the critic has indulged an overfamiliar interpretive heuristic or because the critic generalizes too quickly about a film's characterizations or formal properties. Most film scholars seem to acknowledge that the discipline is awash with weak interpretations of films. *Making Meaning* allows us to identify and catalog specific ways in which readings of films go horribly awry.

Making Meaning also proves quite useful for understanding blacklist and Cold War interpretations. Early in his book, Bordwell draws an important distinction between comprehension and interpretation. On one hand, comprehension involves the viewer's or critic's construction of referential and explicit meanings that are cued by the formal properties of the film. Referential meanings are built up by the viewer in the process of constructing the film's fictional world and the events of the story. Explicit meanings are a literal construal of a film's meaning, the message or "point" of the story that the film overtly communicates. Interpretation, on the other hand, involves the viewer's or critic's construction of a text's implicit and symptomatic meanings. Implicit meanings are covert or symbolic and are typically expressed as themes that the film critic explicates in reading the film. Symptomatic meanings are repressed, unspoken meanings in a text that critics extract by uncovering structuring absences within the work, which are then traced back to economic, political, or ideological factors.

The two main critical lenses used in blacklist and Cold War interpretations correlate with these processes of comprehension and interpretation. The postwar cycle of anti-Communist propaganda films, for example, fall under the concept of critical comprehension insofar as propaganda depends on an overt, didactic appeal to spectators. By identifying this cycle as propaganda, film critics acknowledge that the referential dimensions of these texts involve characterizations and story events that depict Communist Party members as duplicitous, subversive, and criminal agents of the Kremlin. The explicit message of these films is that Communists pose a dangerous threat to U.S. security. In contrast, films seen as blacklist or Cold War allegories fall under the concept of interpretation. In revealing the allegorical dimensions of these films, critics must "decode" meanings that are disguised through particular figurations, such as synecdoche and personification. Because these allegorical meanings are seen as expressions of their creators' political discontent, these readings, more often than not, seek to explicate implicit meanings of such films.

PULLING BACK THE IRON CURTAIN: POSTWAR ANTI-COMMUNIST PROPAGANDA

Despite important differences in their form and their overall aims, propaganda and allegory share one important characteristic, namely their didactic function. Although they communicate in a less direct manner, allegories traditionally have functioned as a form of moral instruction and educational tool. Not surprisingly, *fable* and *parable* are cognate terms for allegory, further indicating this shared propensity for conveying moral lessons. This sense of allegory as a didactic form dates back at least to the time of the ancient Greeks. Aesop, a Greek slave who lived about six hundred years before Christ, is credited with writing a number of popular fables that have been collected, translated, and revised in several guises all the way up to the present day. Indeed, the notion of "Aesop language" has long been associated with allegorical forms of expression intended to evade political censorship and would play an important role in the Smith Act prosecution of Communist Party leadership in 1949.[6] This didactic function of allegory would hold until the early nineteenth century when romantic poets like Wordsworth and Coleridge self-consciously rejected allegory in favor of symbolism, which was viewed as a more organic deployment of figurative language.

Like allegory, propaganda is a discursive form distinguished from other types of communicative acts on the basis of its didactic intent. Unlike allegory, however, propaganda's polemical qualities are much more overt and more explicitly directed toward social instruction and political persuasion. More important, the term *propaganda* also functions pejoratively. Used in a present-day context, *propaganda* usually refers to discourse that advances a position on the basis of misstatement, distortion, and untruth.

The idea that propaganda is a derogatory term is largely a twentieth-century invention. As J. Michael Sproule points out, this modern conception of propaganda derives from Progressive efforts in the 1910s and 1920s to analyze the dissemination of public information in search of nationalist or political bias. Describing the change in public understanding of propaganda augured by World War I, Sproule writes, "Before the war, propaganda, if it had any meaning for an ordinary American, signified chiefly the spreading of self-interested opinions through publicity. Under the influence of anti-German exposés, however, the term by 1915 had begun to take on more sinister connotations of manipulations and half-truths secretly sowed by society's avowed enemies."[7] According to Sproule, the negative connotations of propaganda were promulgated through the emergence of specific institutions created to combat foreign propaganda and root it out of the public sphere. These institutions include Woodrow Wilson's Committee on Public Information, which sought to counter the dark shadow of German propaganda and, thus, build support for America's entry into World War I, and the Institute of Propaganda Analysis, founded in 1937 and charged with thwarting the efforts of "special interests to monopolize the channels of public communication."[8] Along with these institutions, prominent public intellectuals like Walter Lippman, Gilbert Seldes, and John Dewey also contributed to the pejorative understanding of propaganda as self-interested expression colored by bias and untruth.

During the late 1930s the Institute for Propaganda Analysis (IPA) not only strove to uncover the most egregious examples of propaganda in the public marketplace but also sought to educate citizens about the best methods to detect propagandistic material. For example, in a November 1937 bulletin published by the IPA, Clyde R. Miller identified "seven common propaganda devices" that readers of the bulletin should watch for. Although Miller's schema was widely criticized for its oversimplification and logical fallacies, it nonetheless guided public understanding of propaganda analysis as a useful primer. Indeed, although there is no specific evidence that later film critics employed this framework in their treatment of anti-Communist films, the fact that many reviews call attention to these devices suggests that the wide circulation of Miller's ideas contributed to a common fund of knowledge about the way propaganda operated. Among the devices highlighted by Miller were the following:

1. *Name-calling*—the propagandist applies such bad names as "fascist" or "communist" to the opponent to stimulate hate and fear.

2. *Glittering generalities*—"the propagandist identifies his program with virtue by use of 'virtue words,'" such as truth, freedom, justice.

3. *Transfer*—"the propagandist carries over the authority, sanction, and prestige from something we respect and revere [often church and nation] to something he would have us accept."

4. *Testimonial*—to bolster an idea or plan by using a statement from someone recognized by the public.

5. *Plain folks*—when members of society's political or social elite court the public by appearing to be just ordinary folks and therefore wise and good.

6. *Card stacking*—the propagandist relies upon half-truths, distractions, and omissions, using "under-emphasis and over-emphasis to dodge issues and evade facts."

7. *Bandwagon*—the propagandist works to make us "follow the crowd, to accept the propagandist's program en masse."[9]

The ability to detect propaganda qua propaganda proves to be one of the most important traits of analysis. By its very nature, propaganda does not advertise its rhetorical appeals but rather conceals them under the guise of public information. For this reason discourse only achieves the status of propaganda when one recognizes its attempt at persuasion. Propaganda, thus, might be defined as a type of discourse that tries, but fails, to conceal its didactic intent. In contrast, undetected propaganda is received as mere information.

This understanding of propaganda as a form of failed rhetoric, though, is not shared by every political theorist who has attempted to define it. In the early 1960s Jacques Ellul argued that modern propaganda is an almost necessary aspect of governance in contemporary societies insofar as all modern political systems depend to a greater or lesser degree on some form of public participation.[10] Drawing on broad psychological appeals, propaganda works by making individuals feel a sense of belonging within the body politic and helps them conform to broad cultural norms. For Ellul, modern propaganda emerged as a response to the disintegration of smaller social groups, such as the family, the village, or the church. It supports governance by helping to organize society and creating a national sense of cohesion.

Because Ellul focuses so strongly on the sociological and psychological dimensions of propaganda, the question of its truthfulness is more or less irrelevant to its functions. Propaganda is defined by its effectiveness and utility rather than its veridicality. Some propaganda is factually accurate; some propaganda is based on false facts; and some propaganda falls somewhere between these two poles—that is, it is based on factually accurate information but is deceptive in the way it is used. In the latter case propaganda is based on some piece of factual information but encourages individuals to draw obvious, if wrong, conclusions from it.[11]

Ellul's conception of propaganda has been influential in some academic circles, but it has not been widely adopted in film studies. I believe that one reason for this is that Ellul's definition of propaganda overlaps significantly with post-Althusserian theories of ideology. Indeed, by developing an extremely capacious and multifaceted concept of propaganda, Ellul identifies several aspects of propaganda that later scholars are more likely to identify as ideological in their nature. For example, Ellul distinguishes between political propaganda and sociological propaganda, describing the latter as diffuse and spontaneous, not the result of deliberate actions: "It is rarely conveyed by catchwords or expressed intentions. Instead it is based on a general climate, an atmosphere that influences people imperceptibly without having the appearance of propaganda; it gets to man through his customs, through his unconscious habits. It creates new habits in him; it is a sort of persuasion from within. . . . Sociological propaganda produces a progressive adaptation to a certain order of things, a certain concept of human relations, which unconsciously molds individuals and makes them conform to society."[12]

Because Ellul sees the circulation of specific ideologies as the output of propaganda, his conception does not square with modern usage of these terms. Consequently, contemporary film scholars seem reluctant to embrace his theory of propaganda for fear of muddling their own theories of film as an ideological form. Instead, most current film scholars rely on a common-sensical definition of *propaganda* as something significantly different from *ideology*. For example, discussing the postwar anti-Communist cycle, Thomas Doherty writes: "Ironically, then, while in self-conscious service to an (overt) political ideology, the anti-communist films failed to fulfill the traditional (covert) ideological function of American cinema. This peculiarity arises not from their anti-communist content as such—after all, *Ninotchka* has that— but by their failure to achieve the two different 'ideological' missions simultaneously: to be both 'Hollywood' and 'agit-prop.'"[13] As Doherty's usage makes clear, propaganda is overt and self-consciously strives to be persuasive while ideology is covert and lacks a particular message. Propaganda is prone to failure if audiences recognize its rhetorical tactics too easily. In contrast, ideology maintains its epistemic status even when it is analyzed.

As a rule of thumb, Hollywood filmmakers generally avoided making films that could be identified as propagandistic. The reason was fairly simple: making propaganda films was bad for business since such product inevitably alienated a significant portion of the public put off by such overt polemicism. As Ruth Vasey points out, the major studios recognized that political messages in films have the potential to generate controversy. Such controversy sometimes leads to consumer boycotts or resistance from exhibitors. By staying politically neutral, Hollywood attempted to preserve an audience for its products that was as large as possible.[14]

Warner Bros.' release of *I Was a Communist for the FBI* in 1951 illustrates some of the risks in making anti-Communist films for a mass audience. The production file for *I Was a Communist* contains several letters to Jack Warner showing the divisive effect the film had on viewers. A number of letters praise Warner for his bravery in throwing a spotlight on the scourge of Communism in the United States. Bernice Mertes wrote, "It takes courage to make such a picture as this. . . . You have blazed the trail with a fine picture that was not only educational, but superb entertainment as well."[15] Similarly Nancy Olwine of Trotwood, Ohio, lauded Warner for making a magnificent movie, adding, "I hadn't realized how much power the Communist party had in the United States until I saw this picture."[16]

Yet an almost equal number of letters were extremely negative. Jack D. Zeldes of Galesburg, Illinois, attacked the film for misrepresenting basic legal principles: "My suggestion: When you are making a motion picture which involves Constitutional rights, please keep a copy of the Constitution handy. Any United States Senator or Representative will furnish Warner Brothers, or any citizen, a copy of the Constitution free of charge."[17] Several other letters criticized *I Was a Communist* for its anti-Semitism, holding Warner himself personally responsible for whipping up hatred against Jewish people. In a protest from "a Jew to a fellow Jew," Julius Newman of Roxbury, Massachusetts, wrote, "What the hell are you trying to prove or do? I demand that this dangerous, rotten, + libelous bit of propaganda be withdrawn immediately before some Jewish mother somewhere, gets her son's cracked skull for Mother's Day."[18] These polarized responses illustrate the problem that propaganda films had from a market perspective. Although it is impossible to measure the number of people who decided not to go to *I Was a Communist* on the basis of such comments, one might surmise that such negative word of mouth essentially cut the film's potential audience in half.

This perception was reflected in contemporaneous discussions of the anti-Communist cycle. In 1956 Dorothy B. Jones observed, "With a few exceptions, these films were not good motion pictures as judged by one of the industry's own criteria—box office success."[19] Jones goes further, though, noting that studios continued to make these films despite their poor financial prospects. The reason Hollywood continued to place these losing bets had much more to do with response to external pressures than to the studios' usual development process. After the initial flurry of anti-Communist films made in 1948 and 1949 as a direct response to the HUAC investigations, their production slackened in 1950 and 1951. HUAC's return to Hollywood, though, led to renewed interest in anti-Communist projects in 1952, a year that saw the release of some thirteen films in the cycle. According to Jones, this number constitutes about 37 percent of the total number of anti-Communist films produced in the eight-year period covered in her study.[20] Yet the cycle remained unpopular, as evidenced by Paramount president Barney Balaban's comments after the premiere of *My Son John* (1952). When an executive from a rival studio showered Leo McCarey's fervid family melodrama with praise, Balaban responded, "I'm glad you feel that way. I wish you had made it."[21]

Jones doesn't mention it, but this anti-Communist cycle also failed on another important criterion for success: critical response. Although most films expect their share of bad reviews, there is some evidence that the negative response received by most anti-Communist films affected the distribution patterns for later entries in the cycle. In an item in the *Indianapolis Star*, Harold Heffernan noted that producers John Wayne and Robert Fellows opened *Big Jim McLain* in every key city in the United States before it went on to New York, hoping to avoid, or at least delay, the kind of critical lambasting that *My Son John* received. By saving New York until last, Wayne and Fellows tried to reap the benefits of the film's appeal to middle America before that appeal could be tainted by eastern elite tastemakers.[22]

Additionally, anti-Communist propaganda films also faced challenges in international markets. Such overt partisan politics invited censorship from other countries when a film's political line ran counter to a nation's official foreign policy positions. As Gordon Mirams, censor of cinematograph films in New Zealand, explained in a letter to Warner Bros. distribution offices in Auckland, the New Zealand government expressed concern about the implication that criminal actions depicted in *I Was a Communist for the FBI* were performed under "direct instructions or guidance from the Kremlin, from Stalin, or from Moscow." Mirams added that "the Censor's official position here confers on him a special responsibility to take careful note of any references (whether in action, dialogue or commentary) as might conceivably be the subject of diplomatic protest or controversy and a consequent source of embarrassment to the Government."[23]

I Was a Communist for the FBI was not alone in risking the approbation of foreign censors. *Variety* claimed that Sam Fuller's submarine thriller *Hell and High Water* (1954) was almost certain to run into difficulties in India, the Middle East, and the Netherlands because of its anti-Communist slant.[24] A *Variety* editorial made Hollywood's stakes quite clear. With nearly 40 percent of a film's revenues coming from foreign rentals, "Hollywood-made jibes at the Soviet Union are poison for the box office" in countries that "cherish their neutralism or have sensitive political balances to respect."[25]

The critical recognition of Hollywood's postwar anti-Communist cycle as propaganda developed quite early and has been steadily maintained all the way to the present. *Time* magazine, for example, described William Wellman's *The Iron Curtain* (1948) as "top notch anti-Communist propaganda."[26] Moreover, in a 1953 issue of Britain's *Sight and Sound*, the journal's editors wrote: "The Western world has never been very adept at propaganda, and it was not as propaganda but as entertainment that most of the films in which Hollywood has concerned itself with the cold war were conceived. But on such a subject every statement, of the dangers to be fought, of the values to be supported, is bound to be propagandist. Against the dynamic, growing force of Communism, Hollywood, as powerful a shaper of public opinion as any in the western world, has put up the weakest of counter attacks."[27]

Even when critics and reviewers of the period didn't use the word *propaganda*, their comments often framed these anti-Communist films as failed polemics. In a review of John Wayne's *Big Jim McLain*, Milton J. Shapiro wrote, "The film's theme is anti-communism, the anti-communism popular today—thoughtless, hysterical, breast-beating anti-communism."[28] Summarizing this cycle's long-term legacy, Tony Shaw contends that such "clumsily produced, overtly propagandistic Red-baiting material . . . may even have hindered rather than helped the anti-Communist cause by bluntly depicting Fifth Columnists as moronic and easy to spot."[29]

To a certain degree the promotion of the films in the postwar anti-Communist cycle participated in their critical construction as propaganda. Advertising material created for the espionage thriller *Walk East on Beacon* (1952) invited audience members to participate in a national surveillance campaign: "The FBI needs your help in its fight to guard our freedom."[30] Echoing the language of post-9/11 warnings from the Department of Homeland Security, the *Walk East on Beacon* ad asked viewers to report:

- Espionage, sabotage, or subversive activities
- Possession and distribution of foreign-inspired propaganda
- Chartering of aircraft for flights over restricted areas
- Unusual fires or explosions affecting vital industry
- Suspicious individuals loitering near restricted areas
- Theft or unauthorized possession or purchase of large quantities of firearms, ammunition, or explosives, or short-wave radio devices
- Foreign submarine landings
- Suspicious parachute landings
- Poisoning of public water supplies
- Possession of radio-active materials

Undoubtedly, such pressbook materials were shaped by the FBI's cooperation with the Louis de Rochement production, but the overt attempt to recruit citizens as surrogate agents certainly enhanced the film's reception as anti-Communist propaganda.

Many of these films also employ the kinds of devices that Clyde R. Miller of the Institute for Propaganda Analysis saw as central to its appeal. "Name-calling," for example, was a common rhetorical device in anti-Communist cinema. Films like *The Red Menace* and *I Was a Communist for the FBI* depict party leaders as racists, catering to a sense of political alienation and anomie among racial minorities at the same time that they privately harbor prejudices toward these groups. Similarly, *The Red Menace, My Son John, Red Planet Mars* (1952), and other anti-Communist films utilize the device of "transfer" by relying on the authority and sanction of the church as part of their rhetorical appeal. Finally, as some critics of the period recognized, all of the films engaged in "card stacking" by dramatizing incidents that were riddled with half-truths and distortions.

Among critics the most serious objections involved the films' systematic association of the Communist Party with sex and criminal violence. Dorothy B. Jones, for instance, notes that the films themselves rarely offer an explanation for Americans' attraction to the Communist movement. "But in more than a few instances," adds Jones, "the main attraction is shown to be a woman, a formula which not only conforms to the Hollywood tradition, but often underscores the 'free love' viewpoint associated with radical movements."[31] Likewise, as Karel Reisz observed in 1953, the cycle puts forward the contention that the "American Communist Party is run by a gang of cheap though diabolically clever crooks, distinguishable from other hoodlums only in that their boss lives in the Kremlin."[32]

Jones's and Reisz's comments are a reminder that these films draw on traditional patterns of storytelling as much as they do the ideological mission implicitly mandated by HUAC. As Daniel J. Leab notes: "There can be no doubt that these post–World War II anticommunist films are clearly a product of the cold war. Yet it is important to note that the themes highlighted, the characters portrayed, the story lines set forth, and the images presented all had their roots in films produced twenty years earlier in the United States. Because of the cold war, these movies heavily emphasized certain aspects, but the concept of the films was in the mainstream of American filmmaking."[33] As we will see, in their reliance on the conventions of crime melodramas, legal thrillers, and social problem films, Hollywood's genre norms inflect the political message of these films in unusual and sometimes surprising ways.

MOVING PICTURE PARABLES: BLACKLIST CINEMA AND POLITICAL ALLEGORY

While a sizable corpus of anti-Communist films has been read as propaganda, a similar number of films have been read as political allegories offering disguised commentary on the operation of the blacklist, both pro and con. It is fair to say, however, that film critics and reviewers do not employ a precise concept of allegory for the films under consideration. The term *allegory* tends to be used very loosely and is often treated as though it were synonymous with other symbolic or figurative forms of storytelling, such as fables or parables.

Allegory itself has a complex history that stretches back at least to the ancient Greeks. Yet the term's current meaning also proves to be remarkably fluid as several modern film scholars are drawn to the concept through its usage by twentieth-century thinkers such as Walter Benjamin, Fredric Jameson, Paul de Man, and Gilles Deleuze.[34] Whether it is conceived as a rhetorical device, a narrative genre, or an aspect of deconstruction, allegory remains an important interpretive filter for critics writing about American cinema during the Cold War. In each of these interpretive contexts, allegory is viewed as a tool for filmmakers interested in offering indirect political commentary on the institutions and operations of the Hollywood blacklist.

One of the simplest definitions of allegory, going back to Quintilian, describes it as saying one thing but meaning another.[35] Although such a definition captures something necessary about allegorical narratives, it does not provide sufficient grounds for distinguishing allegory from other tropes, such as hyperbole or understatement, that also involve indirect forms of expression. To define allegory more precisely, literary theorists frequently point to the importance of extended metaphor as a distinctive trait of allegorical expression.[36] In allegorical literature or allegorical paintings the literal surface of the text contains representations that are metaphorical substitutes for persons, places, things, ideas, concepts, or values not explicitly represented.

Indeed, for some critics one of the most distinctive traits of allegorical expression is that the text signals these patterns of substitution to the reader in a way that effectively channels its own preferred interpretation. According to Northrop Frye, "We have actual allegory when a poet explicitly indicates the relationship of his images to examples and precepts, and so tries to indicate how a commentary on him should proceed."[37] Although a definition of *allegory* based on this conceit is likely too narrow to cover all cases, it is nonetheless true that this kind of figuration is common to core examples of allegory, such as *The Romance of the Rose*, *Piers Plowman*, and *Pilgrim's Progress*.

These different definitions of *allegory*, though, skirt an issue that many critics see as central to traditional definitions of the form. As Jeremy Tambling notes, classical Roman writers initially treated *allegory* as a term that refers to both the mode of writing or rhetoric that employs allegorical tropes and to a particular form of interpretation. Modern writers, though, have tended to split off the latter element from allegory, referring to it as *allegoresis*—that is, the practice of interpreting a text in an allegorical manner.[38] For texts conceived as allegory there is a fairly unproblematic fit between allegory and allegoresis since such works typically prescribe their interpretations through their use of extended metaphor, linguistic punning, or visual iconography.

Yet, having split off allegoresis from allegory, there is nothing to prevent the critic or reader from applying allegorical interpretation to any text. Because allegories are thought to conceal their didactic message to a greater or lesser degree, allegoresis can lead to a search for hidden meanings that is maddening at best and impoverished at worst. As Maureen Quilligan puts it, "Hunting for one-to-one correspondences between insignificant narrative particulars and hidden thematic generations, he [the reader] is frustrated when he cannot find them and bored when he can."[39]

Quilligan's implicit condemnation of allegoresis, however, begs an obvious question: how do allegories produce a degree of intersubjective meaning in their texts such that there is wide public agreement about what they signify? In an attempt to establish allegory as a particular literary form, Quilligan notes the importance of linguistic cues in allegorical literature, arguing that its status as genre arises from "the generation of narrative structure out of wordplay."[40] Quite often, this wordplay is evident in the naming of characters and settings. A canonical example is Prudentius's *Psychomachia*, in which the characters are named after virtues and vices, such as Chastity and Lust, and their battles come to represent the inner struggle for their souls.[41] John Bunyan employs a similar strategy in *The Pilgrim's Progress*, where the protagonist, Christian, must bypass the Slough of Despond, Vain Confidence, and Mr. Worldly-Wiseman in his journey to the Celestial City.[42] As Quilligan notes, such naming conventions are a defining characteristic of premodern allegories, but they also crop up in the work of some modern writers. Quilligan cites Thomas Pynchon's novels as emblematic of this strategy, particularly *The Crying of Lot 49* and *Gravity's Rainbow*.[43]

Very few of the films commonly deemed blacklist allegories employ the kind of wordplay or allusion that Quilligan sees as characteristic of literary allegories. Moreover, films like *Quo Vadis* and *The Robe* depart from the model established by *The Pilgrim's Progress* insofar as the diegetic content used to dramatize Christian martyrdom and salvation serves as an extended metaphor for the blacklist rather than the other way around. Punning or other forms of wordplay crop up from time to time as a localized feature of blacklist allegories and interpretations, but we must look elsewhere for a device that establishes the patterns of extended metaphor that link together textual features with their implicit meanings.

Besides the emphasis on wordplay in literary allegory, Quilligan further notes that allegories commonly contain a pretext, an embedded feature that channels the text's preferred interpretation. Quilligan describes the relationship between pretext and text in allegory:

> By pretext, I mean the source that always stands outside the narrative. . . . The pretext is the text that the narrative comments on by reenacting, as well as the claim the narrative makes to be a fiction *not* built upon another text. The pretext thus names that slippery relationship between the source of the work and the work itself; this relationship deserves a special term, for it is more complicated than the usual connection between a work and its sources, which are often no more than places where the author found stimulating ideas for fictional treatment of a given subject.[44]

In the case of medieval and Renaissance allegory, the Bible is the pretext. It need not be the whole of the Bible but rather may be simply an individual book or some passage within it.[45] Because of its wide circulation within medieval and Renaissance culture, the Bible furnishes a set of shared assumptions about the universe's origin, the nature of sin, and the future rewards that await those who live a pious life and take Christ as their Savior. Indeed, one reason why texts like *The Psychomachia, The Romance of the Rose, The Inferno, and The Pilgrim's Progress* all function as canonical narrative allegories is that their manifest contents ultimately lead back to the Bible as a pretext, one that furnishes latent signifieds that can be mapped in one-to-one correspondence with the manifest signifieds that constitute the surface text of such works. As Quilligan further notes, the Bible also functions as a pretext for many modern allegories, such as Hawthorne's *The Scarlet Letter* and Melville's *The Confidence Man,* that tell stories of sin and redemption or the search for spiritual meaning. Many films made by Vittorio De Sica, Ingmar Bergman, Luis Buñuel, and Federico Fellini also have a distinctly allegorical cast, in part because they either employ Christian iconography or because they pose questions about the possibility of grace and salvation.[46]

Yet given the multiplicity of contexts in which political allegories circulate, it seems clear that the Bible cannot provide a consistent frame of reference in all cases, even for texts that make use of Christian themes or iconography as part of their manifest content. Instead, in political allegory the relation between text and pretext is much more topical, with the pretext furnished by the reader's awareness of current events or policies. Indeed, it has become a truism to note that allegory is commonly used by artists laboring under oppressive regimes.[47] In these circumstances the relationship between manifest content and latent signifieds proves useful to the artist since it circumvents the official censorship of political speech while at the same time it shrouds the artist in a veil of plausible deniability.

Often cited as a canonical example of political allegory, L. Frank Baum's *The Wizard of Oz* offers a useful illustration of the way artists make reference to recent political events. Indeed, the story is now routinely taught in introductory economics courses to explain the history of monetary policy. While many readings of Baum's book differ slightly in their details, all authors agree that *The Wizard of Oz* offers disguised commentary on Democratic presidential candidate William Jennings Bryan's "free silver" campaign of 1896.[48] In this reading the colors green, gold, and silver serve as coded references to money: green refers to greenbacks or paper money, gold refers to the gold standard that was then current monetary policy, and silver—especially Dorothy's silver shoes—refers to Bryan's desire for the Treasury to coin silver bullion as a way of increasing money supply. A linguistic pun further supports Baum's allegorization of debates about a bimetallic money standard; the name *Oz* is inspired by the conventional abbreviation for ounce, the basic unit of measure for pricing precious metals.

The Wizard of Oz is a particularly lucid example of political allegory, but it is hardly the only one. Indeed, if we focus just on some recent examples, several films have been read as allegories of the 9/11 attacks. In these cases the U.S. battle against jihadists provides the pretext for the allegorical meanings of these works. Douglas Kellner, for example, describes contemporary alien invasion films like *The War of the Worlds* (2002) and *Cloverfield* (2008) as allegorical representations of Al Qaeda's attacks on the World Trade Center.[49] Andrea Comiskey summarizes the work of several reviewers and pundits who argue that Christopher Nolan's *The Dark Knight* (2008) functions as an allegory of Bush-era Homeland Security policies.[50] Even trade publications like *Variety* are not immune from this tendency. As Justin Chang said in an editorial that examined Hollywood a decade after 9/11, "Serious-minded fantasy films such as Peter Jackson's 'The Lord of the Rings' trilogy and the later installments of the 'Harry Potter' series (both franchises hit theaters in 2001) are informed by a sense of evil palpable yet elastic enough to invite a host of allegorical readings."[51]

During the period of the blacklist two texts were widely understood as Cold War–era political allegories: George Orwell's *Animal Farm* and Arthur

Table 1 Allegorical Parallels in *Animal Farm*

Animal Farm	*Soviet History*
Napoleon	Josef Stalin
Snowball	Leon Trotsky
Old White Boar	Karl Marx / Vladimir Lenin
Squealer	Vyacheslav Molotov
Moses the Raven	The Russian Orthodox Church
The Puppies	The Secret Police

SOURCE: Wikipedia, http://en.wikipedia.org/wiki/Animal_Farm.

Miller's *The Crucible. Animal Farm* was first published in Britain in 1945 and appeared in the United States about a year later. Within just a few months of its U.S. debut *Animal Farm* became a publishing sensation.[52] The book received several favorable notices from mainstream critics, and nearly all of these initial reviews identified recent Soviet history as the target of Orwell's satire. The fashion magazine *Vogue*, for example, featured a profile of Orwell in which the magazine attributed *Animal Farm*'s success to its trenchant critique of "the policies and philosophies of Soviet Russia."[53] Indeed, the anti-Stalinist message of *Animal Farm* was so widely recognized that Daniel J. Leab concludes, "No reader, either then or now, with even a smattering of knowledge of Soviet history from 1917 to 1944 could miss Orwell's obvious targets."[54]

Using Soviet history as the allegorical pretext for Orwell's zoomorphic fable, one can readily identify *Animal Farm*'s various characters as stand-ins for important figures in the Russian Revolution (see table 1). Although, in principle, the text of *Animal Farm* and its allegorical pretext function at discrete levels, Orwell deploys several references and allusions to Soviet history that connect the two levels:

- The farm animals' use of the term *comrades* as a form of address to one another

- The citation of October 12 as the anniversary of the Battle of Cowshed, a reference to the Bolshevik's October Revolution

- The episode of the confessions and executions overseen by Napoleon, a barely disguised allusion to the Soviet "purge" trials of the late 1930s

Through such references to these aspects of Soviet politics and history, *Animal Farm* easily fits Quilligan's definition of allegory as a literary genre that signals its preferred interpretation to the reader.

If *Animal Farm* is the prototype of anti-Communist allegories of the Cold War period, Arthur Miller's *The Crucible* is perhaps the era's quintessential anti-McCarthy or anti-HUAC allegory. Miller's play debuted on Broadway in January of 1953, just a few years after the publication of Marion L. Starkey's popular history of the Salem witch trials, *The Devil in Massachusetts* (1949). As Brenda Murphy points out, *The Crucible* essentially formalized parallels between past and present that were already well established in the critical reception of Starkey's history.[55] In a 1949 review of *The Devil in Massachusetts* McAlister Coleman wrote, "In this time of the prevalence of witch hunters the book should serve as a horrible warning, but it won't be read by those who most need warning."[56]

The renewed interest in the witch trials proved to be a crucial factor in Miller's decision to dramatize them on the Broadway stage. As Miller recalled in his memoir, "as though it had been ordained, a copy of Marion Starkey's *The Devil in Massachusetts* fell into my hands."[57] Starkey's book was like a bolt of lightning for Miller, who had dimly remembered learning about the witch trials in his college days but now saw the contemporary relevance of the story. Noting similarities in the way that HUAC informers and accused witches recanted their earlier statements, Miller wrote, "The hearings in Washington were profoundly ritualistic. . . . The main point of the hearings, precisely as in seventeenth-century Salem, was that the accused make public confession, damn his confederates as well as his Devil master, and guarantee his sterling new allegiance by breaking disgusting old vows—whereupon he was let loose to rejoin the society of extremely decent people."[58]

After reading Starkey's history, Miller traveled to Salem, where he spent three weeks conducting research in the village records. Drawing on this archival material and on Charles Upham's two-volume history of Salem witchcraft, Miller found all the details he needed to fashion a historical allegory that indirectly represented the events of the postwar Red Scare. When Miller found himself the target of HUAC's inquiry in 1956, Richard Arens directly asked the playwright about his awareness of the drama's allegorical dimensions: "Are you cognizant of the fact that your play *The Crucible*, was the case history in a series of articles in the Communist press drawing parallels to the investigation of Communists and other subversives by Congressional Committees?" Miller responded, "The comparison is inevitable, sir."[59]

Like Arens, several contemporary critics recognized the analogy that Miller drew between HUAC and the Salem witch trials. Eric Bentley, later an important historian of the HUAC hearings, wrote, "At a moment when we are all being 'investigated' or about to be 'investigated,' it is moving to see images of 'investigation' before the footlights."[60] In its review of *The Crucible* the *New York Post* added, "It is inconceivable that Miller is unaware that the year is 1953 and that a play about Salem's witch hunt was inevitably bound to stir contemporary echoes."[61] Even reviewers who disparaged Miller's treatment of his historical subject grasped his overall intent. Robert Warshow, for example, wrote, "Mr. Miller has nothing to say about the Salem trials and makes only the flimsiest pretense that he has. *The Crucible* was written to say something about Alger Hiss and Owen Lattimore, Julius and Ethel Rosenberg, Senator McCarthy, the actors who have lost their jobs on radio and television, in short the whole complex that is spoken of, with a certain lowering of the voice, as the 'present atmosphere.'"[62] Warshow's summary of *The Crucible*'s message follows the pattern I discussed earlier for other political allegories such as *The Wizard of Oz* and *Animal Farm*. He reads the text of *The Crucible* allegorically by bringing together a group of recent historical events that then serve to endow the play with covert significance.

Notably, though, Miller himself preemptively attempted to distance himself from the rather straightforward allegorical readings later offered by contemporaneous theater critics. In a 1953 profile of Miller written by Henry Hewes just prior to *The Crucible*'s premiere, the playwright averred:

> I am not pressing a historical allegory here, and I have even eliminated certain striking similarities from *The Crucible* which may have started the audience to drawing such an allegory. For instance, the Salemites believed that the surrounding Indians, who had never been converted to Christianity, were in alliance with the witches, who were acting as a Fifth Column for them within the town. It was even thought that the outbreak of witchcraft was the last attack by the Devil, who was being pressed into the wilderness by the expanding colony. Some might have equated the Indians with Russians and the local witches with Communists. My intent and interest is wider and I think deeper than this.[63]

Although *The Crucible* is undoubtedly the most widely recognized allegory of McCarthyism and the Hollywood blacklist, the Salem witch trials also proved to be fodder for political commentary on the small screen just weeks after the play's premiere. On March 29, 1953, *You Are There*, a CBS program devoted to recreating historical events as though they were breaking news stories, broadcast its own dramatization of the Salem witch trials.[64] Unbeknownst to viewers at the time, the teleplay for *You Are There*'s dramatization of the Salem witch trials was written by the blacklisted screenwriter Arnold Manoff.

In fact, Manoff was one of three blacklisted screenwriters—the others being Walter Bernstein and Abraham Polonsky—who collectively contributed more than fifty scripts during the show's five-year run. The trio worked through fronts and pseudonyms to deliver their scripts to the show's producer, Charles Russell, who in turn concealed the writers' identities from the show's sponsor. Manoff, Bernstein, and Polonsky's clandestine participation in the show lasted until 1955, when a CBS executive, William Dozier, revealed to the brass that Russell had deceived the network about the provenance of these scripts.[65] By then, though, the trio had written several additional episodes that offered allegorical commentary on McCarthyism and the HUAC investigations, including shows on Galileo, Joan of Arc, Socrates, and the Dreyfus case. Summarizing *You Are There*'s political slant, J. Hoberman writes, "Blacklisted writers managed to suggest that Communists or suspected Communists were being treated like the great martyrs of history; from McCarthy's point of view, Joan, Galileo, and Socrates were Commies avant la lettre."[66] Or as Bernstein colorfully put it, with Russell running interference for CBS, "we fought a kind of guerilla war against McCarthyism."[67]

Scholars have noted that a similar sort of political critique pervades producer Hannah Weinstein's series, *The Adventures of Robin Hood*. Since the series was shot in Britain, where the blacklist was not enforced, Weinstein was able to hire several blacklisted screenwriters, such as Ring Lardner Jr., Adrian Scott, Norma Barzman, and Ian McLellan Hunter, to pen individual episodes under pseudonyms.[68] Because of these writers' backgrounds, some critics discern a clear left-wing perspective in the way medieval England is depicted. Michael Freedland, for example, notes *"Robin Hood* stands out today as the finest hour of the 'Fronts.' It was perhaps the most popular black-and-white series of the 1950s in Britain and did well in America, too. What few Americans realised was that the fictional stories had as many left-wing sentiments in them as the statements the Hollywood Ten were unable to deliver when called to HUAC hearings."[69] James Chapman adds, "As well as responding to British society in the 1950s, *The Adventures of Robin Hood* can also be read in relation to Cold War America. The influence of the blacklisted writers is very apparent in the prominence of the recurring motifs of tribunals, inquisitions, witch hunts and informers that seem nothing if not an explicit commentary on HUAC and McCarthyism."[70]

As we will see, film critics performed a very similar operation in readings of dozens of films as blacklist or Cold War allegories. These films cut across a wide range of genres and cover the entire gamut of the political spectrum. Yet they all share at least one thing. They rely on a similar set of events to heighten and strengthen the analogies drawn between the film's dramatis personae and the totems of Cold War political culture.

A COGNITIVE APPROACH TO ALLEGORICAL READING: THE ROLE OF BIASES AND HEURISTICS

In *On the Origin of Stories* Brian Boyd notes that several academic critics have read Dr. Seuss's famous children's book *Horton Hears a Who* (1954) as a political allegory. The justification for this approach comes partly from Theodor Geisel himself, who acknowledged that the inspiration for the story came from his travels to Japan in 1953, just after the end of the Allied occupation. The story's theme ("A person's a person, no matter how small") reflected Geisel's perspective on the importance of voting in a new democracy, particularly among young people who had been indoctrinated by Japan's imperialist ideology during the war. Drawing out the implications of Geisel's comments, some critics have read *Horton Hears a Who* as an allegory about U.S.-Japan relations, with the elephant standing in for the United States and the tiny dust speck containing Whoville as a stand-in for Japan.[71]

Boyd is fairly critical of this interpretation of *Horton Hears a Who*, perhaps with good reason. He argues that this glib analogy fails to consider the allegorical significance of several of the story's other characters, such as the monkey family, the Wickershams, and a mother-child pair of kangaroos. It also elevates the causative dimension of local cultural influence at the expense of other levels of explanation. These include universals, such as Dr. Seuss's engagement of cognitive play and the interest in opposites and contrast frequently exhibited during early childhood development. These also include individual factors, such as Dr. Seuss's penchant for end rhyme and anapestic rhythm in his verse. For Boyd the reading of *Horton Hears a Who* as allegory is ultimately reductive in that it ignores these other levels of explanation.[72]

In contrast to reflectionist approaches, Boyd argues that we should see aesthetic choices operating within the framework of a problem-solution model. Such an approach is consistent with Boyd's evolutionary account of literature in that all biological organisms are problem-solvers and evolution itself actually generates both problems and solutions in the very process of generating life. The theory also explains very specific choices that writers make as they seek to gain the reader's attention, establish particular expectations, and decide whether to work within the constraints provided both by institutions and aesthetic traditions. As Boyd demonstrates, the analysis of such choices proves very illuminating in the case of Dr. Seuss, who by 1954 had not only developed a distinctive style but was reviving a character featured in his breakthrough success, *Horton Hatches the Egg* (1940). Thus, at least one of the challenges faced by Geisel involved the problem of returning to a familiar character without simply recycling the situation depicted in the earlier story.

As David Bordwell has argued, though, this problem-solution framework is equally applicable to the practice of film criticism. The critics identified by Boyd analyzed *Horton Hears a Who* as political allegory because they faced the same four problems that all critics face:

1. The problem of appropriateness (i.e., how to construct arguments for the significance of the text chosen for critical interpretation)

2. The problem of recalcitrant data (i.e., how to adjust one's critical concepts and methods to the specific features of the text)

3. The problem of novelty (i.e., how to avoid the replication of existing interpretations of the text under consideration or others like it)

4. The problem of plausibility (i.e., how to make the critical interpretation sufficiently persuasive)[73]

Although these goals are specific to the practices of critical interpretation, they fit quite easily into the multileveled biocultural approach outlined by Boyd. Critics, like fiction writers, must gain the reader's attention. Critics seek status and recognition within their respective communities. Critics must deal with the weight of tradition, particularly the norms and conventions established within particular critical institutions. Critics also must understand what counts as a "good" interpretation—that is, novel, persuasive, and well supported by evidence drawn from the text. As Bordwell puts it, "The critical institution—journalistic reviewing, essayistic writing, or academic criticism—defines the grounds and bounds of interpretive activity, the direction of analogical thinking, the proper goals, the permissible solutions, and the authority that can validate the interpretations produced by ordinary criticism."[74]

In addition to these general problems, critics performing allegorical interpretations face two more challenges. The first is the problem of differential levels of meaning (i.e., how to connect the latent, implicit meanings of the allegory to the manifest, referential meanings of the text). The second is the problem of framing (i.e., how to establish the appropriate critical frame for the narrative's allegorical pretext). Unlike medieval or Renaissance allegories that rely on Christianity as a common, widely understood pretext, contemporary political allegories rely on topical references that are part of the text's historical and cultural background. In blacklist and Cold War allegories the pretext is provided by HUAC's investigation of Hollywood in the late 1940s and early 1950s and by McCarthy's Senate investigation of alleged Communists working within American government.

Critics performing allegorical interpretations relied on a repertoire of particular textual components that could connect the latent and manifest meanings of Cold War–era films. This repertoire of elements aids the critic in solving two particular problems: the problem of plausibility and the problem of differential levels of meaning. These textual components include such elements as authorial intent, the political activities of personnel involved in the film's production, and specific genre conventions that lend themselves to the activation of the allegory's latent significance.

Not surprisingly, one of the easiest ways to support an allegorical interpretation is to assert that it was the author's intent to use the work as a comment on current political events. This way of motivating an allegorical interpretation proved to be important for certain canonical blacklist-era texts. In interviews conducted in the early 1970s, screenwriter Carl Foreman repeatedly asserted that he intended *High Noon* as a critique of HUAC's incursion into Hollywood. Similarly, although the politics are a good deal more complex, many critics argue that Elia Kazan's *On the Waterfront* is the director's cinematic defense of his testimony as a cooperative witness.

At first blush the documentation of a filmmaker's intentions seems to provide a straightforward warrant for a critic's allegorical interpretation of a work. Yet in practice the issue becomes far more complicated. For one thing, the number of examples where a filmmaker's intentions are known or documented proves to be rather small in comparison to the overall corpus of blacklist allegories. For another, even when a filmmaker aims to use allegory to offer political commentary, such intentions cannot cover every aspect of a film text, and those elements motivated by another rationale may confound or muddle its allegorical implications. This was the case with Brian Boyd's analysis of *Horton Hears a Who*, where it was difficult to explain the function of other characters in allegorical terms.

Because appeals to authorship often prove to have quite limited explanatory power, other critics cite the political commitments of a film's cast members or creative personnel as evidence for a text's manifest and latent meanings. These political actors essentially fall into three groups:

1. HUAC Witnesses, both "Friendly" and "Unfriendly." Many blacklist allegories feature the work of individuals subpoenaed to testify before HUAC. Some of these individuals were blacklisted writers who wrote new screenplays using fronts or pseudonyms to hide their participation. Others were cooperative witnesses, whose testimony is used to support allegorical readings of films about informers. In the case of *On the Waterfront*, for example, the warrant for allegorical interpretation depends not only on Elia Kazan's participation in the production but also on the contributions made by Budd Schulberg and Lee J. Cobb, who also testified as "friendly" witnesses before HUAC.

2. Conservative Members of the Motion Picture Alliance for the Preservation of American Ideals (MPAPAI). During the first round of HUAC hearings in 1947, many of the "friendly" witnesses were culled from the membership of the MPAPAI, which formed in 1944 to counter the left-wing influence of Communist Party members and Popular Front groups. The allegorical implications of several blacklist-era films devolve on the participation of MPAPAI members. Stuart Heisler's *Storm Warning*, for example, features two prominent MPAPAI stalwarts: Ronald Reagan and Ginger Rogers. Cecil B. DeMille's participation in the organization is widely seen as a warrant for the interpretation of *The Ten Commandments* (1956) as an anti-Communist allegory. *Johnny Guitar*, however, is read as an anti-HUAC tract, partly owing to the casting of MPAPAI member Ward Bond as one of the film's main villains.

3. Liberal Opponents of HUAC, like those who made up the Committee for the First Amendment (CFA). Like the MPAPAI, the CFA formed largely as a response to contemporary political events. Unlike the MPAPAI, though, the CFA was created to challenge the authority of HUAC as an investigative body and to provide public support for the Hollywood Nineteen. Humphrey Bogart's participation in the CFA—and, later, his status as a suspected Communist— is key to the articulation of blacklist subtexts in Nicholas Ray's *In a Lonely Place* (1950). More generally, though, any form of public opposition to HUAC or McCarthyism has provided the basis for allegorical interpretations of the blacklist. John Ford, for example, famously challenged the institution of loyalty oaths in the Screen Directors Guild. Ford's public stance in opposition to MPAPAI loyalists, like De Mille, encouraged his biographer,

Joseph McBride, to see several Ford films in the 1950s as disguised commentary on the blacklist. These include *Wagonmaster* (1950), which uses Mormons as allegorical stand-ins for suspected Communists, run out of town by a bigoted sheriff who is himself a surrogate for HUAC chair, J. Parnell Thomas (R, NJ). It also includes Ford's 1955 half-hour television program *The Bamboo Cross,* in which local Communist leader King Fat pressures a missionary, Sister Regina, to give false testimony against one of her fellow clergy. Although the politics are reversed, for McBride this scenario begs comparison to the plight of HUAC witnesses.[75]

Besides the critic's appeal to a film's personnel or to the authorial intention expressed through the text, a film's genre conventions also supply a set of "ready-made" tropes that can be used to connect the manifest and latent levels of allegorical meaning. Indeed, this means of connecting the manifest and latent levels of allegorical texts is inherent in several examples I have already discussed. It, for example, is implicitly part of the interpretation of *The Robe* as blacklist allegory. It also informs the aesthetic strategies of allegorists like Arthur Miller and the teleplay writers of *You Are There.* The use of Roman tribunals or Joan of Arc's martyrdom to comment on the HUAC investigations depends quite particularly on the juxtaposition of past and present events that exists as a potentiality of all historical films.

FRAMES AND REFERENCE POINTS IN THE INTERPRETATION OF POLITICAL ALLEGORIES

By using these strategies to connect the manifest and latent meanings of allegory, the critic creates a frame for the interpretation of specific features of a cinematic text. More important, as several experiments conducted by Daniel Kahneman, Amos Tversky, and others have demonstrated, such framing can have profound effects on judgment and decision making.[76] Several of these experiments examine "risky choice" scenarios, where the frame provides a shift in reference points that affects the way outcomes are perceived as gains or losses. The most famous example of risky-choice framing is the "Asian disease problem," which asked subjects to imagine an outbreak of an unusual Asian disease that is expected to kill six hundred people.[77] In each condition of the experiment, subjects were asked to evaluate two possible protocols for responding to the disease. In one version subjects were asked to consider the following:

If program A is adopted, two hundred people will be saved.

If program B is adopted, there is a one-third probability that no one will die and a two-thirds probability that six hundred people will die.

In this version of the problem, the initial condition established by program A emphasized a positive outcome, namely that a substantial number of lives would be saved. In a second version of the problem, however, the outcomes were framed differently:

If program A is adopted, four hundred people will die.

If program B is adopted, there is a one-third probability that no one will die and a two-thirds probability that six hundred people will die.

In the first version of the problem 72 percent of subjects chose option A. In the second version 78 percent chose the gamble expressed in option B , this despite the fact that the consequences established in both scenarios are identical. Kahneman and Tversky hypothesized that the discrepancy in responses can be attributed to prospect theory. Decision makers tend to be "risk averse" when the outcome proposed is good, but they tend to be "risk seeking"—that is, much more willing to accept a gamble—when both outcomes are framed as negative.

The experiment described above shows that judgments can be cognitively biased in situations that involve rational deliberation, but Kahneman and Tversky also showed that such biases exist even when the framing effect is created by an apparently random reference point. In a striking illustration of such influence Kahneman and Tversky rigged a wheel of fortune that was marked from 0 to 100 so that it would stop at either 10 or 65. The experimenters would spin the wheel and then asked subjects to write down the number that the wheel landed on, which, of course, could only be either 10 or 65. The experimenters then asked their subjects to estimate the percentage of African countries in the United Nations. As Kahneman explained, "The spin of a wheel of fortune—even one that is not rigged—cannot possibly yield useful information about anything, and the participants in our experiments should have ignored it. But they did not ignore it. The average estimates of those who saw 10 and 65 were 25% and 45% respectively."[78]

No matter how it is generated, framing effects research has repeatedly shown the importance of reference points in judgment and decision making. As Gideon Keren points out, reference point hypotheses are "based on the assumption that our perceptual and judgmental apparatus is attuned to process changes (rather than absolute terms)—hence any evaluation is relative to a reference point."[79] In fact, the influence on attentional processes may be the most fundamental component of framing effects. As Keren puts it, "Given the capacity limitations of the cognitive system, some selection has to be made and different frames evidently direct attentional resources to different aspects by cueing the system toward one or the other attribute."[80]

What does this research tell us about the way critics interpret texts as political allegories? I argue that critics deploy frames and reference points, like those used in experimental research, as a way of directing attention to specific aspects of cinematic texts. Obviously, critics are different from these experimental subjects in that they are not exploring risky-choice problems or performing tasks specifically assigned to them. Rather, critics create these frames in response to the institutional demands for novel interpretations described earlier. Moreover, critics' interpretations of texts represent a higher-order cognitive activity than the simple selection of option A or B found in many scenarios used in this type of empirical research.

Yet, because interpretation is dependent on underlying perceptual and judgmental processes, we should not discount the effects of framing on film interpretation simply because the critic's activity is self-directed and involves more complex forms of abstract reasoning. Instead, drawing on the insights of social and evolutionary psychology literature, we ought to consider the ways critics deploy frames to construct analogies between narrative elements and contemporary politics. Usually, this involves the selection of topical reference points that function as an allegorical pretext, which then guide the reader's attention to specific textual features while suppressing attention to others. In doing so, the critic provides a link between two types of framing effects: *frames of communication,* which center on the linguistic aspects of frame construction, and *frames of mind,* which center more on the mental processing of information. In the case of allegorical interpretation critics communicate both the way they have framed the text and the effects this framing has on their own processing of it as allegory.

Because blacklist allegories depend on specific political events as reference points for the interpretive frame, they are particularly prone to frame switching—that is, the same text can be interpreted in diametrically opposite ways. For example, such frame switching characterized the critical reception of *The Crucible.* In an editorial published in the *New York Post,* the newspaper noted that the play seemed to be intended as an indictment of McCarthyism but added that Miller's "loaded allegory" appeared to create more confusion than clarity in its disguised commentary on contemporary politics. Arguing that the international spread of Communism, unlike witches, constitutes a genuine threat to our national security, the *Post* editorial declared, "It is ironic that Miller's most fiery lines seem designed to caricature America's jitters rather than Prague's terror."[81] The reference to Prague's terror is telling in that it suggests that *The Crucible* might just as easily be read as a comment on Soviet show trials in Eastern Europe as it was a comment on McCarthyism.

Films like *High Noon* and *Invasion of the Body Snatchers* have been read as both anti-Communist and anti-HUAC, depending on the way the critic has assembled the topical reference points that serve as the text's allegorical pretext. This aspect of allegorical interpretation is consistent with a much larger ability to switch frames in the perceptual and cognitive processing of information. Such frame switching is evident in certain perceptual illusions, such as the famous Jastrow "duck-rabbit" picture. It is also evident in the relation between *content-locative* and *container-locative* linguistic constructions. As Steven Pinker demonstrates, in such constructions ordinary language serves as a means of framing the meaning of a statement:

> Imagine that the meaning of a content-locative construction is "A causes B to go to C," but the meaning of the container-locative is "A causes B to change state (by means of causing B to go to C)." In other words, loading hay onto the wagon is something you do to hay (namely, cause it to go to the wagon), whereas loading the wagon with hay is something you do to the wagon (namely, cause it to become loaded with hay). These are two different construals of the same event, a bit like the gestalt shift in the classic face-vase illusion on which the figure and ground switch places in one's consciousness.[82]

For Pinker, such frame switching is evident across a wide variety of mental activities. Commenting on a lawsuit involving insurance payouts related to the attacks on the World Trade Center on September 11, 2001, Pinker writes, "And the ability to frame an event in alternative ways is not just a reason to go to court but also the source of the richness of human intellectual life. As we'll see, it provides the materials for scientific and literary creativity, for humor and wordplay, and for the dramas of social life. And it sets the stage in countless arenas of human disputation."[83] One of those arenas involves dichotomous interpretations of Cold War–era films as allegories.

Although framing effects are evident in individual interpretations of specific films, other cognitive biases and heuristics are evident in the collective work of the critical community. As I noted earlier, the development of particular interpretive strategies in relation to Cold War–era cinema took place over time. Appearing around the same time as a more general rapprochement with the blacklist era, these critical commentaries contributed to the elaboration of a specific reading formation that allied Cold War cinema with allegorical expression. After the establishment of a small group of canonical Cold War allegories, such as *The Crucible* and *High Noon*, later critics who engaged in this critical enterprise relied on the availability heuristic to expand the category to include other members.

The availability heuristic describes a tendency in the human mind to react more rapidly and more strongly to information with which we are already familiar. In *You Are Not So Smart*, David McRaney offers a simple and elegant example of the availability heuristic. Most people, when asked whether there are more words in English that begin with *r* or have *r* as their third letter, believe the first of these two premises. But that belief turns out to be wrong. The fact that so many people guess wrong—that is, well beyond the level predicted by chance—reflects the availability bias. It is much easier to recall words that begin with *r* (rap, return, ring, rope, rude) than it is to remember words that have *r* as their third letter (hard, term, bird, coronation).[84] Sociologist Barry Glassner offers another example of the availability heuristic that is arguably closer to the kind of interpretive practices engaged by allegorical interpretation. Examining research on school violence, Glassner found that media coverage of school shootings in Kentucky, Mississippi, Arkansas, Oregon, and Colorado conveyed the impression that violence in schools had increased. It hadn't. In fact, as Glassner points out, violence in schools decreased by more than 30 percent throughout the 1990s. Yet the easy recall of these shootings—and the copy-cat crimes committed almost immediately afterward—intensified the belief that school violence was on the rise.[85]

When applied to the interpretation of blacklist allegories, we might hypothesize that critics are more likely to believe that such allegories were commonplace largely because of the ease with which a few prominent examples can be called to mind. This familiarity then leads them to propose new examples of blacklist allegory, which themselves function as additional prototypes of the phenomenon. The process might easily devolve into a vicious cycle as the gradual enlargement of the category creates an ever larger number of easily recalled examples. But the institutions associated with film criticism eventually provide a check on the infinite expansion of the category. Once the number of blacklist allegories achieves a sort of critical mass, the familiarity of the examples reduces the novelty value of any new cases that are nominated. By that point, however, the sheer number of familiar examples reinforces the impression that such allegories were commonplace, and the belief begins to take on the force of received wisdom.

The power of the availability heuristic is evident in Michael Freedland's brief analysis of screenwriter Carl Foreman's inclusion of "The Colonel Bogey March" in *The Bridge on the River Kwai*. Knowing Foreman's history with *High Noon*, Freedland speculates that the music functions as a kind of coded message to Foreman's inquisitors: "The traditional lyrics were obscured in the on-screen singing. But almost everyone seeing the film realised that the number was a verbal two fingers to the tormentors. It wouldn't take too much of a stretch of the imagination to believe that Foreman was directing his digits toward HUAC."[86] Arguably, Freedland came to this judgment based solely on his knowledge of the meaning of "The Colonel Bogey March." Yet the psychological studies demonstrating the availability heuristic suggest that Freedland was already attuned to the music's significance thanks to his preexisting knowledge of Foreman's history with HUAC.

During the period when the canon of blacklist allegories was enlarged, the availability heuristic was buttressed by other cognitive biases that tended to favor the inclusion of additional examples: the representativeness heuristic and confirmation bias. The representativeness heuristic refers to the tendency to perceive a greater probability for a statistically unlikely exemplum based on the fact that the data associated with it matches our preexisting schemas. Daniel Kahneman and Amos Tversky have demonstrated the importance of the representativeness heuristic in a series of experiments that asked subjects to predict the likelihood of a person's major on the basis of a personality sketch. For example, they showed that subjects predicted that someone who was intelligent and tidy, but wrote dully and mechanically, displaying a penchant for corny puns and science fiction references, was more likely to be a computer science major. This was despite the fact that the base rate for computer science enrollments was actually lower than several other fields. For most people, the degree to which the person conformed to our already existing prototypes for computer science majors outweighed the fact that it was statistically less probable. More tellingly, Kahneman and Tversky showed that representativeness affected judgment even for individuals who had experience working with statistics. Describing the outcome of this experiment when it was replicated with 114 psychology graduate students, Kahneman writes, "Substitution was perfect in this case: there was no indication that the participants did anything else but judge representativeness. The question about probability (likelihood) was difficult, but the question about similarity was easier, and it was answered instead."[87]

Here again, although allegorical interpretation involves a type of judgment different from that used in these experiments, the representativeness heuristic is suggestive for what it tells us about habits of mind, including those that inform film criticism. Once a film like *High Noon* is established as a familiar example of blacklist allegory, we are more likely to see other westerns that take up similar themes as representative of the category. Our intuitions about probabilities should tell us that there are far more westerns produced that have nothing to do with the blacklist. Yet when it comes to films that appear to match our schema for blacklist allegory—a schema that is shaped to a considerable degree by common conventions of the genre—we ignore that base-rate scenario and judge instead on the representativeness of the case. As a factor in the development of blacklist allegory as a specific reading formation, the representativeness heuristic favors the inclusion of an ever larger number of members in the corpus.

In a somewhat convoluted way the representative heuristic is an example of one last habit of mind that is important to the development of blacklist allegory as a particular reading formation: confirmation bias. Put simply, confirmation bias refers to a tendency to accept evidence that conforms to what we already believe and to ignore evidence that challenges these preconceived ideas.[88] According to Daniel Gilbert confirmation bias is produced through both the associative operations of memory and by the fact that we can only understand a proposition if we initially attempt to believe it. To understand an idea, we must know what the idea would entail if it were true. Only after this initial belief in the proposition can we decide whether we should disbelieve it. This need for initial belief extends even to propositions that manifestly appear nonsensical. Gilbert's example of this is the statement, "Armadillos relish imported cheeses." According to Gilbert, before we reject this idea as ludicrous, the associational processes of memory search for links between armadillos and imported cheeses in an initial effort to make sense of the senseless premise.[89]

Confirmation bias explains how critics engaged in the interpretation of films as blacklist allegories were predisposed to see specific examples as members of the category. If Gilbert is right, one initially would have to believe the proposition "*Warlock* is a blacklist allegory" before one could unbelieve it. In that moment when the mind strives to understand the proposition, the associational processes of memory attempt to forge connections between *Warlock* and the larger category of blacklist allegory. Such associationally linked aspects of the film might include (a) its resemblance to other westerns identified with that category, such as *Broken Arrow* or *Johnny Guitar;* (b) the participation of director Edward Dmytryk, one of the original members of the Hollywood Ten, in the film's production; and (c) Dmytryk's autobiographical comments on the film, which he saw as a critique of fascism.[90] Once these associative connections are made in the conscious mind, the critic then can mine the film for evidence that confirms this initial predisposition while ignoring any aspects of the film that appear to challenge it.

The cognitive biases and heuristics that I've described are not only key components of a biocultural approach to allegorical interpretation; they are also entirely compatible with the problem-solution model advocated by Boyd and Bordwell. Political allegories pose a specific problem for critics in that, unlike other allegorical texts, they do not rely on a widely disseminated body of knowledge that can serve as the pretext for the work's allegorical meanings. Instead, critics cite a set of topical reference points, which, in turn, endow specific features of a text with salience and significance. In the case of blacklist or Cold War allegories these reference points include the HUAC investigations of the 1940s and 1950s, the rise of McCarthyism, and the geopolitical tensions that existed between the United States and the Soviet Union. Besides the selection of reference points, critics engaged in allegorical interpretations also seek specific ways to connect the text's manifest and latent levels of meaning. To forge those connections for blacklist allegories, critics frequently appeal to the authorial intention behind a specific film or to the political commitments of those involved in its production. All of these specific challenges for critics would seem to fall on the "cultural" side of the ledger insofar as they are informed by the goals and protocols established within the larger institutions of film criticism.

Yet in seeking to meet those institutional goals, the particular interpretive strategies employed by critics are derived from habits of mind that are rooted in biological processes. These habits of mind are a consequence of the ways different parts of the brain interact with one another, a process that is itself the outcome of thousands of years of human evolution. Perceptual pattern-seeking, cognitive fluency, frame switching, and the associative processes of memory are all hardwired aspects of our brain's functions that will predispose critics to attend to films in a certain way. The development of blacklist allegory as a specific reading formation was itself produced by a unique combination of biological predispositions, cultural influences, institutional protocols, and large-scale historical processes. In laying out the way these elements interact, I argue that the understanding of allegorical interpretation as a critical practice requires a multileveled explanation akin to those proffered by other cognitivist scholars.

CONCLUSION

The institution of the Hollywood blacklist in 1947 remains one of the most noteworthy cultural events of the postwar era. The blacklist influenced the lives of Hollywood's labor force in myriad ways, nearly all of them bad. Careers were destroyed, friendships ruined, moral codes compromised, and individual directors and screenwriters were forced to work in exile. The divisive atmosphere created by the blacklist shrouded the entire industry with an aura of paranoia, suspicion, and fear.

Given its importance as an aspect of the industry's politics, it is not surprising that so many critics see it as a salient element in the meaning of particular film titles. Indeed, our evolved social intelligence makes it relatively easy to infer the intentions of individuals on both sides of the political divide. For those victimized by the blacklist, particularly those compelled to testify before HUAC, it requires little imagination to assume that "friendly" witnesses will seek to use their film projects as a way of justifying their own actions and that "unfriendly" witnesses will try to dramatize the individual and social costs paid by those who resisted the committee's tactics. Working within the chill created by the blacklist, such sentiments could not be expressed directly, though, and instead took the form of political allegory, a form commonly used by artists as a way to evade the strictures of institutional censorship. Similarly, for the studio heads placed under HUAC's spotlight, one readily surmises that the production of anti-Communist films served both as a response to public pressure and as a means of forestalling further investigations. In Hollywood's effort to demonstrate its political loyalty, the industry made a cycle of overtly didactic anti-Communist films that were widely and easily recognized as propaganda.

Yet while it is easy to understand the larger political motivations, one must also recognize that the expression of political views and attitudes was constrained by larger institutional forces, namely the narrative and stylistic conventions that constitute the classical Hollywood cinema as a particular mode of production. No matter how strongly one felt about the events of the blacklist, even the most blistering critique of "Red Scare" tactics had to be expressed in stories organized around goal-oriented protagonists who were engaged in agonistic conflicts with other characters that were structured in a causally linked series of dramatic events. The insertion of political content into these canonical story schemas was not always smooth, though, as the conventions of Hollywood narratives and genres exerted their own influence on the shape that these political sentiments took. In the next chapter I look at a prime example of the ideological confusion produced in such attempts to graft political views onto existing Hollywood conventions when I examine the function of the femme fatale as a character type in the cycle of anti-Communist films noir produced in the late 1940s.

2 I Was a Communist for RKO

Hollywood Anti-Communism and the Problem of Representing Political Beliefs

In the wake of the 1947 hearings conducted in Washington by the House Committee on Un-American Activities (HUAC) Hollywood produced several overtly anti-Communist films. Film historians have offered slightly different accounts of the number of anti-Communist films made during the late 1940s and early 1950s, but most estimate that close to fifty such films were produced.[1] Brian Neve, for example, suggests that the height of the cycle occurred during the three-year period from 1951 to 1953, when some forty-one anti-Communist films were released.[2]

As I noted earlier, these titles display many of the devices and techniques that were commonly associated with propaganda during the late 1930s and early 1940s. Films like *The Red Menace, My Son John,* and *Red Planet Mars* employ "transfer" techniques by associating anti-Communism with the sanction and authority of Christianity. *Red Planet Mars,* for example, tells the story of two American scientists, whose efforts to contact Mars inadvertently lead to the overthrow of the Soviet government by the Russian Orthodox Church. Hollywood's emphasis on Christianity as a counter to Communism may have been cued by HUAC itself. In a particularly notorious speech on the floor of the House, Mississippi congressman and HUAC member John Rankin said, "Communism is older than Christianity. It is the curse of the ages. It hounded and persecuted the Savior during his earthly ministry, inspired his crucifixion, derided him in his dying agony, and then gambled for his garments at the foot of the cross; and has spent more than 1900 years trying to destroy Christianity and everything based on Christian principles."[3] It may surprise some readers to learn that Marxist ideas predate Marx's birth by almost eighteen hundred years, but Rankin's comments nonetheless illustrate the extent to which Christianity, rather than capitalism, was viewed in the 1940s as Communism's natural ideological rival.

In addition to these "transfer" techniques, several anti-Communist films make use of "testimonials" that rely on recognizable public figures to bolster the film's political message. *Big Jim McLain*, for example, featured cameo appearances of the real-life members of HUAC, including Congressmen John Wood (D, GA) and Donald Jackson (R, CA). Presumably, the producers of *Big Jim McLain* believed that the brief appearance of HUAC members at the start of the film would enhance its anti-Communist message by associating it with the imprimatur of the committee.

Although the studios regularly produced anti-Communist fare during the Cold War period, the films themselves posed certain problems for their makers. For one thing, most of the early films in this cycle enjoyed little box-office success, an observation not lost on the studios themselves insofar as their own surveys demonstrated little to no interest in anti-Communist films on the part of film audiences.[4] By far the easiest solution to soft consumer demand was to simply stop making them. This, however, was not a viable solution as long as the films themselves served an alternate function in mollifying tensions between the industry and the American government.[5] Consequently, to minimize the economic risks of these films, the studios kept their production costs low. Of the fifty or so films that make up this cycle, relatively few had budgets resembling that of A pictures of the period, and relatively few featured top directors or stars.

A more vexing question for the studios was how to incorporate anti-Communist plots and characters into their standard fare. While Hollywood routinely capitalized on hot political issues and contemporary social problems, the threat of Communism posed certain problems from a dramaturgical perspective. This is because the defining characteristic of a Communist was not something that someone did or possibly even said but rather an underlying, unobservable set of political principles and beliefs.[6] As screenwriter Richard Collins observed: "Many Americans have never known a Communist personally. I'm afraid they won't recognize the girl next to them on the assembly line, or the old farmer next door as Communists because they haven't a real picture of what a Communist is. They have rather a bogey-man image. They expect a 'Communist type.' There is no such type any more than there is a Methodist type, or French type or capitalist type. *The only thing all Communists have in common is the way they think.*"[7] As a character trait or plot element, this, of course, leaves a lot to be desired. The easiest solution to this dilemma would be to have characters espouse their beliefs, but this in turn encourages screenwriters to commit the worst of transgressions in Hollywood, the unpardonable sin of "talkiness."[8] In the case of *I Married a Communist* this became a major concern during rewrites as screenwriter Robert Hardy Andrews was encouraged to "cut down on the talk" and to eliminate "'soapboxing' from any point of view."[9]

Indeed, the anti-Communist film's implicit reliance on dialogue became especially evident in *The Thief* (1952), a film that is generally regarded as a somewhat eccentric example of this cycle. Although the film is a fairly standard espionage thriller in terms of its plot, it attained a certain novelty status as one of a few films made during Hollywood's sound era that contains only a single word of dialogue. The film itself is not "silent" insofar as it makes use of sound effects and a synchronized music track, but it nonetheless harks back to Hollywood's silent era in its emphasis on an almost purely visual storytelling. *The Thief*, however, raised an interesting problem: if the characters don't speak, how does the film communicate its anti-Communist political slant?

The answer is it doesn't. Ray Milland plays a scientist who passes along atomic secrets to other members of a spy ring, but the film gives no verbal or visual reference to the ultimate recipient of this stolen information. Even Harry Popkin Productions' synopsis of *The Thief* omits any specific mention of the group or the country that operates the spy ring.[10] As a result of this circumspection, the critical reception of *The Thief* presented a range of responses to the film's political subtext. Most reviewers treated *The Thief* as a generic spy story and focused attention on its unusual approach to the soundtrack. Others simply assumed that the spy ring was working for the Communists.[11] Still other items, however, belie a certain hesitancy about assuming the identity of the film's villains. A *Los Angeles Times* story published a few months before *The Thief*'s release said, "[Clarence] Greene, who wrote the story with [Russell] Rouse, wouldn't divulge much of what it's about. I gleaned, however, that Milland plays a government scientist who becomes involved with foreign (Russian?) spies."[12] Similarly, the *Saturday Review* noted, "'The Thief' presents Ray Milland as an atomic scientist in the government's employ who, somewhat unwillingly, passes along top secret information to the agents of an unnamed (though reasonably obvious) foreign power."[13] Because *The Thief* rather self-consciously avoided the kind of soapboxing described earlier, reviewers were left to surmise that the film's villains were Soviet agents.

Rather than using dialogue to express a character's political beliefs, Hollywood more customarily presented figures who simply embodied certain political values through their demeanor or even physical stature. This is how, for example, the characters played by Gary Cooper and James Stewart in Frank Capra films were able to espouse the values and principles of 1930s populism.[14] The notion that political values can be communicated through a character's very mode of being raises certain questions about cinematic representations of Communism, however. How, for example, might a character embody the basic precepts of Marxist or Leninist thought? Is there a way to communicate one's belief in collective action and dialectical materialism through behavior or demeanor? Can one display one's misgivings about capitalism and class privilege through one's mode of being? Clearly filmmakers like Sergei Eisenstein thought so, but for various reasons their approach to a historical materialist form of film narration was never adopted by Hollywood.[15]

More typical of Hollywood's representation of Communists is the titular character of *Ninotchka* (1939), who embodies facets of Soviet Communism through her sobriety, humorlessness, and brusque interactions with others. When we are first introduced to Ninotchka, her simple, unadorned clothing and her unremittingly rational outlook mark her as a model of bureaucratic efficiency whose sole purpose in life is to labor in service to the state. As a caricature of Communism, Ninotchka lacks the nuances that might reflect more complex principles of Marxist philosophy. Still, she embodies certain political values associated with the Soviet Union as a carefully planned, centralized socioeconomic system.[16]

Although *Ninotchka* was rereleased after the HUAC hearings of 1947, the character did not appear to serve as a model for later screenwriters faced with the challenge of developing Communist characters. The parody of Communist ideology was an option for filmmakers, but such an approach risked alienating HUAC by making light of what the committee argued was a serious threat to American democracy. Instead, Hollywood more or less did what it always did with highly charged, controversial, or topical material: adapted it to the norms of Hollywood film style and narration. In fulfilling HUAC's ideological imperative, filmmakers formulated a set of interrelated narrative and representational strategies for incorporating anti-Communist subject matter into their work. On one hand, some films, like *The Thief,* treated the topic as the equivalent of Hitchcock's "MacGuffin," something that concerns the characters but to which the audience should pay no attention. Using this strategy, Communism itself becomes a detail that is more or less incidental to the plot and does not become an integral part of the themes or meanings of the work.

On the other hand, other filmmakers tried to integrate Communist characters or anti-Communist subject matter with existing generic and narrative formulas. More often than not, this involved a process of "shoehorning" anti-Communism into a preexisting mold. In this chapter and the next I explore Hollywood's attempts to create a strain of explicitly anti-Communist political propaganda by looking at four representative examples of this cycle: *The Red Menace, I Married a Communist, I Was a Communist for the FBI,* and *Big Jim McLain.* Of particular concern here are the ways in which Hollywood adapted anti-Communism to the generic constraints of film noir, the detective film, and the courtroom drama respectively, as well as the ways these strategies reciprocally inflected each film's representation of Communism. By bending anti-Communist subjects to these ideologically loaded genres, the films transformed political attitudes and beliefs into criminal behaviors. More important, the attempt to represent the lure and appeal of the Communist Party gives voice to more pertinent and relevant social concerns of the late 1940s and early 1950s. Ironically, by attempting to combat the threat of Communism in these films, Hollywood provided unwitting justification for its continued existence by acknowledging the pervasiveness of particular gender and racial biases.

THE RHETORIC OF REPRESSION: ANTI-COMMUNISM AND THE U.S. GOVERNMENT

Communism in the United States has never been a major political force, nor has it ever constituted a genuine threat to the security of the U.S. government. Despite its status as a minority voice in American politics, though, the American Communist Party (CPUSA) experienced unprecedented growth during the 1930s. Spurred both by the Depression and the growth of fascism in Europe, CPUSA membership increased from seventy-five hundred at the start of the decade to nearly seventy-five thousand by 1938.[17] At least some of the CPUSA's popularity during this period derived from its links to the Popular Front, a loose coalition of political groups united by their opposition to Nazism in Germany and fascism in Italy and Spain. The CPUSA also attracted members through its activist stances on a range of social issues. Along with other politically progressive groups of the period, the CPUSA marched on behalf of the unemployed in Chicago; it protested the lynching of young blacks in Alabama; and it supported labor strikes among farmworkers in California.[18] Communists in Hollywood shared the CPUSA's penchant for activism. Through the leadership efforts of screenwriters such as John Howard Lawson, Lester Cole, and Dalton Trumbo, Hollywood Communists participated in the formation of the Screen Writers Guild and the Hollywood Anti-Nazi League, and they organized benefits on behalf of the Loyalist cause in the Spanish Civil War.

Although anti-Communism did not emerge as a major political force in Hollywood until the mid-1940s, the roots of the Red Scare can be traced back to previous efforts to regulate domestic Communism, such as the establishment of the Fish Committee in the U.S. House of Representatives in 1930. Eight years later, Congress established a special committee to investigate un-American propaganda, naming the bill's sponsor, Representative Martin Dies (D, TX), chair after it passed the House by a vote of 194 to 41. Although the committee was ostensibly charged with investigating all types of anti-Americanism, Dies made left-wing extremism a central focus of the committee's first set of public hearings.

In 1940 Congress enacted still another measure aimed at limiting Communist influence on American politics when it passed the Smith Act, which made it unlawful to knowingly or willfully advocate overthrowing any level of government within the United States. By proscribing such activity, the Smith Act made it a crime to belong to any group that espoused revolutionary rhetoric, regardless of whether one individually subscribed to such beliefs.[19] The passage of the Smith Act had little immediate effect on domestic Communism. Although the FBI amassed evidence that could be used in prosecutions, no members of the American Communist Party were charged with violating the Smith Act until 1948. Most historians have explained this delay by appealing to changes in the political climate that occurred when the United States entered World War II. With the Soviet Union as an ally, the prosecution of American Communists was no longer a prudent political objective, and anti-Communists bided their time until the war's end.

The eventual indictment of Communist Party leaders for Smith Act violations proved to be the coup de grace for an organization that already had seen a mass exodus of members after the Nazi-Soviet Non-aggression Pact of 1939. In July of 1948 officials arrested twelve committee members of the CPUSA, including the party's general secretary, Eugene Dennis, and chair, William Z. Foster, for conspiring to advocate the violent overthrow of the government. The party's leaders were tried and convicted in 1949, and by the end of the year, both the defendants and their lawyers, who were cited for contempt of court, found themselves in jail. An appeal of the verdict went to the Supreme Court, which upheld the decision on June 4, 1951. Chief Justice Fred Vinson, who wrote the majority opinion, relied on a lower court precedent revising the interpretation of the "clear and present danger" doctrine to justify the Smith Act's restriction on free speech.[20]

Even prior to this prosecution, however, the Smith Act had already had an impact on the Hollywood blacklist. As several film historians point out, the lawyers for the Hollywood Ten rejected the use of the Fifth Amendment during the 1947 HUAC hearings because they feared that admission of Communist Party membership might result in Smith Act indictments for "unfriendly witnesses." The decision to go forward with the First Amendment defense had not been an easy one. By refusing to answer the committee's questions, the Hollywood Ten also rejected a third possible legal strategy, which was to admit party membership but in a way that tried to forestall Smith Act prosecutions.

Dalton Trumbo's preparation for his testimony before the committee indicates that this tactic was given serious consideration by the "unfriendly witnesses." In a document that appears to be a trial run for the hearing, Trumbo wrote the following as a reply to a potential query about the United States' form of government: "It is my conviction that the United States will, by constitutional amendment and popular vote, become a socialist state in one form or another."[21] As Trumbo's response indicates, had the Hollywood Ten cooperated with HUAC, they would have been at pains to emphasize their hope to change government by working within the system rather than by overturning it.

Besides influencing the legal strategy of witnesses before HUAC, the Smith Act also impacted Hollywood by serving as something of a rhetorical model for anti-Communist films. What proved to be particularly crucial about the Smith Act is that it did not outlaw the American Communist Party per se, a measure that would have been blatantly unconstitutional and would have alienated much of the bipartisan congressional support for the anti-Communist cause. In theory Smith Act violations could apply to anyone advocating political revolution, no matter what political party they belonged to. By focusing on a single aspect of Marxist-Leninist dogma, the Smith Act effectively criminalized membership in the Communist Party without actually attacking the core of Communist ideology. According to the law, Communists could freely criticize class privilege and capitalist exploitation. Communists could also advocate the redistribution of wealth and the elimination of personal property rights. What they could not do was advocate the overthrow of the government, and it mattered little whether individual members actually believed this principle. To put it bluntly, if you were a Communist Party member and had a copy of Marx and Engels's *The Communist Manifesto* on your bookshelf, then you were probably guilty of violating the Smith Act.

This still left those prosecuting Smith Act violations with a problem, namely how to rebut testimony by the accused that they never advocated or even believed in the overthrow of the American government. To solve this problem, prosecutors exploited a phrase used by Lenin that would allow judges and jurors to effectively discount such denials. Historian Ellen Schrecker describes the strategy:

> Enter "Aesopian language." The phrase refers to a statement by Lenin in the preface to a later edition of one of his early works in which he discussed how, in order to avoid Tsarist censorship, he had to make political observations "with extreme caution by hints in that Aesopian language—in that cursed Aesopian language to which Czarism compelled all revolutionaries to have recourse whenever they took to their pens to write a 'legal' work." Could it be that the troublesome language in the CP's constitution was just an Aesopian subterfuge designed like Lenin's language to protect the party from the hand of the law? Such a formulation would solve the government's problems; it would let future prosecutors claim that whenever the CP's leaders denied they advocated force and violence they were simply using "Aesopian language."[22]

Anti-Communist filmmakers pushed the rhetorical strategy employed in Smith Act prosecutions even further. Using a "dumbed-down" version of this logic, anti-Communist films employed representational strategies that almost literally "criminalized" membership in the Communist Party. In films like *I Married a Communist* and *The Red Menace,* Communist characters were not suspect because of their political beliefs but rather because they were gangsters, blackmailers, and murderers. To illustrate how these representational strategies were employed, I turn now to RKO's *I Married a Communist,* a film that draws heavily on the generic prototype established by the studio's earlier film noir classic *Out of the Past* (1947).

COMMUNISM AS GANGSTERISM: *I MARRIED A COMMUNIST* AS FILM NOIR

I Married a Communist (a.k.a. *The Woman on Pier 13*) was released in 1949 as RKO owner Howard Hughes's contribution to Hollywood's war on Communism. According to Larry Ceplair and Steven Englund, the film's script achieved a certain notoriety as something that served as a loyalty test for RKO directors. Hughes offered the project to any director who he suspected was a Communist, and if the director turned the project down, it confirmed for Hughes that he actually was one. The project is alleged to have been rejected by at least a dozen different directors, including such notables as John Cromwell, Nicholas Ray, and Joseph Losey, before it was finally helmed by future Disney auteur Robert Stevenson.[23]

Like other films in the anti-Communist cycle, *I Married a Communist* was a commercial and critical flop. When the film's first showings garnered little return at the box office, the film was retitled *The Woman on Pier 13* in hopes of downplaying the film's status as political propaganda and highlighting the romance and crime elements of its story line. Perhaps because of Hughes's personal interest in *I Married a Communist*, the film is one of the most frequently cited by scholars who have written about the blacklist. Yet despite its notoriety, the film has received almost no sustained critical attention. More often than not, *I Married a Communist* is simply dismissed as, in the words of Andrew Velez, "a museum piece, an odd *noir*-like propaganda document of nearly desperate and simplistic melodrama."[24]

I Married a Communist merits closer inspection, though, if only to reveal the ways in which Hollywood attempted to devise an aesthetic solution to potentially conflicting aims. If we situate this dilemma within the problem-solution model discussed in the previous chapter, it becomes evident that films like *I Married a Communist* tried to satisfy public expectations about Hollywood's role in the anti-Communist crusade while still trying to deliver an entertaining product to a large, politically diverse audience. Perhaps the most salient characteristic of *I Married a Communist* in this regard is the extent to which it derives its narrative strategies and visual style from another important cycle of the postwar period: film noir. It is the somewhat strange status of *I Married a Communist* as an amalgam of propaganda and noir that makes the film such a conundrum. Put simply, if one aims to use film to build political consensus, why borrow devices and storytelling strategies from the bleakest and most pessimistic films Hollywood ever made?

I should emphasize here that the identification of *I Married a Communist* as an example of film noir is by no means a controversial or even novel idea. In fact, the film is listed as an example of film noir in several reference works on the subject.[25] Moreover, James Naremore, Frank Krutnik, and Steve Neale have all identified *I Married a Communist* as part of a cycle of anti-Communist noir that includes titles such as *Big Jim McLain, I Was a Communist for the FBI*, and *The Thief*.[26] What none of these previous scholars have done, however, is to *analyze I Married a Communist* as a film noir. By addressing the question of the relationship between the film's generic status and its propaganda function, my argument parallels that of Thomas Doherty in "Hollywood Agit-Prop." Doherty argues that this cycle of films faced the double pressures of politics and the marketplace and thus strained to fulfill the expectations of being both propaganda and entertainment.[27] Doherty traces this problematic back to the films' adherence to classical Hollywood narrative strategies. I, however, wish to emphasize the ways in which specific genre conventions deform anti-Communist noir's ideological mission.

To call *I Married a Communist* a film noir, though, raises the question of whether one can meaningfully describe film noir as a film genre at all. This is by no means a simple question insofar as various attempts to define film noir as a genre are often as murky as the visual style of the films they seek to categorize. For the past several years various theorists have questioned the imprimatur of noir's most fundamental characteristics. Frank Krutnik, for example, challenges the idea that film noir is associated with a particular visual style by suggesting that "the elements identified by such critics as Paul Schrader and [Janey] Place and [Lowell] Peterson— compositional imbalance, *chiaroscuro* lighting, night-for-night shooting, etc.—are not specific to the *film noir*, nor to the crime film, nor to 1940s cinema."[28] Marc Vernet disputes the notion that German expressionism and hard-boiled literature should be seen as constituent influences on film noir's visual style and narrative strategies.[29] Michael Renov and Elizabeth Cowie question the extent to which the femme fatale is a character trope specific to film noir.[30] Finally, Steve Neale argues that flashbacks, temporal manipulation, and voice-overs are not typical traits of film noir narration in that many films appearing on canonical lists of the genre do not deploy them.[31]

Given these problems, the trend in recent research on film noir, and in genre theory more generally, has been to treat genres as discursive constructs that are inherently mixed and heterogeneous.[32] In *More Than Night: Film Noir and Its Contexts,* James Naremore makes just such a claim for film noir by treating the term not as an essentialist category, with clearly defined traits and boundaries, but rather as an ideological concept, with its own social and cultural history. Drawing on the work of Gregory Lakoff, Ludwig Wittgenstein, and Jacques Derrida, Naremore accepts their premise that concepts are formed out of "networks of relationship, using metaphor, metonymy, and forms of imaginative association over time."[33] In the case of film noir the category developed as a complex structure with fuzzy boundaries but with a core set of influential members at its center. By treating film noir in this way, Naremore acknowledges that certain canonical films are recognized as such by persons who use the term but that this is more because the term has a heuristic value within the linguistic community than because of any inherent meaning of the concept.

As a discursive construct, film noir maintained a complex relationship with both Communist and anti-Communist discourses of the period. As

Naremore suggests, the first decade of film noir was mostly the product of a vaguely leftist group of directors and screenwriters, who had previously supported Popular Front causes and New Deal programs.[34] Viewed from this perspective, film noir emerged in the late 1940s as a kind of outlet for this political ferment at a time when left-wing filmmaking was coming under fire both from HUAC and from Hollywood's MPAPAI. For other critics, like Paul Schrader, the Red Scare provided the ground for noir's prevailing mood of fear, suspicion, and paranoia while simultaneously giving voice to the sense of bitterness, defeat, and cynicism that resulted from the failure of 1930s progressivism.[35]

Both Naremore and Richard Maltby note that HUAC's efforts to monitor liberal and radical elements in Hollywood were mirrored by campaigns against film noir waged by sociologists, "psychocultural" analysts, conservative interest groups, and even liberal-minded film producers. What united all of these disparate groups was a distaste for films that focused on the base, elemental human passions that drove their characters to commit adultery and murder. Describing what we now refer to as film noir, these cultural commentators decried the films for their lack of socially redeeming values and for their sensationalistic treatment of the more vile and barbaric aspects of humanity. Chief among these attacks was John Houseman's broadside against "tough" movies in which he argued that films like *The Postman Always Rings Twice* (1946) will give future historians the impression that the United States in 1947 "was a land of enervated, frightened people with spasms of vitality but a low moral sense . . . a hung-over people with confused objectives groping their way through a twilight of insecurity and corruption."[36]

Yet, as Naremore also points out, the Communist Party itself joined this chorus of critics in questioning the social merits of film noir. This leftist criticism of the genre was related to the criticisms cited above, but it focused more specifically on the psychoanalytic dimensions of film noir characterizations. John Howard Lawson, perhaps the most ideologically committed member of the Hollywood Ten, argued that the purpose of revolutionary drama was to "circumvent a Freudian escape from truths people wished to avoid."[37] Embedded within Lawson's critique is an assumption that film noir emphasized individual psychological motivations at the expense of larger and more relevant social conditions. For Lawson and other leftist critics, the overheated crime melodramas of the 1940s laid the blame for social ills on psychological drives toward greed, lust, and murder rather than examining their root causes within the structures of capitalism, racism, and domestic fascism. Because it depicted irrational behaviors that were out of the individual's conscious control, film noir's treatment of social issues left no possibility for radical change.

All of these things suggest that film noir is a rather curious choice as a vehicle of anti-Communist propaganda. In fact, the social problem film seems a much more likely vehicle for anti-Communist sentiment based on the genre's tendency toward an earnest and sober treatment of issues and the greater sense of cultural legitimacy it derives from that approach. On closer inspection, though, it becomes clear that film noir offered certain rhetorical advantages to right-wing ideologues in Hollywood that the social problem film did not. By emphasizing the irrational causes of human behavior, film noir could illustrate how Communism "dupes" red-blooded American males. More important, by equating Communists with gangsters, thugs, and petty thieves, film noir could do something that the American government struggled to do, namely to "criminalize" membership in the Communist Party.

As a prototypical anti-Communist noir, *I Married a Communist* follows in the footsteps of *Out of the Past*, itself a widely recognized model of noir style and storytelling. Several factors account for the "family" resemblance between the two films. Both were produced and distributed by the same studio (RKO). Both feature some of the same personnel (cinematographer Nicholas Musuraca and production designer Albert D'Agostino). And both films treat characteristic noir themes, such as the threat of an enticing but malevolent female sexuality, and of a past that, in the words of Richard Maltby, contains "dark and menacing secrets that can no longer remain hidden, but must surface and find resolution."[38] In fact, this family resemblance might have been even stronger if *I Married a Communist* had used some of the personnel proposed during earlier stages of its production. In December of 1948 RKO announced that the female lead in *I Married a Communist* would be played by Jane Greer, who was so memorable as Kathie Moffatt, in *Out of the Past*.[39] Moreover, Howard Hughes asked the screenwriter of *Out of the Past*, Daniel Mainwaring, to work on the script for *I Married a Communist*. When Mainwaring refused, Hughes elected not to renew his option at RKO.[40]

As is typical of film noir, the character haunted by the past is *I Married a Communist*'s protagonist, Bradley Collins (Robert Ryan). In the film's first sequence Brad is shown registering at a hotel to celebrate his honeymoon with his new bride, Nan (Laraine Day). Later, in the hotel bar, Brad has an apparently chance encounter with his old girlfriend, Christine Norman (Janis Carter), who poses as a San Francisco magazine writer. As we subsequently learn, Christine is actually a Communist Party operative who uses her sexual allure to encourage young men to become party members. After a couple of scenes in which Christine investigates Nan's background and targets her brother, Don Lowry (John Agar), as her next conquest, Vanning (Thomas Gomez), the leader of the local Communist cell, visits Brad while the latter is working at the Cornwall Shipping Company. Vanning also poses as a San Francisco journalist, and during his brief meeting, he tries to blackmail Brad into rejoining the party. Unbeknownst to Nan, Brad was formerly known as Frank Johnson, an idealistic young Communist who participated in New Jersey labor strikes as a member of the party and who may have been criminally involved in the death of a shop steward.

Meanwhile, as Vanning utilizes Brad's criminal past to embroil him in party activities, Christine continues to mold Don into a model Communist. Soon both men use their positions at the Cornwall Shipping Company to create a deadlock in negotiations between labor and management and promulgate a strike that ties up the entire waterfront. After Don asks Christine to marry him, Jim Travis, the local union leader, accuses Don of letting Christine use him as a party stooge. Don confronts Christine about her politics and learns of Christine and Brad's past relationship as party members. Christine and Don's argument is interrupted by Vanning, who then arranges for Don to be killed in order to silence him. Despite a late warning from Christine, Nan watches helplessly as Bailey, a thug who operates a carnival shooting gallery, runs down Don with his car in an event staged to look like a "hit-and-run" accident. Because of Christine's phone call right before Don's death, Nan quickly surmises that Don was murdered because of his involvement with Christine. Nan then confronts Christine, who admits that Don was killed by Bailey to prevent him from revealing Brad's past association with the Communist Party. After Nan leaves Christine's apartment, Vanning enters and discovers Christine writing a suicide note that details her involvement with Communism. Vanning then throws Christine out the window of her apartment and destroys all evidence of her party affiliations. Vanning thus makes her death appear to be a suicide, one caused by the loss of a lover rather than her involvement in political blackmail and conspiracy.

Armed with the knowledge that Bailey functions as a hired assassin for the Communists, Nan goes to the carnival hoping to find information that will implicate Don's killers. To elicit a confession from Bailey, Nan poses as an unhappy housewife looking to have her husband killed to collect on his insurance policy, a scenario, of course, reminiscent of another canonical film noir, *Double Indemnity* (1944). In the midst of their conversation Bailey receives a phone call that warns him of Nan's true identity and is ordered to bring her to the warehouse that serves as party headquarters. Brad follows Nan both to the carnival and the warehouse. During a series of fistfights and gun battles, Brad rescues Nan by vanquishing Bailey and Vanning; the latter is killed with a cargo hook that reminds us of Brad's past status as a stevedore and labor organizer. Brad is wounded in the scuffle and lies dying on the floor of the warehouse. Surrounded by Nan, Jim, and various police officers, Brad offers a deathbed confession and tells Nan to accept Jim as a more appropriate romantic partner. In the film's last shot Brad grins in medium close-up and just before dying says, "I—always told you—you came along too late for me."

As is evident from this plot summary, the narratives of *Out of the Past* and *I Married a Communist* are structured around a similar set of characters and character functions. Like Jeff Bailey (Robert Mitchum) in *Out of the Past*, *I Married a Communist*'s protagonist, Brad, is someone whose position at the start of the film is threatened by his past identity and by a past murder he fears will be pinned on him. Like Kathie in *Out of the Past*, Christine is an archetypal femme fatale whose sexual allure drives men to foolish and self-destructive behavior. Like Ann in *Out of the Past*, Nan is the morally virtuous counterpart to the femme fatale, the figure who represents the protagonist's hope for a happy and secure future. Like Whit (Kirk Douglas) in *Out of the Past*, Vanning is the power outside the law, the figure who heads an underworld organization and who exploits the protagonist's past mistake for his own ignoble ends. Finally, like Joe in *Out of the Past*, Bailey is the underworld enforcer, the hired gun who helps to achieve his boss's objectives by intimidating, threatening, or murdering any character who stands in their way.

Besides sharing these character types, both films also share certain stylistic traits more generally associated with film noir. Much of this can be traced to the influence of cinematographer Nicholas Musuraca. Although Naremore notes that Musuraca's work displays very few of the traits highlighted by Janey Place and Lowell Peterson in their groundbreaking essay, "Some Visual Motifs of Film Noir," he nonetheless admits that the cinematography of *Out of the Past* "seems definitively noir-like, chiefly by virtue of its low-key deeply romantic 'painting with light.'"[41] The visual style of *I Married a Communist* may not be as celebrated or influential as that of *Out of the Past*, but it, too, displays a tendency toward low-key, "mystery lighting." As Patrick Keating notes, the lighting style of films noir was quite variable, exhibiting a tension between the realism and expressionism that informs its visual style in almost equal measure. Still, to the extent that films noir were melodramas, they were lit the way that cinematographers

Figure 1. This frame from *I Married a Communist* illustrates the moody look of Nicholas Musuraca's cinematography, a key aspect of the film's critical reception as an anti-Communist film noir.

had been lighting melodramas for many years: with, in Keating's words, "low-placed key lights, strong contrasts, and hard cast shadows on the walls."[42] Whether one views *I Married a Communist* as either noir or melodrama, Musuraca's camera work displays the kind of heightened expressivity that is associated with both forms.

Several sequences in the Collins's home use menacing shadows to suggest the threat Communism poses to Brad's marriage and home life. As in *Out of the Past*, Musuraca's lighting setups for these scenes in *I Married a Communist* motivate the key light in an apparent source, creating a visually striking chiaroscuro in which patches of light and dark fall over the walls of the Collins's den and staircase (fig. 1). Unlike *Out of the Past*, however, in this setup Musuraca places the sources above eye level rather than below. Thus, when combined with the shot's high-angle framing, Musuraca's setup suggests the forces of light and darkness pressing down on the film's characters. This motif is especially clear in the final shot of the sequence, when Brad returns home after being ordered by Vanning to tie up the waterfront. After Brad tells Nan to go back to bed, the film cuts of a medium close-up of Brad's face, a bright light from the couple's bedroom providing the source of illumination. As the camera holds on Brad's troubled visage, darkness passes over him and completely envelops him as the bedroom door closes offscreen. Throughout these sequences Musuraca's lighting scheme functions as something of a visual pun. By moving toward an increasingly shadowy mise-en-scène within the Collins home to parallel Brad's growing entanglements with the film's Communist thugs, the film visually reminds us of Communism's threat to Brad's "domestic security," a metaphor that equates Brad's marriage and family life with the nation at large.

Other sequences are even more striking in their use of noir lighting. Two scenes set in elevators, for example, utilize the confined space and mobility of the elevator car to create unusual lighting effects. In the second of these two scenes Brad scuffles with Arnold, one of Vanning's henchmen, in the warehouse freight elevator. Our view of the fight is obscured at several points by the alternating flashes of light and dark caused by the elevator's movement past the dimly lit floors of the warehouse. The lighting scheme for this shot not only heightens suspense by restricting the spectator's knowledge to what is heard on the soundtrack, but it also remains unusual for its almost stroboscopic effect.

By borrowing certain devices associated with film noir's visual style, anti-Communist noir gives a particular political valence to certain conventions associated with the genre. Darkness here becomes not just a metaphor of existential being, nor is it a mere signifier of noir's bleak worldview. Rather, darkness takes on a pragmatic aspect by cloaking political subversion within a shroud of secrecy. Anti-Communist rhetoric echoed this cinematic linkage between "shadows" and political conspiracy, ironically even as it pushed Communists further underground for fear of prosecution. According to Irwin Gellman, Richard Nixon believed that "Communists had to be forced into the sunlight, for the way to destroy a subversive philosophy was to sell democracy and the American way of life."[43] For Nixon darkness and shadows were associated with danger and conspiracy while light was associated with truth, knowledge, and public discourse.

Despite the similarities in plot and visual style, *Out of the Past* and *I Married a Communist* differ in some important respects. For one thing, because *I Married a Communist* does not use flashback structures, the genre's emphasis on "pastness" is something that is only thematized rather than functioning both at the level of theme and narration. Moreover, by giving us not one but two characters who are "duped" by Christine's political influence and sexual allure, *I Married a Communist* splits some of the film noir protagonist's narrative functions into two separate roles. Of the two, Brad more closely resembles archetypal film noir heroes, like Jeff Bailey and the Swede (Burt Lancaster) from Robert Siodmak's *The Killers* (1946), insofar as he is threatened at the start of the film by a guilty secret buried in his past. Don, however, more closely resembles these characters as they are depicted in flashback: weak males who are susceptible to the charms of attractive women and who are lured by them into a world of crime and corruption. By dramatizing Don's indoctrination into Communist Party rhetoric, the film implies that Brad underwent a similar transformation during his affair with Christine. Thus, the narration of *I Married a Communist* alludes to Brad's past as "Frank Johnson" without having to actually show it.

Perhaps the most salient difference between *I Married a Communist* and other films noir is the one most commonly cited by those film historians who have written about the Hollywood blacklist, namely the emphasis on the criminal underworld in the representation of Communism. Brian Neve, for instance, writes, "The equation of domestic communism with gangsterism is a feature of a number of films that picture an 'enemy within.'"[44] Likewise, Andrew Velez notes in his introduction to the published screenplay of *I Married a Communist*, "Set on the San Francisco waterfront, the Marxist heavies in the story are portrayed in much the same style as Depression-era gangsters and wartime-movie Nazis."[45]

Critical attention to the cycle's equation of Communism and gangsterism is nothing new, though. In fact, it was an important feature of the initial reception of films like *I Married a Communist*. The *New York Times* review of the film began, "An old story formula has been given a new look by R.K.O. Radio Pictures simply by substituting Communists for gangsters in 'The Woman on Pier 13.'"[46] Likewise, *Time*'s review claimed, "*I Married a Communist* is a celluloid bullet aimed at the U.S.S.R.—a stock gangster film with Communists dubbed into the underworld roles."[47]

Several instances of "gangsterism" occur in *I Married a Communist*, but certainly the most vivid is the sequence in which Bailey and Grip kill Ralston, a party member suspected of providing information to the FBI regarding the San Francisco cell's activities. The murder is staged for Brad's benefit and is performed with a particular sense of viciousness and cruelty. The murder scene begins with two shots of Bailey and Grip walking Ralston toward the end of a pier. The film then cuts to an eyeline match of Brad and Arnold as they quietly watch Bailey perform the preparations for the murder. This is followed by a brightly lit medium shot in which Bailey puts a belt around Ralston's torso to hold his arms close to his body. After another brief shot of

Brad and Arnold looking on, the film then cuts to a shot of Bailey binding Ralston's legs together, after which the two thugs carry their victim toward the left part of the frame. Then, in the most dramatic shot of the sequence, the film cuts to a shot that is roughly perpendicular to the previous setup that shows Bailey and Grip carrying Ralston toward the camera. The camera pans left and then holds as Ralston is brought directly into the foreground. The shot ends in a blurred close-up of Ralston's face as he screams for help. We then cut to a high-angle long shot at the end of the pier that shows Bailey and Grip throwing Ralston's body into the water. This is followed by a reverse-angle cut in which we see Bailey's and Grip's reactions as Ralston struggles helplessly to stay afloat. After a medium shot of Ralston bobbing up and down in the water, the film cuts to another medium two-shot of Grip and Bailey that shows a sadistic smile slowly creeping over the latter's face. The scene concludes with a shot of the water as Ralston's body finally sinks below the surface for good. Even for other films noir of the period, the murder is depicted as especially cold-blooded and is perhaps only surpassed by the famous scene in *Kiss of Death* (1947) in which Tommy Udo (Richard Widmark) gleefully pushes an old woman in a wheelchair down a flight of stairs. In fact, although the Production Code Administration (PCA) ultimately approved the scene, they expressed concern about the sequence's excessive brutality when the screenplay was submitted during preproduction. Even after the film was released, censorship boards in Australia and Ohio cut certain shots from the sequence, including that of Bailey's sadistic grin, as well as shots of Ralston struggling to stay afloat.[48]

Many historians and critics have identified this substitution of Communists for gangsters as an important feature of anti-Communist film noir, but few have broached the cultural implications of this generic trope. By juxtaposing seemingly antithetical discourses, the substitution of Communists for gangsters results in some basic ideological contradictions within the cycle. Many early critics of the gangster film noted that the genre derives much of its power and resonance from its situation within a capitalist economic and social order. As Robert Warshow so memorably put it, the gangster hero is "the 'no' to that great American 'yes' which is stamped so big over our official culture."[49] By taking American myths of individualism, opportunity, and hard work, and turning them on their head, the classic gangster film offers viewers its own variation of a "rags to riches" narrative, one in which the heroes achieve their position through ruthless ambition and brute force rather than through pluck, luck, and American ingenuity.

Unlike Communism, which advocates collective ownership and a classless society, the gangster film is not a negation of capitalism but rather its *reductio ad absurdum.* It thus presents us with the dark shadows of the American economic system, where market forces operate in their purest form. Unchecked by law, government regulation, or individual conscience, competitors are eliminated through deadly force, violence and intimidation serve as barriers to entry, and personal loyalties can always be exchanged for the promise of greater wealth and power.

Although film noir differs in important ways from the gangster film proper, it nonetheless inherits certain elements of its predecessor's treatment of capitalism. Like gangsters, film noir heroes and heroines are often driven by forces of greed and ambition. In *The Killers* and *Criss Cross* (1949) the characters attempt to outmaneuver one another for the loot from a heist. In *Out of the Past* Jeff's investigation is initiated by Whit's desire to recover $40,000 that Kathie has stolen but has not spent. In *Double Indemnity* and *The Postman Always Rings Twice* insurance money plays a large role in the characters' motivations. In its own way the very idea of "life insurance" offers a perfect condensation of film noir's attitudes toward capitalism insofar as it involves quantifying the exchange value of a human life. Film noir never questions the notion that life insurance can provide for an individual's economic security; rather, it merely suggests that there are legitimate and illegitimate ways of collecting it.

By juxtaposing an ideology of radical social and economic equality with one governed by self-interest, anti-Communist film noir pushes the contradictions inherent in this mismatch to the point of logical absurdity. In one particularly odd scene in *I Married a Communist* Vanning is shown paying off Bailey for killing Don. After receiving $1,000 for the contract killing, Bailey asks for a little extra for doing such a clean job. The negotiation between the two seems unintentionally humorous insofar as it invokes a much older version of a market economy, in which the barter system determines the exchange of goods and services. Far from the planned economies of socialist states, the bartering between Vanning and Bailey seems like an almost pure application of the capitalist principles of supply and demand.

The promotional material for *I Married a Communist* adds further confusion to this already muddled ideological mix. Rather curiously, a caricature drawing of the film's principal characters depicts them as though they were members of high society rather than thugs and common laborers. Don, who works as a stevedore on the docks, is shown grinning happily and dressed in a somewhat dapper suit and tie. Nan and Christine are shown in elegant, strapless evening gowns. Christine holds a cigarette and martini glass. A far cry from the drab uniforms and peasant dress worn by Russian communists in films like *Mission to Moscow* (1943) and *Song of Russia*

(1944), the drawing of the characters in *I Married a Communist* evokes the wit and sophistication of the Algonquin Round Table or, at the very least, the guest list at Sardi's.[50] Although the image is motivated by the cocktail parties that Christine throws to draw new members to the Communist Party, as an image circulated among potential filmgoers, the drawing reminds us of the difficulties inherent in representing a group defined by its political beliefs. Since cinematic representations of American Communists had not been codified in terms of dress or physical appearance, one might just as easily use the iconography of the romantic comedy as the iconography of the gangster film.

Operating within a broader cultural context, Hollywood used the representation of Communists within fictional contexts to provide the connection between political belief and criminal activity that HUAC sought in its investigations but was generally unable to prove. Curiously, though, in *I Married a Communist*, characters such as Vanning and Christine bear little resemblance to the Communists envisioned by the architects of the Smith Act and the McCarran Internal Security Act. Although they employ the trappings of conspiracy (microfilm, secret hideouts), they do very little that might be construed as sedition or sabotage. Rather, by conflating discourses of Communism and gangsterism, these films show Communists performing acts of extortion, blackmail, and murder, acts more appropriate to Al Capone than to Leon Trotsky.

In fact, because of this conflation of discourses, some contemporary reviews of anti-Communist film noir suggest that the films fail in their propaganda aims. The *New York Times* reviewer for *I Married a Communist* wrote: "Although there is a strong resemblance between the tactics used by Communists and those generally accredited to gangsters on the screen forcing reformed associates back into evil ways of life, this similarity would not be objectionable in itself. After all outlaws are pretty much the same no matter what their objectives. But current events are making too sharp an impression, and, as a consequence, certain mental barriers work against a picture such as 'The Woman on Pier 13,' in which the cards are so obviously stacked."[51] Similarly, in his review of *The Red Menace* Bosley Crowther wrote: "Pardon us for pointing—but if the Communist party in the United States is as lacking in discipline and cohesion as it is made to appear in the picture entitled 'The Red Menace,' . . . then we need have no great anxiety of it fouling our American way of life."[52]

Perhaps the most peculiar reference *I Married a Communist* makes to contemporary events, however, is found in the published screenplay for the film, where the San Francisco cell leader is named Nixon. The character's name likely alludes to future president Richard Nixon, who by 1949 was established as one of the nation's most important Communist hunters. The film's release predates Nixon's notorious "Red-baiting" campaign against Helen Gahagan Douglas in the 1950 California Senate race, but Nixon was already well known as a member of HUAC and as the political force behind the prosecution of Alger Hiss for perjury.

According to Daniel Leab, the character's name went through several incarnations and was changed to "Nixon" in the penultimate draft of the script by Robert Hardy Andrews. In correspondence between RKO and the Pacific American Steamship Association, which was vetting the names of characters to avoid any resemblance to an actual person, the association commented, "If your central character is to bear the name 'Nixon' and if you are portraying him as a communist, you might be in for a ribbing in view of the identical name of a Congressman from your own district who introduced into the 80th Congress a bill controlling the red brethren."[53]

Although Leab offers no explanation for why the name "Nixon" was chosen by Andrews nor any indication of why it was subsequently changed to "Vanning," the name change raises the tantalizing possibility that Andrews intended to subvert the film's putative ideological mission by establishing an implicit parallel between HUAC and the Communists depicted in the film. A metaphorical reading of the scene where Brad is taken to the warehouse would seem to support this possibility. In Andrews's script Brad is brought before Nixon, who questions him about his Communist past as "Frank Johnson" and confronts him by producing a copy of Brad's party membership card. If the final film had not changed the villain's name to "Vanning," it would have effectively suggested that the real-life California congressman employed tactics similar to the political blackmail and extortion depicted in the film.

POLITICAL DIFFERENCE AS SEXUAL DIFFERENCE: THE "RED SPY QUEEN" IN *I MARRIED A COMMUNIST*

A more important ideological contradiction in *I Married a Communist* is evident in the film's treatment of gender. Just as anti-Communist film noir conflates politics and criminality, it also conflates politics and sexuality through the archetypal figure of the female Red agent, who functions much like the femme fatale of film noir. Although the femme fatale is described in myriad ways by film scholars, the female Red agent is often discussed simply as a stock character in anti-Communist films. Nora Sayre, for example, writes, "In these movies, there is a figure whom my notes identify as the Bad Blonde: in the 1950s, you knew there was something wrong with a woman if her slip straps showed through her blouse; in this context, it meant treason."[54] Similarly, Dana Polan argues that "the forties film noir seems to offer a malevolent image of a seductive femininity little different from the malevolence of a postwar communism (with the two frequently combined in the representation of the dark-haired, exotic Russian agent out to trap American men in such films as *The Woman on Pier 13* [*I Married a Communist* (1949)] or *The Red Menace* [1949])."[55]

Although Christine Norman is neither Russian nor dark-haired, her character in *I Married a Communist* shares many traits with the femme fatale. Like Kathie in *Out of the Past* or Kitty (Ava Gardner) in *The Killers*, Christine is a woman of dubious virtue who uses her sexuality to achieve her aims. As several feminist scholars have argued, women like Christine retain a fascination despite the apparent misogyny of the genre.[56] Much of this fascination derives from the genre's tendency to invest the femme fatale with sexual power and thus treat her as a narrative agent with clearly defined goals. Unlike the male heroes, though, the femme fatale rarely takes direct action herself but instead manipulates the male characters by encouraging them to commit acts that go against their better judgment—in this case, to abandon their political beliefs to become members of the party. As the professor says of Don during Christine's party, he is "ideologically uninformed but emotionally receptive." By emphasizing the notion of emotional receptiveness, the film suggests that Christine's sexual attraction paralyzes men's intellectual and critical faculties. As an embodiment of the party's allure, Christine literalizes the metaphor of political seduction. She indoctrinates members not on the basis of political issues or policies but rather as compensation for the sexual favors she dispenses. The poster art of *I Married a Communist* featured copy highlighting this aspect of Christine's character by indirectly describing her as a prostitute: "Nameless, shameless woman. Trained in an art as old as time."

In fact, this advertising campaign was so explicit about Christine's sexual appeal that it caused concern within the Advertising Code Administration. In a letter from Gordon White of the administration to S. Barret McCormick, RKO's director of advertising and publicity, White indicates that he received a number of complaints regarding *I Married a Communist*'s campaign and that he never approved the copy in the form that it appears on the film's poster. White goes on to say that he reluctantly approved the ad in its original form, where the objectionable copy was "followed by text which ties it in with a story of mob violence and crime."[57] In a separate letter to Perry Lieber, McCormick admitted that the two phrases had been removed from their original context. In its original form the two headlines read: "Nameless, shameless woman—she served a mob of terror and violence whose mission is to destroy" and "Trained in an art as old as time—she follows a vicious pattern, first an innocent flirtation, then pretended love, then disgrace, finally murder."[58] As this correspondence suggests, the Advertising Code appeared to have no problem with the insinuation of prostitution as long as it was linked to a downward spiral of violence and did not imply the woman's profiting from her activities.

While Christine, in many ways, fits the archetype of the femme fatale, her image also evokes a more topical and more concrete reference point: the "Red Spy Queen" Elizabeth Bentley, whose cooperation with U.S. officials created a minor media frenzy in the late 1940s. As Kathryn Olmsted points out, two veteran anti-Communist journalists—Nelson Frank and Frederick Woltman—hyped Bentley's story, describing her as a "svelte and striking blonde" who had mysteriously turned informant, providing the FBI with material about the Russian spy ring she ran. Although Frank's image of Bentley was an attempt to "sex up" his story to sell papers, other journalists followed his lead, embroidering the image of her as a "red spy queen."[59]

According to Olmsted, the newspaper coverage of Bentley's exploits drew heavily on an existing repertoire of representational tropes for international espionage and political subversion: "To explain her [Bentley] to their readers, journalists fell back on popular stereotypes of female spies and Communists. Depending on which newspaper they read, Americans learned that Elizabeth was either a sex-starved, man-eating temptress or a sexually repressed man-eating spinster."[60] In fact, while I have found no evidence that Bentley was a specific role model for Christine, J. Hoberman reports that RKO initially planned to feature Bentley in a topical prologue to *I Married a Communist*.[61] Bentley's "party girl" image, which was augmented by rumors of alcohol abuse and sexual promiscuity, seems consistent with certain aspects of Christine's character that were played up both in *I Married a Communist*'s promotional material and in the film itself.

As Sayre and Polan seem to indicate, Christine is not unique in this regard. The metaphor of indoctrination as sexual seduction was a frequent trope of anti-Communist cinema and encompassed several different kinds of films in the cycle. On one hand, in *The Red Menace* one of the main supporting characters, Mollie O'Flaherty, is described in the film's shooting script as "man bait" for prospective Communists.[62] As a result of this description, the Production Code Administration cautioned the screenwriters of *The Red Menace* that "extreme care" should be exercised in Mollie's characterization and that the film should not suggest that "she promiscuously dispenses her virtue as a tool of the party."[63] On the other hand, *Walk East on Beacon* draws a figurative analogy between Communism and seduction in a speech given by Matt Foss, a cab driver operating as a courier in a Communist spy ring. In a scene midway through the film, Foss describes his early involvement with the Communist Party to his wife, Rita. As a kid growing up during the Depression, Foss "wanted to help get the world back on track." Foss's association with Communism began innocently enough as he attended meetings, listened to speeches, and sang songs at party functions. Describing what followed, Foss says, "When I came to, I had a card in my pocket. My party name was Vincent." On the word *Vincent*, director Alfred Werker cuts to a close-up of Foss, who exclaims, "It was like waking up finding yourself married to some woman you hate, so you start hating yourself."

An even more striking conflation of sexuality and Communism occurs in a rather different dramatic context near the beginning of *Jet Pilot*, Howard Hughes's other major foray into anti-Communist cinema, made in 1951 but not released until 1957. Shortly after her mysterious arrival at an Alaskan air base, Anna, a Russian fighter pilot played by Janet Leigh, asks to take a shower after being searched by her American counterparts. After some flirtation between her and American pilot Jim Shannon (John Wayne), Anna comes out of the bathroom, draped only in a towel, and proceeds to dress in front of the two men assigned to question her. Director Josef von Sternberg handles this sequence by alternating medium shots and medium close-ups of the two men gawking at Anna with medium shots and close-ups of Anna putting her clothes on. The sequence culminates with a shot of Anna, now clothed in long underwear, coming around a pot-bellied stove in the middle of the room and turning her backside toward it to get warm. After an eyeline match to a two-shot of the two men followed by still another shot of Anna warming her fanny, Sternberg cuts to a medium close-up of Jim as he leans in and says, "This might be some new form of Russian propaganda." By describing Anna's coy flirtation as "propaganda," Jim implies that his arousal constitutes a kind of political engagement in which his judgment and critical thought processes have been impaired.

The trope of Communism as a form of seduction even includes much later films that were ostensibly critical of Hollywood's actions during the blacklist. In *The Front*, for example, there is a scene in which Hecky Brown (Zero Mostel), the popular television host of *Grand Central*, explains to a HUAC investigator why he marched in a May Day parade and subscribed to the *Daily Worker*. In an attempt to absolve the character of any possible guilt in the eyes of the audience, the film has Hecky declare that he never actually read the *Daily Worker* and that he only participated in these activities to impress a cute young Communist woman with a "big ass." In their attempt to forestall criticism from the right and the suggestion that hardcore Communists were rightly blacklisted, director Martin Ritt and screenwriter Walter Bernstein make Hecky a character that is not only apolitical but also lacks judgment and self-control. Ritt and Bernstein's way of rendering Hecky politically innocuous is to blame the woman with the "big ass" and to suggest that his activities as a Communist sympathizer were all part of an elaborate, but ultimately innocent, game of seduction.

Christine's "bad girl," though, is counterbalanced in *I Married a Communist* by another recurrent character in film noir, the archetypal "nurturing woman" who provides an explicit contrast to the femme fatale's dangerous sexuality.[64] In *I Married a Communist* this generic and ideological role is filled by Nan Collins, who, in this respect, is similar to other generic prototypes, such as Lola Dietrichson in *Double Indemnity* or June Mills in *Fallen Angel* (1945). By pairing Nan with Christine, *I Married a Communist* establishes a set of structural oppositions at the start of the film that define each woman's role according to its relationship to both home and work.

Two early sequences involving the film's representation of domestic space serve to underline the contrast between Nan and Christine. During an early sequence we learn that Nan operated her own business as an interior decorator and that the couple met when Nan was hired to redecorate Brad's office at the Cornwall Shipping Company. After returning from their honeymoon, Nan and Brad receive a Ming vase as a wedding gift from the Cornwalls. As Nan is opening the gift, Don asks Nan if she will redo the living room. Nan replies that just as it is too late to change Brad, it is too late to change the room. This brief exchange economically delineates both the Collins's home as a stable domestic space and Nan's place within it. Not only does Nan give up her career to become Brad's wife, but she is also deterred from employing her professional skills in her own home. Nan's entry into the "marriage contract" defines her role as strictly a domestic partner, and as such her professional skills are laid to rest in favor of her "wifely duties," which involve maintaining the family home in accordance with her husband's wishes.

The sequence preceding this one, however, features a rather different treatment of domestic space and femininity. Here Christine's kitchen, a space strongly coded as feminine, is transformed into a makeshift darkroom in order to process microfilm obtained by the party. Unlike the Collins home, which is initially treated as a kind of domestic sanctuary, Christine's apartment collapses the distinction between public and private spheres in that it functions as both her home and her workplace. As a party functionary, Christine is something of a "career woman," but her effectiveness as such depends on her apartment's appearance as a space of ordinary domesticity. Christine's kitchen is used for food preparation but is also used for purposes of espionage. Her bedroom appears to be a place to sleep, but it is also the film's primary site of party indoctrination.

Unlike other films noir, however, the narrative trajectory of *I Married a Communist* problematizes any simple opposition between femme fatale and "nurturing woman." For one thing, Christine is differentiated from her generic prototype by the fact that she does not operate in her own interests but rather serves the interests of others. In several canonical films noir, greed is a motivating factor for nearly all the characters and applies equally to both the duped hero and the manipulative heroine. This is not the case with Christine, however, who subordinates her desire for personal gain, emotional well-being, and even sexual fulfillment to the particular needs and goals of the Communist Party.

Christine's difficulty in controlling her feelings and sexual desires becomes an important source of dramatic conflict that serves to motivate her later conversion. This theme comes to the fore in a scene midway through the film, when she argues with Vanning about her right to a private life. When Vanning accuses Christine of bugging Brad just for the emotional satisfaction, Christine responds, "And emotion is something you are not built to understand or appreciate." To this, Vanning answers that Christine has responsibilities to the party that are "not to be endangered by personal entanglements." Later, the conflict will resurface when Christine tries to refuse a party assignment. When Vanning indicates that her assignment was intended to separate her from Don so that she may gain proper perspective on their relationship, she responds, "I will worry about my private life." To this Vanning retorts, "You *have* no private life."

These two scenes raise two important issues concerning Christine's relationship to the femme fatale figure. First, they suggest that Christine is finally never as coldly calculating as other femme fatales. Second, unlike other femme fatales, Christine's position within the film undergoes an important shift that enables her character to experience a kind of political redemption. Kitty, the duplicitous heroine of *The Killers*, is perhaps the *locus classicus* of the calculating and manipulative antiheroine who remains unchanged throughout the course of the film. In the final scene of *The Killers* Kitty begs her dying husband to proclaim her innocence to Riordan, the insurance investigator played by Edmond O'Brien. In contrast, Christine goes through a transformation linked to the film's treatment of public and private spheres. Whereas Communism itself is shown to blur the boundaries of public and private life such that one's service to the party or the state effectively erases the latter, Christine's feelings for Don encourage her to reclaim her private life and to join Don in a romantic, rather than strictly sexual, union. The prospect of becoming Don's wife—and being something other than a party agent—suggests Christine's gradual alienation from the party and her desire to return to a normative notion of femininity. When Don is murdered by party thugs, Christine confesses her role in his death to Nan. Her actions thus effect a kind of betrayal that is typical of the femme fatale, but rather than betraying the trust of the duped hero, Christine betrays the principles and beliefs she espoused at the start of the film.

Like Christine, Nan also undergoes a major shift in the course of *I Married a Communist*. As the archetypal "nurturing woman," Nan initially is identified with notions of domesticity and is rarely shown outside of the Collins's home. As the film progresses, Nan becomes less an unsuspecting and supportive wife and more an investigative agent within the film's narrative. Midway through the film, Nan begins to question Brad about Communist influence on the union, about Brad's past relationship with Christine, and about Christine's politics. Her brother's death also signals an important change in Nan's relation to the narrative. Where she had previously been content to simply asks questions, she now takes it on herself to infiltrate the Communist ring in order to learn the truth about Don's murder.

Just as Kansas did in *Phantom Lady* (1944), Nan adopts the persona of the femme fatale to enter several settings that are iconically and narratively linked to noir as a genre, namely the carnival midway, the nightclub, and the warehouse that serves as the party's base of operations. Liberated from the confining space of the home, Nan plays the "bad girl" in an attempt to trick Bailey into acknowledging his culpability for Don's death. This shift in the film's representational strategies is signaled most clearly when Nan picks up the rifle in Bailey's shooting gallery. Framed in a two-shot, Bailey moves from the right-hand part of the frame to a position directly behind Nan. Bailey uses the same pickup line here that we've heard him try earlier on two other women: "You need practice, baby, lot's of practice." Positioned behind her, Bailey is unable to see the evident discomfort on Nan's face. Despite her distaste for Bailey, Nan gamely plays the interested suitor in order to maintain Bailey's interest. The dangerous sexuality associated with Nan's femme fatale pose is metaphorically suggested by her marksmanship. Impressed by her shooting skills, Bailey drily remarks, "Who d'ya wanna kill?"

Nan's role-playing continues in two later scenes at the Gay Paree, a seedy nightclub patronized by Bailey. In one sequence Nan pretends to have a friend who wants her husband killed so that she may collect the insurance money. Bailey agrees to do the job for a thousand dollars, but Nan insists that the death be made to look like an accident. In fishing for information about Don's death, Nan asks Bailey for some proof that he can pull off such a job. Bailey's response to Nan covers the next eight shots of the sequence, which are edited in a conventional shot/reverse shot pattern. In the medium shots of the sequence, each character plays his or her role in a prototypical film noir scenario: Nan plays the femme fatale looking to get rid of her husband and Bailey plays the two-bit Lothario, who hopes to seduce his counterpart by impressing her with his toughness. In the close-ups, however, Bailey and Nan each reveal the true nature of their characters. On one hand, Bailey reveals himself as a cold-blooded killer, who smiles and even laughs at the recollection of another man's brutal death. Nan, on the other hand, reveals herself in her reactions to Bailey's description of the hit-and-run accident. Her performance as a "bad girl" is just that—a performance—but it has allowed her to get the admission of guilt from Bailey that she sought.

By the end of *I Married a Communist* Nan and Christine have exchanged places within the film's configuration of sexuality, femininity, and domesticity. Where several other films noir are structured around the stable opposition between the femme fatale and the nurturing woman, *I Married a Communist* problematizes such a simple binarism. Although this representational strategy serves to differentiate *I Married a Communist* from other films noir, it also raises a larger question about the film's broader function as propaganda. In other words, what does the film's representation of women tell us about the potential appeal of Communism as political discourse, and why is this more dynamic treatment of gender roles linked with the film's delineation of public and private spheres?

Perhaps the simplest element to explain is Nan's masquerade as a murderous seductress. Feminist critics have long argued that such characters bespeak a kind of cultural fascination with sexually aggressive and dangerous women. Christine's movement, though, from "bad girl" to "nurturing woman" demands a more complex explanation. At one level it is not uncommon for propaganda films to feature a character who serves as a kind of surrogate for the audience's political, rather than social or aesthetic, experience of the film. This character is typically distinguished from others by the way he or she gradually comes to grips with the film's moral or political lessons. Christine would seem to serve that ideological function in *I Married a Communist*. She begins the film as a somewhat committed Communist agent but comes to realize the evils of the party's activities. The way Christine comes to this realization, however, indicates *I Married a*

Communist's limits as propaganda. Christine gradually comes to resent the demand for unquestioning loyalty to the party, yet she only takes action after it orders her boyfriend's death. Moreover, because Christine's death occurs as a result of defenestration, it might well remind viewers of Jan Masaryk, the Czech minister of foreign affairs widely believed to have been assassinated by a Soviet agent. Consequently, it is almost impossible to disentangle whether the lesson Christine learns is one that involves the dangers of political obeisance or one that involves political extortion and assassination.

At still another level there is a dimension to Christine's experience that is related to her attempts to balance her public and private life. Through her work indoctrinating members of the party, Christine enjoys a certain status within the cell and has been given, in Vanning's words, important responsibilities. Christine also works as a newspaper photojournalist as a cover for her party activities. Although *I Married a Communist* complicates Christine's professionalism by creating a narrative conflict between work and romance that ultimately is only resolved through her death, her characterization nonetheless reminds us that one reason for the Communist Party's appeal is that it promised a greater measure of political and social equality to its female members.

More important, the depiction of Christine's status within the party is entirely consistent with both earlier and later Hollywood representations of the social and political status of women within Communism. In *Ninotchka*, for example, director Ernst Lubitsch exploits and overturns our assumptions about gender roles in the Communist Party for the titular character's introduction. The film's trio of Soviet envoys—Iranov, Buljanov, and Kopalski—go to the train station in Paris to greet a special envoy from Moscow whom they have never seen. In a lateral tracking shot framed as a medium long shot, the trio approach someone they believe looks like a Russian envoy but are taken aback when the gentleman turns to another person on the platform, raises his arm, and says, "Heil Hitler." Lubitsch then cuts to a long shot of a lone woman standing in the deep background, who we soon learn is Ninotchka. Much to the surprise of the trio, the envoy is a woman. This simple misrecognition gag contains several elements related to the representation of gender in Soviet Communism. First, as I noted earlier, the gag is predicated on the notion that there is nothing special or unusual about a person's appearance, physiognomy, costume, or bearing that would differentiate a Communist from a non-Communist. As William Paul points out in his analysis of the scene, since the trio simply assumes the envoy to be male, they approach someone who is revealed to be a Nazi, a person who represents the Communist's most bitter political rival in Europe during the 1930s.[65] Second, the trio appears to make the assumption that the envoy is male because the communiqué from Moscow gives no evidence to the contrary. The inference we might draw from this is that Moscow offers no comment on Ninotchka's gender since women's presence in the Soviet political system is commonplace enough that it need not be specified. When the trio finally meet Ninotchka, they do indeed comment on her gender, but this seems more to register our surprise at this turn of events than to imply that Ninotchka holds a unique or unusual position. In fact, Lubitsch has coyly used viewers' tendency to employ the representativeness heuristic against us. Just because male political envoys are the norms both in the United States and in the Soviet Union, we should not automatically assume that an individual envoy is male.

Warner Bros.' wartime paean to the Soviet Union, *Mission to Moscow*, also contains several sequences that refer to the different social statuses of Russian and American women. The film was an adaptation of a best-selling book by former ambassador Joseph Davies and recounts his experiences as a diplomat in the Soviet Union. The film became something of a cause célèbre after its release in 1943 because of its gross distortion of Stalin's purge trials of the 1930s. Later, in October of 1947, HUAC would grill Jack Warner about his involvement with *Mission to Moscow* and even targeted the film's screenwriter, Howard Koch, as one of the nineteen "unfriendly" witnesses subpoenaed to testify.

In a sequence from *Mission to Moscow* that contains echoes of *Ninotchka*, the Daviesses' butler, Freddie, approaches a woman standing in a locomotive cab and asks if she likes to ride with the engineer. Much to his surprise, the woman replies that she is the engineer. Interestingly, this misrecognition gag is predicated on the fact that Freddie is an American and has certain preconceptions about the role of women in the workplace. The implication of the gag is that no Russian would make the same mistake since it is relatively commonplace in the Soviet Union to see women in jobs that, in the United States, are typically held by males. Later, Mrs. Davies meets her counterpart, Mrs. Litvinov, the wife of the Russian president. After a series of shots that orient us to the space of Mrs. Litvinov's cosmetics shop, the two women sit down for tea. In a series of shot/reverse shots, Mrs. Litvinov and Mrs. Davies explain their preconceptions about Russian and American women. Expressing surprise that Mrs. Davies once ran her father's business, Mrs. Litvinov says, "We were under the impression that American women were ornamental and not useful. And you thought that our women were functional but not ornamental." In a sequence that parallels the one between Mrs. Davies and

Mrs. Litvinov, the Davieses' daughter, Emeline, meets the Litvinovs' daughter, Tanya. Whereas Emeline is characterized as a typical American teenager, Tanya is a paratrooper and is active in the Soviet military. Finally, *Mission to Moscow* also includes a montage sequence that shows Davies inspecting various aspects of Soviet industry. As part of his tour, Davies talks with a Russian woman who works as a coal miner. When the woman asks Davies if there are any female miners in America, Davies retorts with a shockingly cavalier comment linking American women to both domesticity and death: "Well, there's no law against it, but we don't like to put them underground until we have to."

While *Mission to Moscow* might seem exceptional in that it was made at a time when the Soviets were American allies, one can find plenty of other working women in the cycle of anti-Communist films produced during the late 1940s and early 1950s. Echoing the representational strategy seen in *Mission to Moscow*, women are depicted as spies, political operatives, and military personnel in films like *The Red Menace, Walk East on Beacon, I Was a Communist for the FBI, Red Planet Mars*, and the aforementioned *Jet Pilot*. Christine's characterization in *I Married a Communist* is consistent, therefore, with the broader image of women Communists seen throughout the 1940s and 1950s. This is not to say that real-life Soviet women somehow had it better than American women, nor is it to suggest that Russian women did not suffer in their own way under the structures of patriarchy. What it does suggest, however, is a sense that, in the popular imagination of Americans, Communists treated women differently, more as active and productive members of society and less as wives and mothers.

This articulation of female professionalism would have special resonance for American movie audiences of the late 1940s. As many historians have noted, women entered the workforce in unprecedented numbers during World War II, thus bringing them closer to the social position of women in the Soviet Union. Many of these jobs as machinists or assembly line workers were previously held by men, who became either volunteers or conscripts in the U.S. military. The "Rosie the Riveter" phenomenon was seen as a shift in employment policies that was primarily motivated by wartime conditions, but it accorded women an unusual degree of importance and status within the workplace.

As was the case with female Communists, the "Rosie the Riveter" phenomenon was also subject to cinematic treatment. Perhaps the best example of Hollywood's representation of wartime working women was RKO's *Tender Comrade* (1943). Directed and written by two members of the

Hollywood Ten, Edward Dmytryk and Dalton Trumbo, the film is an archetypal example of the Hollywood "home-front film" that details the travails and sacrifices of those who supported America's war efforts by their activities at home. *Tender Comrade* stars Ginger Rogers and tells the story of four women who work in an airplane factory and live together in a large old house. The women ostensibly move in together to save money, but their communal living situation quickly reveals the filmmakers' leftist political sensibilities.[66] The house itself becomes a metaphor for a model society in which all decisions are made collectively and all responsibilities are shared equally among the tenants. Disputes arise, but they typically are related to broader wartime concerns, such as rationing and hoarding, and are mediated within the context of the group's needs rather than as a matter of individual rights and responsibilities.

Not surprisingly, *Tender Comrade* would come under suspicion during the HUAC hearings of 1947 and would be singled out by the star's mother, Lela Rogers, as an example of Communist propaganda being smuggled into a film. At issue was a scene in which Manya, an older immigrant woman who cooks and cleans for the other women in exchange for room and board, receives a medal that her husband has earned during his tour of duty. Although Manya initially proposes that she keep the medal in her room, Doris, one of the other tenants of the house, suggests that she display it on the living room mantle where it can serve as a symbol of war sacrifice for the entire group. Doris justifies her request by appealing to the house's system of democracy, saying that it is "share and share alike, isn't that right?" Manya assents to the request by replying, "Uh huh. Democracy." For Lela Rogers the redefinition of democracy as a form of collective ownership epitomized the threat that Communist screenwriters posed to the industry and the nation as a whole. Though less obvious, what may also have been at issue is not merely how *Tender Comrade* redefined democracy but how the film redefined gender roles within that democracy.

As both a working woman and a femme fatale, Christine Norman necessitates a double strategy of ideological containment that goes beyond that normally associated with film noir. On one hand, by restoring the boundaries between public and private, *I Married a Communist* strives to align Christine with emerging ideological norms of femininity. On the other hand, since her politics are seen as inextricably linked to her excessive and threatening sexuality, *I Married a Communist* eliminates her in the most brutal fashion possible at the very point that she comes to espouse the film's larger political message. As is typical of film noir, Christine's femme fatale is no less doomed than the film's duped heroes.

CONCLUSION

I Married a Communist's conflation of professionalism, gangsterism, femininity, and sexuality reveals the paradox that exists at the heart of anti-Communist film noir. Communism becomes suspect not merely because it will overturn our country's political and economic structures but also because it threatens to alter the very social fabric of our nation. In articulating the reasons for Communism's appeal as a political philosophy, the anti-Communist film noir provides inadvertent justification for the party's importance. Although the CPUSA was certainly not a paragon of political progressivism in the area of gender issues, it nonetheless offered small hope—more than the traditional two-party system offered—to those who believed that women might be something other than wives, mothers, and domestic custodians. This was achieved less through party politics than through the images of Communist women circulated in popular texts of the period. Although anti-Communist film noir attempts to dismiss those who fall prey to Communism's allure as being, like Brad Collins, weak-willed and weak-minded, it ultimately betrays its own principles by caricaturing the party's operations as political blackmail and extortion. If most film audiences saw through this rhetorical strategy as easily as most reviewers did, then one must posit another underlying, more genuine, reason for the party's appeal. As we will see in the next chapter, the reason may be that anti-Communist films unwittingly gave voice to those most marginalized by American politics: women and people of color.

3 Reds and Blacks

Representing Race in Anti-Communist Films

In a 1953 article for *Sight and Sound*, critic and future director Karel Reisz offered a catalog of various features common to anti-Communist films made in Hollywood. Besides the element of gangsterism, Reisz noted several other traits, including Communism's relationship to science, intellectualism, neurosis, and megalomania respectively. In the middle of Reisz's list, however, is a particularly incisive, if often overlooked, aspect of Hollywood's representation of Communism, namely its inclusion of Jews, African Americans, and other people of color in the Communist cells depicted onscreen. Interestingly, Reisz distinguishes this subtype of Hollywood Communist from the others by suggesting that their motivations for joining the party are untainted by neurosis or power madness: "There are only three ways a normal, honest person can become a communist. He may be temporarily discontented by some social injustice. . . . He may be a Jew or a negro—if so, the film will patronise him and he will leave in the final reel. Or, most reliably, his clean animal instincts will let him down."[1]

Reisz's observations are interesting for several reasons, not the least of which is that he associates "animal instinct" with people of color. More to the point, this emphasis on instinct is set in opposition to the intellectualism regularly found in representations of party leadership. As a result, racial difference is, at least within the limited context of Hollywood's portrayal of the Communist Party, associated with honesty and normality, a striking shift away from the way Anglo-European whiteness establishes the normative terms for society as a whole. Reisz implies that white European Communists are cold-hearted, twisted freaks, but African American and Jewish Communists are good-hearted folk, driven to join the party out of feelings of social unrest.

In establishing this division within the Communist Party between whites and people of color, Reisz insinuates that some reasons for joining the party may be more legitimate than others. Although it is easy to dismiss those drawn to the party because of some personality flaw or psychological disorder, it is less easy to dismiss people driven by their political discontent. The latter are shown to be misguided souls, but one can understand their dissatisfaction, especially those who faced racial discrimination on a daily basis and were confronted by social structures that offered little redress and even less hope. For this reason Jewish and African American Communists engage our empathy insofar as their motives for joining the party arise from their hope for sweeping social change, a change they believed would never come from America's two-party system.

Reisz, however, stops well short of making a much more startling observation about Hollywood anti-Communist cinema, namely that lurking somewhere behind the cycle's simplistic politics and ham-fisted characterizations lies a kernel of genuine political and social critique. If one grants that blacks and Jews had legitimate reasons for becoming Communist Party members—reasons that have nothing to do with the violence, extortion, sabotage, and blackmail that function as propagandistic "name-calling" in anti-Communist films—then one must also grant that the basis for this social discontent was quite real. In an odd way, anti-Communist films became strange bedfellows of the liberal social problem films of the 1940s to the degree that both were part of a small group of Hollywood films that openly addressed racism as a social and political concern.

In this somewhat narrow aspect Hollywood anti-Communism generally sought to distinguish itself from the right-wing extremism that aligned with the anti-Communist movement more generally. As historian Ellen Schrecker points out, white supremacists, segregationists, and Dixiecrats had a natural affinity with the anti-Communist sentiments of HUAC and McCarthy.[2] HUAC member John Rankin (D, MS) was one of the most vicious anti-Semites in American politics. In a particularly notorious speech before the House of Representatives, Rankin attacked members of the Committee for the First Amendment, who had lobbied on behalf of the Hollywood Ten in 1947, because their Anglicized names hid their actual Jewish origins: "One of the names is June Havoc. We found that her real name is June Hovick. . . . Another one is Eddie Cantor, whose real name is Edward Iskowitz. There is one who calls himself Edward Robinson. His real name is Emanuel Goldenberg. There is another here who calls himself Melvyn Douglas, whose real name is Melvyn Hesselberg."[3] Generally speaking, segregationists greatly benefited from the emergence of anti-Communism as a political force since they could dismiss any effort to overturn the Jim Crow laws of the South as the result of the international Communist conspiracy.

Given this larger political picture, Hollywood's avoidance of anti-Communist race-baiting seems even more remarkable. Whereas Washington's most vocal anti-Communists saw the participation of blacks and Jews in the Communist Party as symptoms of Communism's malignant infiltration of front groups, Hollywood saw the participation of blacks and Jews as symptoms of larger underlying social problems. In anti-Communist films people of color may be "dupes," but they were sincere and well-intentioned dupes. The political task of Hollywood anti-Communism was subtly altered by this assumption. Instead of demonizing persons of color, Hollywood sought to show that Communists cynically used them as political pawns.

Despite the suggestiveness of Karel Reisz's analysis of anti-Communist films, subsequent scholars and historians generally have ignored this component of Hollywood's propaganda. Although some scholars have addressed the relationships between Communism and sexuality in Hollywood's Cold War films, there has been relatively little consideration of the relationship between race and anti-Communism. In this chapter I examine this relationship in more detail by looking at two pertinent issues of Hollywood's anti-Communist films: (1) what are the predominant strategies that Hollywood's anti-Communist films used to represent race and ethnicity; and (2) in what ways have Hollywood films sought to discredit the Communist Party's appeal to people of color.

In my discussion I attempt to chart the range of approaches Hollywood anti-Communist films took to these issues by examining three films thought to be prototypes of the cycle: *The Red Menace, I Was a Communist for the FBI,* and *Big Jim McLain.* Through these three case studies, I hope to elucidate subtle differences in rhetorical strategies found in Hollywood's anti-Communist propaganda. Additionally, I show how these anti-Communist films sometimes borrowed from the tropes and conventions of the liberal social problem films of the late 1940s. Although many historians argue that films like *Crossfire* and *Gentleman's Agreement* were the real targets of HUAC's investigations of 1947, I contend that these films nonetheless supplied a template for Hollywood's representation of race in anti-Communist films.[4]

RACIAL ISSUES AND THE COMMUNIST PARTY IN AMERICA

Although the CPUSA always subordinated it to other concerns, the fight against racial prejudice had been a plank in the Communist Party's political platform since the late 1920s. In an attempt to bring greater numbers of minorities into the fold, the CPUSA enacted several measures designed to improve the party's appeal, particularly to African Americans. In 1928 the Comintern took the rather unusual step of identifying southern blacks as an "oppressed nation" within the United States and argued that African Americans in the "black belt" deserved the right of self-determination because they represented a majority of the rural southern population.[5] Three years later, in a further effort to show that the party was hospitable to people of color, the CPUSA mounted a series of show trials that exposed the problem of "white chauvinism" within their ranks. The most famous of these was the trial of August Yokinen, a janitor for the Finnish Workers Club of Harlem, accused of barring blacks from a party-sponsored dance and for harboring reservations about blacks and whites bathing together in the club's sauna.[6]

Besides its focus on "white chauvinism," the CPUSA also featured an African American vice-presidential candidate during the 1932 elections. James Ford, described variously as a former postal worker from Chicago and a former steelworker from Alabama, had been an active member of the party since the late 1920s and had served on the Comintern's Negro Commission at the Sixth World Congress. With Ford running alongside William Z. Foster, the Communist ticket received barely more than a hundred thousand votes to Franklin Roosevelt's plurality of seven million, but a disproportionate number of these came from black voters. Although the CPUSA's inclusion of Ford was largely a matter of political symbolism, it nonetheless functioned as an act of affirmation for thousands of African Americans.[7]

Perhaps the most important component of the party's campaign to attract African American members was its highly publicized support in the Scottsboro case. In 1931, nine young black males were charged with raping two white women during a train ride through northern Alabama. After the nine were convicted and sentenced to death on questionable medical evidence, the Communist Party sent attorneys from its International Labor Defense (ILD) to Scottsboro to make contact with the defendants and to organize protests on their behalf. By making the case central to its anti-lynching crusade, the Communist Party greatly increased its visibility within various African American communities around the United States.[8]

In the decades that followed, the CPUSA continued the struggle against racial prejudice as part of its Popular Front and wartime political strategies.[9] In 1936, for example, Communists helped to organize the National Negro Congress, which convened to explore several issues pertinent to the "betterment of the race," such as the participation of blacks in labor unions, the problems of the Jim Crow system of the American South, and the threat of fascism, especially the then recent invasion of Ethiopia. Additionally, much as they had in the Scottsboro case, Communists organized on behalf of defendants of color in several highly publicized trials, including the Sleepy Lagoon case in 1942, the "Martinsville Seven" case in 1951, and the "Trenton Six" case also in 1951.

For their part Communists in Hollywood participated in many aspects of the party's fight against racial prejudice. Although much of their attention was devoted to labor issues, Hollywood Communists lent support to a number of other causes, promoting civil liberties legislation, antilynching laws, and the defense funds of the Scottsboro and Sleepy Lagoon cases. Beyond that, many Communists in Hollywood sought to use their films as vehicles for a more progressive approach to the representation of persons of color. Much of the literature created by the Hollywood Ten pointed to its interest in these issues, citing the critical acclaim received by *This Gun for Hire* (1942) and *Crossfire*—the former was written by Albert Maltz, and the latter was produced by Adrian Scott and directed by Edward Dmytryk— for their treatment of Nazism and anti-Semitism respectively. Moreover, the Hollywood Ten were also fond of citing John Howard Lawson's screen-play for *Sahara* (1943) for its landmark depiction of a Sudanese soldier, who symbolically pummels a German Nazi in a fistfight.[10] Later, after they were blacklisted, director Herbert Biberman and screenwriters Paul Jarrico and Michael Wilson collaborated on *Salt of the Earth* (1953), a film that recounts the real-life story of a miner's strike in New Mexico that involved several Hispanic men and women.[11]

Despite the CPUSA's efforts, though, the number of blacks who became members of the party remained relatively small. In 1935, after the party's initial recruiting efforts, African Americans made up about 8 percent of the party's members.[12] That number grew slightly throughout the 1940s, but the party experienced great difficulty retaining African American mem-bers; many dropped out after only a few months. The reasons for this turn-over were complex, but they are evident in the complicated, and often dif-ficult, relationship black Communists maintained with the larger structures of the party. During the CPUSA's early attempts to recruit African Americans, its interest in class solidarity often pitted members of the black working class against members of the black middle class. Moreover, black Communists were expected to give up important aspects of their cultural life in obeisance to the party. This was especially evident in Communist attacks on black popular culture, such as jazz, which the party at one point believed to be irredeemably hedonistic. Finally, try as it might, the CPUSA could not completely eradicate the racist views held by its individual mem-bers. In his repudiation of his Communist past, author Richard Wright complained of the condescension aimed at blacks in the party when he described the tone of a black Communist organizer as "more patronizing than that of a Southern white man."[13]

During the highly contentious debates surrounding the Scottsboro case, NAACP leaders accused the Communist Party of opportunism. Such charges would recur throughout the 1930s and 1940s and would ultimately find their way into various anti-Communist discourses of the Red Scare period. Perhaps the best known example of this criticism is Winston Record's *The Negro and the Communist Party*, which condemned the CPUSA for its cynicism and deception in its treatment of African Americans.[14] The taint of these charges continued well into the civil rights era as many historians characterized the Communists' relations with African Americans as "manipulative" if not completely exploitative. Some historians and commentators accused the CPUSA of misusing funds raised for the Scottsboro case and other high-profile trials. Others even went so far as to suggest that the ILD's legal strategies may have jeopardized the lives of their defendants.

All of these charges would appear, in one way or another, in anti-Communist films made between 1949 and 1955. That said, these films offered a range of approaches in their efforts to discredit the Communist Party's appeal to African Americans. Some, like *I Was a Communist for the FBI* and *Trial* (1955), portrayed Communists as jaded, self-interested con artists, who took advantage of black Americans' guileless idealism. Others, like *The Red Menace*, offered a more sympathetic treatment of African Americans' and Jews' political aims but ultimately suggested that they would never be fulfilled by an organization as dogmatic, rigid, and autocratic as the Communist Party. Still others, like *Big Jim McLain*, avoided overt statements on racial issues despite the fact that those issues strongly, if implicitly, informed the depiction of their film's settings. These discourses problematized the rhetorical strategies of anti-Communist films. By addressing the party's appeal to blacks and Jews, anti-Communist films were placed on the horns of an ideological dilemma. Even as they vilified the Communist Party, these films acknowledged the extent to which racism and anti-Semitism were serious problems in American society. Ironically, anti-Communist films gave implicit and sometimes unintentional support to a civil rights struggle to which most anti-Communists were rather resolutely opposed.

THE RED MENACE: ANTI-COMMUNIST NOIR AND THE LIBERAL MESSAGE MOVIE

Released by Republic Pictures in June of 1949, *The Red Menace* was among the first anti-Communist films made by Hollywood after the HUAC hearings of 1947. The film was preceded by only a couple of other anti-Communist films, including *The Iron Curtain* and the reissue of *Ninotchka*. When HUAC returned to Hollywood in the early 1950s, Republic reedited and reissued *The Red Menace* under a new title, *Underground Spy*, thereby maximizing the public relations value of its early contribution to Hollywood's war on Communism.[15]

Produced by Herbert Yates and directed by R. G. Springsteen, *The Red Menace* tells the story of Bill Jones (Robert Rockwell), a World War II veteran cheated by real estate developers building a new housing project for returning GIs. When Bill fails to get help from his local Veterans' Services Center, he becomes mixed up in a local Communist cell that promises to assist him and other victimized veterans. Although initially skeptical about the party's politics, Bill continues to attend cell meetings because of his attraction to Mollie O'Flaherty (Barbara Fuller), a young Irish woman used to lure new members to the party. Bill quickly grows disaffected with Communism but is afraid to leave it after party leadership kills one member and drives another to suicide. Having reached his breaking point, Bill takes flight with his new girlfriend, Nina Petrovka (Hanne Axman). Hungry and exhausted, Bill and Nina stop in a small Texas town, where they relate their experience with the party to the local sheriff. The kindly sheriff counsels them on the blessings of the American system and invites them to stay on and live in the town. The film ends with Bill and Nina basking in the promise of a new start and a hopeful future.

In its promotion of the film, Republic circulated a flyer that featured a picture of the studio and copy that explained, "Why Republic Studios Produced 'The Red Menace.'"[16] The flyer called attention to the dangers posed by "fifth column" organizations and featured quotes from unnamed "great Americans" regarding Communism's threat to the American way of life. The flyer also noted the attacks on the film made by the *Daily Worker* and *People's World,* and it used these to buttress its claims that Communists threatened to "destroy our form of government by force and violence, bloodshed and terror."[17] These attacks were published prior to the film's release and were based on script pages that had been leaked by members of *The Red Menace*'s production team. The attention given to *The Red Menace* by these Communist publications must have seemed like a godsend to Republic's publicity department. Not only did it make the film appear timely and credible by providing implicit evidentiary support for the charges made by HUAC and the MPAPAI (after all, someone had surreptitiously disseminated the script), but it also enabled Republic to appear courageous by standing up to a virtually nonexistent campaign to threaten and intimidate the studio. Later, after the film was in general release, Republic followed up its flyer with a poster that reprinted the reviews from the *Daily Worker* and *People's World* in their entirety. The reviews were bracketed by various images of the film and were juxtaposed with an editorial from a "legitimate" mainstream newspaper that praised both the film and the studio.[18] While the leftist reviews lambasted *The Red Menace* for its simpleminded and grossly caricatured characterizations of Communists, Republic used this denunciation to its advantage by circulating the reviews as evidence that the film had struck a nerve. As an additional part of its promotional campaign, Republic sought and received the public support of the California Senate Fact-Finding Committee on Un-American Activities (i.e., the Tenney Committee), which issued a resolution that recognized Republic Studio's great contribution to the fight against Communism and urged every American to see the film.[19]

Like *I Married a Communist*, *The Red Menace* is linked to the 1940s cycle of film noir in various ways.[20] Indeed, the film opens with the use of a nondiegetic voice-over, a device commonly used in the semidocumentary cycle of film noir that arose in the late 1940s.[21] Moreover, the film begins with a close-up of Nina that quickly pulls back to a two-shot of her and Bill seated in the front seat of their automobile, a setup that evokes a similar shot from *Out of the Past*. Bill is seated on the driver's side on the right part of the frame, and Nina is seated in the background of the shot on the left part of the frame. The image's composition and its dark, moody lighting recall an almost iconic image of Jeff and Kathie from the latter film, one that occurs just moments before the climactic police ambush that will leave both characters dead. Besides its use of omniscient voice-over narration and its noirish look, *The Red Menace* includes several other elements that link it to film noir, such as its treatment of gangsterism and of female sexuality. Whereas *The Red Menace* generally eschews the gangster film iconography found in *I Married a Communist*, it nonetheless characterizes the Communist leadership as a group of goons who use violence and intimidation to uphold the party line. When Reachi, a young student, disputes a point of party dogma by arguing that Communism is itself a denial of democracy, he is brutally beaten to death for his dissent. Similarly, *The Red Menace*'s characterization of Mollie and Nina is consistent with film noir's trope of the femme fatale insofar as they both function as seductresses who embody the dangerous lure of the party.

The reception of *The Red Menace* also indicates that the film differs significantly from *I Married a Communist* in its treatment of persons of color. Several reviews of *The Red Menace* called attention to this aspect of the film and even suggested that it played an important part in the film's propaganda functions. In a review for the *Citizen News*, Lowell Redelings wrote, "There are a certain number of scenes involving the reaction and rebellion of certain minority group representatives to Party dictatorship. . . . The lesson taught is that all races and creeds are exploited by the Party toward advancing the one great cause of revolution in all non-Communist nations."[22] *The Red Menace*'s rhetoric, though, made it a target of criticism among the radical left, who, not surprisingly, bashed the film for its chauvinistic representations. Sidney Burke of the *Daily People's World* wrote:

> The picture puts the foulest white chauvinistic phrases into the mouths of leading Communists while at the same time unconsciously revealing the real white chauvinism of the film makers in its patronizing, contemptuous treatment of Negro characters.
>
> One scene is typical. It shows a Negro man standing cap in hand in the apartment of a white woman party member, and quotes him as saying "Miss O'Flaherty," although she calls him by his first name. This is despite the fact that the two are longtime co-workers.[23]

In addition to racism, Burke also calls attention to the film's anti-Semitism and male chauvinism.

Why did some critics praise the film's varied characterizations while others blasted its racism and "chauvinism?" To some degree the contrasting reviews of *The Red Menace* suggest that each side simply seeks to uphold its side of the party line. Yet to get a complete picture of the film's complex and contradictory treatment of race, it is necessary to take a closer look at *The Red Menace*'s production history.

According to studio documents, racial and ethnic difference was an important consideration for the filmmakers throughout *The Red Menace*'s development. The shooting script, for example, contained capsule descriptions for each of the main characters, many of them calling specific attention to the character's racial or ethnic background. The description for Henry Solomon reads, "An emotional young Communist poet of Jewish extraction. His story is one of deep tragedy and pathos."[24] Similarly, the summary for Sam Wright says, "Negro re-write and office man on the Party newspaper. He approves of the theories of Communism, until he learns that it is using the colored American for its own sinister ends."[25]

With such an ethnically diverse cast of characters, it is not surprising that the Communist Party's stance on racial issues proves to be an important motif in *The Red Menace*. The film introduces this motif in an early scene in Mollie's apartment, where Bill notices several books on Marxism sitting on Mollie's bookshelves. After Bill remarks that he finds it funny that someone as cute as Mollie might be a Communist, she responds, "Nothing so funny about it. Not if you stop to realize that the party's been behind every decent cause in this country. The war against fascism and the Labor Movement. Look what it's doing today fighting for the minorities, the Jews and the Negroes." In this scene Mollie succinctly summarizes one popular view of the Communist Party as an organization that supported several progressive causes, racism among them.

In countering this view, *The Red Menace* includes several episodes that strive to undermine the party's credibility on racial issues by suggesting that it only pays lip service to progressive causes. During an argument about the meaning of democracy in Communist political theory, Yvonne Kraus calls the student, Reachi, a "Mussolini-spawned dago." Later, in a meeting of the cell's top members to censure Henry Solomon, the poet responds to the party's accusations of ideological deviance by saying, "You pretend to fight racial discrimination, but you keep reminding me that I'm a Jewish American, that Sam down in the office is a Negro American, and that Mollie is an Irish American" (fig. 2). Lastly, after Sam leaves *The Toilers* office to return home to his family, Martin Vejac, the paper's publisher, comments on Sam's departure by grumbling, "Wasting our time on those African ingrates." In all of these episodes Communists reveal their deep-seated hatred for people of color the minute that they question or challenge some aspect of party dogma.

The shooting script for *The Red Menace* also thematized the issue of racial tolerance through its use of a nondiegetic narrator. Although handled differently in the finished film, the script included the narrator in its cast of characters and further stipulated that the voice used to read the narration would be that of a woman. The use of an omniscient female voice-over was unusual for this period, but *The Red Menace*'s screenwriters, Albert Demond and Gerald Geraghty, defended their gambit as something that would maintain audience interest throughout the film: "She is an important character whose warm and human voice ties the episodes of the picture together. Although she is never seen, she is a definite personage, and speculation as to her identity enhances the picture's suspense."[26]

The identity of the narrator was to remain concealed until the film's last shot. In the penultimate shot of Bill and Nina walking hand in hand toward the sunrise, the voice-over narration would read, "And so the fears of Bill and Nina melt away, as they walk into the flame of the torch ever held upraised." This hopeful, if clichéd, image was to be followed by a close-up of "the torch in the hand of the Statue of Liberty. As the voice continues, the CAMERA PANS DOWN to the rest of the statue. The lips of the face in shadow or turned away so that they cannot be seen, but the voice seems to come from them."[27]

Figure 2. In *The Red Menace* Communist Party leadership admonishes Jewish poet Henry Solomon (right) for deviating from official dogma regarding Marx's concept of dialectical materialism. Solomon responds by implicitly accusing the party of using racial difference for its own political ends.

The idea that the Statue of Liberty would narrate *The Red Menace* is typical of the film's obvious jingoism, but it also serves an important rhetorical function. As our nation's most obvious symbol of the "melting pot" that unites various racial and ethnic groups in a shared sense of American identity, the Statue of Liberty offers a handy icon to counter the purported appeal of Communism to people of color. American democracy and anti-Communist ideology, the film seems to say, may have problems concerning racial discrimination, but notions of equality among races, classes, and immigrant groups is a foundational myth that is part of our nation's core beliefs. While the film offers no real solutions to the problems of race hatred and discrimination, it nonetheless uses the Statue of Liberty as a reminder that American democracy, like Communism, promises equal opportunity to all its citizens, even if it doesn't always fulfill those promises. According to press reports, this fatuous, flag-waving ending was cut when cast members of *The Red Menace* complained to Springsteen that the scene went well beyond the bounds of common sense and good taste.[28]

Table 2 Ethnicity as a Marker of Difference in *The Red Menace*

Character	Heritage	Age	Politics
1 Mollie O'Flaherty	Irish	Young	Communist
Father Leary	Irish	Old	Non-Communist
2 Sam Wright	African American	Young	Communist
Tom Wright	African American	Old	Non-Communist
3 Nina Petrovka	Middle European	Young	Communist/ Non-Communist
Yvonne Kraus	Middle European	Old	Communist

Instead, the producers opted to use the voice of Lloyd G. Davies, a member of the Los Angeles City Council, to burnish the film's political credibility.

At a deeper level the treatment of ethnic difference also informs the thematic and ideological structures of *The Red Menace* by establishing oppositions between characters who share an ethnic or racial heritage but are divided along political and generational lines. This is most clearly evident in three sets of characters whose stories are subordinate to the central plotline involving Bill Jones (table 2). Although the characters in *The Red Menace* are hardly "three dimensional," the subplots involving these secondary characters deepen and enrich the film's political message by exploring other motivations for joining, and ultimately leaving, the Communist Party.

Sam Wright's disaffection with Communism begins after the tragic suicide of Henry Solomon. The Jewish poet quits the party after its leaders criticize his work for suggesting that Marxism is an outgrowth of other ideas, such as Hegelianism, rather than a wholly original philosophical system. After leaving the party, Solomon finds himself friendless and poor, cut off from the only social life he has known. Moreover, because he has worked as a poet for the party, Solomon's work is politically tainted in a way that leaves him little prospects for publication in other newspapers. Not satisfied, the party further ruins Solomon's reputation by smearing him in their newspaper, which describes him as a hack poet writing libertine verses.

Quite remarkably, *The Red Menace* acknowledges the discrimination Solomon faces for having been a party member. The film even goes so far as to suggest that Solomon faces greater persecution as an ex-Communist than he does as a Jew. During a montage sequence, we see Solomon performing office work and learn from the voice-over narration that this is one in a series of office jobs that he has taken. Each time, however, Solomon is dismissed when his bosses discover his Communist past. As the voice-over makes clear, Solomon is fired despite the fact that his job performance is fine and he no longer associates with the party or its members. As if that weren't enough, Mollie is investigated for her brief interaction with Solomon on the street, an encounter that the Communists interpret as fraternization with a party enemy. When Solomon's status also threatens Mollie's position, he confronts Vejac about *The Toilers'* smear campaign. Vejac says that the best thing for Mollie would be for Solomon to leave her alone, to go away and not come back. Moved by Vejac's prodding, Solomon hurls himself out of the office window and plummets to his death.

As a staffer for *The Toilers,* Wright had been friendly with Solomon and is emotionally shaken by his suicide. He knows that the party drove Solomon to his death, yet he is asked to cover up its involvement by writing a laudatory piece that laments the loss of a promising talent. Wright's alienation from the party reaches a breaking point during a visit from his father, Tom, described in the script as a "philosopher gifted with old-fashioned 'horse sense.'"[29] Tom reminds Sam of his son's admiration for Solomon's poems, and he appeals to Sam's religious upbringing by discussing a recent sermon delivered by Deacon Smith at the Wrights' church. As Tom recounts the Deacon's sermon, which accuses the Communist Party of exploiting racial issues for its own political agenda, he notes that slavery in America ended eighty years ago but that Communist countries have effectively enslaved their peoples by denying them basic civil rights. The combination of Communist dishonesty and religious guilt proves too much for Sam, who leaves the newspaper office with his father. Before going, Sam types an introduction to the article on Solomon's death, even though he knows it will never be printed. In it, Sam links Solomon's sacrifice to that of other American patriots, such as Nathan Hale and Colin Kelly.

In this sequence and others in *The Red Menace* Communism finds its ideological inverse in Christianity. Here again, Christianity, like ethnic difference, functions as an important narrative and thematic motif in the film, one that goes beyond any individual character. This is especially evident in an early montage depicting the party's indoctrination of its members. During Nina's lesson, for example, voice-over narration explains the Communists' belief that "Man and his world are the product of natural forces that are constantly changing." After explaining Communism as a form of ethical relativism in which there are no eternal verities of right and wrong, the voice-over adds, "Actually, it is the old doctrine of atheism sugar-coated in highbrow terms." A little later, the voice-over continues over shots of Earl Partridge's lesson: "Partridge sneers at democracy as a delusion created by Christians. He sings the old Marxian song that religion is a narcotic devised to make workers endure their chains."

Yet, although the film's voice-over is broadly aligned with a faith-based anti-Communism, *The Red Menace* also uses Father Leary to personalize these issues and to dramatize atheism as an adventitious consequence of Communist belief. During a fairly early scene in which Father Leary visits Henry and Mollie at the latter's apartment, the poet questions the clergyman about his belief that a neighbor's drinking problem might be cured by prayer and Christian charity. Implicit in Henry's question is the belief that social problems are caused by social conditions and thus cannot be solved by religious belief. To this, Father Leary responds by defining God in distinctly secular terms as a collective wish for social justice. Pointing to his chest, Leary says, "God is the being that puts something in here that makes you want a better world. The atheistic systems are always founded on hatred. Race hatred when they are Nazi; class hatred when they are Communist." Leary's little homily strays pretty far from normative theological conceptions of God, but it nonetheless serves an important rhetorical function in the film. By abjuring conventional religious explanations, Leary's definition of God sounds an awful lot like Henry's and Mollie's reasons for joining the party, namely their Utopian wish to make the world a better place. In doing so, Leary espouses a political position somewhat similar to Communism in order to undermine the very basis for believing in it. Before leaving Mollie's apartment, though, Leary rather brazenly takes a quarter from Henry's hand to give to the church poor box, an act that almost seems like a tacit admission of the emptiness of the church's promises.

Father Leary represents a tradition and ethnic heritage from which Mollie has turned away. Although much of the scene is cast as a debate between Henry and Father Leary, Mollie remains its focal point. This is expressed partly through Springsteen's framing and composition, which frequently places Mollie on the opposite side of the frame from Leary, a strategy that highlights the pair's generational, gender, and political differences even as it underlines their shared ethnicity. As an Irish Catholic, Leary is a substitute father figure for Mollie, one whose paternalism acts as an inducement for her to reunite with her actual parents.

This early scene motivates Mollie's political conversion later in the film. After Henry's suicide, Mollie seeks out Father Leary and asks for forgiveness. Leary grants it but also offers Mollie a political lesson: "The best way to defeat Communism is for us to live Christianity in an American democracy every day of our lives." The film then cuts to a long shot of Mollie entering the church with the music of the church organ swelling in the background. As Mollie nears the altar, the film cuts to an almost perpendicular angle from the previous long shot. In a medium long shot, Mollie notices her mother seated in one of the pews. The two embrace as the church organ continues to play. The shot ties family, religion, and democracy into an ideological knot in which each element is inextricably linked to one another and all are opposed to Communism. Ironically, though, the film substitutes this image of family unity for a more substantive analysis of Mollie's reasons for joining the Communist Party in the first place. Nothing really changes in terms of her family's economic conditions and none of the political causes that Mollie cites in praise of the Communist Party—the labor movement, racism—are any less vital or urgent. Christianity and American democracy are simply lesser evils in *The Red Menace*. Both philosophies may give rise to attendant social problems, but they are less brutal and authoritarian than the Communist rule Mollie has experienced.

The third, and final, ethnically linked pair in *The Red Menace* is Yvonne Kraus and Nina Petrovka. The difference between these two, however, is less a matter of politics or religion than a question of Communism's relation to pleasure. This issue is especially evident in the script's description of Kraus as "an intense and fanatical Communist—frustrated sexually and emotionally, her outlet being a consuming hatred for America."[30] This aspect of Kraus is manifested in a couple of different dramatic contexts in the film but is mostly expressed as a kind of jealousy directed at other female Communists. Kraus, for example, expresses a romantic interest in Bill early on but defers for the good of the party when it appears that Mollie stands a better chance of attracting him. Later, when Yvonne complains that Nina has taken a personal interest in Jones, and thus has placed her desires above that of the party, Vejac remarks that a little romance would help to calm Kraus down. Kraus's self-denial and sexual frustration, ostensibly for the good of the party, makes her a bitter and unhappy woman, more than ready to chastise others for their romantic endeavors.

Nina, in contrast, is depicted as a sensualist with an Epicurean appreciation for life's finer things. When Nina takes Bill to an Italian restaurant, she is revealed to be knowledgeable about food and wine, and a medium close-up of her seated at the table shows her entranced by the music playing in the background. The sequence is important both because it displays Nina's growing affection for Bill and because it further differentiates her from Yvonne. In its own way the sequence foreshadows the next scene in which *The Toilers* reports that Henry Solomon has been censured for his "libertine" poetry. By bracketing the scene in the restaurant with scenes of Solomon's comeuppance, *The Red Menace* suggests that Nina's enjoyment of life shares something with the poet's celebration of truth and beauty. For Nina, food, wine, music, and romance offer intrinsically valuable experiences whether or not they fulfill the larger aims of the party. The juxtaposition of Yvonne's ideological rigor with Nina's deepening relationship with Bill motivates Nina's flight from the party during the film's last act, this despite the fact that she was born and raised a Communist and has long embraced the party's core values.

By film's end, though, *The Red Menace*'s use of generic tropes ultimately undermines its ostensibly progressive stance on issues of race. While much of the film combines aspects of film noir and the social problem film, *The Red Menace* somewhat inexplicably borrows from the western to achieve narrative closure. In the film's final scenes Bill and Nina stop in a small Texas town. The couple's situation appears hopeless as they try to elude both the Communists who have driven them from Los Angeles and American immigration officials who are likely to deport Nina if they are captured. Tired from their long drive, their spirits broken, Bill and Nina turn themselves in to the sheriff of this small town and throw themselves on the mercy of the American legal system.

When they enter the sheriff's office, however, it as though Bill and Nina have entered a completely different film. The mise-en-scène strongly evokes the iconography of the western in the office's simple layout and modest decor. It contains a large desk and a few chairs. The sheriff's gun belt and a .45 caliber pistol sit atop the desk. The sheriff does not wear a uniform but rather is dressed in shirtsleeves, trousers, and a vest on which is pinned a six-pointed star. Described as a "big, rangy man," the sheriff is dressed like the typical western lawman and embodies the rugged individualism and quiet authority frequently associated with the cowboy as a figure of American mythology.[31] Without apparent ties to any larger law enforcement organization, the sheriff displays some of the same qualities as the frontier hero; a loner and a man of few words, he is a shrewd judge of character and a repository of folk wisdom. The sheriff may lack the cultivation and manners of high society, but he makes up for this through his kindness, honesty, and openness.

After listening carefully to Bill and Nina's story, the sheriff reassures them that the law will deal fairly with them and that, unlike Communist countries, the United States gives a second chance to those who deserve it. According to the sheriff, although Nina may have perjured herself on her immigration form when she claimed that she wasn't a Communist, the American government is likely to overlook that legal infraction owing to Nina's political conversion. As he puts it, because of the valuable lessons

Nina has learned, she is apt to be "a better citizen than lots of us, because she has learned somethin' that Bill Jones was tryin' to throw away." After the sheriff gives the couple his political and moral sanction, he takes his leave to pick up a drunk from a neighboring town. Realizing that they never got the sheriff's name, Bill and Nina stop a small boy passing by. The boy, who is dressed as a slightly more garish version of the sheriff himself, says that, because he has a long name, the kids just call the sheriff "Uncle Sam." The film closes with a series of lap dissolves of the Statue of Liberty in New York harbor accompanied by a nondiegetic choir singing the hymn "America."

The final revelation that the sheriff is, indeed, "Uncle Sam" is likely intended as a substitute for the earlier ending, which revealed the Statue of Liberty as the source of the film's voice-over narration. The actual ending of *The Red Menace* may lack the absurd jingoism of the ending in the shooting script, but both seek to elevate the film's narrative closure to a kind of allegorical status. By naming the sheriff "Uncle Sam," the film implies that the traits we identify in this kindly, understanding, and good-hearted sheriff are the same characteristics of the country as a whole. In striving for this pointedly symbolic ending, though, *The Red Menace* also carries the perhaps unintentional connotation that the mythology of the frontier is the ideological cornerstone of American modernity. As such, the cultural perception of the American West—a perception that was largely molded by Hollywood's images of it—emerges in the final analysis as the dominant vision for an America no longer beset by the Communist threat.

In sum, *The Red Menace* contains several subplots that bind together the various strands of the film's ideology. By organizing these subplots around African American, Irish, and middle European characters, the film strives to repudiate American Communism by demonstrating the ways in which it is antithetical to religious belief, political dissent, romance, and even cultivated tastes. More important, by resolving these conflicts through characters marked by their ethnic or racial difference, *The Red Menace* co-opts the representational strategies of contemporaneous "social problem" films such as *Crossfire, Gentleman's Agreement, Intruder in the Dust* (1949), *Pinky* (1949), *Home of the Brave* (1949), *Lost Boundaries* (1949), and *No Way Out* (1949). Unlike most Hollywood films of the 1940s, which frequently place African American actors in small parts as porters, butlers, and maids, *The Red Menace* gives fairly prominent roles to two African American actors, who portray a talented young journalist and his father respectively. Admittedly, the Communist press was right to call attention to Sam's deferential treatment of Mollie, an element likely included to avoid alienating southern theater owners and audiences, but they ignored several other aspects of the film's characterization that broke with Hollywood conventions. Indeed, what is particularly remarkable about the film is that its political message is largely expressed through characters who are intended to represent the ethnic and racial diversity of America in 1949. *The Red Menace*'s anti-Communist ideology is undoubtedly expressed through the film's voice-over narration and central plotline, but it is reinforced along the way in speeches made by a Jew, an Irishman, an African American, and a white southern sheriff.

Yet the film's final narrative detour through Texas seems to undermine the liberalism of its anti-Communist message. More than any other film genre, the Hollywood western is the one most clearly invested in the meanings of "whiteness." As several film scholars have pointed out, this is not only evident in the genre's treatment of American Indians but also through a more systematic marginalization of cultural difference.[32] By invoking the western in its final scenes, *The Red Menace* moves, both literally and figuratively, from a multicultural space to one that has eliminated nearly all traces of cultural difference. Bill and Nina's decision to remain in this small, rural, presumably all-white community represents more than a repudiation of Communism; it signifies an almost total assimilation to the dominant elements of American politics and culture. In the long view *The Red Menace* doesn't merely fail to offer its minority characters an efficacious political alternative to the Communist Party. Rather, by appealing to the mythology of Manifest Destiny, and its attendant policies of racial and cultural genocide, *The Red Menace* manages to void their presence altogether.

THE CYNICISM OF ANTI-COMMUNISM: *I WAS A COMMUNIST FOR THE FBI*

If *The Red Menace* evinces at least some sympathy for the reasons African Americans and Jews joined the Communist Party, *I Was a Communist for the FBI* differs markedly from its predecessor by treating African Americans and Jews as complete outsiders, tools of the party's leadership who had been unwittingly duped by Communist promises of advances in civil rights. Given this change in representational strategies, one might surmise that, just a few years after the 1947 HUAC hearings, anti-Communist filmmakers no longer needed to explain the party's political appeal. With anti-Communist purges taking place in several professions and with further investigations of Hollywood in the offing, anti-Communist filmmakers could simply assume some measure of support for both their politics and their films. With no compunction to demonstrate a legitimate basis for Communism's allure, films like *I Was a Communist for the FBI* depicted Communist leaders as vicious, callous, and venal panderers, manipulating the hopes and dreams of people who are either too idealistic or too stupid to recognize they are being used.

Released by Warner Bros. in 1951, *I Was a Communist for the FBI* is based on the real-life experience of Matt Cvetic, an agent who became a minor celebrity after his testimony before HUAC.[33] Cvetic posed for nine years as a Pittsburgh steelworker and Communist Party organizer. During that time Cvetic collected an enormous amount of information about the party's structure and its inner workings. His experiences were turned into a series of articles for the *Saturday Evening Post,* and the film was subsequently adapted from those articles. Somewhat strangely, *I Was a Communist for the FBI* was nominated for an Academy Award for Best Documentary, despite the fact that several events were fictionalized for the sake of the film. In 1952 the film also provided the basis for a successful radio series with Dana Andrews playing the role of Cvetic. By this time Andrews himself had become something of an anti-Communist icon starring in such films as *The Iron Curtain, I Want You* (1951), and *Assignment Paris* (1952).

In seeking to carve out a coherent narrative line for *I Was a Communist,* producer Brian Foy and screenwriter Crane Wilbur focused on three subplots that would serve to unify the film's episodic structure. The first subplot involved the difficulties in Cvetic's family life caused by his undercover work. Early in the film, Cvetic attends a birthday for his mother but is called away by party officials to attend a meeting with Gerhard Eisler, the real-life brother of film composer Hanns Eisler. Before Cvetic leaves, he is berated by his brother, who accuses him of putting party business above the needs of the family. A little later, Cvetic learns that his son, Dick, has been involved in several fights at school because the other kids tease him about his dad being a Red. In each of these scenes Cvetic is driven by a desire to put things right with his family but is prevented from doing so by his guise as a Communist organizer. Afraid of being exposed, Cvetic leaves a letter with his parish priest that would explain the true nature of his FBI work in the event of his death.

When this letter is discovered by Eve Merrick, Dick's Communist schoolteacher, it initiates *I Was a Communist*'s second subplot: the threat of Cvetic's exposure as an undercover agent. Although viewers are mostly aligned with Cvetic throughout the film, the break from that pattern of focalization functions here to add some modicum of suspense to the film. Because the film's narration does not communicate Eve's motivations, the spectator does not know how she plans to use this information. As it turns out, Eve seeks to use Cvetic's FBI connection to escape the party's clutches. Much of the middle section of the film concerns Cvetic's efforts to smuggle Eve to safety without blowing his cover. In this respect this subplot is a variation of central character types and narrative tropes of the espionage thriller: the undercover agent who must covertly assist a fellow spy to flee from enemy territory.

The film's other main subplot involves Cvetic's investigation of party malfeasance and his surreptitious efforts to combat a rising tide of Communist violence. In one scene, for example, the party discusses a new plan to discredit HUAC by describing the committee as "fat-headed politicians whose only aim is to crash the headlines." As one party bigwig explains it, "We want them laughed at, ridiculed. If we start the ball rolling, there are plenty of big-mouthed suckers in this country who will do the rest." In another scene the party is shown fomenting violence on a Pittsburgh picket line. To make the strikers appear to be victims of management's strong-arm tactics, the party imports several thugs who bludgeon picketers with steel pipes. And in still another scene two Communist hit men murder an FBI agent brought in to protect Eve.

Unlike *The Red Menace*, which received a mixed response from critics, contemporary film reviewers were almost effusive in their praise of *I Was a Communist*. *Variety*, for example, described the film as a "forceful and exciting true-to-life melodrama" and stated that it was as "timely as today's newspaper headlines."[34] The topical nature of the film was also highlighted by *Motion Picture Herald*, which wrote, "Snapping with action and crackling with tension, this Warners production comes popping out of the headlines at one of the most appropriate moments in the history of the industry."[35]

As was also the case with *I Married a Communist* and *The Red Menace*, most reviewers called attention to *I Was a Communist*'s employment of gangster film tropes to depict Communist leaders as a group of hardened criminals. Richard Griffith, for example, noted *I Was a Communist*'s debt to Warner Bros.' earlier gangster cycles and cited an unnamed critic's colorful assessment of the film's formulaic qualities: "The gunplay and violence are so familiar we half expected George Raft to turn up flipping his famous quarter."[36]

Despite the film's factual pedigree, most of these gangster tropes were added to *I Was a Communist* to enhance its value as both entertainment and propaganda. In testimony the real-life Cvetic admitted that while the party frequently talked about assassinations, he never actually saw anyone commit a murder. As Stephen J. Whitfield notes, the actual experience of most American Communists was hardly as exciting or as dangerous as the image projected in *I Was a Communist:* "Consisting mostly of meetings, the life of the Party was in fact rather dull; the typical Communist was far more familiar with the mimeograph machine than the machine gun."[37]

In some ways, though, *I Was a Communist* goes beyond other anti-Communist films by using conspicuous consumption to indicate the greed and corruption of American Communist leaders. During the meeting for Gerhard Eisler, party leaders feast on champagne and caviar. Warner Bros.' production notes even attested to the authenticity of this scene's opulence by emphasizing that the filmmakers used real caviar. Ostensibly this was done because it is difficult to "imitate caviar for the cameras," but the filmmakers were at pains to note that they used good American caviar rather than the imported Russian variety. When Cvetic comments on the well-appointed buffet table—complete with candlesticks, silver service, and a stuffed bird—a party comrade responds, "Better get used to it, Cvetic. This is the way we're all going to live once we take over." When Cvetic asks if that includes the workers, too, his comrade says, "The workers will always be workers."

Interestingly, Warner Bros.' promotional material for *I Was a Communist's* provenance extended beyond its gangster film roots, suggesting that the film also followed in the footsteps of past studio exposés, like *I Was a Fugitive from a Chain Gang* (1932), whose title it seems to deliberately echo, and *Confessions of a Nazi Spy* (1939).[38] The studio additionally sought to link *I Was a Communist* to its most prestigious current offerings. In a telegram sent on April 7, 1951, Jack Warner suggested including the film in individual screenings of their big quartet of pictures: *Strangers on a Train* (1951), *Captain Horatio Hornblower* (1951), *A Streetcar Named Desire* (1951), and *Jim Thorpe, All-American* (1951).[39]

Within this heterogeneous mix of genre conventions race also emerged as an important cultural aspect of *I Was a Communist's* critical reception. The *Hollywood Reporter,* for example, noted that the film shows how the Communist Party uses "union men and minority groups as pawns in their grandiose ambitions toward political supremacy."[40] Similarly, while citing the film's basis in real-life events, *Cue* describes a litany of party abuses that include "the stirring of racial hatreds and conflicts when it suits party purpose."[41]

While these reviews rarely discuss specific scenes that depict the party's manipulation of racial hatred, the theme of race was an important aspect in *I Was a Communist's* development. In Crane Wilbur's story outline the following passage describes a speaker at a rally: "His declarations are frequently interrupted by applause, and in close shots we see the dupes and dopes thus affected, victims of frustration in one form or another, all the white, black and off-color, that go to make up the so-called American strain. There are youths of both sexes, many of the unfortunately under-privileged, some of who are patently well-off intellectuals. Most of the girls are starry-eyed with neurotic enthusiasm, but nearly all have faces that would stop an eight-day clock, which is one of the potent reasons why we find them where they are."[42] Aside from Wilbur's insulting references to female party members, the passage is also notable for its reference to the "dupes and dopes" who make up the "American strain," a melting pot of youths who are "white, black, and off-color." Wilbur's outline continues this motif of Communist exploitation in a later scene where Matt Cvetic meets a couple named Lola and Joe: "When they are gone Matt Cvetic turns to Hudson in shock and asks, 'Is that guy really her friend?' Hudson laughs, 'Look, kid, Moscow has ordered a special drive to stir up the negroes. We pick up a few frustrated suckers here and there, but in the mass they shy away from us. So we use the dames to play up the racial equality line.'"[43]

This emphasis on race carried over into subsequent drafts of the screenplay. In a draft dated December 21, 1950, Wilbur included an early scene in which an ice cream man talks to a racially mixed group of children. Initially, the ice cream man lectures the white boys in the group, saying, "Don't you kids know better than to play with niggers? That's bad—you're better than they are—don't forget that." Then, he hands out papers of penny ice cream to a group of African American youths. In an effort to gain their confidence, he says, "This is on the house fellers. (half whispers) Keep away from those white kids. They hate you—they'll gang up on you every time." If the political point of the scene was not clear enough, nondiegetic voice-over narration adds, "Kind of slimy, huh? Nothing's too low for these guys. They never miss an angle."[44]

The revised final screenplay draft also included a specific reference to the delicate issue of miscegenation. In the big scene of the Communist rally, Blandon addresses an audience that Wilbur describes as "some whites present, the audience in the main is composed mostly of negroes."[45] The text of Wilbur's screenplay includes an exchange between Blandon and a few of the audience members in attendance. Blandon says to the crowd, "You've been oppressed so long you've grown used to it—but when a Communist heads the government of the United States you will be granted the natural rights of free men—the right to pick and choose the mate with whom you wish to spend your days." During this line of dialogue there is a cut to a reaction shot that shows an African American man and his white girlfriend seated together. Wilbur's description adds, "the negro's arm possessively across the back of her chair." In response to Blandon's pledge a second African American man leaps to his feet in anger and says, "I *am* a member of the Party, but I don't go along with that. Every right-thinkin' member of my race hates the thought of mixin' black and white—!"[46] By making reference to African American disapproval of interracial relationships, Wilbur's screenplay shows still another way that the Communist Party was thought to exploit racism as a political issue. By encouraging race hatred among blacks and whites over the issue of miscegenation, the Communist Party could undermine the social fabric that holds American democracy together.

In the finished film two scenes from *I Was a Communist* stand out for their treatment of racial issues. The first is an early scene of a party meeting. An establishing shot of Freedom Hall dissolves to a long shot of the hall's interior that shows a large audience in the foreground listening to a speech delivered offscreen. Cvetic and Gerhard Eisler enter in the background of the shot, and the camera tracks and pans left to follow them as the two men are seated among other party members. Although this description suggests that this shot could be one of thousands of crowd shots in Hollywood films, it differs from the vast majority of these shots to the extent that Cvetic and Eisler are made conspicuous by their skin color. Even in this very distant view of the crowd, Eisler and Cvetic appear to be among a small number of white men in a predominantly African American crowd. This shot is then followed by a medium long shot of the speaker among other party leaders. Behind the group on the dais hangs a large photo of Stalin flanked by smaller portraits of George Washington and Lincoln.[47] The American flag occupies the right third of the frame (fig. 3). A cut to a more distant view of the dais reveals two African American men seated on its edges. On its own the visual organization of the scene would seem to make a simple point, namely that African Americans compose a large segment of the Communist Party's membership and even hold lower-level leadership positions within the party structure. To ensure that audiences don't misread the scene, though, the film employs Cvetic's voice-over to secure the intended ideological point. According to Cvetic, this was "the same old line used on racial minorities to create unrest and confusion," part of a recipe for a "Hell-brew of hate from the Kremlin" that applies the political strategy of "divide and conquer." The combination of image and sound here makes the point crystal clear: large numbers of African Americans may join the Communist Party, but they remain marginalized and excluded from the central power symbolized by the small cadre of whites in the center of the dais.

Figure 3. This shot from *I Was a Communist for the FBI* typifies the film's treatment of racial issues. It suggests that Communist Party leadership exploits racial divisions in society as a means of fomenting social unrest. Despite the fact that people of color constitute a large segment of party membership, they remain marginalized from its center of power, symbolized here by the small cadre of whites who sit beneath the portraits of George Washington, Josef Stalin, and Abraham Lincoln.

The ensuing scene elaborates on this theme of racial manipulation. The sequence begins with a medium shot of Blandon, one of the party leaders, packing his briefcase. Eisler congratulates him on his speech, and Blandon responds, "Those niggers ate it up, didn't they?" Cvetic politely chastises Blandon for his racial epithet: "You mean Negroes, don't you, Jim?" Blandon retorts, "Only when I'm trying to sell them the party line." As Blandon turns away to get a drink, Cvetic asks him about the potential for racial violence caused by the party's fiery rhetoric. Blandon responds that even if a Negro gets angry and kills a man, then the party can go to bat for him by raising a legal defense fund. The film then cuts to a medium shot of Eisler, who says, "Just like in the Scottsboro case." After a return to the previous setup, Blandon explains that the party raised $2 million for the Scottsboro defense fund, even though the actual legal costs were only

$65,000. As Blandon walks away from the group, he says, "Yes, we made a tremendous profit on that deal."

In still another scene, just prior to the strike at the steel mill, Blandon instructs his hired thugs to wrap their steel pipes in Jewish newspapers. In this way a harmless-looking object is turned into a lethal weapon. Beyond that, Blandon also hopes that American Jews will be blamed for the labor violence, which in turn will stir up anti-Semitic sentiment. When Jews are attacked, both verbally and physically, the party will rush to their defense in order to gain favor within Jewish communities.

Playing on widespread suspicions about Communist manipulation of people of color, these scenes suggest that the party's stance against racial prejudice is part of a Machiavellian scheme to inflame racial hatred. By supporting defendants in high-profile trials and by advocating for racial equality, the Communist Party appears to be the cure for society's racial ills when, in fact, it is their cause. Paradoxically, if Communists secretly aggravate the existing biases against persons of color, then the party's utopian promises of racial equality resonate even stronger within these groups. The effect of this racist rhetoric is, of course, to cast doubt on all forms of racial protest. Commenting on the scene where party operatives wrap steel pipes in Jewish newspapers, one reviewer wrote, "Watching this scene unfold, the public may well consider just how much intolerance in America today has been created for the evil purposes of the Communists."[48]

Bosley Crowther strongly dissented from his peers, questioning both *I Was a Communist*'s documentary aura and its rhetorical strategies. Arguing that the film only "pretends" to tell the "true story of Matt Cvetic," Crowther points out that the film seems calculated to create a backlash against other political interests: "The sketchy demonstrations of Communist infiltration within the ranks of labor, school teachers, and Negroes tends to build up current suspicions in all these groups. Many ideas that are liberal—such as defense of our civil liberties or criticism of some of the methods of the House Committee on Un-American Activities—are made by this film to seem 'pink.'"[49] Unfortunately, few other movie critics in America showed Crowther's political perspicacity.

Ironically, by lumping together Communists, racists, and well-meaning civil rights advocates, anti-Communist filmmakers engaged in the same kinds of political practices as the groups they were criticizing. If part of the anti-Communists' complaint was that Communists were using racial issues instrumentally—that is, as a means to a larger political end—then anti-Communists were no less susceptible to the same charge. Anti-Communist films like *I Was a Communist* did not show interest in racism and civil rights issues per se but rather used them to discredit Communism as a means of achieving racial and social justice.

The strongest evidence that anti-Communist filmmakers used the issue of race instrumentally is found in *I Was a Communist*'s cinematic treatment of the film's African American characters. Unlike *The Red Menace*, which at least dealt with the experiences of black, Jewish, and Irish Communists in its subplots, *I Was a Communist* generally treats its minority characters as scenery, an undifferentiated mass of people that help expose the party's hypocritical handling of racial issues. As the PCA's content analysis of *I Was a Communist* indicates, African Americans appear in the film as party members, students, and porters, but all of these characters are identified as "incidental" (i.e., narratively insignificant).[50]

Perhaps because they viewed these characters as incidental, the PCA also made several recommendations for script changes that would downplay the film's racial themes. In a letter to Jack Warner, Joseph Breen asks the filmmakers to eliminate the use of the word *niggers* and to excise a newsreel shot of a race riot.[51] These requests, however, show the extent to which the Production Code Administration sought to mollify both sides of the political aisle. The former request probably was made to allay the concerns of liberals and interest groups, like the NAACP, while the latter request was made as a concession to state censors, who the PCA claimed would "generally delete scenes of actual race riots."[52]

The major exception to the film's superficial treatment of racial and ethnic characters is, of course, the protagonist, Matt Cvetic, who identifies himself in the film's opening voice-over as a Slovenian. Curiously, though, contemporaneous reviews generally treated the hero's Slovenian background as an extraneous detail, something included largely as tacit motivation for Cvetic's ability to infiltrate the Communist cell in Pittsburgh. Though it is never stated as such, one might surmise that Cvetic gains the Communists' trust because he comes from immigrant stock and thus differs little from the thousands of other foreign-born laborers who join the Communist Party. More important, though, Cvetic's Slovenian background also hints at a racial code in the film that ultimately reinforces the very racial hierarchies that other anti-Communist films, such as *The Red Menace*, sought to question. As a white European, Cvetic is smart enough to see through Communism's lies while the masses of African American members are depicted as being too gullible and too trusting to be anything but party shills. In *I Was a Communist for the FBI* the fevered imaginations of its makers produced a vision of Communism that showed the party bent on subverting and manipulating persons of color in an effort to overturn America's political structures. Yet at the end of the day it was anti-Communists themselves who tried to use the party to destroy any and all forms of political opposition.

BIG JIM MCLAIN: COMMUNISM AS EXOTIC DETAIL

As a star vehicle for John Wayne, *Big Jim McLain* is one of the films most frequently cited in histories of the Hollywood blacklist and of the anti-Communist cycle of films that resulted from it.[53] *Big Jim McLain* would be the first in a series of films for Wayne that established his credentials as a cinematic bulwark against the Communist threat. Besides this film Wayne battled Communism in *Blood Alley* (1955) and *The Green Berets* (1968). Moreover, in his most personal project, *The Alamo*, Wayne produced, directed, and starred in a film that some critics read as an allegory of America's containment policies of the postwar period.[54] As an MPAPAI member, as an icon of the American West, and as a cinematic combatant of Communism, Wayne became an important symbol of American patriotism and of the Cold War policies and military buildup established during the postwar period.

As I mentioned earlier, *Big Jim McLain* is also notable for its inclusion of footage showing real-life members of HUAC. Although several anti-Communist leaders, such as J. Edgar Hoover, made cameo appearances in films and HUAC activities were amply documented in newsreels, the appearance of HUAC in *Big Jim McLain* was one of the rare instances in which the committee's hearings were presented within a fictional context. Since the committee appeared only at the film's beginning and end, however, HUAC's cameo functioned as little more than an endorsement of Wayne's cinematic politics.

HUAC's cooperation with Wayne's production company, however, caused some serious concerns for *Big Jim McLain*'s distributor, Warner Bros. Much of this concern involved the need to get clearances from the various real-life government agents, officials, and institutions depicted in the film. A memo from Carl Milliken Jr., head of Warner Bros.' research department, to Finlay McDermid, dated March 18, 1952, lays out the studio's concerns: "One way or another we show the investigations which are made in behalf of this Congressional Committee as being done in illegal and offensive ways and by individuals of a rather low caliber. While I appreciate that the writers' endeavor is to laud and not demean these activities, I submit that this story could backfire in its present form—even to the possible extent of placing *us* in contempt of Congress."[55] Milliken's language rather cleverly references the types of criminal charges levied against those witnesses who refused to cooperate with HUAC. Milliken followed up this memo with another to studio lawyer Roy Obringer that was even more explicit about Warner Bros.' problems with the script. Milliken's memo indicates that the studio was bothered by the apparent lack of progress in getting HUAC's approval and that they blamed this reluctance on certain elements of the script:

> The script shows the investigators as using illegal and criminal methods in obtaining their evidence. They are shown as "bugging" premises and as installing wire-tapping devices in a house. We show them as searching Communist Party headquarters apparently without the benefit of a search warrant and after having gained entry through the expert use of a jimmie. In this last endeavor, we show the Honolulu police as assisting them on orders from the Chief of Police.
>
> Whether or not such evidence is obtained in the ways shown, the Judith Copland conviction (which was thrown out by the Supreme Court because of this illegal sort of evidence) is probably a sore point with such agencies. Neither the Committee nor the investigators will want—in all probability—to have such activities detailed.
>
> The investigators are shown using coercion on informants and the threat of physical brutality after suspects are in custody.
>
> Several times in the course of the story, the investigators express the feeling that Constitutional safeguards for the individual should be abandoned in the case of Communists. The Committee may hold to the thinking that these Constitutional guarantees, frustrating as they some-times are in their workings, are provided not only for the few culprits who hide behind them but for all of us.[56]

Although these concerns were never completely allayed, Milliken appears to have dropped the matter when he learned from producer Robert Fellows that HUAC and the Naval Intelligence Office approved the inclusion of "illegal procedures" that Milliken recounted in his previous memos.[57]

Set in Hawaii in 1952, *Big Jim McLain* treats the island as a kind of liminal space, both physically and geopolitically. As a territory between Asia and North America, Hawaii is an area of prime importance to the Asian American diaspora that extends beyond the Pacific Rim to include major cities on the coasts and in the heartland. Because it was not yet a state, though, Hawaii took on some of the aspects of the American frontier as a site of struggle, both culturally and politically. As the events of Pearl Harbor had shown in 1941, Hawaii was especially vulnerable to enemy attack because of its isolation from the mainland and its proximity to unfriendly nations. More important, as a boundary space between East and

West, Hawaii also was viewed as particularly susceptible to Communist influence arising from Asian countries, such as Red China and North Korea. The island's retention of indigenous customs would place it under suspicion as an area not entirely assimilated to all aspects of mainstream Americanism.

Given Hawaii's status as a liminal space, one might expect *Big Jim McLain* to employ some of the familiar tropes of the "yellow peril." In stories by Sax Rohmer and Robert Chambers, Asians constitute an insidious threat to various aspects of American politics and culture, one made worse by the seeming foreignness of Asian traditions and philosophy. Yet *Big Jim McLain* generally resists this type of xenophobia in favor of a more familiar linkage between Communism and European immigration. Inverting some of the usual hierarchies of white supremacism, in *Big Jim McLain* the threat of Communism arises not from the Hawaiian natives and Japanese Americans living there but from the cultivated English gentlemen who so easily assimilate into American society.

The film begins with an exterior long shot of a rural road bracketed on one side by a grove of trees and on the other by an open field of grass. The bucolic landscape, however, is beset by a thunderstorm as rain and flashes of lightning spread across the screen. The film's title card appears with the first flash of lightning, and subsequent flashes serve as transitions for some of the later credits as they unspool. On the soundtrack a medley of classic American songs, such as "Yankee Doodle" and "Dixie," accompanies a nondiegetic voice-over that quotes from Stephen Vincent Benet's poem "The Devil and Daniel Webster." Through this overdetermined concatenation of Americana and nature's fury, the film's title character is linked simultaneously to a disembodied voice of democracy and to the primordial power of the American landscape.

Almost immediately after the credit sequence, though, the film disentangles these thematic motifs, albeit in sometimes contradictory ways. After the opening images of storm and land, the film dissolves to an extreme long shot of the Capitol Building in Washington, D.C. The camera then pans to the right to reveal a sign indicating the entrance to the HUAC hearing room. This is followed by still another dissolve to an establishing shot of the hearing room itself. After indicating the roots of democracy in the American landscape and our nation's founding fathers, the film then moves to modern-day Washington, a gesture that rhetorically links HUAC's investigations with Daniel Webster's famous query about the status of the Union and analogizes Communism to the temptations of Satan. The change in settings, however, appears to sever the connection between nature and democracy. The move to a modern, urban setting suggests that our nation's liberties are now the province of bureaucratic functionaries rather than the rugged individualists who carved out their existence in the American wilderness. Public hearings and congressional investigations now play the roles once served by militias and lawmen.

Yet if the preservation of the Union is now the domain of institutional bureaucracies, then so, too, is the threat of domestic Communism. During *Big Jim McLain*'s opening sequence a witness being questioned by HUAC responds by taking the Fifth Amendment. The witness's refusal to answer questions is depicted as a legal loophole, a procedural filigree knowingly used to thwart further investigation. Thus, the very legal processes and protections purportedly embodied in the congressional inquiry offer security to those who would continue their nefarious activities. The witness himself, we are told, is a university professor, who will return to his post teaching economics. Taking its cue from Marx himself, *Big Jim McLain* depicts Communism as the ideological terrain of modern, urban intellectuals, who have brought their dissident and subversive philosophies with them from Europe. This motif will be picked up later in the film's characterizations of Doctors Gelster and Mortimer, whose gray suits, spectacles, and mustaches mark them as sophisticated and well-educated gentlemen, figures who provide a distinct physical contrast to the beefy American investigators played by Wayne and James Arness.

In efforts, though, to adhere to broader conventions of Hollywood entertainment, *Big Jim McLain* implies that the HUAC investigations themselves are something of a failure. When the hearings are stalled by witnesses' legalistic tactics, it falls to investigators like McLain and his partner, Mal Baxter, to carry the committee's mission forward. At this point one might well expect *Big Jim McLain* to adhere to conventions of the "G-Man" cycle that emerged in the late 1930s as a more positive alternative to the classic gangster film. Not surprisingly, many other anti-Communist films, like *Walk East on Beacon*, revel in the FBI's use of wiretaps and hidden cameras to reveal the sinister activities of seemingly ordinary people. Surprisingly, though, *Big Jim McLain* mostly eschews that kind of investigative technophilia. Instead, McLain and Baxter employ more mundane investigative techniques, such as tracking down leads, conducting interviews, and liaising with local law enforcement and union officials.

The reasons for this shift in cinematic rhetoric are twofold. First, by emphasizing more traditional alliances among law enforcement agencies, *Big Jim McLain* avoids the impression that Communism is endemic to Hawaiian politics and culture. Communist subversion remains a localized threat that has the potential to create a great deal of social mischief, but it has not yet infiltrated the true centers of local power, which are symbolized by real-life Honolulu police chief Daniel Liu and union leader Max Venaby, respectively. Second, by emphasizing traditional investigative methods, the film enables Big Jim McLain to function as a mediating figure who operates between the Edenic natural setting of Hawaii and the social, legal, and political orders represented on the mainland in Washington, D.C.

If the first sequences of *Big Jim McLain* establish Washington as the site of the civil and social, subsequent sequences establish Hawaii, the film's principal setting, as the locus of the natural. Unlike the western, however, which defines nature as uncivilized wilderness, *Big Jim McLain* sees its tropical setting through tourist eyes, highlighting the unspoiled tropical splendor of the islands and the exotic customs of its people. This tourist perspective is established early on in a scene showing McLain and Baxter's plane journey to the isles. During the flight an attendant directs the passengers' attention to prominent tourist attractions in Hawaii, such as Diamond Head. Later scenes take place at other well-traveled sites, such as Pearl Harbor and Waikiki Beach.

In addition to highlighting particular tourist destinations, the film also uses Hawaiian natives to add local color to the setting. When McLain and Baxter arrive in Hawaii, the film includes a scene of them deplaning in order to show the locals greeting visitors with leis, hula dancers, and native musicians. At other times, native singers and strolling musicians provide atmosphere for McLain's romantic dinners with Nancy Valens, a woman he has met in the course of his investigation. In all of these ways the landscapes and people of Hawaii emerge as *Big Jim McLain*'s primary signifiers of the natural, albeit in a conception of nature as quaint and idyllic rather than wild and forbidding.

Whereas the film's Hawaiian locations offer the beauties of unspoiled tropical vistas, McLain himself is linked to nature in several ways, thereby complicating his status as an agent of the political and legal structures mentioned above. For example, the film frequently makes reference to McLain's size, six foot four. As a physical trait, McLain's impressive size is something that cannot be achieved through education, culture, or social engineering. Moreover, a flirtatious, blonde boardinghouse owner nicknames McLain "76" in reference to his height. The number thus comes to signify both McLain's masculine potency ("76 inches is a lotta man") and his link to American history by referencing the year 1776 and its almost mythic status in American ideology.

Costume also serves to link McLain to nature. Unlike the Communists, who almost always appear in drab gray suits, McLain is often clothed, like the native Hawaiian males we see, in print shirts and casual slacks. Typically, McLain dresses in this manner for his dates with Nancy Valens, but he also wears informal clothing for his police work. Mixing the modes of dress appropriate to both Washington and Hawaii, McLain sometimes simply puts a sports jacket over his Hawaiian print shirt. In its use of Hawaii as a modern "frontier" setting and Wayne as a mediating figure between nature and society, *Big Jim McLain* establishes parallels between its titular protagonist and Wayne's more familiar guise as a western hero.

The tropical splendor of Hawaii undoubtedly enhances *Big Jim McLain*'s production values, but the film's natural settings also serve as a perfect breeding ground for Communist activities. The film suggests this link primarily through the use of leprosy as a metaphor for the spread of subversive ideology. The leprosy motif is introduced early in the film during the aforementioned flight from Washington to Hawaii when the flight attendant also directs the passengers' attention to the island of Molokai, describing it as the home to one of the nation's only leper colonies. This is followed by an insert that reveals an aerial view of the island. The leprosy motif returns when McLain goes to Molokai to interview Willie Namaka's estranged wife, who works at the leper colony as a nurse. During her interview with McLain, Mrs. Namaka describes her past association with the Communist Party but says that she now recognizes the party's agenda as "a vast conspiracy to enslave the common man." Asserting her loyalty to the nation, Mrs. Namaka says that she "wouldn't lend a hand to a conspirator any more than she would to a . . ." Mrs. Namaka pauses here before admitting that she was going to say "a leper," a comment that concretizes the metaphorical link between contagion and Communism.

In fact, an earlier draft of the screenplay makes this metaphorical link even more explicit. In a scene where McLain meets with a doctor in Molokai, the doctor says, "Dan Liu told me the score. Are we hiding a Communist here?" McLain responds, "I don't think so. I'm just hunting information." In an effort to underline a similarity between himself and McLain, the doctor adds, "We have something in common. We both seek out lepers. . . . Good luck."[58]

This "Communism as contagion" motif recurs near the end of *Big Jim McLain* when the film's chief villain, Sturak (Alan Napier), reveals the other members of the Communists' "seventh cell," one of whom is a bacteriologist. As Sturak outlines the plans to isolate Hawaii, it becomes clear that even Communists view the spread of their philosophy as akin to germ warfare. Their ultimate plan is to place Hawaii under quarantine, both medically and economically.

Metaphors of disease and epidemic were quite common in descriptions of the Communist threat, but in *Big Jim McLain* the equation of Communists as lepers also hints at the film's treatment of racial and ethnic minorities. As part of the Asian diaspora that includes elements of Japanese, Chinese, Filipino, and Polynesian cultures, Hawaii is thus a ripe climate for the importation of Communist philosophies that move both westward from their point of origin among European intellectuals and eastward from the Maoist strains arising from both mainland China and North Korea. By failing to individuate any of its native Hawaiian characters, *Big Jim McLain* preserves the sense of ethnic difference among Hawaii's Asian diaspora while also suggesting that its native populations are a faceless mass, ready and waiting to be colonized by European Communists. It is through this particular articulation of race that John Wayne's dual status as anti-Communist icon and western hero is most deeply felt. As another kind of "native American," the dark-skinned Hawaiian natives may be subject to the predations of European Stalinists, but they must also be protected by people like McLain and Mal Baxter, descendants of America's great white settlers, whose belief in Manifest Destiny allowed them to conquer a continent. Within this battle against Communism, which here is construed as America's nightmare inversion of Manifest Destiny, the Hawaiian natives depicted in *Big Jim McLain* emerge as both the hapless victims of international conspiracy and the helpless beneficiaries of American democracy.

The investigation itself, however, proves fruitless as those apprehended by McLain and the Hawaiian police, once again, take the Fifth in their testimony before HUAC. As Thomas Doherty points out, McLain appears to take comfort, in the film's final scene, both from his girlfriend's supportive love and from the awesome sight of American military might on display.[59] Cued by the sounds of "Anchors Aweigh" playing offscreen, McLain and Nancy glance off left. The film then cuts to an extreme long shot of an army brigade marching toward the camera, its members surrounded by a fleet of battleships and destroyers. The film cuts to a medium close-up in which various soldiers answer the roll as their names are called. According to Doherty, the group that passes before the camera is similar to the typical, ethnically diverse platoon of a Warner Bros. combat film.[60] What Doherty fails to note, though, is that the moment's egalitarian spirit is quickly undercut by the film's final shots, which reveal its true ideological underpinnings. Over a long shot of a vessel slowly leaving the harbor, its passengers waving to McLain and Nancy in the distance, the voice-over narration reiterates the question posed in Benet's famous poem: "Neighbor, how stands the Union now?" The film then dissolves to a lateral tracking shot that shows the mostly white military personnel who occupy the territory as a security force. As the camera moves past the smiling faces of U.S. sailors and soldiers, McLain replies, "There stands the Union, Mr. Webster. There stands our Union, sir." McLain, who serves as a proxy for Wayne's right-wing ideology, aligns the strength of the Union with America's military might rather than the "melting pot" to which the Hawaiian peoples would be joined. For Wayne and other anti-Communists, the Union stands on the shoulders of the protectors rather than in the heritage of those protected. In this way *Big Jim McLain* unintentionally expresses the link between white racism and anti-Communism that permeated America's Cold War culture.

CONCLUSION

After the landmark *Brown v. Board of Education* decision, the emerging civil rights movement confronted many challenges posed by its relationship to the Communist Party. Although many viewed the party as a civil rights organization, the purge of Communists around the country encouraged many African American activists to sever their ties to it. Of course, this trend had already been established in the late 1940s when Red-baiting contributed to the NAACP's firing of its founder, W.E.B. DuBois. But the *Brown* decision reinvigorated the anti-Communist campaigns in the mid-1950s by establishing new arenas for their activities in which civil rights leaders would find themselves as targets.[61]

Much as the NAACP did in the 1930s, civil rights leaders in the 1950s tried to distance themselves from Communist support. For example, at a Harlem rally protesting the acquittal of two white defendants in the murder of Emmett Till, the rally's organizers warned against accepting help from Communists, saying that "their support is the kiss of death."[62] Later, Martin Luther King Jr. submitted to pressure from the Southern Christian Leadership Conference, firing two of his top aides because they once had been Communist Party members.[63]

Characterizing the 1950s as an era of "lost opportunities," Ellen Schrecker argues that McCarthyism had a multifaceted impact on the direction of the civil rights movement by limiting its potential for political alliances and by minimizing the movement's emphasis on class issues and economic equality.[64] In doing so, McCarthyism placed civil rights leaders in an ideological bind; although anti-Communist groups could not prevent African Americans from voicing their concerns about policies on segregation, voting rights, and Jim Crow, they nonetheless forced them to attest their loyalty to the very government and nation that oppressed them. By dismantling whatever coalitions remained in the Popular Front's remnants, McCarthyism effectively forestalled a more radical and more progressive solution to the problems of racial discrimination.

The ambivalence evident in the civil rights movement's attempts to negotiate a position somewhere between the radical left and the McCarthyist right is paralleled by the ideological confusions and contradictions present in Hollywood anti-Communism's treatment of race. In seeking to explain away the Communist Party's stance on civil rights issues, Hollywood anti-Communist films raised the specter of race as a significant social problem. Although these films consistently portrayed Communist Party leaders as puppet masters, controlling and manipulating the people who followed them, the rhetoric of these films implied that Communist leaders merely fomented a problem that already existed. At their worst these films suggested that the solution to society's racial ills could be found in prayer and Christian belief, a trope that perhaps suggests why religious leaders like Martin Luther King Jr. and Jesse Jackson have proven to be more acceptable to mainstream America as the public face of the civil rights movement.

Some of these films, like *I Was a Communist for the FBI*, treated their African American characters as part of an undifferentiated Communist mass, a pliable body that could be bent and twisted to fit the party's will. Others, like *The Red Menace*, placed unusual emphasis on race as a cinematic theme and gave fairly prominent supporting roles to African American actors. By exploring the plight of these supporting characters, Hollywood anti-Communist films illustrated the extent to which race was a double-edged sword as a weapon in the industry's arsenal. As Henry Solomon, the Jewish Communist poet of *The Red Menace*, puts it in referring to the party's minority members, "We're none of us hyphens; we're just plain Americans." Solomon's desire to rise above this divisiveness resonates beyond the simplistic anti-Communist rhetoric that encapsulates it. His plea for unity is a backhanded retort to Communist Party officials, but it applies just as easily to America as a whole.

4   Stoolies, Cheese-Eaters, and Tie Sellers

Genre, Allegory, and the HUAC Informer

No issue related to the Hollywood blacklist has been as contentious or as emotionally charged as the question of "naming names." Although many of those blacklisted felt anger toward the studio executives and producers who callously cast them aside, a special sort of contempt was reserved for HUAC informers. Consider, for example, the infamous controversy surrounding Elia Kazan's Lifetime Achievement Award at the 1999 Academy Award Ceremony. Kazan is among the most honored filmmakers in the Academy's history, having won three Oscars for Best Director, but many jeered the announcement of his award, saying that the moral cowardice he displayed as a cooperative witness before HUAC made Kazan unworthy of such a distinction. Victor Navasky quotes one of those objectors, who claimed that "since part of his lifetime achievement was to cost others in the profession their jobs, he shouldn't be honored."[1] Thus, when Martin Scorsese presented Kazan with his award on Oscar night, many prominent actors, such as Nick Nolte, responded by quite literally sitting on their hands. That this event would stir such passions nearly fifty years after Kazan's testimony is but a small indication of the emotional wounds caused by HUAC informers.

Victor Navasky's *Naming Names* remains the definitive analysis of this issue. Navasky's landmark book systematically examines the specific reasons why people in Hollywood cooperated with the committee and the extent to which these justifications correspond with the record of their actual testimony. Although it is clear that Navasky has a political axe to grind, his analysis is remarkably cogent and evenhanded. Navasky admits at the outset that there may be perfectly valid situations, such as the threat of murder, in which informing is completely defensible. Moreover, Navasky also acknowledges that some informers, such as Larry Parks, became victims of the blacklist despite their cooperation and notes that the humiliation and self-loathing involved in informing might be seen as mitigating circumstances for those who caved in to HUAC and to studio pressures to cooperate.

Interviews, memoirs, and committee transcripts have left a rich chronicle of the circumstances faced by witnesses testifying before HUAC, and historians have plumbed the depths of these documents in a variety of secondary works. Likewise, a handful of films made decades after the Hollywood blacklist was established—including *The Way We Were, The Front, Guilty by Suspicion,* and *The Majestic* (2001)—dramatize witnesses' moral and professional quandaries. Yet although these books and films constitute two nodes of our collective memory of the Cold War era, a question emerges in their interstices: how was the dilemma of the HUAC informer represented in films made during the blacklist period?

A survey of blacklist film criticism suggests that Hollywood films rarely offered explicit representations of HUAC's activities and almost never referred directly to the investigations taking place within the film community. Films like *Big Jim McLain* were very much the exception rather than the rule. Instead, as countless essays on Cold War cinema have shown, filmmakers typically used allegorical narratives to draw analogies between situations depicted onscreen and the dilemmas faced by HUAC witnesses. These allegorical structures cut across a wide variety of genres, including the courtroom drama, the espionage film, the docudrama, the historical film, the western, and the science fiction film. As such, the Cold War and the Hollywood blacklist constitute an important semantic field for the implicit and symptomatic meanings of dozens of Hollywood films made during this period.

In this chapter and those that follow I map the various ways in which allegory has functioned as a part of blacklist criticism. A careful reading of this criticism reveals that film historians have sometimes made questionable assumptions about the actions and intentions of those involved in making these films. The production histories of these blacklist texts show that the bases for these interpretations are much more complex than is traditionally thought. Moreover, a historical overview of this criticism shows a stark difference between the contemporaneous and long-term reception of these films. At the time of their release, reviewers made scant reference to their blacklist subtexts. Allusions to the blacklist in contemporary reviews, if they were made at all, take the form of oblique traces that must be read symptomatically to discern any sense of the film's allegorical functions. In contrast, in the 1970s critics began to call attention to these subtexts at about the time that Hollywood itself started acknowledging the blacklist's role in the industry's history. By exploring both real and possible interpretations of these blacklist allegories, one gets a sense of the often disputed, contested, and multivalent qualities these films hold for critics and historians.

This chapter examines the way in which certain films addressed the ethical and moral dilemmas faced by HUAC informers. I selected six films as case studies of this type of blacklist allegory: *Storm Warning* (1951), *Viva Zapata!* (1952), *Man on a Tightrope* (1953), *On the Waterfront* (1954), *Pickup on South Street* (1953), and *I Confess* (1952). The first is a piece of florid propaganda that metaphorically justifies the acts of HUAC informers by situating them within larger notions of social evil and civic duty. The last is sometimes read as a sympathetic portrait of an "uncooperative witness," one that ennobles the silence of those who resisted HUAC by exploring the pressures caused by community suspicions and an uncaring, ineffectual legal system. The remainder fall somewhere in between these ideological poles.

Critics often develop allegorical interpretations by comparing the films' characters and plot events to historical personages and events roughly contemporaneous with the films' release dates. By drawing analogies between the films and the political contexts in which they were produced, critics treat these events as topical reference points that provide a pretext for the work's allegorical meanings. Taken together, these topical reference points "frame" the meanings of the film by acting as corroborative evidence supporting the critic's interpretation. In the case of these "informer" allegories, the topical reference points are derived from the testimony of witnesses who appeared before HUAC. Indeed, in critically analyzing these films, scholars typically gesture to the political commitments of their makers, especially those who appeared as cooperative witnesses.

This is especially true of Elia Kazan's films of the 1950s. Given his prominence as someone who "named names" to the committee, it should surprise no one that virtually his entire output during that decade has been interpreted as a reflection of his decision to cooperate. But most critics don't stop there. Rather, they additionally appeal to Kazan's collaboration with other "friendly" witnesses, such as screenwriter Budd Schulberg and actors Adolphe Menjou and Lee J. Cobb, as further evidence of the films' blacklist subtexts. Critics have adopted similar rhetoric in relation to the other films discussed in this chapter. The casting of Ronald Reagan and Ginger Rogers in key roles in *Storm Warning* is taken to be an important clue to the film's politics. The anti-Communism featured prominently in Sam Fuller's *Pickup on South Street* is consistent with the director's work as a whole. And, in a remarkable display of the "guilt by association" tactics that guided HUAC's own investigations, one reading of *I Confess* as blacklist allegory rests partly on screenwriter George Tabori's previous work with Elia Kazan.

Although the HUAC hearings themselves figure prominently as a "frame" for these "informer" allegories, further support for these analogies arises from genre conventions that are a standard part of Hollywood story-telling. Many of these elements—informers, reluctant witnesses, Fifth Amendment defenses—were common to courtroom dramas, detective films, and police procedurals long before the HUAC hearings were even contemplated. When they appeared in films made during the blacklist period, though, these genre elements took on a different resonance for film critics and historians. The historical context for these films may have furnished the reference points that anchor their meanings as blacklist allegory, but the genres themselves served as a natural ground, one that set the political significance of these works into relief. In the case of these "informer" allegories, these critical interpretations suggest that filmmakers themselves were simultaneously both the strongest defenders of the industry's cooperation with HUAC and the most subtle critics of the "Red-baiting" hysteria that gripped the nation for nearly a decade.

CAN ONE EQUATE RACISM WITH COMMUNISM? *STORM WARNING* AND THE CASE FOR CIVIC DUTY

J. Hoberman describes *Storm Warning* as "the first movie to focus on an unwilling informer," and he notes that the film was producer Jerry Wald's "comment on post-HUAC Hollywood."[2] Directed by Stuart Heisler, *Storm Warning* tells the story of a small-town prosecutor's battle against the Ku Klux Klan. As the film begins, Marsha Mitchell (Ginger Rogers) comes to town to visit her sister, Lucy Rice (Doris Day). While trying to find her way through town, Marsha inadvertently stumbles upon the murder of a journalist sent to write a story about Klan activities. Before she can report the crime to authorities, Marsha learns that the perpetrator is her sister's new husband, Hank Rice (Steve Cochran). Out of family loyalty, Marsha remains silent about the murder. In this respect Marsha differs little from the rest of the town's denizens, who keep quiet as a result of Klan intimidation. When prosecutor Burt Rainey (Ronald Reagan) learns that Marsha may have witnessed the crime, he pressures her to give up the killer's identity in an effort to pin the crime on Klan leadership. Rainey even subpoenas Marsha to testify at an inquest, but she lies on the stand in order to protect Lucy's husband. Marsha's loyalties change, though, when Hank attempts to rape her. When Marsha threatens to go to the police, she is abducted and taken to a Klan rally, where she is horsewhipped for her intended betrayal. Rainey leads a raid on the Klan's rally, and although he saves Marsha, Hank and Lucy are both killed in the ensuing gun battle. As Marsha kneels over her dying sister, she realizes the price of her silence.

Produced by Warner Bros. during 1949 and 1950, the film was made prior to the committee's specific request to "name names." Consequently, it seems to be a reaction to the public resistance of the Hollywood Ten rather than to the more extensive HUAC investigations that resumed around the time of the film's release. That said, the film contains several elements that appear to link it to the larger issues surrounding the Hollywood blacklist. These elements are not always mentioned in critical commentaries on the film, but they provide underlying support for the parallels that critics have drawn between *Storm Warning* and the anti-Communist crusade. For one thing, the production of *Storm Warning* was overseen by Jack Warner, one of two studio executives who testified during the 1947 hearings. For another, *Storm Warning* was produced near the start of the postwar anti-Communist cycle by the studio most strongly invested in anti-Communist filmmaking. Finally, *Storm Warning* stars Ginger Rogers and Ronald Reagan, two of the MPAPAI's most vocal and prominent members. Like Jack Warner, Reagan was one of HUAC's friendly witnesses during the 1947 hearings as was Ginger Rogers's mother, Lela.

At least one of these elements was the result of fortuitous circumstances rather than preproduction planning. Rogers was offered the role of Marsha only after Lauren Bacall turned it down.[3] Bacall's action resulted in her suspension from the studio and opened the door for Rogers to assume the role. Although Bacall's motivations were reportedly more financial than political, there is little doubt that her presence in the cast would have altered *Storm Warning*'s political valences. As a member of the Committee for the First Amendment, who participated in protests on the Hollywood Ten's behalf, Bacall would have counterbalanced the overtly anti-Communist public postures of many of the film's chief participants.

Besides the film's cast, two other elements help to support the reading of *Storm Warning* as a blacklist allegory. The first is Rainey's oblique dialogue reference to investigative bodies in Washington and "points north." Explaining his dilemma to the town's deputy, Rainey says that the townspeople refuse to come forward with information about the crime but then also cry "Foul!" when someone from the outside "starts poking his nose in our affairs." In his brief speech Rainey not only speaks to the need to "clean up our own messes" but also implicitly endorses the legitimacy of federal investigative bodies as necessary tools in the fight against certain kinds of organizations. In this respect Rainey's speech might be read as a defense of the MPAPAI's invitation to HUAC to investigate Hollywood when the industry's policy of self-regulation failed to deter the threat of Communism within its ranks.

The second element supporting the interpretation of *Storm Warning* as blacklist allegory is the metaphorical substitution of the Klan for the Communist Party. This analogy rests on a series of rather loose parallels evident in the public perceptions of both Klansmen and Communists. Both groups were viewed as politically extremist, radicals operating on the far right and left wings of mainstream American politics. Both groups also were thought to operate in the shadows and dark corners of American society. In the case of the Klan this secrecy was emblematized by the hoods worn to protect the identity of their members. In the case of the Communist Party the apparently clandestine nature of the organization was substantiated by the party's desire to keep membership rolls secret and by suspected Communists' resistance to official investigations. During the HUAC investigations of the Hollywood Ten, the political claim to both free speech and the secret ballot fueled speculation that the "unfriendly witnesses" had something to hide.

In addition to secrecy, each group was also perceived as potentially threatening as a result of the seeming ordinariness of its membership. Because Communist Party members were identifiable only through their party card or their publicly espoused affiliations, they could "hide in plain sight," passing as ordinary Americans in their daily interactions with others. As Robert Corber points out, in this respect, "Red-baiting" is not unlike homophobia in that it attacks a group whose difference is not readily apparent in their language, dress, or outward behavior.[4] The same is true of Klan members insofar as their identifying marks—their white robes and hoods—are not worn during day-to-day activities. Commenting on this aspect of the Klan, Rainey says, "Here we are trying to find a bunch of murderers, but when we find them, who will they be? Probably friends of ours. Fellas we went to school with."

In still another filmic parallel between the two groups, *Storm Warning* implies that Klan members, like members of the Communist Party, are motivated by a kind of misguided idealism. Just after Rainey's remarks on the likely identity of the murderers, the deputy admits that he was once a member of the Klan. When Rainey asks the deputy why he joined, he responds, "Oh, I thought it was something to do good. You know, help people. Get 'em out of trouble, keep 'em out." The deputy's language here is strongly evocative of similar scenes in anti-Communist films where party members justify the organization's activities by appealing to a desire to help the disadvantaged and downtrodden.

Storm Warning establishes still another parallel by suggesting that the Klan, like the Communist Party, differs little from a gang of criminals. When Rainey asks the deputy why he left the Klan, he says it was "just a racket, a bunch of hoodlums dressed up in sheets." This is then borne out in the rest of the film as we see Klan members commit acts of fraud, extortion, and physical intimidation, a dramaturgical strategy not unlike that used for Communist Party members. In this respect *Storm Warning* harkens back to a broader pattern of representational strategies used by Hollywood to depict political radicalism.

Indeed, certain aspects of the film's style seem to strengthen its connection to these other cycles. In a memo to *Storm Warning*'s cinematographer, Carl Guthrie, Jerry Wald wrote, "Please try to get as many shadows and as much dramatic light as possible into the scenes you're shooting in the house. I would like to see some of the faces in the scene in shadow, and at times in darkness."[5] This emphasis on shadows and darkness lends a noirish atmosphere to the scenes inside Hank and Lucy's house, a creative choice that makes *Storm Warning* a companion to the anti-Communist films noir produced just a few years earlier.

Despite these loose parallels, the equation of Communists and Klan members ignores an obvious and fundamental difference between the two groups, namely their attitudes toward racial equality and civil rights issues. Anti-Communist films frequently acknowledged the party's image as a champion of civil rights, even if they suggested that this image does not accord with the private beliefs or political strategizing of party leaders. In marked contrast to the party's record on civil rights, the Klan's long history of lynchings, anti-Semitism, and virulent racism is well-documented and needs no elaboration here.

What is important is the fact that *Storm Warning*'s treatment of racial issues serves to conceal, or at least weaken, this difference between the two groups. This is because *Storm Warning* is that rare beast in Hollywood, an exposé of the Ku Klux Klan that ignores the issue of racial prejudice almost entirely. The Production Code Administration's content analysis of the film reveals that race was not viewed as a significant story element of *Storm Warning* and that the only African American characters in the film were incidental to the narrative.[6] Indeed, the only time we see a black character onscreen is during a scene outside the courthouse, when an African American woman crosses the frame in a crowd shot. Although Warner Bros. production notes trumpeted the fact that *Storm Warning* had sixty-three different speaking parts, not a single one was given to an African American actor.[7]

The avoidance of racial issues was reinforced by two related aspects of its depiction of the Klan. First, although Rainey makes a vague reference to lynching, the only acts of violence shown in *Storm Warning* are directed against white characters. The reporter whose murder initiates the action of the film is white, as are *Storm Warning*'s other two victims of Klan violence, Marsha Mitchell and Lucy Rice. Second, as several reviewers noted, *Storm Warning* avoids certain markers of geographical specificity. *Time*, for example, observed that "producer Jerry Wald also manages to make the picture inoffensive, and even palatable, to most Southern moviegoers. To do so, he passes up chances to give authentic flavor to the movie's locale."[8] Likewise, the reviewer for the *New Yorker* wrote, "Although the locale of the picture is supposed to be the south, I gather from the title that the lesson we are all meant to take home is that the Klan spirit is not circumscribed by geography. In any case, the producers seem to have worked toward that point by cutting down on ripe Southern dialect and magnolia atmosphere."[9]

At first blush it might appear that Warner Bros.' obscurantism was the result of a desire to assuage southern theater owners and audiences. But internal correspondence shows that the studio's legal department requested a deliberately ambiguous depiction of the film's setting and characters because it feared being sued by the Klan. In a memo to Wald, Carl Milliken Jr., head of the Warner Bros. research department, wrote:

> From the information that I have at hand it is not possible for me to say whether or not the Ku Klux Klan has a national organization which is in a position to sue us. Possibly the threat of such a suit is less than the threat of a suit from an individual klan or its officers should we inadvertently establish such a group in our fictional story.
>
> So long as the community described in this story and its exact location is kept indefinite (as it is now in the script) it would seem to me that no particular klan could establish the fact that we had them in mind in making this picture.[10]

The reason for concern about a potential lawsuit stemmed from an earlier case brought against Warner Bros. for its 1936 film *Black Legion*. In a memo to Milliken, R. J. Obringer explained that the Georgia chapter of the Ku Klux Klan had successfully sued the studio for patent infringement. In preproduction on *Black Legion* Warner Bros.' costume department used the Georgia Klan's hood and robes as the model for the Legion's costumes in the film. In doing so, the costume department replicated a badge that had been patented by the group several years earlier. As Obringer noted, the legal protection given to the group by the U.S. Patent Office was important since it provided precedent for the Klan's legal rights.[11] Milliken reiterated this point in his own memo to Obringer, calling the Klan a "corporate organization" implicitly endowed with the same rights as any other business entity, including the right to sue the studio if it believed Warner Bros. deliberately defamed individual members or chapters.[12]

The overarching concern about potential lawsuits, though, not only shaped *Storm Warning*'s treatment of its setting but also influenced the film's characterization of its fictional Klan members. Under advice of Warner Bros.' legal counsel, Wald and company attempted to avoid any dramatic situation that might resemble a real-life Klan murder for fear that they may be sued by the person accused of the crime. Here again, the roots of this trepidation reach back to *Black Legion*. When that film was released, a Black Legion member on trial for murder in Detroit sued the studio, alleging that the story of the film was too similar to the facts of his own case. Worried that showing crimes against Jews, Catholics, or African Americans might invite lawsuits on similar grounds, Wald went in the opposite direction, making his murder victim a white journalist, killed not because of his race but rather to stop him from publicizing the Klan's activities. In a remarkable bit of self-justification, Wald defended this strategy in a letter to Irv Kupcinet of the *Chicago Sun-Times:* "I also feel that there are too many minority problems being put on screen and not enough majority race problems. Most of the agents in Hollywood spend their time trying to find a new minority race to do a film about; and it's getting so that every time an agent says, 'I have a new subject matter for you,' I shudder and say, 'Now what new race of people has this gent dug up?'"[13]

Of course, by deliberately evading the subject of race, *Storm Warning* avoids the very thing that makes the Klan the Klan. The end result is that *Storm Warning* is a rather tepid potboiler, a film that is all muffled bark and toothless bite. Paradoxically, though, the idiosyncrasies of *Storm Warning*'s depiction of the Klan only served to strengthen the analogies that film critics draw between the film's characters and members of the Communist Party. *Storm Warning*'s lack of specificity about setting and theme renders the Klan a constitutively ambiguous symbol, one open to multiple interpretations. As Wald said in a letter to Cameron Shipp of Glendale, California, "Our basic theme is 'who is more guilty, the Klan and its members, or the people who turn their backs on the Klan, all of them to grow and flourish, figuring what the heck, I'm not a Catholic, or a Jew or a Negro.'" By elevating the themes of silence and collective guilt over the theme of race hatred,

Wald constructs a scenario that, at least superficially, evokes the dilemma of witnesses before HUAC.

In sum, because of its casting and because it was produced at the height of the Red Scare, a handful of critics identify *Storm Warning* as a paean to HUAC informers that might easily be read as a defense of the investigations themselves. These interpretations work like other political allegories in that they involve identifying particular topical reference points that furnish a pretext for understanding the allegory's latent meanings. In the case of *Storm Warning* this pretext involves the testimony of "friendly witnesses," such as the film's star, Ronald Reagan. It also includes the hearings themselves insofar as they provide analogical similarities to the standard conventions of the courtroom drama. Both of these elements allow critics to "frame" Ginger Rogers's character, Marsha, as a stand-in for witnesses who refused to cooperate with HUAC.

Yet because *Storm Warning* disregards the issue of southern racism, the film simultaneously highlights and downplays the parallels between the Communist Party and the Klan as subversive groups. While elements of secrecy and gangsterism create certain similarities in their cinematic depictions, the public perception of each group's stance on racial issues made it possible to ignore *Storm Warning*'s blacklist subtext. As Stephen Vaughn points out in his book on Ronald Reagan, "When *Storm Warning* opened in Miami, a local paper assailed Hollywood for exposing domestic fascism while neglecting 'the equally ugly and dangerous other extreme—Soviet-directed Communism.'"[14] Instead of seeing their metaphorical similarities, the aforementioned editorial described the groups as two sides of the same coin.

These divergent readings of *Storm Warning* point to the duality of many blacklist allegories in cinema. Some films, like *Storm Warning,* seem to play a game of "hide and seek" in appearing to both reveal and conceal the possibility of allegorical readings. Others create allegorical subtexts with such ambiguity that the films themselves can be interpreted in diametrically opposite ways. As we see in the next section, even the most seemingly obvious blacklist allegories are subject to multiple interpretations, a further indication that the critic's framing of a film's characters and events ultimately shapes the interpretation of its meanings.

PARABLES OF COOPERATION AND RESISTANCE IN THE FILMS OF ELIA KAZAN

Of all the people in Hollywood who cooperated with HUAC, Kazan is perhaps the figure most tainted by his decision to "name names." As Victor

Navasky, Brian Neve, and countless other commentators note, the director had been a member of the Group Theatre in the 1930s. In the production of Clifford Odets's *Waiting for Lefty*, Kazan played a taxi driver who led the audience in the call to strike at the play's conclusion.[15] By Kazan's own account of events, he was a member of the American Communist Party from 1934 to 1936. Kazan claims he left the party after being frustrated by the strictures of party discipline and his "firsthand experience of dictatorship and thought control."[16]

When HUAC revived its investigation of Hollywood in 1951, Kazan quickly emerged as a particularly attractive target. At the time, Kazan was one of the most acclaimed directors in Hollywood, a figure whose stature might have enabled him to mount a serious challenge to the committee's authority. As the director of *Gentleman's Agreement, Boomerang* (1948), *Pinky* (1949), and *Panic in the Streets* (1950), Kazan was a filmmaker who possessed both a wealth of talent and a genuine concern for social issues. Kazan's films received several Oscar nominations, and *Gentleman's Agreement* took home the prize for Best Picture in 1948.

Thus, when Kazan was subpoenaed by HUAC, many people looked to him as a potential champion of those who had been blacklisted. If Kazan had refused to answer the committee's questions, he would have forced 20th Century–Fox and Spyros Skouras to make a very difficult choice: suspend Kazan and lose the services of a widely respected director, or defy the committee by keeping Kazan on the roster of studio talent. The dilemma for Fox would be worsened by the eleven Oscar nominations received by Kazan's latest film, *A Streetcar Named Desire*, which Warner Bros. debuted in September of 1951, just a few months before Kazan's first appearance before HUAC. Indeed, the acclaim for *A Streetcar Named Desire* should have altered the debate about the merits and effectiveness of the Hollywood blacklist. Given its industry accolades, Kazan's film would surely pass any political litmus test that the committee or industry might use, thereby foregrounding the issue of whether the blacklist was founded on the threat of questionable films or questionable filmmakers.

Kazan's acquiescence to the committee made all this a moot point. During his first appearance before HUAC, Kazan answered all of the committee's questions, except for the one that required him to "name names." When Kazan testified a second time before HUAC in April of 1952, he not only admitted his membership in the party during the 1930s but also identified eight party comrades from the Group Theatre and a handful of functionaries from his cell.[17] What appalled leftists even more than Kazan's cooperation, though, was his post hoc rationale for doing so. In a *New York*

Times ad printed two days after his testimony, Kazan argued that the atmosphere of "mystery, suspicion, and secrecy" had given rise to a sense of hysteria that could only be cured by the dissemination of the cool, hard facts of Communism. Urging other liberals to speak out, Kazan identified Communism as an "unprecedented and exceptionally tough problem," and he related his own unhappy experiences regarding the impact of party discipline on open political debate. Kazan also railed against the abuses of power by foreign Communist governments and argued that their elimination of free speech, a free press, and individual rights made Communist doctrine fundamentally incompatible with the tenets of American democracy.[18] For many in Hollywood it was one thing for Kazan to turn informer but entirely another for him to justify and rationalize his perfidy.

Objections to Kazan's actions appeared almost as soon as he gave his testimony before HUAC. In a scathing critique of Kazan and *Viva Zapata!* John Howard Lawson, a member of the Hollywood Ten, wrote, "We are accustomed by this time to the dreary spectacle of frightened men and women, who lie and supplicate and repent, denying all that is decent and progressive in their professional and personal lives in order to secure absolution from the ignorant politicians who have become the arbiters of culture in the United States. But Kazan seemed determined to outdo other informers, both in treachery to his friends and in personal abasement."[19]

Given the great lengths to which Kazan went to explain his actions, many later film critics have interpreted his directorial output in the 1950s as yet another attempt to justify his cooperation with HUAC. Much of this critical attention has centered on *On the Waterfront,* but some of Kazan's earlier films, particularly *Viva Zapata!* and *Man on a Tightrope,* have received consideration as well. If one accepts these films as political allegories, however, they reveal a profound ambivalence about the blacklist and the extent to which it involved the untrammeled exercise of power. Much of this doubt can be traced to Kazan's status as a liberal anti-Communist, a centrist position that deplored the exercise of totalitarian power at both ends of the political spectrum. As Kazan himself put it, "I was bewildered. I was anti-Stalinist and anti-McCarthy at the same time. It was difficult to reconcile the two."[20] Describing his HUAC testimony, Kazan adds, "I don't think there is anything in my life towards which I have more ambivalence."[21]

Viewed in this respect, any reading of Kazan's films that reduces them to anti-Communist tracts ignores an important aspect of their double-coding; they are as much anti-HUAC as they are anti-Communist. As Brenda Murphy observes, "In making *Man on a Tightrope,* he could attack the repression of artistic freedom by a Communist regime, thus answering his critics on the Left, at the same time that he was celebrating the power of art to resist authoritarian repression, thus divorcing himself from the extremists on the Right."[22]

While some, like Murphy, see Kazan as expressing a profound ambivalence in all three of these films, this position is a much more modern facet of critical discourse on Kazan. Earlier critics, by and large, were content to see the filmmaker's work as an apologia for his HUAC testimony. Paul J. Vanderwood, for example, argues that *Viva Zapata!* was an anti-Communist clarion call to postwar America disguised as a historical recreation of the Mexican revolution. Vanderwood notes that the project had long been tainted by its association with left-wing politics, both as a depiction of a revolutionary political figure and as a project that involved screenwriter Lester Cole, a member of the Hollywood Ten blacklisted in 1947. Cole had been attached to a Zapata project while at MGM, but the studio ultimately dropped the film following his HUAC testimony. MGM then sold the rights to the project to 20th Century–Fox, which was already developing its own Zapata biopic entitled *The Beloved Rogue*.[23]

In taking over the project, Fox's studio chief, Darryl Zanuck, hired Kazan and John Steinbeck to collaborate on the screenplay but was cautious about developing a Zapata film in such a sensitive political climate. According to Vanderwood, Zanuck expressed concern that the film could be construed as advocating civil war and further encouraged Kazan and Steinbeck to emphasize the role of free elections and a democratic government in Mexico's political transformation. Moreover, in his correspondence with Kazan, Zanuck warned against the possibility that Communists might use the film as a platform for their own beliefs. For his part, Kazan viewed Zapata as a social-climbing New Dealer who led a failed revolution because he was corrupted by power.[24] As Kazan stated in a 1952 letter to the *Saturday Review of Literature*, he initially was drawn to the project by Zapata's renunciation of power: "The man who refused power was not only no Communist; he was that opposite phenomenon: a man of individual conscience."[25]

In his screed against *Viva Zapata!* John Howard Lawson focuses on this act of renunciation, claiming that there is no evidence in the historical record that Zapata voluntarily gave up power; in reality Zapata fled Mexico City when his troops were greatly outnumbered by enemy armies approaching from the south and east.[26] Lawson goes further, though, saying not only that Kazan fabricated this episode in his characterization of Zapata but also that he did so self-servingly to justify his decision to cooperate with HUAC: "Kazan elucidates his meaning most forcefully in his testimony before the Un-American Committee. He performs an act of renunciation, subtly connected with the meretricious 'renunciation' which he imposes on the celluloid Zapata. Kazan renounces political struggle, denies even the right to conduct struggle or hold opinions. Just as his false Zapata abandons land-reform to avoid any suspicion of Communism, Kazan discards all pretense of personal or artistic independence in order to retain whatever shreds of 'dignity' the Committee will grant him."[27] Lawson's comments on *Viva Zapata!* introduce an important element in the literature on Kazan's work, namely a tendency to see the protagonists of his 1950s films as surrogates for the director himself.

While Vanderwood is right to highlight liberal anti-Communism as the overarching political orientation of *Viva Zapata!*, his reading also neglects the profound ambivalence that sits just below the film's surface. As Nora Sayre points out, "Kazan claimed that his movie about the Mexican revolutionary was an 'anti-Communist picture.' He has since called it 'progressive.' The film's highly confused romanticism did invite conflicting interpretations."[28] Sayre's observation about Kazan's shifting perception shows that cognitive frame-switching is not solely the purview of critics but extends to filmmakers as well.

This ambivalence is best understood in two important parallel scenes in the film that depict the peasants' demands for land reform. The first scene follows the credits and begins with an explanatory title stating that a delegation of Indians from the State of Morelos is meeting with President Porfirio Diaz. It is followed by an establishing shot that shows the delegation being led into the Capitol by a group of guards. The sequence's third shot is taken from inside a guard's station and shows the peasants being searched for knives and other weapons.

The next series of shots shows the peasants entering a large hall and waiting for Diaz to come in. Through the use of classical Hollywood decoupage, Kazan establishes the regal interior of the Capitol, as well as the peasants' wide-eyed response to their surroundings and to Diaz's brusque entrance. In a series of shot/reverse shot figures the peasants complain that their land is being taken away and ask for government assistance in protecting it. Diaz responds that such land disputes are a matter for the courts. As the peasants begin to leave, Kazan cuts to a complex deep-focus composition that shows the back of Diaz's head in the left foreground, Zapata standing alone in the midground with the other peasants off to his right, and a presidential portrait in the deep background of the shot that is spatially aligned with Zapata's position within the frame (fig. 4). The shot nicely captures Zapata's problematic status within his social structures. By

Figure 4. In this shot from *Viva Zapata!* director Elia Kazan neatly foreshadows his protagonist's rise to power as a populist leader, as well as Zapata's later betrayal of his political principles. It also illustrates Kazan's ambivalence about his subject. The director admired Zapata largely for his renunciation of the power he had amassed but that personally corrupted him.

refusing to move along with the other peasants, Zapata's isolation from the group suggests that he is the only one among them with the strength to defy the current government and challenge its failure to protect the rights of the underclass. At the same time, the visual juxtaposition of Zapata and the presidential portrait foreshadows the former's problematic rise to power. Reflecting the director's own ambivalent political status, Zapata is shown caught between two factions, defying the existing power structure, on one hand, and sympathizing with the plight of the politically disempowered, on the other. Crucially, Zapata is visually separated from those whose rights he defends, suggesting in the immediate context that he rejects their timid acquiescence but foreshadowing Zapata's later betrayal of his political principles.

Following this deep-focus composition is another shot/reverse shot figure that depicts Zapata verbally jousting with Diaz. When Zapata complains that the patience that Diaz expects of the peasantry will not fill hungry bellies or cross disputed boundaries, Diaz demands the name of the one who defies him. After Diaz hears the response, an insert shows him circling the name Emiliano Zapata. At the time of the film's release, any insert shot displaying names on a list would have special resonance, especially coming from a director like Kazan, who himself was threatened by the blacklist. The shot suggests that Zapata, like Kazan, is a troublesome political subject, one potentially in need of special attention and legal constraint.

This scene is paralleled by a later scene in which a delegation of Morelos Indians visits the Capitol; only now it is Zapata who occupies the position previously held by Diaz. Both visually and narratively, the latter sequence contains several echoes of the former. Like Diaz in the earlier sequence, Zapata is seated at a desk that signifies his place of power, and the camera frequently adopts his vantage point with government officials in the foreground and the peasantry in the middle and background planes of the composition. As before, the Indians seek government assistance to resolve a land dispute, although in this case it involves Zapata's brother. Just as Zapata confronted Diaz in the earlier scene, Zapata himself is confronted by a member of the delegation named Hernandez. In rhetoric similar to Zapata's, Hernandez presses for a resolution by claiming that the ground is ready for planting, that seeds cannot wait, and that stomachs cannot wait. And much as Diaz did, Zapata demands Hernandez's name and then circles it on a list.

In all of these respects the parallels between Zapata and Diaz reinforce Kazan and Steinbeck's ostensible theme, namely that power corrupts those who gain it. This reading, however, is overly simplistic and ignores several differences between the two sequences. Most obviously, the two rooms that serve as political arenas are different. While the hall in the latter sequence is decorated apropos of a palatial government building, there is nothing comparable to the presidential portrait that looms so large in the earlier sequence. Consequently, Hernandez, the moral conscience of the latter sequence, is never aligned with power in the same way that Zapata was in the former.

Second, the latter sequence is spatially organized such that Zapata's adviser serves as a mediating presence between Zapata and the Morelos delegation. The master shot of the latter sequence places Fernando, played by Joseph Wiseman, in the middle ground, quite literally between Zapata in the foreground and the Morelos in the background. Fernando is, of course, the personification of American colonial influence on Mexican politics, and Kazan's composition underscores this point by suggesting that his influence over Zapata alienates the Mexican from his own people.

Finally, the latter sequence merely depicts Zapata circling Hernandez's name; there is no insert showing the name itself. The latter sequence, thus, lacks the kind of identificatory alignment between spectator, narrator, and character that makes the earlier shot from Diaz's point of view so powerful. The earlier sequence quite explicitly situates Zapata as an object of government scrutiny and uses the list as a metaphor for Hollywood's own surveillance of its personnel.

All of these differences function narratively to prepare for the scene's conclusion, in which Zapata rejects the trappings of presidential power and returns to the Morelos as a populist leader. This is signified by the sequence's final shot, which shows Zapata toting a rifle and leading the delegation out of the room in the Capitol. Despite this ostensibly upbeat ending to the sequence, the apparent triumph of Zapata's political conscience hides a deeper ambivalence at its heart. After all, Zapata's return to his people results only in his martyrdom as a political hero. By explicitly comparing Diaz and Zapata, the film hints that the corruptive influence of power nearly transforms a populist revolutionary into a collaborator, a political despot little different from his predecessors. Viewed this way, it is hard not to see *Viva Zapata!* as Kazan's commentary on his own political dilemma. As a former radical turned anti-Communist liberal, Kazan faced the same prospects as his titular hero; Kazan could become a political martyr to a cause he questioned or he could become a collaborator and betray those with whom he worked.

The film Kazan made immediately after testifying before HUAC, *Man on a Tightrope*, contains a similarly ambivalent political stance. Most film scholars have read the film as a straightforward anti-Communist political tract, a mark of Kazan's almost complete interpellation as national subject.[29] The apparent ideological change in Kazan's filmmaking is evident in the narrative, which tells the story of Karel Cernik (Fredric March), the owner of a small Czechoslovakian circus. Faced with Communist Party pressure to make changes in his performance and threatened with the loss of a business handed down by his father, Cernik leads his circus troupe in a daring escape to the West. Like several other anti-Communist films, *Man on a Tightrope* was ostensibly based on real-life events. Additionally, by utilizing the conventions of espionage films to dramatize Cernik's escape, this film bears more than a passing resemblance to *The Iron Curtain*, which Fox had produced only a few years earlier.

Robert E. Sherwood's screenplay establishes the depredations of Soviet-styled Communism at the outset. The film begins with several long shots of the Cernik circus caravan making its way through the Czechoslovakian countryside. When the caravan nears a roadblock, military police order the wagons off the road and into the ditch. Cernik protests that he has a permit to use the road, but the soldiers ignore his entreaties and repeat their order. The caravan travels only a short distance before one of the circus wagons breaks an axle. Through this introductory episode Sherwood and Kazan affirm a central tenet of anti-Communism, namely that the rigidity and insensitivity of Communist bureaucracy causes hardships for its citizens. Later that night, the circus performs in a rural area outside of Pilsen. As the clowns enter to the strains of "Chattanooga Choo Choo," word quickly spreads throughout the circus that the police are in attendance. A brief series of shots shows two policemen (identifiable by their fedoras, suits, and unsmiling faces) lurking behind the spectators, thereby confirming the rumor circulating among the performers.[30] Through this brief vignette Sherwood and Kazan affirm still another central tenet of anti-Communism, namely that citizens under Soviet rule are subject to constant surveillance and government supervision.

The next day, while the circus is being set up for the next performance, the police return to take Cernik to Pilsen for questioning. After a brief montage depicting the developing romance of Cernik's daughter, Teresa, an establishing shot shows the two policemen escorting Cernik into a dank and dreary office space. People line benches outside the office, trying to avoid the puddles of water that collect in the entryway. The camera pans left, with the police, as Cernik is ushered toward a small desk and seated beneath large portraits of Josef Stalin and Vladimir Lenin that hang on the far wall in the background. The chief inspector (John Dehner) interrogates Cernik while another party official does clerical work and still another lounges on a sofa.

In a series of shot/reverse shot setups, the chief inspector asks Cernik about his ownership of the circus. Cernik explains that although his family owned it for several years, the circus was nationalized in 1948 and now belongs to the state. Instead of being the proprietor of the circus, Cernik is merely its manager. Having avoided one ideological trap, Cernik is then questioned about his employees, one of whom is Chinese and another who pretends to be a French duchess. The party official queries Cernik about his Chinese performer's political beliefs. Is he a Maoist, or does he support the failed fascist regime of the Nationalists? Cernik replies that, like other circus people, the Chinese performer has no politics nor nationality; he is only a juggler. Similarly, the party official questions Cernik about the other circus performer's claims to royalty and her brandishing of a French flag as part of her act. Cernik replies that this was merely a tribute to the performer's late French husband, a sword swallower named "the Duke," and that her lapse was partly caused by mental problems triggered by her husband's demise.

After sidestepping the issues of ownership and personnel, Cernik must respond to questions about his clown routine and whether he has made changes that were ordered by party officials. The routine shows an unwavering Cernik as he receives twenty-seven kicks in the ass from a fellow clown named Jaromir. When Jaromir becomes too tired to inflict any further pain, he stops kicking Cernik, who then turns and kisses his tormentor. After viewing this routine, the Propaganda Ministry ordered Cernik to transform this gag into a political allegory of capitalist exploitation. On one hand, as Cernik explains it, Jaromir's character represents Wall Street imperialism and is to be dressed in a silk hat, spats, and diamond studs. Cernik, on the other hand, was to represent an African American laborer, who is quite literally both the butt of the joke and the victim of capitalist aggression. Cernik adds that although they made the necessary changes, no one in the audience laughed at the clown routine. Consequently, Cernik put back the kiss at the end to restore its comic effect. The chief inspector, however, commands Cernik to comply with the original directives of the Propaganda Ministry and warns him that his circus might be given to a rival ringmaster if he does not obey these orders. Having been chastened by party discipline, Cernik is escorted out of the office and returns to his circus.

Through these expository sequences, Sherwood and Kazan not only provide Cernik with personal motivation for escaping from Czechoslovakia, but they also offer a none-too-subtle critique of the so-called Soviet experiment. Espousing a liberal anti-Communist line, the filmmakers dramatize the repressive nature of Stalinist rule by highlighting its arbitrary authoritarianism, the atmosphere of suspicion bred within a police state, and the limits on creative expression created when propaganda and ideology supplant art and entertainment. In all these respects, the narrative appears to support the reception of *Man on a Tightrope* as an anti-Communist tract, one entirely consistent with Kazan's own politics following his HUAC testimony in 1952.

Still, this reading of the film, especially the scene of Cernik's interrogation, is all too literal. As Brenda Murphy points out, the interrogation scene is both a concrete, visual representation of Communist oppression, on one hand, and a metaphoric representation of HUAC's repression of civil rights and free speech, on the other. Murphy continues the line of argument that identifies Kazan's offscreen role as HUAC informer with his protagonists:

> Kazan most often likened the character of Cernik to the screenwriter Robert Sherwood, proud, aloof, reserved, unyielding. But he also imputed qualities to Cernik that he claimed for himself. Like Kazan's famous "Anatolian smile," which pragmatically hid his feelings of

injury and rage, Cernik's "meekness & humbleness always has
something two-edged about it. . . . It smells not kosher to the
Communists. They resent him without knowing quite why. His PRIDE,
gives them pride. And pride is necessary to go on under humiliating
circumstances." This is most evident in the interrogation scene, where
Cernik plays the cooperative and naive circus owner in order to keep his
circus going. The casting of Adolphe Menjou, one of the prime
cooperative HUAC witnesses, as an agent of the Ministry of Propaganda
and of the formerly blacklisted Fredric March as Cernik has been seen
as an ironic circumstance in the making of the film. Kazan was fully
aware of this, and he makes full use of the resonance of these roles in
his filming of the interrogation scene and in Menjou's own subsequent
arrest by the police, which he plays with the polished sangfroid of
Claude Rains at the end of *Casablanca*.[31]

Of course, Kazan's use of casting as a means of underlining a film's political subtexts was nothing new. During the blacklist the activation of intertextual and extratextual meanings associated with a particular performer
was an especially useful tool insofar as it, like allegory, evaded the official
structures of censorship. Although Kazan's use of Menjou may have been a
means of bolstering his anti-Communist credentials, it nonetheless shaped
the implicit and symptomatic meanings of *Man on a Tightrope*. Through
his presence in the film Menjou serves as a metonymic link between the
Communist officials portrayed onscreen and the real-life HUAC members
that he so publicly supported. With this in mind, certain aspects of the
interrogation scene take on new meanings. The Communists' suspicion of
foreigners, for example, alludes to a similar xenophobia in HUAC discourse,
especially the notorious anti-Semitism of Congressman John Rankin.
Similarly, the Communist Party's desire to regulate Cernik's clown act has
strong parallels with HUAC's efforts to force Hollywood to toe the ideological line. The interrogation scene even hints at the practice of blacklisting
when the chief inspector orders Cernik to fire "*la Duchess.*"

Following the interrogation scene, the rest of *Man on a Tightrope* plays
out in terms of this double discourse. Its explicit and referential meanings
attest to the evils of Communist oppression, but Kazan's film also functions
as an implicit critique of HUAC and the Hollywood blacklist. These multiple levels of meaning are enhanced by the metaphors of theatricality that
are part and parcel of the film's circus setting. As performers, Cernik and his
troupe play public roles that serve to conceal their private motives and
desires, a distinction that accords with a similar division between referential
and implicit meanings in *Man on a Tightrope*. Indeed, the last half hour of
Kazan's film plays as a kind of docudrama version of Ernst Lubitsch's *To Be*

or Not to Be (1942) as the troupe puts on an impromptu show near the border in order to fool their Communist oppressors.

The bittersweet resolution of Man on a Tightrope contains a similarly double-edged quality. Cernik triumphs over his Communist oppressors by leading his troupe to safety, but he is fatally wounded in the process. Although this ending offers a jingoistic dramatization of the price of freedom, its implicit meanings contain an ambivalence regarding the status of other blacklistees. Given the choice between complying with the party's ideological directives and losing his professional livelihood altogether, Cernik seeks a third alternative, namely a desire to escape to another land, another country. This aspect of the narrative suggests that Cernik is a surrogate for people like Dalton Trumbo, Joseph Losey, Michael Wilson, and Jules Dassin, who resisted the committee but then fled to Europe or Mexico in an effort to find employment working within other national film industries. Such a path was not taken by Kazan, although Man on a Tightrope's implicit meanings suggest a sympathy with those who opted for voluntary exile from Hollywood. Yet Kazan's narrative also signifies the price paid by many of these voluntary exiles. Losey and Dassin notwithstanding, many of these blacklisted writers and directors failed to sustain a career outside of Hollywood and were only able to eke out a career by selling black market scripts through fronts and pseudonyms. Cernik's literal death in a foreign land, thus, functions as a metaphor for the "death" of the exiles' careers.

I have elaborated on the political subtexts of Viva Zapata! and Man on a Tightrope to establish a context for Kazan's most famous film, On the Waterfront, which was nominated for twelve Oscars in 1955 and won awards for Best Picture, Best Actor, and Best Director. On the Waterfront achieved renown not only for its critical acclaim but also because the film is widely interpreted as Kazan's cinematic defense of his cooperation with HUAC.[32] In brief, On the Waterfront tells the story of Terry Malloy (Marlon Brando), a washed-up boxer who regains his dignity by testifying against the corrupt leadership of a longshoremen's union. The film opens with the murder of Joey Doyle, a neighborhood kid who is himself expected to testify before the Waterfront Crime Commission. After Joey's murder, Terry becomes involved with the Doyle family when the union's leaders, Johnny Friendly (Lee J. Cobb) and Terry's brother, Charley (Rod Steiger), ask him to keep an eye on the victim's father and sister, Edie (Eva Marie Saint). Both Edie and the local parish priest, Father Barry (Karl Malden), appeal to Terry's conscience by asking him why he continues to protect corrupt and vicious thugs like Friendly. The pressure on Terry escalates when Kayo Dugan is killed by "accident" in a ship's hold, and Charley is murdered for trying to

Table 3 *On the Waterfront* as Anti-Communist Allegory

On the Waterfront	*Hollywood Blacklist*
Terry	Kazan/Schulberg/Cobb
Johnny Friendly	V.J. Jerome / John Howard Lawson
Union leaders/Mobsters	Communists
Crime Commission	HUAC
Longshoremen	American public

protect Terry from mob reprisals. Terry then testifies against Johnny Friendly before the Crime Commission but finds that all of his former friends have turned against him for being a "stool pigeon." In the film's climax Terry confronts and physically attacks Friendly outside the union's waterfront offices. Terry is brutally beaten by Friendly's henchmen but rises to lead the longshoremen to work, an action that collectively defies Friendly and his thugs by asserting the rank and file's control over the union.

On the Waterfront is one of the most widely discussed films in the literature on the blacklist, and I have no desire to belabor points made emphatically by other critics. Suffice it to say that the interpretation of *On the Waterfront* as blacklist allegory devolves on two elements: (1) Kazan's and Schulberg's actions before the film was made and (2) their construction of a narrative that hinges on the question of whether the protagonist will testify against his coworkers before the Crime Commission. From these two elements it would be quite easy for contemporary critics to interpret the film as a blacklist allegory, one that substitutes one much-publicized investigation (Estes Kefauver's Senate Committee Hearings on organized crime) for another (the HUAC investigations of the 1950s).

These allegorical interpretations thus depend on a series of binary terms that highlight latent meanings lurking just beneath the film's manifest content. Following the methodology described in cognitive framing exercises, critics perform this operation by grouping together topical reference points to create a pretext for *On the Waterfront*'s allegorical significance (see table 3).

This reading is supported by additional contextual factors surrounding the film's production, most especially Kazan's well-documented identification with his hero. According to Joanna Rapf and Brian Neve, Kazan's production notebook for *On the Waterfront* contains several instances in which the director, following the dictates established by his own Actors

Studio, makes sense of Terry by drawing on his own life experience. At one point Kazan compares Terry's early bravado with his own youthful aplomb as a "white-haired boy director."[33] Similarly, Neve also implies that the relationship between Terry and Edie depicted onscreen may have been inspired by Kazan's own relationship with his wife, Molly: "In the late fifties Molly Kazan wrote *The Egghead,* a play that was performed in New York and reads in part as a wife's questioning of her husband's naivete about domestic communism."[34] Finally, both Rapf and Neve point out that Kazan draws an explicit connection between Johnny Friendly and American Communist leaders Jerome and Lawson.[35] In an unabashed display of the punning heuristic, Reynold Humphries adds a twist to Kazan and Schulberg's choice of the name "Friendly":

> The film takes up the cudgels in defense of the Constitution and of informing. When served with a subpoena, Terry is told: "You can bring a lawyer if you wish. And you're privileged under the Constitution to protect yourself against questions which could implicate you in crimes." This is a legal argument in favor of the Fifth. However, Terry is a friendly, not an unfriendly, witness and the irony of the statement lies in the fact that what happens to Terry—blacklisted by his union—is precisely what befell those named by Kazan and dozens of others before HUAC. Terry talks and is blacklisted. Kazan talked and got others blacklisted.[36]

Although the interpretation of *On the Waterfront* as Kazan's defense of his HUAC testimony is pervasive among contemporary critics, I contend that the film's politics display some of the same ambivalence that was evident in *Viva Zapata!* and *Man on a Tightrope.* The notion of *On the Waterfront* as an "ambivalent" text is not new; in fact, it has been theorized by critic Kenneth R. Hey in a pioneering essay on the film. Hey's analysis of *On the Waterfront* goes well beyond the issue of authorial attention by attributing the film's ambivalence to several factors, including the collaborative process of film production, Kazan and Schulberg's use of Christian symbolism, and the false optimism of the resolution, which does nothing to challenge the union's larger power structure.[37] Curiously, Hey does not link this ambivalence to the blacklist, suggesting instead that Terry's guilt and confession, both to Edie and to the Crime Commission, is a straightforward justification of Kazan's, Schulberg's, and Cobb's experiences as informers. Hey's interpretation runs counter to my own reading of *On the Waterfront* as a double allegory, one that draws parallels between Communism and McCarthyism, and thus contains an ambivalence about Kazan's cooperative testimony at its very core.

Still other critics, including Schulberg and Rapf, find the analogy between Terry and Kazan to be glib, and they further suggest that the implicit comparison is inconsistent with the film's contemporaneous reception. By far the loudest objections along these lines have come from screenwriter Budd Schulberg in his foreword to the Cambridge Film Handbook on *On the Waterfront:*

> By far the most vexing of all negative comments is the academic fixation that Terry's denouncing the "Pistol Local" to the Waterfront Crime Commission is an apology and metaphor for the House Un-American Activities Committee hearings on Communism in Hollywood. That is not what Elia Kazan asked me to do when he came to see me, and in no way was that my motivation for wanting to write this film. What disturbs me most about this aspersion—repeated in film schools across the country until it's become academic gospel—is that if you think of the longshoremen as merely stand-ins or surrogates for Hollywood testifiers, you trivialize the ordeal of the actual longshoremen who had to overcome their terror in order to testify against the legal thugs who ran the ILA.[38]

While Schulberg makes an excellent point about the tendency to overlook the struggles of the fictional longshoremen's real-life counterparts, his argument is a fairly bald-faced attempt to exert authorial control over the meanings of *On the Waterfront.*

Schulberg's denunciation of academic film criticism, however, feels hollow. He conveniently ignores the substantial evidence that links Kazan's individual history and perspective to a reading of *On the Waterfront* as a blacklist allegory. Just because Schulberg avers that he never intended the film as a defense of his HUAC testimony does not mean that he can blithely dismiss the intentions of his collaborators. Moreover, as was the case with *Man on a Tightrope,* Schulberg's critique of allegorical readings of *On the Waterfront* depends on an all too literal appeal to the factual basis for the film's events. According to Schulberg the major reason that they decided to have Terry testify against his cohorts is that real-life people, like Johnny Dwyer, Tommy Bull, and Tony Mike diVincenzo, testified themselves before the Crime Commission.[39] Whereas this aspect of *On the Waterfront* is often overlooked by modern critics, the reality status of characters and incidents does not logically preclude other types of interpretation. *On the Waterfront* may be an unusual case in this regard since it simultaneously appeals to two different real-life events (the testimony of Dwyer and diVincenzo vs. the testimony of Kazan and Schulberg). Still, as David Bordwell and Kristin Thompson point out, realistic and authorial motivation can reinforce one another within an individual text.[40] In fact, Kazan's own history as a cooperative witness might well have drawn him to the real-life stories of union whistle-blowers. Recognizing the parallels with his own life, Kazan may have been attracted to *On the Waterfront* because of its allegorical subtext, not in spite of it.

Joanna Rapf makes a similar argument in her critique of allegorical interpretations of *On the Waterfront*. Rapf grants that Schulberg and Kazan's testimony makes it "inevitable that their film has been 'read' as a defense of their actions," but she also claims that "if you did not know about the personal backgrounds of Schulberg and Kazan, it would be a stretch to see *Waterfront* as a commentary on testimony before the HUAC."[41] Jeffrey Chown goes even further by claiming that "no general audience in 1954 or in the present would see a connection between Terry Malloy and HUAC testifiers" unless they were "coached by an overzealous film professor."[42] Rapf and Chown seem to side with Schulberg here, albeit on slightly different grounds. Like Schulberg, they attempt to restrict interpretations of *On the Waterfront* to specific textual elements, but they do so by prohibiting the use of certain types of extratextual knowledge. In this respect Rapf's and Chown's comments share something with recent critiques of auteurism that suggest that artists should not be in a position to "dictate the interpretation of their work."[43]

The reviews included in Rapf's Cambridge Film Handbook on *On the Waterfront* seem to support her and Chown's assertions since they make no specific reference to Kazan's, Schulberg's, or Cobb's cooperation with HUAC. Instead, they draw attention to *On the Waterfront*'s journalistic origins and link the film to other social realist pictures, particularly those from Europe. *Harper's*, for example, compared the film to the French poetic realist classic, *Quai des brumes* (1938), while *Commonweal* suggested that Kazan's interest in human dignity made *On the Waterfront* an American counterpart of *The Bicycle Thieves* and *Diary of a Country Priest* (1952).[44] When *On the Waterfront* appeared at the Venice Film Festival in 1954, the festival chairman was even more explicit about its relation to Italian neorealism, calling it "the first Italian film made in Hollywood."[45]

A wider survey of reviews, though, reveals that at least a few commentators did make specific reference to Kazan's and Schulberg's testimony. Surprisingly, the television host and gossip columnist Ed Sullivan made perhaps the most direct connection between Waterfront and HUAC. In an item about Kazan's recent success Sullivan asserts, "In his 'On the Waterfront,' no one has pointed out that Kazan actually dramatized his own denunciation of the Commies. Marlon Brando, in turning against the dictators of the waterfront at the urging of the priest and the girl with whom he was in love, actually was reenacting the role which Kazan played in real life before the Un-American Activities Committee. Kazan named names and dates just as Brando did."[46]

Others also offered offhand allusions to this background. For example, Edwin Schallert writes, "As John Friendly (nice sort of name) Cobb just doesn't stand for that kind of subversive conduct on the part of the men he represents."[47] Given the widespread suspicions that unions were corrupted by Communist organizers in the 1940s, the mention of "subversive conduct" might take on a specific political valence within this context. Similarly, Philip K. Scheuer notes in an article on *On the Waterfront* that Budd Schulberg "is known for his novels, short stories, and, in the last couple of years, his anti-Communist articles."[48]

Besides these allusions to Communism and the Red Scare, still another aspect of *On the Waterfront*'s contemporaneous reception clouds the issue of whether audiences were aware of this blacklist subtext. Whereas almost all of the reviews commented on the film's semidocumentary qualities, several also compare the film to earlier gangster films. *Variety*, for example, suggested that Schulberg's scenario is strongly reminiscent of early James Cagney films, and Philip K. Scheuer and *The Hollywood Reporter* directly compared *On the Waterfront* with *Little Caesar* and *The Public Enemy*.[49] These gangster film references further complicate the reception context insofar as these same comparisons were used in relation to anti-Communist films just a few years earlier. In fact, one might view *On the Waterfront* as a more prestigious version of *I Married a Communist*, which also dramatized the corruption of a longshoremen's union and was a fictionalized account of Harry Bridges's activities as a union organizer in San Francisco.

Unfortunately, the critical reception of *On the Waterfront* in the 1950s does not really offer any conclusive evidence about how a film audience of the time might have read the film. On one hand, unlike other cooperative witnesses, Kazan made his testimony a public issue by taking out an advertisement in the *New York Times* to explain his actions. On the other hand, the mere existence of the ad does not prove that average moviegoers would remember it as they watched *On the Waterfront*. Similarly, one cannot draw any inference from the oblique references to the Red Scare made by a handful of reviewers. After all, reviewers are not average moviegoers; their status as journalists and their relationship to the industry would suggest that they most certainly knew about Kazan's, Schulberg's, and Cobb's experiences as "friendly witnesses."

More important, one would hardly expect to find much beyond individual traces of this reception context if *any* public expression of political dissent was likely to result in reprimands or job loss. Film reviewers would be as prone to these pressures as anyone else and would tread very carefully around a film's blacklist subtext. Ed Sullivan is the exception that proves the rule since his reputation as a "Red-baiter" insulated him from any potential blowback. As such, although I share Rapf's concerns about drawing hasty conclusions about *On the Waterfront*'s contemporaneous reception, I cannot wholeheartedly endorse her viewpoint that allegorical readings of the film are "a stretch."

Still, I do agree with the implication of her critique that most of these allegorical readings are not terribly imaginative. In particular, the equation of union leadership with Communists seems overly neat, reductive, and simplistic. In their rush to condemn Kazan as a traitor to the left, most critics ignore the way *On the Waterfront* draws strong parallels between the union's leadership and the Crime Commission. Indeed, from the perspective of dramatic structure, one group is the inverted mirror of the other, with Terry situated as a mediating figure between the two. One group uses the threat of physical violence to obtain Terry's silence; the other uses the threat of state authority and subpoenas to pressure Terry to talk. One group appeals to Terry's sense of loyalty and brotherhood; the other appeals to his sense of conscience and citizenship. One group coerces Terry's silence in meetings that occur behind closed doors; the other group exerts pressure in public spaces, such as the court system and the workplace.

Kazan himself said that he broke ranks with American Communists largely because of the unrestrained authoritarianism of party leaders. Of course, much the same could be said of Senator Joseph McCarthy and HUAC during the height of the Red Scare. Their invasion of privacy, their desire to censor movies for their politics, and their interference with the creative process were all abuses of power that suggested to liberal anti-Communists that right-wing authoritarianism should be fought as hard as left-wing authoritarianism. Thus, in this somewhat limited respect, Johnny Friendly and his cohorts stand in for anti-Communist demagogues as much as they do Communist cell leaders.

Of particular importance here is *On the Waterfront*'s treatment of dissident speech and public debate. Union leadership efforts to deter whistleblowers in *On the Waterfront* function as a metaphor for a much broader effort to restrain free speech. Friendly and his cohorts interfere with public discussions of the union's violent enforcement of its codes when they disrupt a gathering of the rank and file in Father Barry's church. A similar attempt to constrain free speech occurs during the famous "Sermon on the Docks" sequence. After Kayo Dugan is killed, Father Barry delivers a long speech over his lifeless body in which he compares the struggles of the longshoreman to the martyrdom of Christ. Although Barry uses the discourse of Christianity, Communism's ideological *doppelganger,* he urges their solidarity in order to stand up to the capitalist fat cats represented by Johnny Friendly and Terry's brother, Charley. In response to this, union thugs pelt Father Barry with food and tin cans in order to deter him from publicly denouncing Friendly and Charley. This scene also shows the first evidence that Terry's loyalty is weakening when he punches one of the thugs in order to help Father Barry be heard. Because of the way that the union deals with public expressions of dissent, its leaders serve as stand-ins for the censorship and political repression represented by HUAC or McCarthyism. Friendly and his gang, thus, become a multivalent symbol, one that functions simultaneously to critique the authoritarianism of John Howard Lawson and HUAC chair Harold Velde (R, IL) in almost equal measure.[50]

The sequence that most pointedly underlines the possibility of a double allegory is the one in which Friendly and Charley track down Terry to ask him about the meeting he attended in the church basement. The language of their exchange is particularly evocative of blacklist discourse as Terry is made to answer for attending a secret meeting of dissident union members. In an earlier scene Charley asked Terry to make a note of who was present and to "name names" when he reports back to Friendly. When Terry responds that he is not a "stoolie," Charley's response, once again, echoes HUAC discourse as he says it is not "stooling" when you do it for your friends. After telling Friendly that Father Barry was the only one who spoke, Terry is shocked to learn that Kayo Dugan went straight to the Crime Commission after the meeting and offered them thirty-nine pages of testimony. Terry's lapse in judgment is forgiven, though, when Charley pleads that he has been spending too much time around Edie. Recapitulating the logic of anti-Communist films, Terry's indiscretion is overlooked because he has been "duped" by an attractive woman, a situation that leads to questions about his loyalty. Terry is nonetheless punished for his lapse as Friendly orders him to work in the hold.

Kazan does little to sort out the inherent contradictions of this double allegory. Although the dominant reading strategy interprets the gangsters in *On the Waterfront* as metaphorical substitutes for Stalinist Communism, this does not logically preclude the possibility that they also might symbolize other kinds of repression. As such, this secondary reading suggests the pattern of substitution seen in table 4.

Table 4 *On the Waterfront* as Anti-HUAC Allegory

On the Waterfront	*Hollywood Blacklist*
Terry	An "unfriendly" witness
Johnny Friendly	J. Parnell Thomas/Harold Velde
Union leaders/Mobsters	HUAC
Father Barry	Communist organizer
Longshoremen	American public

In sum, although several critics use Kazan's HUAC testimony to argue that his films justify his decision to cooperate, other critics "frame" Kazan's work as that of an archetypal liberal anti-Communist. The latter critics see Kazan as a figure equally suspicious of political repression coming from either the left or the right, one situated in the "vital center" eloquently described in Arthur Schlesinger Jr.'s famous book.[51] Yet, as Joseph Litvak reminds us, one reason for the ambiguity in Kazan's work is that the blacklist itself discouraged any direct condemnation of it. In a chapter of *The Un-Americans* devoted to Kazan's *A Face in the Crowd* (1957), Litvak writes:

> Obviously, Kazan and Schulberg could not have made a film explicitly criticizing the blacklist, even if they wanted to, since one of the blacklist's principal effects was to police not just film personnel but film content as well, and since the first rule of this censorship was to censor the fact of its own existence. Some might therefore see in *Face*'s strategy of displacement a cunning allegorical indirection. But the "allegory" of *A Face in the Crowd* functions like the allegory of *On the Waterfront*, not like the allegory of, say, *The Crucible*. In changing the subject, that is, the film doesn't transform it; it evades and misrepresents it.[52]

While the bottom line may be that Kazan sacrificed political principle for individual gain, it seems strange to single him out for approbation when so many others did exactly the same thing. In fact, the demonization of Elia Kazan only makes sense if, like his protagonist Terry Malloy, he has come to symbolize Hollywood's own recollections of its darkest period. Kazan stands in for all of those others who made the same choices, engaged in the same betrayals, and tried to make a virtue of political expediency. The acclaim of Kazan's films made him a convenient scapegoat for those who paid the price that he refused. That said, those films also suggest that

Kazan's choice was not easy and was not without personal doubts and reprisals. The allegorical dimensions of *Viva Zapata!, Man on a Tightrope,* and *On the Waterfront* attest to this uncertainty. When one chooses between the lesser of two evils, one is still left with evil.

TRADING INFORMATION: *PICKUP ON SOUTH STREET* AND THE POLITICS OF NAMING NAMES

Samuel Fuller's *Pickup on South Street* is perhaps one of the most overdetermined films made during the blacklist period. The *Village Voice* even went so far as to claim that "Fuller's 1953 masterpiece is the most lyrical celebration of the McCarthyite worldview ever made."[53] Several factors contribute to its importance as a canonical Cold War text. Fuller's film was released in 1953, a period in which HUAC's renewed interest in Hollywood cast a pall over the entire film industry. Fuller himself is widely recognized as one of film history's most dedicated anti-Communists. This aspect of Fuller's work is evident in several films besides *Pickup on South Street*, such as *The Steel Helmet* (1951), *Fixed Bayonets* (1951), *China Gate* (1957), and *Shock Corridor* (1963). *Pickup on South Street* is centrally concerned with the politics of informing, and in Skip McCoy and Moe it offers not one but two characters whose dilemmas mirror those faced by HUAC witnesses.

For dedicated auteurists Fuller's fulsome anti-Communism has proven to be something of a problem, one that the director's most ardent admirers sidestep by focusing on his storytelling and stylistic flourishes. Yet, as several critics point out, Fuller's anti-Communism is far more complex than that found in many other "Red Scare" films of the period. Lee Server, for example, briefly compares *Pickup on South Street* and *Big Jim McLain* and suggests that Richard Widmark's "seedy pickpocket" is a far cry from John Wayne's noble investigator for HUAC. Noting Fuller's interest in outsider figures, Server writes, "Of course Fuller, a radical individualist, was an anti-Communist, but his view of democracy was equally anti-propagandist, focusing on the warts and calluses of an America populated by society's dregs."[54] Nicholas Garnham reinforces this perception of Fuller's politics, saying that "to regard *Pickup on South Street* as an anti-Communist tract is absurd."[55] Garnham adds that Communism plays a crucial role in the dramatic structure of Fuller's films. As an emblem of America's obsessive neuroticism and as a catalyst for characters' actions, Communists function both as an Other through which Americans define themselves and as nightmare figures, especially for characters associated with mental disturbance. For critics like Server and Garnham, Fuller's interest in the problems of individuals avoids simple sloganeering by examining the relationships between national subjects and the institutions that shape and influence them. Fuller's films oppose totalitarianism in all its forms, whether it is expressed as Stalinism, Maoism, Nazism, fascism, or—in the case of *Pickup on South Street*—overzealous American patriotism.

Of course, anti-Communism and the problem of the individual are such important themes of Fuller's films that many critics and historians have more or less assumed that he is the person responsible for their presence in *Pickup on South Street*. Yet the film's production history reveals a more complicated story, one that challenges the dominant critical paradigms employed in its interpretations. Although the film's Cold War themes are consistent with Fuller's larger oeuvre, an examination of studio documents reveals that Darryl Zanuck, rather than Fuller, was the person responsible for both its anti-Communist slant and its tough, politically contemptuous tone. Contrary to the *Village Voice*'s assessment, *Pickup on South Street* was more a matter of a studio matching an existing film project to a director's sensibilities than it was a vehicle for the director's worldview.

Pickup on South Street was based on "Blaze of Glory," an unpublished story by Dwight Taylor optioned by 20th Century–Fox. In Taylor's story small-time hood Skip McCoy steals the wallet of a gentleman riding on a subway train only to find later that it contains a small square of microfilm. Skip then returns to the boardinghouse where he lives and borrows his landlady's magnifying glass and her Bible. Using the glass to examine the microfilm, Skip quickly realizes that it contains government information and that he has accidentally stumbled on a Communist spy ring. Shortly thereafter, Inspector Donnegan accuses Skip of stealing the wallet and says that when he can prove it, he will put Skip away for life as a "three-time loser."

In attempting to ward off the police, Skip conducts his own investigation of the spy ring, and becomes involved with Helen Courtland, a United Nations worker who has gotten mixed up with the Communists. While visiting Helen, Skip encounters Mr. X, the man whose wallet he stole. After making an excuse to leave Helen, Skip tails Mr. X to a photography shop and engineers the spy's capture by starting a fire inside the store. Unfortunately for Skip, Mr. X's apprehension displeases the police, who were hoping that Mr. X would lead them to the leak's source inside the State Department. Skip learns from Inspector Donnegan that the microfilm he possesses is the only way the police can uncover the mole inside the government. After searching his conscience, Skip admits to the theft and turns over the microfilm to police. Taylor's story ends with Skip going back to prison, his fellow prisoners greeting him with a banner that says, "Welcome back."[56]

According to Fuller, Taylor's story was centrally concerned with a female lawyer who falls in love with a client she is defending. Fuller saw the original as a courtroom drama, a genre that generally lacked interest for him.[57] Yet, although Fuller is correct that courtroom scenes dominate the later part of Taylor's story, he conveniently ignores the fact that Taylor established several important elements of Fuller's later film, chief among them Skip's petty theft, his status as a "three-time loser," the microfilm, the Communist spy ring, and Skip's involvement with a woman loosely associated with the spies. More important, both Taylor's story and Fuller's film hinge on an ethical dilemma that resonated with the problems of HUAC witnesses during the blacklist period: should Skip incriminate himself and cooperate with police in order to serve the larger good of national security? Unlike Fuller's film, though, in Taylor's story Skip's dilemma is interwoven with a religious theme that ultimately grounds his ethical quandary within a spiritual context. In this respect Taylor's story is consistent with the Cold War's larger political and cultural climate in which God-fearing Christians and atheistic Communists functioned within a Manichean dichotomy.

This theme of religious belief recurs frequently in Taylor's "Blaze of Glory." For example, after borrowing his landlady's Bible, Skip comes across the passage that says, "Render therefore the things unto Caesar that are Caesar's." This passage is especially pertinent to the film's political subtext since it is commonly read as a religious instruction that encourages Christians to obey Man's law as well as God's law. Within the context of Taylor's story it easily supplies a spiritual motivation for Skip's later cooperation with authorities. Likewise, Skip visits his parish priest, Father Dodd, to seek advice regarding Inspector Donnegan's threats of imprisonment. Here Skip's private confession to both Dodd and God prefigures the more public confession he makes in copping to his theft. Finally, when Skip contemplates cooperating with police, Taylor characterizes his decision as one in which the lowly criminal becomes an instrument of Divine Intervention. Taylor writes that Skip "marveled that God had plucked him out of his obscurity amongst the crowd to be an agent of His cause."[58] By characterizing Skip's decision as an acceptance of God's plan, Taylor suggests that his ultimate imprisonment is a form of Christian martyrdom, albeit one that serves a political agenda defined by American foreign and domestic policy in the 1950s.

Using Taylor's story as a template, Harry Brown completed the first draft of the screenplay for *Blaze of Glory* by January 25, 1952.[59] Brown stayed very close to the contours of Taylor's story but radically changed the story's ending, a move that also downplayed the element of religious sacrifice in Taylor's original. In Brown's screenplay Skip agrees to testify but only in exchange for the police's assurance that they will keep Helen out of their investigation. (In Brown's screenplay Helen is more clearly identified as an unknowing "dupe," who only gets mixed up in the spy ring when she agrees to do a favor for a friend.) Skip then implicates himself in testifying against the spies but is freed by the judge after Inspector Donnegan, Father Dodd, and an FBI agent all speak on his behalf. The script closes with a rather polemical speech that describes Skip as a "soldier" in the Cold War even though he is only a lowly pickpocket.[60] By freeing Skip in the end, Brown's screenplay rewards his willingness to uphold his patriotic duty. As a comment on the dilemma of HUAC witnesses, Brown's screenplay can be read as a call to cooperate with the committee. Like HUAC's friendly witnesses, Skip must own up to his past indiscretions, but his decision to cooperate proves to be both pragmatic and morally justified.

Still, this ending appears to have been a problem for Brown, who devised yet another resolution for a revised draft dated March 13, 1952. Although this version follows the earlier draft very closely, Brown employs an even more obvious deus ex machina to allow Skip to escape punishment. After testifying that he stole the wallet and that the wallet contained microfilm, Skip admits on the stand that he will receive a life sentence as a "three-time loser." This is followed by a dissolve to newspaper headlines reporting not only that the spies are convicted but also that Skip has received a presidential pardon.[61]

The problems with Brown's conception of the project were so severe that 20th Century–Fox's studio head, Darryl Zanuck, suggested that it be completely retooled. In a story conference with director Henry Hathaway and Fred Kohlmar, who had previously collaborated on Fox's *Kiss of Death* (1947), Zanuck criticized Brown's wholly conventional treatment of the subject, one that is entirely predictable and contains no suspense regarding Skip's ultimate actions. Zanuck described Brown's conception as an "Alan Ladd" treatment "when what we really need is a Humphrey Bogart treatment."[62] One might surmise here that Zanuck is trying to draw a distinction between Ladd's fervid anti-Nazi vehicle *This Gun for Hire* and contemporaneous Bogart films, such as *Casablanca* (1942) and *To Have and Have Not* (1944). In making this comparison, Zanuck suggests that Skip should be closer to the latter films' heroes, Rick Blaine and Harry Morgan— cynical and apparently amoral characters who seem to place their own interests and survival above everything else.

Later in the memo, Zanuck complains more specifically about the problems that this "Alan Ladd treatment" creates for the film's romantic subplot. According to Zanuck, Brown's script "should have been a hard-hitting Richard Widmark kind of thing—tough, dirty, full of authority. If this character is not painted as a Tommy Udo, a habitual criminal, then the whole basic situation is worthless."[63] By invoking Tommy Udo, the giggling, psychotic killer from *Kiss of Death*, Zanuck suggests that Skip must be harder, more amoral, more violent, and capable of murder.

Following his suggestion of Tommy Udo as a model for Skip, Zanuck makes an even more startling recommendation when he argues that Skip must not only be tough and unsympathetic but also overtly unpatriotic. Says Zanuck, "There must be enormous doubt in the minds of the audience as to whether this guy, who never even heard of Korea, is going to make the sacrifices which are asked of him. He should laugh at them when they suggest that he do this heroic thing—make a big sacrifice for the sake of his country's safety."[64] Later in the memo, Zanuck reiterates the point about Skip's lack of nationalist sentiment but also suggests that Helen's positive influence ultimately convinces Skip to do the right thing: "The relationship between Skip and Helen: he gets mixed up with her, and her influence on him is the basic motivating factor which eventually makes him realize that he has to do something for his country. Naturally, he never says it in those terms. In fact he even says to Donnegan, 'Don't give me any crap about doing this for the Star Spangled Banner.'"[65]

It might seem surprising that a studio head would suggest an overtly unpatriotic hero for a film, especially an executive as sensitive to political issues as Zanuck was. During his tenure at Fox, Zanuck had overseen such overtly nationalistic films as *Wilson* (1944) and *The Iron Curtain*, generally recognized as the first major anti-Communist film released in response to the blacklist. During a time of heightened political sensitivities, Zanuck's recommendations appear to counter HUAC's ideological mandate.

Yet for Zanuck the problem with Brown's script for *Blaze of Glory* was far more a narrative problem than a political problem. He believed that there was no suspense, and hence no audience interest, in a story that simply moved in lockstep fashion toward a foregone conclusion, even if said conclusion were sanctioned by the country's larger political climate. To preserve some measure of doubt about Skip's eventual actions, it was preferable, indeed even necessary, to make him an unlikable, unsentimental, un-American, and potentially treasonous character. This is especially evident in Zanuck's proposed conclusion, in which he suggests a return to Taylor's original story in which Skip is shown returning to prison. Yet even here Zanuck resists the temptation to have Skip undergo an eleventh-hour political conversion. Rather, Zanuck recommends that Skip should brush off "Donnegan's suggestion at the end that he is a 'good American'" by having Skip reply that he may have gone back to jail for Helen, but that he "would be back there eventually anyway."[66] Zanuck's Skip emerges at the end as a slightly less self-interested character but one who is neither divinely inspired nor transformed into a flag-waving patriot.

More important perhaps, this story conference memo suggests that Fuller may have exaggerated his role in developing the overall dramatic conception for *Pickup on South Street*. In his autobiography Fuller claims that he convinced the studio to make Skip a pickpocket and to set the entire story in the "shadow world of petty criminality," even overcoming Darryl Zanuck's personal reservations in order to develop the project in his own way.[67] The claim is patently false on two counts: first, because the conception of Skip as pickpocket was already present in both Taylor's story and Brown's earlier screenplays; and second, because Zanuck himself advocated developing the elements of petty criminality and clearly had no objections to that type of narrative treatment. Beyond that, Fuller adds that he based Skip, Candy, and Moe on people he met during his years as a crime reporter and further implies that he intended Skip's contemptuousness and irreverence as a counter to the patriotic fantasies of stars like John Wayne.[68] To buttress this claim, Fuller then reproduces the film's most famous dialogue scene in which Skip is confronted by both the police and the FBI. An FBI agent says, "If you refuse to cooperate, you'll be as guilty as the traitors that gave Stalin the A-Bomb!" And Skip responds, "Are you waving the flag at me?"[69] While the words themselves, indeed, are Fuller's, the sentiments they express already had been suggested by Zanuck.

This is not to say, however, that Fuller made no contributions to the development of *Pickup on South Street*'s screenplay. In a story outline by Fuller dated June 25, 1952, several elements of the final film first appear, including Skip's shack; the name changes of "Donnegan" and "Helen" to "Tiger" and "Candy" respectively; and, most important, the addition of Moe to the cast of characters. Here Fuller also embellishes the theme of petty criminality in the script by adding a lengthy discourse on the various working methods of pickpockets, one filled with slang and street argot. Unlike the final film, though, Fuller preserves Zanuck's earlier suggestions about the film's ending in his outline; after beating Joey to death in a train tunnel as revenge for both Moe and Candy, Skip is sent back to jail for life.

Still, although Fuller's story outline was much closer to *Pickup on South Street*'s final form, studio executives expressed concern about the film's tone. A conference memo regarding Fuller's outline is blunt:

The scene between Skip and Candy on page 41 has to be underwritten so that there isn't too much patriotism. Candy should tell Skip she doesn't want him to be a traitor. She loves him too much. Skip tells her not to give him any of that patriotic stuff. She tells him that she went to the FBI because if he were caught, he would be killed. She should be inarticulate in her explanation. We know that to save his life is her main motivation. It isn't patriotism first and then his life, although by trying to save him, she is also being patriotic.[70]

Additionally, the studio now requests a slightly more optimistic note at the end of the picture, saying, "Somehow we get the feeling that Zara may be able to help Skip through J. Edgar Hoover, but Skip and Candy know nothing about this."[71]

By August of 1952 Fuller had completed his first draft of the screenplay for *Blaze of Glory* and had worked out the bulk of the basic story problems to the studio's satisfaction. In attempting to show the high stakes associated with Skip's dilemma, Fuller included a brief scene in which Skip tries to elude the FBI by sneaking into a movie theater. Once Skip has entered, he sees a newsreel that shows scenes from the Korean War and then a "scene of two traitors who were arrested for doing business with enemy Red agents."[72] Furthermore, Fuller's screenplay also reveals the ingenious solution he devised for the film's conclusion. By having Skip's motivation change from avarice to revenge, Fuller allows his hero to avoid prosecution by having him act as an investigative agent to break up the spy ring. In doing so, Fuller gives the film a happy ending while resisting the contrived quality that marked earlier resolutions. In a memo dated August 29, 1952, the studio offers only minor suggestions for revision. These included recommendations to emphasize the "three-time loser" elements in the film's ending and to avoid sentimentality in Skip's speech after Moe's death.[73]

The only major change to the film that remained involved the title, *Blaze of Glory*. Fuller has never indicated why Taylor's original was ultimately rejected, but he nonetheless recounts in his autobiography how the studio finally settled on *Pickup on South Street*. Initially, Fuller suggested *Pick-Pocket* but claims that Zanuck rejected that title as "too European," some years before director Robert Bresson would use it for his own film. Fuller then suggested *Cannon,* a slang term used in the film to describe petty grifters like Skip. This, too, was rejected, but in this case it was because the studio feared that audiences would take the term literally and would come expecting a war movie. Fuller then suggested *Pickup on South Street,* because, as he put it, "New York's South Street had a special memory for me during my newsboy days."[74]

When the film was finally released in 1953, *Pickup on South Street* opened to generally mixed reviews. Most critics praised the film's hard-boiled realism, but many also expressed concern about the story's apparent sordidness and sensationalism. The *Los Angeles Daily News*, for example, described the film as "anything but family fare" and claimed that the characters were just "a notch above the gutter."[75] Besides questioning the film's lurid atmosphere, several critics also expressed concern about its representation of violence. The words *brutality* and *sadism* crop up in many of the film's reviews, and *Variety* panned the film outright as "unnecessarily violent."[76] John L. Scott of the *Los Angeles Times* even suggested that the level of violence was so outlandish that "audiences snicker instead of being horrified," even though Jean Peters's Candy is the "recipient of nine-tenths of the violence."[77]

The emphasis on violence and brutality in the film's reception also led critics to highlight two subordinate themes in their reviews. As Zanuck may well have predicted, the casting of Richard Widmark as Skip led a few reviewers to draw comparisons between his roles in *Pickup on South Street* and *Kiss of Death*. Recalling the famous scene of Udo gleefully pushing an old woman in a wheelchair down a flight of stairs, it seems that Widmark's previous role helped audiences to understand the apparent sadism of Skip, who coldcocks Candy one minute and then caresses her the next. Reviewers' emphasis on sadism and brutality also encouraged comparisons between Fuller's film and Mickey Spillane's Mike Hammer novels.[78] When one considers the wild popularity of Spillane's novels in the early 1950s, his debt to earlier hard-boiled literature, his overt misogyny, and his explicit anti-Communism, the numerous parallels with *Pickup on South Street* make the association seem fairly obvious.[79]

Curiously, although most contemporaneous reviews noted the role of Communist agents as an important story element in *Pickup on South Street*, very few saw anti-Communism as a central theme of the film. Rather, the politics of the film are more manifestly a part of its long-term reception in which its anti-Communism is seen as emblematic of the Cold War period. Instead, most contemporaneous reviews placed far more emphasis on three other themes: the social marginalization of the main characters, the abuse directed at Candy, and the redemptive power of Candy's love for Skip. Indeed, in the rare instance where a reviewer identifies anti-Communism as an important element of *Pickup on South Street*, the reviewer appears to have misread the stated intentions of the film's creators. In a coyly written pan of the film, the *Saturday Review*—contra Fuller, Zanuck, and others—stated that Skip, Candy, and Moe are all "ideologically opposed to Communism, and they patriotically stop their pick-pocketing, stool-pigeoning, and other unsavory activities until the menace is overcome."[80]

Contemporaneous reviews also paid scant attention to the issue of "stool-pigeoning," this despite the fact that the film was produced and distributed during HUAC's most intensive investigation of Hollywood. Between 1951 and 1953, actors, screenwriters, and directors were being pressured to "name names" on an almost daily basis, many of them doing so to save their careers. The issue of informing is slightly more prominent in more contemporary writing on *Pickup on South Street*, but even here the topic is treated abstractly with little or no regard to the parallels that exist between Fuller's characters and HUAC witnesses of the early 1950s. This is regrettable since Fuller's treatment of this issue is richer and more complex than that seen in other films of the period. Unlike *Storm Warning, I Confess,* and *On the Waterfront*, which employ a single character as a surrogate for the HUAC witness, Fuller splits this character function in two. Although Skip and Moe have radically different relationships with institutions and authority, they function as two halves of the same coin insofar as they each embody a part of the ethical dilemma faced by HUAC witnesses.

As described by several historians, the process of clearing oneself before the committee necessitated answering questions related to two separate strands of inquiry. First, witnesses had to admit their past membership in the Communist Party. Second, witnesses then had to identify any other people they remembered from party meetings. Because of the way that these two strands were conjoined, witnesses appearing before the committee basically had four options, three of which would result in their being blacklisted:

1. Witnesses could refuse to answer any questions on Fifth Amendment grounds. This was viewed as a tacit admission of party membership and would result in being blacklisted.

2. Witnesses could refuse to answer questions about their own membership on Fifth Amendment grounds but offer to provide the committee with the names of other members. As in the first case this was viewed as a tacit admission of membership and the end result was the same.

3. Witnesses could admit their past membership in the party but refuse to name other members. Since Fifth Amendment protections were more or less waived by the answer to question 1, the witness had no legal grounds for refusing to answer question 2. The Fifth

Amendment protected witnesses from self-incrimination but not the incrimination of others. Thus, if one refused to "name names," he or she was guilty of contempt of Congress, a situation that also resulted in the witness being blacklisted.

4. Witnesses could answer both questions (i.e., admit their past membership and identify other members). Those who did so were able to continue working in the industry, albeit with the stigma of having informed on friends and colleagues.

In Skip and Moe, Fuller developed two characters whose situations contained strong parallels with witnesses called to testify before HUAC. Skip, for example, attempts to avoid incriminating himself throughout much of the film. As a "three-time loser," Skip could be sentenced to life imprisonment if he admits he committed any crime, even one as seemingly small as pickpocketing. In this respect Skip is like the witnesses who employ the Fifth Amendment in scenarios 1 and 2; just as these witnesses refused to cooperate with HUAC, Skip refuses to cooperate with the police. A legal definition of contempt of Congress is transformed into a literal contempt for authority in Skip. When Agent Zara asks if Skip knows what treason is, he responds, "Who cares?"

Yet Skip's motivation throughout the film strongly diverges from that of uncooperative HUAC witnesses. Although witnesses had many reasons to resist HUAC's inquiries, greed was not among them. Indeed, by refusing to answer the committee's questions, most witnesses knew they would be fired by the studios and sacrificed their financial security as a matter of moral principle. Skip, however, is driven by avarice throughout much of the film. Captain Tiger, for example, offers to clear Skip's previous record, thereby eliminating the threat of life imprisonment for his theft and removing a major obstacle to Skip's cooperation with police. Skip still refuses. When he is apprised of the microfilm's value, Skip tries to extort money from the spy ring by demanding $25,000 for its safe return. In this, Skip is closer to a generic prototype: the small-time hood looking for the "big score" that will enable him to escape his "hand-to-mouth" existence. Although Skip is an emblematic uncooperative "witness" in several respects, his sense of self-preservation and his desire for financial security are motivations much more in line with those of HUAC's "friendly" witnesses.

Similarly, Moe begins the film as an archetypal informer, but her character's actions and motivations become more complicated as the narrative develops. As Fuller describes her, Moe is "an old lady who makes a living by selling information, a stoolie whose one goal is to save up enough money for a cemetery plot."[81] Most previous critics have treated Moe as an ironic counterpoint to Joey, one that establishes parallels regarding the ways in which both institutions and individuals trade information. As Jack Shadoian shrewdly observes, this selling of information is one of the film's dominant themes:

> Everybody sells each other out. Moe sells information to Tiger, and Tiger's professional ethics are bent to keep a kitty for her services. Lightning Louie sells Moe to Candy, Moe sells Skip to Candy, Candy is seduced by Joey's four hundred dollars into going back to get the microfilm from Skip (Fuller brings her from shadow to light, exposing her venality). Skip is playing everybody for his big score. Given what the world is, the behavior of Fuller's people is logical—the Communists are merely at a vile extreme.[82]

Initially, the trading of information appears to be an unseemly epiphenomenon of the "dog-eat-dog" world of industrial capitalism. Whether a big corporation or a lonely old woman, everyone uses cutthroat tactics for personal gain, even if it means selling out or hurting other people. The dynamics of the film change, however, when it is revealed that Joey is, in fact, a Communist agent. Suddenly, for Moe, the issue is less a matter of saving for a burial plot and more about the very definition of Americanism. Moe chastises Skip for "playing footsie with the Commies," a comment that motivates her later unwillingness to give up Skip to Joey.

Although I do not deny the importance of the parallels between Moe and the Communist spy ring, I suggest that previous film scholarship has overlooked the ways in which Moe's activities and motivations parallel those of HUAC informers. In her desire for a comfortable afterlife, Moe resembles those witnesses who cooperated with HUAC in order to salvage their careers. Much like these witnesses, when Captain Tiger and Agent Zara ask Moe about the identity of their pickpocket, Moe provides them with a "list of names," claiming that one of them is bound to be their suspect (fig. 5). And like many "friendly witnesses," Moe attempts to avoid the stigma of being an informer. Throughout the film Moe employs several ruses designed to avoid the appearance of selling out her friends. Echoing the broader political rhetoric of the period, Moe sells ties as a "front" for her activities as a stoolie. Likewise, rather than offer Skip directly to the cops, Moe makes a $35 wager with police that their culprit will be among the list of names she provides. Captain Tiger accepts the bet, knowing that it is one he will lose. Finally, when Candy first meets Moe and describes her as a stoolie, Moe bristles at the epithet and somewhat defensively describes herself as a civic-minded citizen eager to report wrongdoing to authorities. When Candy reminds her

Figure 5. In Sam Fuller's *Pickup on South Street* Moe provides Captain Tiger with a list of possible "cannons" who stole Candy's wallet aboard the subway train. Moe's cooperation with police evokes some of the tactics used by HUAC's "friendly witnesses" who gave the Committee names of suspected Communists who were already known to them as a way of deflecting personal blame as informers.

of the compensation she receives, Moe admits that she sells information in the same way that others peddle apples. Moe's motivations thus function as an inverse of Skip's reluctance to cooperate. While Skip is overtly "unpatriotic," Moe adopts a posture of civic-mindedness in order to downplay the financial benefits she receives from police for her cooperation.

More tellingly, like other "friendly witnesses," Moe attempts to minimize the harm done by her cooperation by suggesting that her actions have no real consequence. When Skip asks her about her dealings with police, Moe offers him a rationalization, saying that they would have caught him anyway. Moe's explanation resonates with the excuses offered by HUAC's cooperative witnesses, especially those who claimed that they only offered up names that the committee already had. By providing the names of those already blacklisted, these witnesses reassured themselves that they really didn't do any harm to others' careers.

Because all are involved in trading information, none of the other characters in *Pickup on South Street* question Moe's activities and seem to accept them as necessitated by her simple needs for food and shelter. Even Skip, who risks a life sentence because of Moe's cooperation with police, acknowledges that her actions are not done out of malice and that "she's gotta eat." As Fuller's most important contribution to the film's screenplay, Moe would seem to be key to understanding the film's ideological stance on HUAC informers. As drawn by Fuller and played by Thelma Ritter, Moe is perhaps the film's most sympathetic character, one whose morality seems dubious when considered in the abstract but whose actions are understandable in light of her circumstances. Seen in this light, Fuller's characterization of Moe might be read as an implicit defense of some cooperative witnesses. Fuller stops short of endorsing the act of "naming names" but acknowledges the reasons for doing so. Instead, Fuller's contempt seems reserved for ideologues who act on principle rather than for survival. This would be especially true of apparent "turncoats," like Kazan, who were believed to be in a position to stand up to the committee but instead cooperated with it out of a misguided sense of patriotic fervor.

Yet any initial judgment of Moe's motivations is complicated by her later refusal to sell out Skip to the Communists. When Joey appears in Moe's tiny apartment, he offers her $500 for Skip's address, an amount vastly larger than the $35 to $50 she usually received for tips. Although this amount would surely defray the rising cost of beans and frankfurters that Moe complains about to Tiger, she nonetheless refuses Joey's entreaties, even though it quite obviously means her premature death and burial in Potter's Field. For the first time acting out of principle rather than self-interest, Moe's refusal to give information links her to those HUAC witnesses who were ultimately blacklisted for failing to play the role of informer. However, even this reading is complicated by Fuller's inversion of political interests in this scene by having a Communist ask the questions rather than the other way around.

While Moe's unstated motivation is her desire to protect Skip, her stated reasons for resisting Joey sound exactly like the sort of mindless flag-waving that both Skip and Fuller despised. In one of the most oft-quoted speeches of the film, Moe says, "What I know about Commies? Nothing. I know one thing. I don't like them." In her admitted ignorance of what Communism is or means, Moe comes across as the worst sort of knee-jerk reactionary, someone who is against Commies but doesn't even know why. In his explanation of the scene, Fuller suggests that Moe represents millions of Americans who saw Communism as a sort of "boogeyman."[83] Thus, in this scene Fuller, like Skip, seems to be playing both sides against the middle. On one hand, Fuller evokes sympathy for blacklistees by acknowledging the complexity of their motivations. Through Moe's tragic death, Fuller appears to recognize the sacrifices made by many blacklistees who refused to sell out their friends and comrades. On the other hand, however, Fuller backhandedly sanctions the larger political project that HUAC represented. By depicting Joey as a venal murderer, Fuller suggests that Communism itself is a threat that must be resisted.

In the end, although Skip and Moe seem to stand in for HUAC witnesses in various ways, their complex and shifting motivations suggest that reading *Pickup on South Street* as an allegory of blacklisting only leads to an ideological muddle. While some critics have read the film reductively as a McCarthyite tract, most others suggest that Fuller's anti-Communism is mollified by a profound suspicion of all institutions. As Fuller himself said of Skip, Candy, and Moe, "They are individualists, trusting no one, beyond politics, changes in governments, intellectual labels, and fashion."[84] Yet if it is wrong to see Fuller as an anti-Communist ideologue, it is equally wrong to see the film as a simple endorsement of Skip's unwillingness to cooperate with authorities and therefore as a testament to those blacklistees who stood up to HUAC.

By distributing the functions of the archetypal HUAC witness across two characters and by treating Skip and Moe as individuals pressured by larger institutions, Fuller may not fully endorse either character's actions over the course of the film, but he expresses great compassion for the reasons they took those actions. Describing the film as being about the "rush to judgment," Fuller implies in *Pickup on South Street* that historians must examine the motivations of HUAC witnesses very carefully before they render any ultimate verdict on them. By acknowledging that everyone has reasons, Fuller's allegory of informing prefigures the political stance taken many years later by Dalton Trumbo in his famous "Only Victims" speech: "Caught in a situation that passed beyond the control of mere individuals, each person reacted as his nature, his needs, his convictions, and his particular circumstances compelled him to. There was bad faith and good, honesty and dishonesty, courage and cowardice, selflessness and opportunism, wisdom and stupidity, good and bad on both sides; and almost every individual involved, no matter where he stood, combined some or all of these antithetical qualities in his own person, in his own acts."[85] As a description of the characters and political stance of *Pickup on South Street*, Trumbo's words seem surprisingly apt.

CLEARANCE AS A FORM OF RITUAL: *I CONFESS* AS
BLACKLIST ALLEGORY

The films of Alfred Hitchcock are undoubtedly the most scrutinized and analyzed in the history of film scholarship. From Hitchcock's notebooks to his treatment of women (both real and fictional) to his cultivation as a television personality, virtually every aspect of the director's career has been examined. Moreover, as David Bordwell has convincingly argued, one can chart shifts in the development of film studies as a discipline by comparing readings of Hitchcock's movies produced at different historical moments.[86]

In perhaps the most important analysis of the political subtext in Hitchcock's films of the 1950s, Robert J. Corber contends that the director's work is symptomatic of the way in which a "Cold War consensus" in America produced a united front against Communism by subordinating the political interests of disenfranchised groups, such as women, gays, lesbians, and African Americans.[87] In his analysis of this consensus Corber draws attention to the historically coincident purges of suspected Communists and homosexuals from the federal government, noting that both were identified as security risks. By taming the "enemy within," McCarthyism effectively accomplished the ideological containment of both Communism and same-sex eroticism by linking sexual identity to national identity. Given Corber's focus on the relations between film and the Cold War, it seems a bit odd that his book makes almost no mention of Hollywood's own purging of Communists during the blacklist period. Likewise, it is equally puzzling that Corber fails to mention *I Confess*, a film that—at first blush—appears to be Hitchcock's most definitive statement on the 1950s Red Scare.[88]

The plot of *I Confess* is simple: in Quebec, Father Michael Logan hears the confession of Otto Keller, who has just robbed and killed a lawyer named Villette. Because Keller disguised himself as a priest when committing the crime, suspicion soon falls on the local parish church. Further investigation reveals that Villette was blackmailing Logan's old flame, Ruth Grandfort, a woman now married to the local prosecutor. With a clear motive and no alibi, Logan stands trial for Villette's murder. Although Logan knows the identity of the guilty party, he cannot divulge it without violating the sanctity and secrecy of the confessional. Logan is later acquitted owing to lack of evidence but is vilified by the community, who remain convinced of his culpability. Moved by Logan's plight, Keller's wife, Alma, reveals her husband's crime but is shot by him while talking to police. A manhunt for Keller follows, and he is soon cornered in the ballroom of the

Chateau Frontenac Hotel. Keller is shot in a brief gunfight with police, and as he lies dying, he offers his final confession to Father Logan.

Perhaps Corber omits *I Confess* because it directly challenges his reading of *Rear Window* (1954), which argues that its oft-cited treatment of voyeurism is, in fact, an embodiment of more nationalized forms of surveillance imbricated within the McCarthyite subject. Yet if this reading casts the film's villain, Lars Thorwald, as the dubious object of Jeff's surveillance, which Corber sees as an expression of a larger national security apparatus, then *I Confess* inverts that relationship by subjecting its hero to the merciless, paranoiac scrutiny of both the legal system and public opinion. As I will argue later, with *I Confess*, Father Logan's situation dovetails with the perspective of McCarthyism's victims by examining the atmosphere of menace engendered by unfounded suspicion, rumor, and innuendo. By pondering the question of whether to testify, Hitchcock's hero in *I Confess* faces many legal and moral quandaries that paralleled those of witnesses before HUAC in the early 1950s.

Considering not only Corber's work but also the sheer volume of scholarship on Hitchcock, surprisingly little has been written about the Cold War subtext of *I Confess*. Indeed, this potentially rich vein of criticism has been more or less summed up by William Rothman's offhand comment that the film is "a thinly veiled allegory of McCarthyism and the blacklist."[89] Theodore Price embroiders this reading slightly, claiming he was initially inclined to simply dismiss Rothman's suggestion of a blacklist subtext: "But as I saw the film again, I realized that this interpretation would surely fit, and with just a little further research I convinced myself that Rothman was quite right." Price goes on to discuss the film's screenwriter, George Tabori, whose attendance at "various fellow-traveling, left-wing cocktail-party gatherings held in and around Hollywood" enhances the film's blacklist subtext.[90] A central element of Price's reading involves Tabori's collaboration with Elia Kazan on *Flight into Egypt*, a New York play that was in rehearsal when Kazan was first subpoenaed to testify before HUAC.[91] All of these offscreen connections among Tabori, Kazan, and Hitchcock lead Price to conclude, "Such then is the first theory of what *I Confess* is 'really' about. The first is to be understood as a political allegory of the McCarthy/HUAC/Hollywood-Ten era, when former Communist Party members of the film community were asked to *confess* their Party membership and to *inform upon* their former comrades."[92]

In contrast, previous Hitchcock scholarship treats *I Confess* as a film that crystallizes the director's preoccupation with the idea of the transference of guilt. On one hand, Eric Rohmer and Claude Chabrol's well-known monograph, the first major scholarly work on the director, says *I Confess* is a particularly apposite expression of Hitchcock's Jesuit upbringing and his Catholic obsession with guilt as an ontological condition of humanity. Far from seeing the film as a blacklist allegory, Rohmer and Chabrol see it as an allegory of original sin and the Fall.[93] On the other hand, Robin Wood argues that the film is a failed reworking of elements from *Strangers on a Train*. Noting that *I Confess* substitutes the priesthood for the political world of *Strangers on a Train*, Wood argues, quite paradoxically, that the latter film benefits from the shallowness and insignificance of Guy's vocation as a tennis player. Father Logan's adherence to church law renders him a less morally complex character than the opportunistic Guy, who genuinely seems to profit from his involvement with a murderer. The same cannot be said of Logan, who acts out of duty and moral necessity rather than from latent psychopathic desires.[94]

Donald Spoto shrewdly observes that *I Confess* is only ostensibly about the notion of "shared guilt" and is perhaps Hitchcock's weakest articulation of that theme. Although Logan clearly benefits from Villette's death insofar as he no longer risks the exposure of his suspected adultery, for Spoto it cannot be said that Logan shares the same desire for murder that Guy has for his wife, Miriam. Instead, Spoto argues that the film's multiple confessions and the mechanics of the plot are aimed at encouraging Logan to divulge a rather different kind of unexpressed desire, namely his continued love for Ruth. As Spoto puts it, "The title of the film, in fact, refers only superficially to Keller's words at the beginning and at the end. Everyone in the film is forced to make a confession, an admission of feeling if not of guilt."[95] Extrapolating from Spoto's reading, one might say that *I Confess* is about two different kinds of guilt rather than the transference of guilt. Logan continues to covet his neighbor's wife, and in the eyes of the church his sin is neither more nor less serious than Keller's murder.

Yet of all the films discussed in this chapter, *I Confess* seems to have the clearest, if quite nominal, connection to the issues of the blacklist insofar as it shares its title with Benjamin Gitlow's exposé of the American Communist Party, first published in 1940. Studio correspondence shows that Warner Bros. was quite aware of Gitlow's book. In a letter to Morris Ebenstein of Warner Bros.' legal department, Fulton Brylawski, a Washington attorney who handled copyright searches for the studios, described Gitlow's *I Confess* as "the history of the Communist Party in the United States, its history, its methods, aims and relations with Moscow."[96] The studio also wrote coverage on Gitlow's book, both in 1940 and 1948, and even considered adapting it to the screen after the 1947 HUAC hearings. In a studio memo written less than six months after the Waldorf Statement, Wes Haynes, one of the studio's story analysts, recommended against Warner Bros.' optioning of Gitlow's book: "If the studio wishes to do a picture with an anti-Communist theme, it seems to me we should seek a sounder, more truly democratic basis than any found in the present book."[97]

By 1952, though, Warner Bros.' interest in Gitlow's book had less to do with any potential overlap with Hitchcock's film than with the simple fact that the studio needed Gitlow's permission to use the title. In a letter to Jack Warner, Harry Mayer and Morris Ebenstein indicated that $2,500 was the minimum amount that Gitlow would accept to allow Warner Bros. to use the name *I Confess*.[98] Warner responded in a telegram back to Mayer and Ebenstein that he would offer no more than $500, adding, "Tell Gitlow if they don't accept it we are changing the title."[99] After initially playing hardball in their negotiations, it appears that Warner Bros. softened its stance, eventually agreeing to pay Gitlow $1,750.[100]

As this correspondence suggests, Warner Bros. acknowledged the possibility that the public might associate the title, *I Confess*, with the recollections of a former Communist Party member. Ironically, though, the few allusions to radical politics that appear in drafts of *I Confess* make reference to Nazis rather than Communists. As one might expect, all of them relate in one way or another to the film's German villain, Otto Keller. George Tabori's draft dated July 3, 1952, describes a late scene in which Alma visits Father Logan in prison to persuade him not to go through with his martyrdom. Like Logan, Alma knows that her husband—here called Hermann—is responsible for the crime with which Michael is charged. When Logan refuses, Alma returns to the church rectory, pulls Hermann's S.S. knife out of her husband's dresser drawer, and stabs him to death with it. In a nifty twist, Alma then goes into Father Benoit's room to confess, suggesting that the cycle could play out all over again in a *mise en abyme* fashion.[101] In a memo to Hitchcock about this draft, associate producer Barbara Keon recommended that Tabori change his "characterization of Hermann, to lose his present quality of psychopath, or Nazism, to make him a more recognizable and less theatric character."[102] Tabori appears to have taken this advice to heart as none of these allusions to Nazis survive in the finished film.

Of course, the very idea that the villain in *I Confess* might be an ex-Nazi rather than a current Communist seems to have escaped the notice of critics like Rothman and Price. Since both critics base their interpretations only on the finished film, they rely primarily on two aspects of *I Confess* to support their reading: the timing of the film's release and its central conceit, namely Logan's status as potential "informer" and witness against Keller. Besides this obvious parallel, *I Confess* also contains other subtler elements that implicitly support Rothman's and Price's interpretations of the film as blacklist allegory. None are cited explicitly by either scholar, but they nonetheless reinforce the analogy between Logan and a HUAC witness.

For example, the name of the film's villain, Otto Keller, supports the allegorical dimension of *I Confess* in various ways. The name *Keller* means "cellar" in German and thus hints at the character's potentially subversive significance by combining the morpheme *cell* with a semantic meaning that refers to an underground space. Moreover, Keller is driven to his theft and murder by the sight of his wife's servitude. This motivation, which explicitly links the issue of class to the film's political subtext, loosely associates Keller with a protorevolutionary ideology. And by framing Logan for Villette's murder, Keller's actions threaten to undermine the church as an institution, which was strongly associated with anti-Communist discourse in the United States.

More important, by directly comparing the worlds of religion and politics, *I Confess* suggests certain continuities and associations between the two. For example, Logan's adherence to church law contains strong parallels with witnesses who invoked the Fifth Amendment to avoid answering questions from HUAC. In both instances, the principles involved are viewed as essential to their respective legal systems, but they nonetheless engender suspicion by appearing to circumvent the search for truth and justice. Additionally, if we accept *I Confess* as a blacklist allegory, then the substitution of religion for politics points up the highly ritualized nature of HUAC testimony. During the hearings of the early 1950s many cooperative witnesses attempted to expiate their own sense of guilt by offering up only the names of colleagues already identified in previous testimony. Yet one wonders what information was actually gained through this type of testimony and furthermore why HUAC and Hollywood were willing to offer clearance to witnesses who offered no new information. Viewed in this light, the question repeatedly asked during the committee hearings, "Are you now or have you ever been a member of the Communist Party?" is nothing more nor less than an attempt to elicit confessions. The oft-noted analogy between the investigations and an inquisition is supported by this aspect of the hearings. In both instances confession, whether spiritual or political, served as a way of "bearing witness" and atoning for past sins. Testimony before HUAC, thus, became an intrinsically valuable form of personal revelation not unlike religious confessions. The recitation of names already known to the committee was HUAC's own peculiar version of Catholicism's "Act of Contrition."

Like the HUAC investigations, *I Confess* is also centrally concerned with the traversal of well-established boundaries between the public and private spheres. The secrecy of the confessional, like the secrecy of the ballot box, is considered an important, indeed inviolate, component of the Catholic faith. By pressuring Father Logan to defend himself, the legal system of *I Confess* threatens to erase the boundary between private and public, the sacred and the secular. For much of the film, Father Logan can escape punishment only by bringing the private disclosures of a parishioner into the very public forum of the courtroom. From a personalized perspective Logan himself becomes the victim of governmental inquisition; he can save himself only by renouncing his faith as a Catholic and his duties as a priest.

Through this articulation of the threat to privacy, *I Confess* both complements and challenges Corber's analysis of the cinematic gaze as an extension of the intrusive surveillance gaze of the national security apparatus. As Corber says of *Rear Window*, "The film's emphasis on the psychopathology of spectatorship implies that the specular logic of the filmic text helped create the conditions of McCarthyism."[103] Yet even if we accept Corber's analysis, *I Confess* is, on its face, an eloquent defense of those who chose not to cooperate and who paid a price as a consequence. Indeed, Hitchcock's sharpest political commentary appears toward the end of the film, after Father Logan is freed by the jury's findings of reasonable doubt. Despite his "not guilty" verdict, we see Logan harassed, taunted, insulted, and physically attacked, moments that would have great resonance for those blacklisted for taking the Fifth. Those who invoked their constitutional rights were not legally guilty of anything, but they were guilty in the court of public opinion and lived their lives under a cloud of suspicion all the same. By dramatizing Logan's public castigation, *I Confess* hints at the injustice of the blacklist by equating it with the knee-jerk fears and potential violence of the unthinking mob.

Moreover, *I Confess* also dramatizes the potential consequences of breaching those boundaries between public and private. Like *The Wrong Man* (1957), a film it resembles in several respects, *I Confess* questions the validity of both eyewitness testimony and Corber's national security apparatus. As an embodiment of this apparatus, Inspector Larrue is a kind of negative mirror image of Jeff in *Rear Window*. Just as Jeff's wild speculations about Thorwald prove to be right despite plausible explanations to the contrary, Larrue's interpretation of the events surrounding Villette's death proves to be equally and disastrously wrong. Hitchcock does not depict Larrue as villainous; he is merely doing his job to the best of his ability. Yet this exposes a deeper flaw within the system. Even when the state is not corrupted by political ambition or paranoia, its panoptic surveillance still leads to the same sorts of faulty inferences. In effect, Hitchcock suggests in *I Confess* that every investigation necessarily disrupts the boundaries between public and private, and threatens to cause serious social harm as a result of that breach. The hearings conducted by HUAC were merely an especially egregious example of that principle insofar as those suspected had committed no crimes, and the concomitant breach in public and private spheres resulted in overwhelming losses of jobs, friendships, and public trust.

Yet even if one reads *I Confess* as a spirited defense of HUAC's resisters, the film remains a flawed critique of blacklist politics insofar as it cannot escape the importance of eliciting confession as an investigative tool. While Father Logan remains heroically silent, the film's moral compass is righted only after Alma does that which Logan refuses to do. Alma's revelation that Otto is the guilty party occurs just after the judge has discharged Father Logan, leaving him free to go. The jury foreman announces that, although they still question Logan's innocence, there was not enough evidence that Logan actually wielded the murder weapon to support a conviction. To this, the judge adds, "Michael Logan, while I have no doubt that the jury must have reached their conclusion in utmost fairness and solemn regard for justice, I cannot help expressing my personal disagreement with their verdict." The feeling that Logan will remain a victim of rumor and innuendo is quickly confirmed when we hear a hissing sound from someone in the courtroom as Michael steps down from the dock where he stood as the accused.

Aided by a phalanx of police, Logan struggles to make his way through the crush of onlookers. Just as Logan disappears into the horde of people, Hitchcock cuts to a medium shot of Otto and Alma as they exit the courthouse. When Logan is pushed into a waiting car and his elbow smashes through one of its windows, Hitchcock cuts to Alma's horrified reaction. Fearing that Logan will be the victim of mob violence, Alma rushes toward him. Otto initially stays behind and, in a panicked voice, shouts at Alma to come back to him. A medium long shot shows Logan fending off the crowd. Alma rushes toward the center of the frame, telling one of the policemen, "He's innocent." The next shot shows Otto, who has remained behind looking offscreen to the right. Hitchcock then cuts to a close-up of Otto's hand as he pulls a German Luger from the pocket of his trousers. The next shot is a medium shot of Alma from Otto's optical point of view. She turns and points directly at the camera, saying, "My husband." Hitchcock cuts back to a close-up as the barrel of the Luger is raised. Otto points and fires. An extreme long shot shows the crowd dispersing in a panic in response to the sound of the gunshot. When Hitchcock later cuts back to Alma, she is doubled over, apparently from a gunshot wound in her abdomen. Logan and Father Millars ease Alma to the ground. Just before dying, Alma asks for Logan's forgiveness. A close-up of Logan shows his eyes welling with tears in response to Alma's confession. Just as Alma expires, Father Millars gives her final absolution of her sins.

Of course, in acknowledging her husband's guilt, Alma violates a legal principle almost as sacrosanct as the secrecy of the confessional, namely that marital partners cannot be compelled to testify against one another. By using Alma's unofficial testimony as the mainspring of the film's resolution, *I Confess* basically sacrifices one legal principle in the service of another. More important, the substitution of Alma for Father Logan as reluctant witness entails a corresponding substitution of ethical and moral issues. While Father Logan's sense of sacred duty is never questioned, Alma's sense of loyalty to her husband sits on shakier ground. Alma's silence throughout much of the film is motivated by a desire to protect a loved one, but it is ultimately superseded by two other ethical questions: (1) should one remain faithful to an evildoer; and (2) should one stay silent as an innocent man is punished for the act of another. When one adds Alma's own sense of personal guilt to the situation—recall that Keller commits the robbery because he hated seeing his wife toil in the church—then her ultimate betrayal of her husband seems completely justified.

Put in these terms, Father Logan's moral dilemma doesn't seem so complex after all. His actions are governed by a clear sense of duty and loyalty to the church, and his silence threatens to harm no one but himself. Logan's potential martyrdom, thus, seems completely reasonable and even consistent with long-standing traditions within Christianity. A more interesting scenario for *I Confess* might have been to have Ruth stand accused of the murder instead of Logan. Like Logan, Ruth appears to have motive and opportunity to commit the crime and is initially considered a suspect. In such a scenario Father Logan's sense of loyalties would seem more conflicted and his situation would more strongly parallel that of Alma. Would Logan's silence seem justified if he believed a loved one, like Ruth, would be punished for a crime for which he could prove her innocence?

As a blacklist allegory, *I Confess* clearly wants to have it both ways. While Logan's dilemma is analogous to the situation of the uncooperative witness, Alma's actions are analogous to the cooperative witness, who ultimately points the finger at another because it is defined morally as the right thing to do. Insofar as both characters' actions are treated as acts of conscience, their political positions both seem equally justifiable. That being said, as an analogy to the blacklist, Hitchcock glosses over some of the moral complexities of the dilemmas faced by witnesses by assuring us of Keller's guilt, thereby making him someone seemingly unworthy of Michael's and Alma's protection. By adopting a "both-and" approach to the HUAC witnesses' dilemma, *I Confess* also elides the most important issue of its real-life counterpart—namely, did HUAC have the authority to conduct its inquiry, and were the studios right to cave in to the committee's political pressure? By focusing on the dilemmas of individuals, *I Confess* never questions the legal and religious institutional framework that provides the context for its characters' actions.

CONCLUSION

Each of the films discussed in this chapter allegorizes the dilemma of a witness subpoenaed by HUAC. Each film also explores the reasons why witnesses might cooperate or refuse to answer questions. Released between 1951 and 1954, these films coincide with the return of HUAC to Hollywood and with the testimony of hundreds of witnesses, each of whom faced the same quandaries presented in the films. At a time when overt representations of the blacklist were virtually impossible, these films employed the familiar tropes of the courtroom drama, the gangster film, and the docudrama to offer disguised commentary on a situation that would emerge as the darkest chapter of Hollywood's long and storied history. Through the use of metaphor and metonymy these films dramatize a range of different responses, all of them consistent with the larger narrative and thematic concerns of their directors.

Made under Jack Warner's supervision and starring two prominent members of the Motion Picture Alliance, Stuart Heisler's *Storm Warning* has been framed by critics as a right-wing fantasy that alerts viewers to the importance of public testimony in exposing subversive groups like the Ku Klux Klan or its metaphoric surrogate, the American Communist Party. In contrast, a small number of critics argue that Alfred Hitchcock's *I Confess* offers a sympathetic treatment of McCarthyism's victims by depicting the destructive power of rumor, innuendo, and the paranoid gaze of both the legal system and the society on which it is founded. The three Kazan films discussed here *(Viva Zapata!, Man on a Tightrope,* and *On the Waterfront)* function as double allegories that simultaneously point toward the equally repressive nature of left-wing and right-wing extremism. Although Kazan couches this discourse within narratives of civic responsibility found in his earlier social problem films, these films also bespeak an ambivalence regarding HUAC and the blacklist as victims become victimizers, artists become exiles, and those who resist institutional imperatives lose their life or their freedom. Finally, in *Pickup on South Street* Sam Fuller, with a major assist from Darryl Zanuck, displays compassion for "friendly" and "unfriendly" witnesses in equal measure. Although ostensibly anti-Communist at the level of plot, Fuller's film opposes all forms of totalitarianism and is profoundly suspicious of the ways in which large institutions dominate, intimidate, and overpower individual citizens.

Although blacklist allegories would continue to flourish as a means of expression within individual generic contexts, like the historical film, interest in the problems of the informer gradually diminished after the mid-1950s. The release of *Storm Center* (1956) signaled the dissolution of this cycle of films. *Storm Center* tells the story of Alicia Hull (Bette Davis), a small-town librarian questioned by the city council for her past participation in Communism after she refuses to remove a book entitled *The Communist Dream*. Throughout the film Alicia is a spokesperson for traditional liberal and democratic values, such as the importance of a free and open exchange of ideas, the dangers of conformity, and the sanctity of human knowledge. Still, the politics of the film are far too explicit for it to be of much interest as an allegory. Wearing its politics on its sleeve, *Storm Center* is a barely disguised critique of HUAC's inquisitorial methods and of Hollywood's acceptance of blacklisting as the cost of self-regulation.

It seems fitting that *Storm Center* acts as an entirely appropriate counterpart to *Storm Warning*. If *Storm Warning* is remarkable in managing to address issues of civic duty, cooperative testimony, the legitimacy of government investigations, and the dangers of secret organizations without ever uttering the word *Communism*, then *Storm Center* is equally remarkable in addressing issues of Red-baiting, censorship, guilt by association, and the relevance of past political memberships without ever asking its heroine to confront the real dilemma of HUAC: the question of whether or not to "name names."

5   The Cross and the Sickle

Allegorical Representations of the Blacklist
in Historical Films

In an essay in *Danse Macabre* best-selling author Stephen King writes, "If horror movies have redeeming social merit, it is because of that ability to form liaisons between the real and unreal—to provide subtexts. And because of their mass appeal, these subtexts are often culture-wide."[1] For King the value of these subtexts is that they endow popular fictions with a social and cultural significance that allows them to tap into their readers' deeply held fears and anxieties. It is through these subtexts that the horror film has commented on a host of social and political issues, including scientism, racism, consumerism, conformism, and, of course, Communism.

Although King only acknowledges it implicitly, these subtexts are also important to the extent that they find expression in allegories, patterns of metaphorical substitution that bridge the gap between the real and unreal, past and present. As I have argued throughout, allegory has been a privileged mode of interpretation both in relation to films made during the blacklist period and later as a facet of postmodernist and deconstructionist criticism. In this chapter I investigate critics' use of allegory to interpret historical films of the 1950s. Through this analysis I address several issues about the way film scholars strive to connect allegorical signifiers and signifieds to the text's referential and implicit meanings. For example, how do critics draw together elements of the blacklist to create a pretext for the work's allegorical meanings? What is the place of authorial intention and audience reception in the encoding and decoding of blacklist allegories? Does this reading strategy privilege certain meanings of the text over others of equal significance?

In an essay on the nature of historical allegory in film, Ismail Xavier notes that the past itself provides the basis for allegorical expression within historical fictions. Describing these as "pragmatic allegories," Xavier suggests that historical novels and films take on allegorical significance insofar as the depiction of prior events offers "disguised comment on the present."[2] As we saw in chapter 1, this approach to history informed the work of the three blacklistees who wrote for the television series *You Are There.*

Both of these points help account for the prevalence of allegorical interpretation in relation to costume pictures and "sword and sandal" epics made at the time of the Hollywood blacklist. The list of titles classified as blacklist or Cold War allegory includes *Reign of Terror* (1949), *Quo Vadis* (1951), *Ivanhoe* (1952), *Julius Caesar* (1953), *The Black Knight* (1954), *The Court Martial of Billy Mitchell* (1955), *The Ten Commandments* (1956), and *El Cid* (1961).[3] In these films the political and religious conflicts associated with the French Revolution, ancient Rome, medieval Britain, World War I, ancient Egypt, and eleventh-century Spain offer disguised commentary on the threat of Communism to American political institutions.

Xavier further notes that personification and extended metaphor have been particularly important strategies in the encoding of a text as allegorical. The former is employed in the creation of national allegories through the use of an individual who stands in for a larger social class or political group and who embodies that group's ethos. The latter involves creating a sort of one-to-one correspondence between particular features of the text and the specific circumstances of the text's historical context. By treating the plot of a film as an extended metaphor, critics construct an interpretive frame around the text, one that pulls together several topical reference points that serve as the allegorical pretext for the text's meanings. In the case of historical allegory the superordinate semantic field that organizes all of the other interpretive elements is the binary opposition between past and present. Through this master opposition the analyst simply maps the points of correspondence between specific features of the text and the particular facets of the film's present context that they seem to symbolize.

In this chapter I examine two historical films that more generally have been interpreted as allegories of 1950s Cold War politics: *The Robe* and *Spartacus.* Not coincidentally, blacklisted writers participated in the creation of these films either by doing first drafts of the films' screenplays or by participating in the screenwriting process at a later stage in the film's production. Despite the involvement of blacklisted screenwriters, however, each film presents a slightly different problem in terms of apprehending the encoding and decoding of allegorical meanings. In some cases the allegorical dimension is understood as a matter of authorial intention; in others it is understood as an aspect of the film's reception, albeit in a highly attenuated form. As such, these case studies not only address the ways in which

American films dealt with Communism as a social and political issue, but they also raise more fundamental issues regarding the role of allegorical interpretation as a kind of critical enterprise. Given allegory's return to prominence in postmodernist theory, one might well want to ask the question: are allegorical readings largely created by the kinds of cognitive biases that occur in the way the mind processes information more generally? To what extent do the allegorical interpretations of historical films reflect the effects of framing or the availability heuristic described in chapter 1?

ARE YOU NOW OR HAVE YOU EVER BEEN A CHRISTIAN?
THE ROBE AS POLITICAL ALLEGORY

The Robe has received attention from several scholars who see it as an implicit critique both of the blacklist and of dominant American Cold War ideology. John Belton, for example, argues that the film "casts Caligula as a witch-hunting, McCarthyesque figure and the Christians as persecuted victims of his demonic attempts to purge the Roman empire of potential subversives."[4] Belton's reading is echoed by Bruce Babington and Peter William Evans, who note the historical parallelism inscribed in the coincidence of *The Robe*'s production with the second round of hearings conducted in Hollywood by HUAC in 1951. Further, Babington and Evans call attention to the contemporary resonance of Tiberius's order to Marcellus to collect information on the early Christians. Says Tiberius, "I want names, Tribune, names of all the disciples, of every man and woman who subscribe to this treason."[5]

Nora Sayre and Maria Wyke, in contrast, see *The Robe* and other biblical epics as tacit endorsements of American anti-Communist ideology at a time when Communists were routinely demonized as godless atheists. As Sayre points out, "Christianity as a commodity—as a wellspring of happiness, as a bulwark against the Red tide—was a boon for Hollywood."[6] In offering this reading of *The Robe* and other biblical epics of the period, Sayre and Wyke implicitly establish a link between their rhetorical strategies and anti-Communist propaganda films like *The Red Menace* and *Red Planet Mars*. As we saw in chapter 4, the theme of Christian redemption also played a prominent role in the anti-Communist message in early drafts of *Pickup on South Street*. Whether one sees *The Robe* as an implicit defense of McCarthyite political tactics or an indictment of them, these readings depend on a series of binary terms that allow for the allegorical substitution of present for past. Most readings of *The Robe* establish a pattern of binary oppositions such as those listed in table 5.

Table 5 *The Robe as Anti-HUAC Allegory*

Past	*Present*
Ancient Rome	USA
Christians	Communists
Caligula	J. Parnell Thomas
Roman tribunals	HUAC
Underground caverns	"Underground" cells
Persecution	Censorship
Crucifixions	Blacklisting

In making their case for an allegorical reading of *The Robe,* Belton and Babington and Evans make reference to screenwriter Philip Dunne's background as a noted Hollywood liberal. Dunne was one of the founding members of the Committee for the First Amendment, a group of Hollywood liberals that protested on behalf of the nineteen "unfriendly" witnesses who were scheduled to appear before HUAC in October of 1947. By referencing Dunne's political credentials, these scholars introduce the possibility that *The Robe's* use of allegory constitutes an intentionalist discourse by suggesting, ever so subtly, that the homologies between past and present may have been planted by Dunne as part of the screenwriting process. This in itself is not surprising, though, since, as Ismail Xavier notes, allegorical discourse is often understood within a framework of intention-utterance-interpretation that presumes that the text contains indices of allegorical intention.[7] Belton pushes the point of intention even further, however, by calling attention to Dunne's claim that he rewrote an existing script by a blacklisted writer. By prefacing this observation with the claim that Hollywood's radical left used the biblical epic to "make a case for the Hollywood Ten and the evils of repressive government," Belton gives at least some credit for *The Robe's* allegorical meanings to the unnamed writer mentioned in Dunne's autobiography.[8]

Dunne's account of *The Robe's* production history and the role of a blacklisted writer in the development process is almost too good to resist. The readings of the film based on this account suggest someone silenced by HUAC had nonetheless found a way to offer a disguised critique of government repression. More important, by endowing the unnamed screenwriter with a kind of subversive agency, these accounts further suggest that the radical left is tweaking the collective noses of Hollywood by using the norms and conventions of Hollywood representation in a manner that counters the ostensible interests of those who instituted the blacklist in the first place.

There is just one problem with this account, though. Although it is true that early drafts of *The Robe* were written by blacklisted screenwriter Albert Maltz, one of the members of the Hollywood Ten, Maltz completed work on the film in September of 1946, more than a year before his HUAC testimony and the subsequent issuance of the Waldorf Statement by the studios.[9] This chronology thus turns commonsense causation on its head insofar as it places the imputed effect of the blacklist—the screenplay and film that is seen as a reaction to it—before its supposed cause. As such, it raises an important question about *The Robe:* can we still see the film as blacklist allegory?

One way to salvage the historical narrative sketched out by Belton and others might be to reread the role of intention to suggest that Maltz is offering a cautionary tale about the Red Scare by situating his adaptation of the Lloyd Douglas novel within an allegorical framework. Certainly, one might make a prima facie case for such a possibility since by 1946 there had been some indications of an impending shift in American politics. Winston Churchill had given his famous "Iron Curtain" speech in July of 1946, and problems within the Screen Writers Guild and the Hollywood Writers Mobilization signaled a rift between liberals and radicals within Hollywood.[10] Besides the immediate postwar context, many state and federal government actions had been taken already to limit Communist influence on American life. HUAC had been investigating Communism on and off since 1938, California's Tenney Committee collected information on Hollywood Communists during the early 1940s, and the right-wing MPAPAI was established in 1944.

Although one cannot entirely dismiss the possibility that Maltz's screenplay was a response to events that foreshadowed the eventual blacklist, several things problematize or complicate this account. First, at least some of the elements that critics have cited in support of *The Robe* as a blacklist allegory are present in Douglas's novel, which was copyrighted in 1942. Caligula's speech in the final scene, which refers to Christians as seditionists, comes directly from the novel, as does the more general equation of Christians with Communists. In chapter 10, for example, in a report to Tiberius about Jesus's crucifixion, Senator Gallio describes Christians as a "small but turbulent revolutionary party." Later, in chapter 21, in a dialogue with Diana, Tiberius characterizes the Jesus movement as having in it "the seeds of revolution" and further suggests that it has aspirations of overthrowing the Roman Empire. Most tellingly, a radical egalitarian spirit is also evident in the proposal Stephanos recounts to Demetrius late in the novel:

> "The whole plan was unsound," he explained disconsolately. "Simon announced that any Christian might sell his property and bring the proceeds to the Ecclesia with the promise that his living would be provided for."
>
> "No matter how much or how little he had?" queried Demetrius.
>
> "Right! If you owned a farm or a vineyard, you sold it—probably at a sacrifice—and brought Simon the money. If you had nothing but a few chickens, and a donkey, you came with the money you'd got from that. And all would live together in brotherly love."[11]

In addition to the suggestive analogies between Christians and Communists, Douglas's novel also contains a reference to blacklisting, once again some five years before the Hollywood blacklist was instituted. Early on, Senator Gallio's wife, Cornelia, expresses fears that the family will be socially blacklisted if her husband continues his outspoken criticism of the government. Thus, when comparing the film to the novel, it becomes clear that determining the intentions of *The Robe*'s screenwriters is problematized by the adaptation process. If the elements that support the allegorical readings of *The Robe* are already present in Douglas's novel, then it is difficult to wholly subscribe to the notion that Maltz or Dunne intended to warn viewers of the evils of repressive government.

A second problem with the "foreshadowing theory" is evident in the subplot involving Marcellus's efforts to gather the names of early Christians. Whereas this subplot appears to be wholly Maltz's invention, the notion of "naming names" would have far less political resonance when it was introduced to the screenplay in 1945 than it would have several years later.

A third problem is evident in 20th Century–Fox's reaction to Maltz's screenplay. Indeed, if the screenplay was intended as an allegorical figuration of both past and future political events, then this dimension appears to have escaped the notice of the film's producers. A conference memo from Darryl Zanuck to Dunne and Frank Ross compares *The Robe* to *David and Bathsheba* (1951) and asks, "Are we again permitting 'talk'—an overabundance of talk—to motivate our climax?" As a means of engendering some suspense in *The Robe*'s third act, Zanuck proposes that Caligula should appoint Gallio, Marcellus's father, as the "head of a committee of the Senators to investigate the case of a traitor. Thus Gallio is forced into [the] position of 'trying' his own son."[12] Zanuck's suggestion to provide a filial pressure on Marcellus not only would complement the legal and political

Table 6 *The Robe* as Anti-Fascist Allegory

Past	*Present*
Ancient Rome	Fascist Italy
Christians	Communists
Caligula	Mussolini
Roman tribunals	Brownshirts
Underground caverns	"Underground" Italian Resistance
Crucifixions	Firing squads

pressures depicted in the narrative, but it also would enhance the parallel between ancient Rome and contemporary America. By placing Marcellus's fate in the hands of his father, Zanuck sought to blame the persecution of Christians on a bureaucratic government committee rather than a power-mad, demagogic, and dictatorial emperor. Although this conference memo raises the unlikely possibility that Zanuck himself sought to use *The Robe* as a vehicle for criticizing American political repression, nothing resembling this subplot survives in Dunne's subsequent drafts or in the finished film.[13]

Finally, a fourth problem with the "foreshadowing" theory is that it ignores other allegorical readings of *The Robe* that are more directly related to the historical context surrounding Maltz's work on the screenplay. For example, since Maltz's first draft was completed during the final stages of World War II, one might just as easily read the film as an allegorical critique of Italian fascism and its hopes of restoring Italy to the glory of the Roman Empire. This alternative explanation of *The Robe*'s significance was more or less endorsed by its producer, Frank Ross, who in 1950 described the film as one that "would show those who caused the death of Our Lord upon the Cross as prototypes of the modern dictators then identified as Hitler and Mussolini."[14]

This analogy also depends on the juxtaposition of past and present, but it puts fascist Italy in place of the United States in terms of the binarisms established by the pattern of substitution (see table 6). Several factors might support this alternative interpretation. For one thing, antifascism was a major political cause for the Hollywood Ten. As members of the Popular Front, many of them participated in the activities of political interest groups, such as the Hollywood Anti-Nazi League. Additionally, in their failed defense during the HUAC investigations, several members of the Hollywood Ten compared the committee's ostensible interest in censorship with similar types of actions taken by fascist governments. Dalton Trumbo, for example, likened the investigation to the Reichstag fire in his prepared statement, saying, "For those who remember German history in the autumn of 1932 there is the smell of smoke in this very room."[15] For another, in his subsequent screenwriting work, Maltz gained renown for examining the perils of fascism. Shortly after his work on *The Robe,* Maltz would coauthor the screenplay for *Cloak and Dagger* (1946), a film that was, according to Bernard F. Dick, "simultaneously an attack on fascism, a tribute to the Italian Communist resistance, an exaggerated account of Germany's attempt to manufacture an atomic bomb, and a plea that the atomic age would not get off to as bad a start as Hiroshima seemed to indicate."[16] Last, although it is a small point, in *The Robe* Maltz's early descriptions of Rome's majesty are suggestive of fascist Italy's interest in monumental political symbolism. Consider page 2 of Maltz's first draft: "As Caligula's voice continues, CAMERA SLOWLY MOVES UP TO the doorway and FOCUSES ON a carved stone Roman Eagle. The claws of the Eagle are holding the 'fasces with the ax.' Rays of carved lightning emanate from the fasces." In ancient Rome the fascis was a bundle of rods that contained an axe and served as a symbol of power when displayed for Roman magistrates. The combination of the fasces with the Roman Eagle and carved lightning seems to take on contemporary resonance here as implicit references to the Iron Eagle of Nazi symbolism and the awesome force of the German blitzkrieg or "lightning war." For all of these reasons, one is tempted to conclude that Maltz's intentions were not to use *The Robe* as a critique of American anti-Communism but rather as a critique of European fascism.

Perhaps the most serious challenge to the foreshadowing theory is found in the differences between Maltz's 1945 screenplay and the 1953 finished film. Ironically, although it is extremely doubtful that Maltz's screenplay anticipated the events of HUAC's investigations and the Waldorf Statement, it includes many more specific and concrete analogies to the Hollywood blacklist than are found in the finished film. For instance, while Caligula's final speech makes reference both to Christian sedition and to Spartacus, who by 1953 was widely viewed as a Marxist hero, the same scene in the screenplay includes three additional references to Christian sedition that were cut from the final film, including Marcellus's denial that he is a seditionist or that he is personally engaged in a plot to overthrow the state.[17] (Instead, Marcellus says that Christians as a group are not engaged in such a plot, an explanation reminiscent of Communist leaders' failed defense of Communism in the Smith Act prosecutions.) Moreover, in a scene in which Marcellus is transported back to Rome to face trial, Maltz includes a line of dialogue that appears to be precisely the kind of "subversive propaganda" that made HUAC appoint itself media watchdog. In the scene a young boy brings dinner to Marcellus's cabin but is asked by the guard whether the prisoner hadn't already received a tray of food. When the boy protests that he is simply following the captain's orders, the guard responds, "What a fine world it'd be if there *were* no captains."[18] Although the line itself is a throwaway, its egalitarian sentiment and its apparent reference to classless society make it similar to the examples of Communist propaganda that HUAC's "friendly witnesses" attested to in 1947. In its own way it is not unlike the "Share and share alike" line from *Tender Comrade* that Lela Rogers found so objectionable.

Likewise, although the film includes Tiberius's charge to find the names of Christians, as well as Abidor's role as informant, it cuts some scenes that further develop the "naming names" motif. For example, in scene 204 of Maltz's screenplay Marcellus pays Abidor a coin for every name the latter gives him to add to his list.[19] Scenes 221 and 222 show Marcellus writing the names of early Christians on a parchment scroll. Maltz's description even includes an insert in which the audience sees four names listed at the bottom of the scroll.[20] Finally, scene 244 of Maltz's screenplay shows Marcellus burning his scroll in a campfire outside his tent:

CAMERA MOVES IN STILL CLOSER. As the flames eat at the paper, it writhes with the heat, and, for a moment, turns toward the camera. We catch a glimpse of part of the list of names

> Reuben . . . Weaver
> James . . . Fisherman

And then the names turn black under the flames.[21]

There are two ways we might account for these changes between Maltz's first draft and Dunne's finished screenplay. One possibility is that some lines and scenes were undoubtedly cut owing to considerations of length. Maltz's screenplay ran 277 pages, and much of Dunne's work on the project involved drastically cutting and reshaping Maltz's material. In comparison, Dunne's final draft of *The Robe* ran only 141 pages.[22] That, however, does not adequately explain why these specific elements were cut. While considerations of length offer a fairly benign reason for the changes in Maltz's script, they do not account for *all* of the revisions, nor do they negate the possibility that these changes were made on political grounds. Indeed, if one ascribes agency to Dunne in shaping the meanings of the text, then one must grant the possibility that Dunne cut these elements to *obscure* the script's political subtext rather than to clarify and illuminate it.

Although my conclusions on this question are tentative, it does not appear that Dunne deliberately sought to becloud *The Robe*'s political subtext. Many of the elements cited above were taken over by Dunne in his drafts of the screenplay and were only cut during the very late stages of the revision process. For example, in his working script dated June 26, 1952, which is more than a hundred pages shorter than Maltz's draft, Dunne cuts the aforementioned line about "captains" but reworks the insert of Marcellus's scroll so that the camera shows him adding Miriam's name to the list in a "shaky sprawling hand."[23] Similarly, Dunne reworked some of the scenes Maltz had written between Marcellus and Abidor but in a manner that preserves the characterization of the latter as a greedy informant. Scene 98, for example, shows Abidor dictating names for Marcellus's scroll:

> *Abidor*
> Benjamin and his wife, farmer
> Marcellus dips his pen in the ink and writes.
> *Abidor*
> Justus, the weaver. It is said he is the leader.
> CLOSE SHOT—Insert
> The list, as Marcellus writes the names.
> *Abidor's voice*
> Hariph, the potter. His daughter, Rachel

Although these sequences appear in Dunne's late drafts of *The Robe*, they were eliminated by the time the shooting script was completed, thereby making the reasons for their exclusion much more difficult to discern.

A more pertinent question, perhaps, is whether Dunne actually understood *The Robe* as a blacklist allegory. Unfortunately the historical record here raises more questions than it answers. Although Dunne does not specifically address *The Robe*'s political subtext in his autobiography, there is at least some evidence that he saw the film as a Cold War allegory. George Custen notes that Dunne pitched the idea of making George Orwell's *1984* to Zanuck by saying, "We could make another *The Robe*, set in the future instead of the past."[24] The problem, as Custen points out, is that Dunne saw these projects as being antitotalitarian, as much against Communism as they were against HUAC. In fact, when one considers the popularity of Orwell's *Animal Farm* as an anti-Communist allegory, one might be inclined to prefer the former reading to the latter. If this is the case, then Dunne's intentions would accord more with Maria Wyke's reading of *The Robe* as a film that defends Christianity as a weapon in the war against Communism. Since the issue of Dunne's intentions gives rise to two seemingly opposed interpretations, one is tempted to ignore the issue altogether as hopelessly confused.

If this complicated chronology and the role of the source novel have prob-lematized an allegorical interpretation based on Maltz's intentions, is there another way we might understand *The Robe* as allegory? The obvious candi-date for an alternative explanation lies in reception theory. According to this line of argument, the process of encoding allegorical utterances has little or no bearing on the meanings created in the process of decoding these structures. Historical, social, and cultural contexts create the conditions for such *allegore-sis*, which in the case of historical films and fictions, involve the understanding of analogies between past and present. As I indicated earlier in this chapter, one can readily adduce this kind of allegorical interpretation in the long-term reception of *The Robe* among film scholars. But are traces of this allegorical framework evident in the contemporaneous reception of the film?

Although it is always difficult to assert and prove a negative proposition, my answer to this question is a qualified no. Rather, as Maria Wyke points out, the technological novelty of CinemaScope overwhelmed the contempo-raneous reception of *The Robe,* such that reviews offer virtually no consid-eration of the film's subtexts.[25] This appears to be true even in publications that one might expect to read the film as a form of political commentary. The review in *Commonweal,* a journal edited by John Cogley, one of the most important early historians of the blacklist, is typical. In the review's first three paragraphs Philip T. Hartung discusses the decision to make *The Robe* in CinemaScope. This is followed by a brief plot synopsis and an assessment of the film's performances. The review concludes by praising the tastefulness and dignity of its depiction of Christ but also complains that the film is not as stirring as it might be owing to director Henry Koster's unfa-miliarity with the new technology.[26] This avoidance of political subtext is evident despite the fact that the same issue of *Commonweal* begins with a discussion of European reactions to McCarthyism and concludes with a book review that addresses the relationship between Communism and reli-gious institutions.

The one major exception to this pattern was, not surprisingly, the review of *The Robe* in the *Daily Worker.* Nearly four months after the film's pre-miere, staff writer Ben Levine published his initial reaction to the biblical spectacle as he watched it in his neighborhood theater:

> The parallels with our own time, it must be admitted, will not be drawn
> by everyone, or even by the majority in our country, and we can be sure
> that the Hollywood producers never intended them to be so drawn. But
> I, for one, could not help thinking of our own Smith Act judges, and of
> the Judge of Ethel and Julius Rosenberg in the scene where Pontius
> Pilate, made absent-minded by his uneasiness, asks for water to wash

Figure 6. Although it is not indicative of the more general critical reception of *The Robe*, the reviewer for the *Daily Worker* specifically called attention to this scene, where the Roman tribune Marcellus pays an informer for the names of Christians. The reviewer claimed that the fat merchant, played by Leon Askin, resembled Whittaker Chambers, the chief witness in the Alger Hiss case.

hands he had just washed thoroughly; or when the argument is given that the proper Roman authorities have already decided that Jesus was guilty and it is treason to question the decision.

And when Gaius Marcellus, in "seeking the names" of Christians, pays a coin per name to a spy, that spy, a fat merchant, looked to me the very image of Whittaker Chambers.[27]

The *Daily Worker* review, and particularly its reference to the scene in which Marcellus and Abidor exchange payment for names (fig. 6), undoubtedly diverged from the pattern found in more mainstream journalistic criticism, but Levine's comments were consistent with the newspaper's editorial line on Hollywood biblical epics as a whole. In an earlier piece on *Quo Vadis*, David Platt makes observations quite similar to those of Levine and additionally cites a much earlier account of "the struggle between the corrupt Roman Empire and subversive Christianity" written by Marx's collaborator, Friedrich Engels, incorporating about eight paragraphs of Engels's prose into his review.[28] This conception of Christians as radicals was further reflected in an Art Young political cartoon first published in *The Masses* in 1917 and later republished in July of 1953, just two months before *The Robe*'s premiere. The cartoon is drawn in the style of a "Wanted" poster, and it depicts Jesus as an outlaw sought on charges of "sedition, criminal anarchy, vagrancy, and conspiring to overthrow the established government."[29]

Besides focusing on CinemaScope as a new widescreen technology, contemporaneous accounts of *The Robe*'s production also effaced Maltz's contribution. Early reports on the film (circa 1945) noted the participation of Maltz, who replaced the first screenwriter on the project, Ernest Vajda.[30] After Maltz completed his work on the script, *The Robe* remained in pre-production limbo until 1948, when Frank Ross announced that RKO was finally ready to make the picture with Victor Fleming and Gregory Peck as the film's director and star respectively. Ross also announced that he hired Maxwell Anderson and Andrew Solt to do the screenplay adaptation despite the fact that he already had Maltz's completed script in hand.[31] The project met another roadblock, though, when RKO canceled the production less than a month later citing the project's $4.5 million budget as too large an expenditure for the studio. After some legal wrangling, *The Robe* landed at 20th Century–Fox when Darryl Zanuck bought out RKO's interest in the project. In a 1952 article detailing the producer's ten-year struggle to bring *The Robe* to the screen, Ross claims that he was not able to hire a top screenwriter during the early 1940s because "most of the good ones were in the service." Ross goes on to say that several lesser-known writers worked on the project until he wrote a scenario himself and hired Philip Dunne to "do a polishing job."[32] This press report corroborates the account of the production offered in Dunne's autobiography and it further points to Ross's role in preventing Maltz from gaining screen credit. In Ross's statements to the press Maltz had gone from an artistic collaborator in 1945 to one of a group of lesser-knowns in 1952, this despite the fact that Maltz had written *Destination, Tokyo* (1943), *Pride of the Marines* (1945), and Ross's own Oscar-winning short, *The House I Live In* (1945). Interestingly, the notes for a 1980 screening of *The Robe* further befog Maltz's involvement by excerpting Dunne's account from *Take Two*, editing it in such a way that it fails to mention the blacklist at all.[33]

Does all of this mean we must reject an allegorical interpretation of *The Robe?* Actually, I think not. Indeed, the strongest evidence to support this model of allegorical interpretation comes not from the possible or deliberate references to anti-Communist repression in the screenplay but to Maltz's implicit conception of Rome as an empire founded on political repression that disregarded constitutional checks and balances to hold power. In his notes for *The Robe* Maltz cited several passages from a book entitled *The Ancient World*. A passage describing the empire's treatment of conquered territories reads: "Rome strictly *isolated* the subject communities from one another. She dissolved all tribal confederacies; she took skillful advantage of the grades of inferiority that she had created among her dependents to *foment jealousies* and to play off one class of communities against another. Likewise, within each city, she set class against class, on the whole favoring an aristocratic organization. In politics as in war, the policy of her statesmen was *'Divide and Conquer.'"*[34] With such a conception of Rome as an underlying element of *The Robe*, one can readily understand how it took on specific political resonance as a text that paralleled anti-Communist policies aimed at America's radical left between 1947 and 1953.

Indeed, the very vagueness of Maltz's notes and research permit a range of possible interpretations of *The Robe*'s subtext. By equating Rome's persecution of Christians with a more generalized notion of political repression, Maltz's dramatic concept was flexible and capacious enough to support myriad readings. Thus, although it is logical to see Maltz's script as an indictment of Italian fascism when it was written in 1945, the changes in the political landscape after World War II make it equally logical to see the 1953 film as either a defense of the Hollywood Ten or as a critique of religious repression in Communist countries. It all depends on the critic's moral intuition about whether Communists are the oppressed or the oppressor, and how the critic then mobilizes topical reference points to frame his or her reading of pertinent events in the film.[35]

In sum, although *The Robe* certainly makes sense as a Cold War parable, that interpretation is supported more by the adaptability of Maltz's scenario than it is by anything in the film's production. Most of the elements cited in support of an allegorical reading of *The Robe* turn out to be far more complicated than first thought. It is true, for example, that the film was coauthored by a blacklisted writer, but that writer's participation in the project occurred before the blacklist was even instituted. It is also true that *The Robe* contains certain textual elements that appear to reference the blacklist, but the early drafts of the screenplay contained many other possible allusions that were gradually eliminated in the revision process. Finally, while Philip Dunne's liberalism and his early defense of the Hollywood Ten may well have encouraged him to see *The Robe* as a scenario of Cold War repression, it appears that he saw the film as being as much a critique of Stalinist totalitarianism as it was a critique of anti-Communism.

The constitutive ambiguity of *The Robe*'s scenario may well have encouraged Maltz himself to reconsider his script's implications in the period immediately after he was blacklisted. In a 1948 speech Maltz spoke of a slippery slope that is established by the illegal and unjust treatment of suspected Communists. It may well have been *The Robe* that Maltz thought of when he warned that soon HUAC will be asking all Americans, "Are you now or have you ever been a Christian?"[36] In making this comment, Maltz may well have been "flipping the frame" for his own script.

SPARTACUS AND THE BLACKLISTEE AS SYMBOL OF
TRUE AMERICANISM

Spartacus, the story of a legendary Roman slave revolt, was released by
Universal-International (U-I) in September of 1960.[37] About a month prior
to the release, Murray Schumach of the *New York Times* reported that U-I
had decided to give blacklisted writer Dalton Trumbo screen credit for
authoring the film's script.[38] *Spartacus* thus became the first Hollywood
film since the 1947 Waldorf agreement to reach the screen with the name
of a blacklisted writer. Although Trumbo's participation in Otto Preminger's
adaptation of *Exodus* (1960) was announced earlier that year, *Spartacus*
was, in fact, the first of these two films to go through the Writer's Guild
arbitration process, the first to face the threatened pickets by the American
Legion and other patriotic organizations, and the first to take on the economic risks entailed by the involvement of a suspected Communist. The
impetus for "breaking" the blacklist appears to have come from Kirk
Douglas, *Spartacus*'s producer and star, but it could not have been accomplished without the support of the film's distributor, Universal-
International. U-I had initially considered releasing the film without any
screenwriter credit, as Allied Artists did with William Wyler's *Friendly
Persuasion* (1957), and only assented to Douglas's wishes after careful consideration of the economic impact of Trumbo's credit.[39]

Because of Trumbo's open participation, the reception of *Spartacus* displays an awareness of the film's relation to the Hollywood blacklist in a
way that was definitely not the case for *The Robe*. Whereas the blacklist
was merely part of the immediate historical context for *The Robe*, *Spartacus*
became a part of that history in a manner that journalists and film reviewers could scarcely ignore. More important, Dalton Trumbo's connection to
Spartacus encouraged an allegorical reading of the film similar to that of its
predecessor. Indeed, in *The Dream Life*, J. Hoberman describes *Spartacus* as
"ready-made for Cold War allegory," not only because of Trumbo's involvement in the production but also because of "the prestige that its protagonist
enjoyed in the Communist world."[40]

The allegorical treatment of *Spartacus* activates roughly the same set of
binary oppositions as those found in the readings of *The Robe* (see table 7).
Maria Wyke's analysis of *Spartacus* is perhaps the chief example of this
type of allegorical reading strategy. As Wyke notes, two particular elements
of *Spartacus* lend themselves to an allegorical treatment of the blacklist.
The first is the film's representation of the slave rebel's camp, which according to Wyke, is "presented as a kind of utopian, proto-Communist society
peopled by whole families who share their work and meager possessions

Table 7 *Spartacus* as Blacklist Allegory

Past	Present
Ancient Rome	USA
Slaves	Communists
Crassus	J. Parnell Thomas
Roman Senate	HUAC
Lists of the disloyal	Waldorf Statement
Crucifixions	Blacklisting

along with a common aspiration to equality and liberation from slave-labor."[41] The second is the famous scene in which Crassus (Lawrence Olivier) confronts Gracchus (Charles Laughton) in the darkened chamber of the Roman Senate. As the victor in the film's political infighting, Crassus reports on the measures taken to ensure loyalty to the empire: "The enemies of the state are known. Arrests are in progress. The prisons begin to fill. In every city and province, lists of the disloyal have been compiled. Tomorrow they will learn the costs of their terrible folly, their treason." With dialogue about treason and lists, one can readily see this scene as a reference to Trumbo's own experience before HUAC and to the personal costs he paid for his purported "disloyalty." Indeed, on the Criterion Voyager DVD edition of *Spartacus*, Kirk Douglas himself describes the scene as Trumbo's "little joke."[42]

Echoing Hoberman's brief description of *Spartacus*, Wyke also points out that its title character carried an awful lot of ideological baggage by the time of the film's production. Spartacus's revolt had been dramatized several times before Trumbo's version, and in each instance, the figure served as an emblem of either national identity, revolutionary consciousness, or class conflict. Bernard Joseph Saurin's tragedy *Spartacus* was first performed in France in 1760 and was later revived during the French Revolution, when it functioned as a commentary on current political events. Later, Raffaelo Giovagnoli's novel *Spartaco*, published in 1874, drew parallels between Spartacus's revolt and the military heroism of Garibaldi. As a figure from Roman antiquity, Spartacus was thus linked to emerging nineteenth-century conceptions of Italian nationalism.[43] Karl Marx himself espoused his admiration for Spartacus's military campaign and described him in a letter to Friedrich Engels as a "genuine exponent of the ancient proletariat."[44] After the publication of Lenin's and Stalin's writings on Spartacus in the

1930s, there was, in Wyke's words, "a constant stream of Marxist historical writings on ancient slavery in the Soviet Union," which canonized Spartacus as a symbol of political revolution for many decades to come.[45]

It was quite specifically this latter conception of Spartacus that informed the Howard Fast novel on which Douglas's film was based. As Fast relates in his autobiography, *Being Red* (1990), he first started thinking about Spartacus while serving prison time following his appearance before HUAC. In deciding to recount the story of Spartacus's slave revolt, Fast hoped to popularize the image of someone he knew to be a Marxist icon of class struggle. In fact, in an episode in the novel after the rebels' monumental victory at Vesuvius, Spartacus gives a speech that echoes the phraseology of *The Communist Manifesto*, urging the "slaves of the world" to "rise up and cast off your chains."[46]

Given the popular association of Spartacus with Marxism, Douglas and U-I faced several potential public relations problems in deciding to make their film. Although complaints about the subject matter could be deflected by emphasizing Spartacus's place within classical antiquity, one could not so easily explain Fast's and Trumbo's involvement. The combination of these factors made a difficult situation that much worse.

In order to combat the likely protests of groups like the American Legion, Douglas's production company, Bryna, sought to link *Spartacus* to American traditions of civil liberty and freedom, a strategy that had already been successfully employed by American abolitionists during the 1830s. Bryna's Stan Marguilies, who was tracking possible protests, obtained a copy of a letter about *Spartacus* being circulated nationally to Legion posts. Attached to the Legion letter was a letter from Marguilies to Bryna management that stated, "It [the Legion letter] is an interesting document both in what it says and the action it implies. I think it provides us plenty of room to defend the picture—if a defense should be needed—on the grounds of its content rather than on contributing personnel."[47]

This is precisely what Bryna did. Months before *Spartacus* was released, Kirk Douglas replied to angry letters regarding Trumbo's employment by stressing the film's weighty themes. Douglas's response to one J. David Johnson was typical: "The movie speaks not only for itself, but for all of us here at Bryna who had a hand in making it. I hope you will see it and then I know you will agree with me that it is a courageous and positive statement about mankind's most cherished goal—freedom."[48] Likewise, a *Spartacus* study guide, published with U-I's participation and designed for circulation in schools, said, "The struggle for freedom, both physical and spiritual, has long interested writers in many lands, and among the fighters for freedom Spartacus for more than two thousand years has remained one of its greatest symbols."[49]

Not surprisingly, reviews of the film picked up on these ideas, which were circulated through Bryna's publicity. *Time* said specifically of Trumbo that he "imparted to *Spartacus* a passion for freedom and the men who live and die for it—a passion that transcends all politics."[50] The *Hollywood Reporter* said, "There is nothing more subversive in 'Spartacus' than contained in the Bill of Rights and the Fourteenth Amendment."[51] Perhaps the most important gesture of public support came from President Kennedy, who crossed American Legion picket lines in Washington, D.C., to attend *Spartacus*.[52] The notion that *Spartacus* presented a particularly American ideal of human freedom was supported by a clever aspect of the film's casting. As Douglas points out in his commentary on Criterion's *Spartacus* DVD, he deliberately used American actors to portray the Roman slaves and English actors to play Roman generals, senators, and patricians. Although Douglas claims that this was done to highlight the class differences depicted in the film, it also serves to highlight America's relation to the British Empire as a particular subtext of *Spartacus*'s image of political revolt.[53]

By the end of 1960, *Exodus* and *Spartacus* occupied the number one and number two spots on *Variety*'s weekly box-office chart, positions that the two films would exchange throughout the early months of 1961. The irony of emphasizing *Spartacus*'s theme of freedom was that Bryna had effectively recast Spartacus as an American hero rather than a Marxist one. When blacklisting began in 1947, it was to keep subversive material, such as *Spartacus*, from reaching American movie screens. In fact, even in 1960 some felt that *Spartacus* was precisely the type of story that threatened American security and thus justified HUAC's incursion on American civil liberties.[54] However, because the American Legion focused on the politics of *Spartacus*'s personnel rather than its subject matter, Bryna used the film's depiction of revolt to deflect criticism of Trumbo's involvement.

Bryna's emphasis on freedom, though, had a curious side effect. Dalton Trumbo, who had been considered "un-American" in 1947, emerged as an American hero in 1960. The *Hollywood Reporter* said of *Exodus*'s New York premiere: "The biggest surprise of the evening came during the credits when spontaneous applause went to script writer Dalton Trumbo."[55] Furthermore, on April 9, 1961, the Teacher's Union honored Trumbo with its Teachers Union Award, saying his "creative gifts as a writer and stalwart stand against the Un-American blacklist have enriched our culture."[56] Ironically, the ceremony took place at the Waldorf Astoria Hotel, where thirteen and a half years earlier, the major studios had declared Trumbo "unemployable."

For Trumbo the validation of his career must have seemed bittersweet. In his own mind neither his politics nor his approach to screenwriting had changed since 1947. Beyond that, he also continued his commitment to American civil liberties, his opposition to domestic fascism, and his resistance to political censorship, all of them beliefs that had underpinned his ill-fated defense before HUAC. Paradoxically, the same rhetoric used to prosecute Trumbo during the Cold War was now invoked to identify him as a champion of free speech.

More than that, Trumbo's screen credit for *Spartacus* had come only after he waged an acrimonious and sometimes bitter struggle to preserve his view of the character. The script had been effectively rewritten by committee during the film's production with Douglas, producer Edward Lewis, director Stanley Kubrick, and costars Peter Ustinov and Charles Laughton making contributions on the set. Trumbo, who as a blacklisted writer was mostly denied access to the set, had serious reservations about the effect of these rewrites on the dramatic conception of the film. After seeing a rough cut of *Spartacus*, he summarized his objections in a now famous eighty page memo to the producers. In a marvelous demonstration of "frame-switching," Trumbo argued that the problems with the film boiled down to an inherent tension between two opposed perspectives on the protagonist. First, there was Trumbo's view of the "large Spartacus," who was a vitally important historical figure, a brilliant military strategist, and a rebel slave whose insurrection shook the Roman Empire to its foundations. Second, there was the "small Spartacus," a view of the character as a more marginal figure, whose rebellion was more like a jailbreak and an attempted escape to freedom. The former was a figure who openly challenged Rome's class and political structures; the latter was a figure who cared only for his personal gain and whose revolt embarrassed Rome's leaders, who then used Spartacus as a political tool in their own schemes.[57]

In making his case for the "large Spartacus," Trumbo indicates that his script employs one of the two basic strategies used in allegorical discourse, namely personification. As Ismail Xavier points out, this technique goes back at least to the time of Greek philosophers, who read narrative agents allegorically as "bodily equivalents for abstract thought."[58] For Trumbo the "large Spartacus" was not a symbol of the United States or even Rome but nonetheless served a similar function by embodying the traits, values, and hopes of the proletariat. As an individual character who represented the experience of thousands of oppressed persons throughout history, Trumbo's Spartacus took part in the ongoing class struggle for economic and political equality that could be—but need not be—viewed as Marxist in origin. In this respect Trumbo's overall conception complements the elements of blacklist allegory that crop up in specific sequences of the film.

As Bernard Dick notes, Trumbo's fight for the "large Spartacus" suggests his desire to use the film as a politically educative project.[59] Yet I contend that it also paralleled his own personal crusade to end the blacklist, a goal itself approached through two seemingly contradictory strategies that mirrored the debate about *Spartacus*'s hero. On one hand, there was a kind of "large Spartacus" way of opposing the blacklist. This consisted of making outraged speeches, offering public pronouncements on Hollywood's hypocrisy, and even making left-wing films outside of the normal production and distribution channels in Hollywood. Herbert Biberman's film *Salt of the Earth* is an example of the latter, but it achieved a certain ignominy as a project that was crushed by Hollywood's powerful, concerted, and carefully orchestrated efforts to prevent the film from being seen. As the *Salt of the Earth* fiasco demonstrated, it is debatable whether open opposition to the blacklist made any measurable political gains or simply hardened right-wing opposition to Hollywood Communism.

Trumbo himself showed little interest in making grand gestures against the blacklist. In fact, as a black market screenwriter, he found it imprudent to badmouth his employers or to question their motives. Instead, Trumbo adopted a more pragmatic strategy and sought to work toward ending the blacklist by making his work ever more valuable to the independent producers who employed him. In Trumbo's view, the blacklist would only end when the interests of the industry finally coincided with the interests of those blacklisted. Producers wanted films that accumulated accolades and box-office revenues. By providing scripts that met those objectives, black market writers moved ever closer to the day when their value to the industry would outweigh their liability as a public relations risk. Wrote Trumbo, "The blacklist will not be broken by the triumph of morality over immorality. It will not be broken by the triumph of one organization over another organization. It will be broken by the sheer excellence of the work of two or three blacklisted writers."[60] (Not coincidentally, the three writers Trumbo had in mind were himself, Albert Maltz, and Michael Wilson, who publicly fought his own war against the industry in trying to get screen credit for his preblacklist script for *Friendly Persuasion*.)[61]

Although the "large Spartacus" strategy was largely ineffective, there was a "small Spartacus" approach to the blacklist that was closer to a covert guerilla attack on Hollywood. Instead of defiantly meeting the blacklist head-on, the "small Spartacus" approach nibbled at its edges and sought to use the film industry's power against itself by letting Hollywood reveal its own hypocrisy. When that hypocrisy was revealed, it was Hollywood, rather than the black market writers they employed, who would have to answer questions from the press and American public. For an example of a "small Spartacus" approach to opposing the blacklist, there is no better than Trumbo's own "Robert Rich" affair on *The Brave One* (1956).

On the same night that *Friendly Persuasion* lost the Academy Award for Best Screenplay Adaptation to *Around the World in 80 Days* (1956), Dalton Trumbo won the Oscar for the Best Original Story for *The Brave One*, a black market script he had written under the alias "Robert Rich." Trumbo took the name as an inside joke, because the film's producers, the King Brothers, had a nephew named Robert Rich who worked for them as a messenger. When Rich was announced as the winner, no one came to the stage to accept the award. In the midst of the confusion, Jesse Lasky Jr., vice president of the Screen Writers Guild, accepted the award on Rich's behalf, who he claimed was at the hospital for the birth of his first child. Adding to the confusion was the fact that the King Brothers' nephew, Robert Rich, had called the Academy earlier that day hoping to wheedle free tickets to the ceremony, apparently confirming the existence of the phantom screenwriter.[62]

Reporters quickly seized on the question of Rich's true identity. On April 1, 1957, the *New York Times* suggested that "Robert Rich" was in fact a pseudonym for a blacklisted writer. Two days later, Trumbo was on the front page of *Variety* refusing to either confirm or deny that he was Rich.[63] Meanwhile, producer Frank King insisted that Robert Rich did exist but was unable to attend the Oscars because he was performing military service in Europe.[64] Far from clarifying the situation, the press's speculation only deepened its mystery.

Unable to identify the true author, the King Brothers faced plagiarism suits from some five different people claiming Rich stole the idea for the story. According to the King Brothers, these suits had no basis, but unless Trumbo testified that he was Rich, they could not fight them. Although they considered such suits a form of blackmail, the King Brothers settled the first of them for $750,000 just thirteen days after the Oscars.[65] To quell further speculation, the King Brothers asked Trumbo to be interviewed by Los Angeles newsman Bill Stout on April 10, 1957. During the interview Trumbo admitted that he had been working on the black market for years and claimed that he had received Oscar nominations but refused to specify which films had been nominated. When asked about allegations that he was Rich, Trumbo once again refused to either confirm or deny.[66] As Trumbo put it, his evasion of the question allowed him to dissociate himself from

bad films that he had written while, at the same time, linking himself to
excellent films with which he actually had no connection.

By the end of 1957 the incident achieved enough notoriety that CBS
planned a comedy based on Robert Rich for early in the week of the 1958
Academy Awards.[67] Recognizing the public interest in Rich, Trumbo
planned to use the controversy as a way to receive screen credit. At the
time, Trumbo was writing *Mr. Adam* for the King Brothers under the pseudonym of "Beth Fincher." If the King Brothers agreed, Trumbo's scheme
called for them to keep the pseudonym throughout the film's cutting,
advance publicity, and press screening. "However," Trumbo wrote, "on the
night the picture opens, there will be a switch. The credit will read: screenplay by Robert Rich." Trumbo suggested that the movie's ads would feature
a drawing of the enigmatic Oscar winner. He also suggested that title
designer Saul Bass could sketch the Oscar itself for the ads, which would be
shown "covering its eyes with its two hands. Or in some other kind of
secretive or furtive pose . . . peering back at the imaginary Rich."[68] Trumbo
hoped the resulting publicity furor would culminate with the revelation
that he was Robert Rich. Unfortunately, *Mr. Adam* had so many problems
with censors that it was never produced.

Trumbo's playful manipulation of the Rich affair makes it a quintessential example of what Michel de Certeau describes as a tactic. For de Certeau,
a tactic is a means of contesting existing power structures through trickery
and legerdemain: "It [the tactic] must vigilantly make use of the cracks that
particular conjunctions open in the surveillance of the proprietary powers.
It poaches in them. It creates surprises in them. It can be where it is least
expected. It is a guileful ruse."[69] The tactic is an art of the weak, but it is
precisely this dissembling quality that endows it with political effectiveness. The tactic achieves political gains by causing power to turn in on itself
and by exposing the fault lines that exist within power structures.
Commenting on the Rich controversy, the *Louisville Gazette-Courier*
described it in terms reminiscent of de Certeau: "Now, perhaps, the official
recognition that some of the film colony's best writers cannot even
acknowledge their work may kill the blacklisting system by ridicule, since
more elevated weapons have failed."[70]

At the height of the Rich affair, Trumbo also publicized the existence of
the black market through two articles he had written for *The Nation* and
Frontier respectively. The first of these articles portrayed the Hollywood
black market as a thriving underground enterprise, one whose very existence proved that the blacklist had not stopped members of the Hollywood
Ten from working in the industry.[71] More than that, the article also argued

that if black market scripts were winning the industry's top awards, then exactly how subversive were the screenwriters who were blacklisted. By demonstrating the blacklist's impracticality and irrationality, Trumbo showed that Communists in Hollywood were never really a threat in the first place.

The second article was entitled "Who Is Robert Rich?" It treats Rich as an everyman, a handy icon of all those blacklisted from their chosen professions. In a particularly eloquent passage Trumbo writes: "Out of this morass of censorship, of suppression, of inquisition, of proscription which is today's official American policy—out of this swamp has risen a dim figure who has done something, who has even won something, yet who cautiously and cunningly refuses to emerge from those mists which obscure his hunting grounds and veil him from his enemies. Robert Rich, therefore, is the generic name of all persons who must somehow escape their individual identities if they are to continue working at their chosen professions. As such, he has as many faces as the blacklist itself."[72]

By downplaying Rich's comical origins, Trumbo elevates Rich to an almost tragic dimension as a symbol of all the blacklist's faceless victims. More important, in doing so, Trumbo also turns Rich into the "large Spartacus" envisioned in his screenplay.

Indeed, although Trumbo never mentions it in his own writings, it seems that the Rich affair may have informed one of the most famous scenes in his screenplay for *Spartacus*. After Crassus's victory over the rebels, he promises his prisoners that their lives will be spared if they identify which among them is Spartacus. The film then cuts to brief close-ups of Antoninus (Tony Curtis) and Spartacus in succession. After an extreme long shot of the prisoners the film returns to a close-up of Spartacus. Just as he begins to stand to identify himself, the film cuts to a long shot of the crowd with Spartacus, Antoninus, and David (Harold J. Stone) in the foreground (fig. 7). Before Spartacus can speak, first Antoninus and then David proclaim, "I'm Spartacus." Kubrick then cuts to a close-up of Spartacus's reaction as he overhears another rebel claim himself as Spartacus and realizes that his comrades in arms will not betray him. In a series of long shots and medium shots, four more rebel slaves proclaim, "I'm Spartacus." Kubrick then returns to the extreme long shot of the rebels as hundreds of voices claiming to be Spartacus become a deafening din in the ears of the Romans.

The sequence lends itself to conventional blacklist allegory by establishing parallels between Crassus's offer of clemency and the pressures on HUAC witnesses to name names, but it is also possible that the scene had a more idiosyncratic and highly personal significance for Trumbo. Some

Figure 7. Although some critics view the famous "I am Spartacus" scene as a straightforward celebration of those who courageously refused to "name names," it also tacitly endorses Dalton Trumbo's own use of deception and misdirection to mock and ridicule the blacklist's mendacity.

three years after the controversy had ended, the question of "Who is Robert Rich?" is answered with "I am Spartacus." As Peter Hanson observes:

> Aside from its dramatic importance in the film, the scene is notable for its perfect representation of Trumbo's vision of personal honor. It involves a rebel hero poised to take responsibility for his actions, and acolytes so moved by his dignity that they offer themselves in sacrifice. Spartacus's soldiers are infected with the sense of honor displayed by their leader. Because Trumbo was ever willing to make grand displays himself—his defiance before HUAC; his model behavior in jail; his principled stands on behalf of unjustly accused individuals; even his controversial "only victims" speech—the moment when the slaves put themselves between death and Spartacus is inspirational on myriad levels.[73]

Monica Silveira Cyrino echoes Hanson's equation of Crassus's offer of clemency with HUAC's interrogation tactics, stating bluntly, "The scene recalls and celebrates the heroism of artists who refused to 'name names' when ordered by the committee to inform on their associates, and so faced the vindictive reprisals of incarceration and the blacklist."[74]

By demonstrating their unity in the face of death and their collective hunger for freedom, these rebel slaves, each in his own small way, embodied the heroic spirit Trumbo envisioned for the "large Spartacus." They achieved it, though, through the denials and evasion that made the Rich affair such an effective weapon in the first place. Trumbo championed the idea of a "large Spartacus" as a figure who might educate and inspire the masses, but he achieved his greatest political gains as a "small Spartacus," a gadfly that used the blacklist's secrecy to mock and ridicule Hollywood's mendacity. By framing *Spartacus* as Trumbo's response to the blacklist, the film's critical reception hints at larger questions regarding the way it was ultimately broken.

CONCLUSION

Using *The Robe* and *Spartacus* as case studies, I have argued that allegorical interpretations of the blacklist—and the models for making sense of them—draw on rather basic aspects of cognition, such as framing and pattern seeking. In the case of the historical film, the analogical equation of present and past is the central semantic field and thus serves to organize the text's patterns of extended metaphor. In each film the presence of a social outlier group (early Christians in *The Robe* and Roman slaves in *Spartacus*) enables the critic to ally this faction with suspected Communists. This comparison is given further support in each film through scenes that provide loose correspondences between real and fictional events, especially those showing Romans instructing their underlings to gather names of the disloyal.

The fact that each film was written by a blacklisted writer further enables the critic to appeal to authorial intention as a warrant for their interpretation. As I have noted, such appeals do not require veridical status to become salient. Emphasizing the role of pragmatics that is a common aspect of framing effects research, the critic merely needs to infer the intent of the author for it to function as part of the analyst's rhetorical strategy. In blacklist allegories these intentions are usually ascribed to blacklisted writers, particularly those working on the black market, who were thought to offer disguised commentary on the industry's politics.

Whereas this model of allegorical significance is one implicitly questioned by poststructuralist critiques of authorship, it is also a model that doesn't work very well for the films discussed in this chapter. Of the two, *Spartacus* is the only film for which there is some evidence that the blacklisted writer who worked on the project sought to encode the text with allegorical significance. Trumbo may not have wanted to make the film an overt political lesson, but it seems quite clear from the historical record that he desired to elevate Spartacus to an almost mythic status as a leftist emblem of class struggle and political revolution.[75] More important, some of Trumbo's collaborators, like producer-star Kirk Douglas, claim that certain key scenes of *Spartacus* contain dialogue references to the blacklist's politics. Picking up on these cues, reviewers consistently highlighted

Spartacus's themes of freedom and political revolt and, on occasion, even linked these to screenwriter Dalton Trumbo's participation in the film. In its critique of slavery and its depiction of the thirst for freedom, *Spartacus* seemed so quintessentially American that it encouraged some reviewers to ask why the blacklist had silenced Trumbo for nearly thirteen years.

The production history of *The Robe*, however, raises more questions about the authors' intentions than it answers. Although the adaptation of Lloyd C. Douglas's novel involved the participation of a blacklisted writer and a noted Hollywood liberal, the final film was based on a six-year-old script written well before its author was blacklisted. Thus, while it is tempting to interpret both films as allegories of the Cold War and the Hollywood blacklist, it is extremely unlikely that Albert Maltz or Frank Ross could have envisioned the allegorical significance that *The Robe* would take on when released during the height of the Cold War. Moreover, in the case of *The Robe* any traces of allegorical significance were mostly absent in the film's contemporaneous reception. Besides offering standard evaluations of performances, production values, and narrative interest, reviews typically called attention to CinemaScope enhancement of the film's spectacle as well as to its dignified, tasteful, and sensitive depiction of Jesus Christ. The majority of allegorical interpretations of *The Robe* did not appear until several years after the film's release, most coming after Maltz's participation in the film became publicly known.

The fact that many critics abstained from reading *The Robe* as blacklist allegory raises a larger question by reminding us that allegorical interpretations often adopt the rhetoric of analogical argument. This is symptomatically illustrated by the language commonly used by critics to express allegorical meanings ("This film is an implicit critique of . . ."; "The movie makes the case for . . ."). It also begs the question, however, of whether allegories, in fact, are a valid form of analogical argument. When the differences detected in the implied comparison outweigh the similarities, should one still accept the critic's framing of the text as allegory? Or should we see this move as something largely activated by the film's relationship with its historical context? In the next chapters we will examine this question more fully by exploring westerns and science fiction films as blacklist allegories. In each case we will confront an important issue: to what extent do the conventions and meanings associated with these genres reshape the films' rhetorical strategies as blacklist allegories?

6 Roaming the Plains along the "New Frontier"

The Western as Allegory of the Blacklist and the Cold War

As *Time* magazine's review of the 1952 western *California Conquest* notes, the plot covers a period between 1825 and 1841, when "Mexico-ruled California was torn by internal strife, and Russia, France, England and the U.S. were trying to take over the territory."[1] Within this political tumult conflict emerges between two factions led by ambitious and wealthy Spaniards. The first, Don Arturo Bordega (Cornel Wilde), hopes to bring "peace and freedom" to the territory by placing it under U.S. rule, while the second, Don Fredo Brios (John Dehner), plots to turn the territory over to the Russians, who will then set him up as governor. The Tsarist Russians of *California Conquest* serve as obvious allegorical stand-ins for the Soviets, and their conspiracy to take California hints at widespread fears that a "fifth column" could overthrow American democracy.[2] By depicting California as a frontier territory subject to a number of competing national interests, *California Conquest* used little-known events of our nation's past to offer cautionary commentary on contemporary foreign policy.

California Conquest is among a large group of westerns widely seen as allegories of Cold War politics in the 1950s. Fred Zinnemann's classic western *High Noon*, for example, is—along with *On the Waterfront* and *Invasion of the Body Snatchers*—one of the films discussed most frequently by scholars as a blacklist allegory.[3] As with *On the Waterfront*, much of the commentary on *High Noon* was spurred by the circumstances surrounding the film's production. In April of 1951 HUAC issued a subpoena to screenwriter Carl Foreman, requesting that he appear before them as a suspected member of the Communist Party. Because of delays, however, the hearings themselves did not occur until September, after *High Noon* had already entered production. On September 24 Foreman appeared before HUAC as an "unfriendly witness," refusing to either confirm or deny he had been a member of the Communist Party. (In fact, Foreman was a member from 1938 to 1952.)

The fallout from Foreman's appearance resulted in both professional and personal difficulties. Stanley Kramer, *High Noon's* producer, initially supported Foreman but did an abrupt about face prior to the screenwriter's testimony. According to the 2002 documentary *Darkness at High Noon*, Kramer fired Foreman from his duties just days before the latter's HUAC appearance. Kramer also tried to strip Foreman of his associate producer title on *High Noon*, but pressure from Zinnemann and Gary Cooper, who played sheriff Will Kane, forced Kramer to back down. Because of Zinnemann's and Cooper's support on the set, Foreman received a letter from Kramer reinstating him as a producer and further promising that no statements about Foreman would be issued until two months after the screenwriter's testimony.[4]

Within a week, however, Kramer returned to his earlier hard-line posture. Despite their written agreement, Kramer issued a press release the day after Foreman's testimony, announcing that he would seek to remove the screenwriter from his official duties as company treasurer. Moreover, following a few weeks of negotiation, Kramer bought out Foreman's financial interest in the company for a sum of $250,000.[5] As part of the latter agreement, Foreman once again lost his associate producer credit on *High Noon*.

Despite the rancorous negotiations with Kramer, Foreman continued to count *High Noon's* star, Gary Cooper, among a small group of supporters. On October 25 the *Los Angeles Times* reported that Foreman planned to start up his own production company after his unceremonious ouster and that Cooper would be one of the company's stockholders.[6] John Wayne, Hedda Hopper, and other members of the Motion Picture Alliance for the Preservation of American Ideals (MPAPAI) waged a bitter campaign against Foreman, however, and the unfavorable publicity soon took its toll on Cooper. Producer Walter Wanger and MGM executive Louis B. Mayer even cautioned Cooper that the taint of Foreman's association would harm the actor's future employment prospects. Consequently, just ten days after the *Times* announcement, Cooper withdrew his resources from Foreman's business venture.

Beyond the very public disputes regarding Foreman's involvement in *High Noon*, the screenwriter's own comments reinforce its status as blacklist allegory. After Foreman received HUAC's subpoena, he began to see his own situation reflected in that of the film's hero, Will Kane (Gary Cooper), the retiring marshal of a small western town called Hadleyville. As the film opens, Kane is marrying Amy Foster (Grace Kelly), a Quaker woman from

Figure 8. Screenwriter Carl Foreman later claimed that the scene from *High Noon* in which Will Kane goes to Sunday morning services to ask for help was inspired by comments made in meetings he had with business associates and lawyers just prior to his testimony before HUAC.

St. Louis. After the wedding ceremony Kane learns that Frank Miller, a man he had earlier sent to jail, is arriving on the noon train. Along with his brother Ben and two other outlaws, Frank Miller plans to exact vengeance on the town. Kane initially agrees to leave Hadleyville with Amy but soon turns back in the hopes of recruiting new deputies to thwart the Millers' scheme. Since Amy's religious belief's proscribe the use of violence and deadly force, she disapproves of Kane's plans and opts instead to return home to St. Louis. As Amy waits to leave, Kane tries to rally support among the townspeople. One by one, though, the men each rebuff Kane's request for assistance. Left completely to his own devices, Kane walks the empty streets of Hadleyville to face Miller and his gang in a deadly showdown.

Foreman later claimed that the scene in which Kane goes to Sunday morning services to ask for help (fig. 8) was inspired by the screenwriter's own meetings with "partners, associates, and lawyers."[7] Moreover, in a series of interviews given in the early 1970s, Foreman went further, saying that *High Noon* was about "Hollywood and no other place but Hollywood and about what was happening in Hollywood and nothing else but that."[8] The fact that Foreman resorts to this mixture of allegory and genre conventions to convey his message was largely the result of the repressive climate created by the blacklist. As Paul Buhle and Dave Wagner note of Foreman, "Naturally, his technique combined indirection and disguise. Given the times, with coworkers and friends being hauled up in front of committees and thrown out of the artistic enterprise they had come to master just a few years earlier, it would have been a greater surprise if his technique had been more overt."[9]

A critical consensus about *High Noon*'s status as anti-HUAC allegory emerged in the years following Foreman's comments about the film. John Belton's *American Cinema / American Culture* typifies this interpretive strategy: "*High Noon* emerges as an obvious example of resistance within the industry to outside investigators, such as HUAC. The film's hero, ironically played by a real-life friendly witness, Gary Cooper, is threatened by a gang of cutthroats (HUAC) who are on their way to town (Hollywood). The sheriff-hero is unable to find allies to help him within the (Hollywood) community. He nonetheless confronts and defeats them, waging a battle alone that the townspeople ought to have fought together."[10] Belton's reading resembles readings of several other notable critics, including Stephen Whitfield, Brenda Murphy, Richard Slotkin, Philip Drummond, Leonard Maltin, and Peter Biskind.[11]

Not surprisingly, given Foreman's troubled history on the project and the documented evidence of his intent, *High Noon* remains one of the most robust examples of the western as blacklist allegory. Indeed, when critics attempt to expand the canon of blacklist allegories to include other 1950s westerns, they often rely on the "availability" and "familiarity" of *High Noon* to suggest it is indicative of a more widespread trend. Moreover, some early academic scholarship on the western argues that, owing to the familiarity of its lore and mythology, the genre is especially useful for allegorical narrative structures, blacklist or otherwise. Comparing *Animal Farm*'s allegorical techniques to those of Hollywood westerns, Philip French writes:

> *Animal Farm* exists in its own right, independent of its easily definable
> political provenance, in the way that all great satire does from
> Aristophanes through Dean Swift. By analogy and with certain
> reservations, the same is true of the Western movie. Unlike *Animal
> Farm* and *Gulliver's Travels*, however, the film-maker is drawing on a
> body of established knowledge readily accessible to the audience—in
> the same way, though for different reasons, that playwrights in, say,
> German-occupied France of World War II resorted to themes from
> classical mythology, or Eastern European dramatists and movie

directors have reworked historical subjects or used Aesopian language in handling ambiguous contemporary fables. An immediate judgment, often rendered between the lines rather than explicitly, might acknowledge the dangerousness and present value of the enterprise, and this can be as true of Hollywood as of Hungary.[12]

French's comments on the allegorical possibilities associated with the western are telling, not only because he cites *Animal Farm*, which, as I have already noted, is among a handful of paradigmatic examples of Cold War allegory, but also because he sketches out several situations in which artists have used political allegory to evade forms of official censorship. Under normal circumstances Hollywood's politics are not like those of Hungary. But they are if one considers the rather limited instance of blacklist allegory.

Unlike the historical film, which relied almost exclusively on the interplay between present and past events to create allegorical signifiers and signifieds, the western allows critics to draw on a range of generic tropes to connect the film's referential and implicit meanings. Such genre elements are not ideologically neutral but rather are invoked in such a way that they clearly signal the political slant of the particular interpretive frame being used. For example, the frontier is often mobilized in readings of westerns as allegorical representations of U.S. "containment" policies aimed at limiting Communist influence around the globe. Similarly, lynch mobs figure prominently in readings of westerns as allegories of McCarthyist repression. The remainder of this chapter illustrates the way in which this combination of generic tropes and topical reference points informs the critical reception of Cold War–era westerns.

THE WESTERN FRONTIER AS THE "NEW FRONTIER"

It almost goes without saying that the frontier is the dominant trope in both the mythology and historiography of the American West. In both instances the concept of the frontier serves as a justification of American exceptionalism in that the experience of frontier life is thought to have helped shape and influence the nation's *ethos*. This emphasis on the frontier is commonly traced to Frederick Jackson Turner's famous address to an American Historical Association meeting at the Chicago World's Fair in 1893. Yet it remains a touchstone of much modern historical writing on the West, as evidenced by Richard Slotkin's monumental three-volume work on the subject.[13]

Not surprisingly, the concept of the frontier has also played a central role in criticism and scholarship on art, literature, and films about the American

West. Jim Kitses argues that Henry Nash Smith's pioneering work furnished the central antinomy of the western genre: the dichotomy between the garden and the desert.[14] Within the thematic matrix established through the western's treatment of setting, the frontier exists as an intermediate space on the borders of both civilization and the untamed wilderness. Following in Smith's and Kitses's footsteps, film scholars have produced an almost limitless stream of analyses that map this set of interrelated semantic fields onto specific titles. During the so-called structuralist phase of film genre criticism, these studies of the western focused on particular themes associated with the frontier, such as the social role of violence and the primacy of rugged individualism as a quintessentially American trait.[15] More recent work on the western takes a different approach by focusing on the frontier's role in fostering specific ideologies of race and gender, more specifically the association of women with the values of civilization and American Indians with traits of the "savage" wilderness.[16]

The notion of the frontier, though, has also served a productive role in blacklist criticism. Defined as an intermediate boundary space between two opposing forces, the frontier proves to be a flexible, dynamic, and dialectical concept, one capacious enough to support several rather divergent reading strategies. On the whole the structural function of the frontier within the genre seems relatively stable; the only real question for critics is how one identifies the entities that are metaphorically counterposed along its border.

In *Cowboys as Cold Warriors* Stanley Corkin examines a number of postwar Hollywood westerns in order to demonstrate the ways in which these films reflect American foreign policy initiatives related to anti-Communism and global economic expansion. Adopting this approach, Corkin frequently treats the archetypal frontier town as a surrogate for places where the Truman Doctrine was employed as a means of containing Communist influence around the globe. Towns in Old West territories, like Arizona and Colorado, thus come to stand in for places like Korea and Greece.

In a particularly telling example, Corkin situates *High Noon* in relation to the outbreak of the Korean War. Corkin cites the work of diplomatic theorist Franz Schurmann, who characterized the underlying assumptions of containment thusly: "There were only two great powers in the world, America and Russia. . . . As American military advantage went either up or down, Russian expansion was correspondingly either encouraged or discouraged. If an ally of America faltered, this could create a vacuum inviting the Russians to step in. The logical conclusion of containment was that if the building blocks of the free world were secure and structures erected with them solid everywhere along the perimeter where the free and communist worlds meet, then world stability will ensue."[17.]

This definition of containment furnishes Corkin with several semantic fields that he maps onto the already existing generic elements of the western. Through a pattern of metaphorical substitution, the two great postwar superpowers, the United States and the Soviet Union, become the forces of law and lawlessness. The western frontier, the mythic boundary between civilization and the wilderness, is thus remapped as the "perimeter where the free and communist worlds meet." Additionally, the western's interrogation of the socially legitimate and illegitimate uses of violence is reconfigured as a question of geopolitical ideology, a defense or critique of the use of American military power in areas prone to Communist influence or incursion.

Having established these links between genre conventions and geopolitics, Corkin then examines the way in which *High Noon* activates these specific elements in its narrative structure. For Corkin, Marshal Will Kane is both the iconic gunfighter of the western and the embodiment of American foreign policy initiatives. Kane's imminent departure from Hadleyville threatens to leave the town with a "power vacuum" that will be filled by the lawlessness and brutality of the Millers, who function as symbols of the Communist threat. Noting that Miller and his cohorts are given few character traits beyond a vague aura of menace and a desire for revenge, Corkin concludes that texts like *High Noon* do not engage the specific doctrines, theories, and principles of Marxism or Leninism but rather treat "the *idea* of Communism" as a "philosophical desire to level human society."[18] In this respect the threat embodied by the Millers is not merely that of social disorder but rather a disorder that potentially undermines the natural social hierarchies that result from property ownership, free markets, and capitalist enterprise.[19]

Throughout his analysis of *High Noon* Corkin shifts between metaphors of external and internal security. The notion of containment would seem to place the frontier outside of America's borders during the 1950s and situate it instead within various political hotspots around the world, like Berlin or Vietnam. But Corkin also sees Hadleyville as an allegorical representation of American borders, one that simultaneously positions Kane as the "world's policeman" at the same time that he protects and upholds the nation's existing social and political structures. Countering earlier policies of appeasement and isolationism, Kane's decisiveness acts as a contrast to the dithering and hand wringing of Hadleyville's community leaders, who symbolize the impotence and failure of political consensus and civic institutions. If this is true, though, Kane is hardly the embodiment of American democracy; instead, his will to action positions him as a militaristic, fascist demagogue. If *High Noon* is, indeed, a critique of consensus, then the film allegorizes the very thin line between assuming civic responsibility and usurping the power of the polity. Corkin's interpretation of *High Noon* counters more traditional accounts of the film that emphasize screenwriter Carl Foreman's authorial intentions. But because he generally elides the issue of domestic anti-Communism, Corkin's reading of *High Noon* positions it as a "Cold War" text rather than a blacklist text proper.

Still, the terms of Corkin's allegorical reading could easily be transposed to semantic fields associated with domestic strategies of containment rather than international geopolitics. Within this thematic nexus *High Noon*'s frontier town, Hadleyville, would stand in for Hollywood, much as it does in Foreman's account of the film's production history. Whereas the latter functions as a form of allegorical autobiography, this approach to *High Noon* treats Will Kane as a brave defender of American values against Communist subversion in Hollywood. This reading is abetted by the casting of Gary Cooper, an MPAPAI member and a friendly witness at the 1947 HUAC hearings. It obviously emphasizes Kane's role as guardian of the community and thus suggests that the character's function is to thwart the influence of "outside agitators" like Frank Miller.

If Corkin's reading of *High Noon* aligns it with the initiatives of right-wing anti-Communist ideologues, Delmer Daves's *Broken Arrow* (1950) recasts the western as a somewhat Utopian allegory of U.S.-Soviet relations. Stanley Corkin and John Belton both identify *Broken Arrow* as a film that proposes "social alternatives to Cold War xenophobia and militarism."[20] Belton even goes so far as to characterize *Broken Arrow* as a film that subverts the dominant ideology of Hollywood, a claim implicitly supported by the fact that a blacklisted writer penned the film's script, even though Michael Blankfort received the credit after acting as a front on the project.[21]

Set in Arizona around 1870, *Broken Arrow* tells the story of Tom Jeffords (James Stewart), a former scout who develops a friendship with the Apache chief Cochise (Jeff Chandler). The studio synopsis of Jeffords's character describes him as "tall, sinewy, fearless," and says that the frontiersman has "long believed that the white man has not dealt fairly with the Apaches."[22] Disturbed by Apache attacks on mail carriers, Jeffords learns to speak the Apache language, and through smoke signals he requests a meeting with Cochise. After discussing the possibilities of peaceful coexistence, Jeffords convinces Cochise to allow an easement through Apache territory to U.S. mail carriers.

Having negotiated this concession, Jeffords returns to Tucson, where he relates the details of his arrangement. Despite assurances to the contrary, Jeffords's news is met with great suspicion within the community; people fear that the proposal may be a trick to lure travelers into an Apache trap. To dispel such qualms, Jeffords agrees to wager $300 that five mail carriers will make their deliveries without being attacked. Although the townspeople express incredulity at Jeffords's truce with Cochise, the five carriers complete their routes without incident, and Jeffords claims his stakes. The last carrier's arrival, however, occurs in the midst of Apache attacks on a military wagon train. Instead of being vindicated, Ben Slade (Will Geer) claims that Jeffords is in cahoots with the Apaches and that the bet was fixed. More seriously, one of the townspeople, Lowrie, charges that someone in the town gave the Apaches inside information about the wagon train's battle tactics. Calling Jeffords an "Indian-lover," the townspeople nearly lynch him, but he is saved by the timely arrival of the U.S. Cavalry. Tragedy is averted but only when General Oliver Howard, also known as the Christian general, brings news that President Grant has ordered him to negotiate a peace treaty with the Apaches.

Jeffords initially believes that Howard came to his defense in order to pressure him to act as an Indian scout. Instead, the general wants Jeffords to serve as an intermediary between himself and Cochise. The pair travels to the Apache camp, and with Jeffords operating as a translator, Cochise agrees to a three-month cease-fire. Cochise's acquiescence comes at a political cost, though. Several of his tribe members desert him, saying that they will not lay down arms for the white man.

As is typical of most classical Hollywood films, *Broken Arrow* also contains a romantic subplot, in this case Jeffords's efforts to woo Sonseeahray, a young woman betrothed to an Apache warrior named Nahilzay. Sonseeahray's parents have already promised her to Nahilzay, but Cochise intercedes on Jeffords's behalf. Angered at this betrayal, Nahilzay sneaks into Jeffords's wickiup and attempts to kill him. Jeffords thwarts the attack, but Cochise catches him fighting with Nahilzay. Jeffords persuades Cochise that he was only acting in self-defense, and the chief kills Nahilzay for violating the tribe's promise of sanctuary.

The two plotlines finally come together in the film's conclusion, as Ben Slade leads a renegade band of townspeople in a raid on Cochise's traveling party. Sonseeahray is killed, and Jeffords is wounded during the gun battle that ensues. Angered by his wife's senseless murder, Jeffords vows to mete out revenge against the lone white survivor of the renegade band. But Cochise stays Jeffords's hand and asks him to let the law take its course in punishing the offenders. "I do not betray my people or their children," Cochise says to Jeffords. "And no one in my territory will open war again— not even you."

Most of the commentary on *Broken Arrow* has focused on its sympathetic treatment of American Indians and its message of peace, hope, and understanding. Philip K. Scheuer's article on the film's production begins with a description of a young Indian boy's contemplative silence after seeing *Broken Arrow* in a projection room on the 20th Century–Fox lot. When pressed for comment by one of his elders, the youth responded, "For the first time in my life I'm proud to be an Indian."[23] *Broken Arrow* even received official sanction from the Association on American Indian Affairs, which cited it as "one of the first films since 'The Vanishing American' (1925) to attempt a serious portrayal of the Indian side of American history and to show the Indian as a real human being the same as a white man."[24]

Although *Broken Arrow*'s sympathetic portrayal of Indians was the dominant theme of its critical reception in the 1950s, the film also received praise for its dramatization of the peaceful coexistence of Apaches and white settlers. Producer Julian Blaustein noted, for example, that the film's title was suggested in passing by some of the Apaches who worked as extras, adding that "the broken arrow is a symbol of peace."[25] In an even more elegant formulation, *Boxoffice* concluded its synopsis of *Broken Arrow* by stating simply, "Thus, peace comes to Arizona."[26]

Perhaps because of its theme of racial tolerance, *Broken Arrow* has engendered a number of divergent allegorical interpretations, all of which are linked to aspects of its contemporaneous reception. Angela Aleiss, for example, reads *Broken Arrow* as a parable of postwar racial assimilation for African Americans. To support her argument, Aleiss cites the Truman administration's endeavors in assigning blacks to government jobs and its policies eliminating segregation within the federal bureaucracy.[27] Aleiss also locates this cultural desire for assimilation within a larger context of white conformity. For Aleiss, this latter concept is synecdochically represented by Senator Joseph McCarthy's use of the label "un-American" to demonize individuals and groups that differed from the norm.[28] Through this somewhat specious series of critical maneuvers, Aleiss's argument about *Broken Arrow*'s civil rights subtext becomes logically dependent on a more fundamental articulation of Communist witch-hunting.

A similar pattern pervades other readings of *Broken Arrow* that interpret it as an allegory of U.S.-Soviet relations. For these critics *Broken Arrow*'s early reception as an argument for peace gets enlarged into a more assiduous commentary on Cold War politics of the early 1950s. Given his emphasis on the frontier as a symbol of geopolitics, Stanley Corkin, not surprisingly, is the chief exponent of this particular take on *Broken Arrow*. The film, according to Corkin, speaks more directly than most other westerns to "the international terms of the Cold War, as it offers a range of analogies between the American West and the world, between Native Americans and other presumed adversaries of the United States, between the nativists of the nineteenth century and the cold warriors of the twentieth."[29] Corkin traces these parallels to the participation of blacklisted screenwriter Albert Maltz, who collaborated with Delmer Daves on earlier "Popular Front" titles. Corkin even suggests that Jeffords's advocacy of treaty negotiations makes him a mouthpiece for party line politics dating back to the 1920s. Corkin's interpretation of *Broken Arrow* corroborates Angela Aleiss's reading to the extent that the Communist Party identified the African American community as a nation within a nation at its 1927 Congress. Thanks to Maltz's Communist credentials, *Broken Arrow*'s frontier setting proves open to multiple interpretations as the film's Apache tribe simultaneously serves as a metaphorical stand-in both for the Soviet republics and for the burgeoning civil rights movement.

Whereas Corkin's reading of *Broken Arrow* treats Native American "otherness" as a symbol of international Communism, John Belton's similar interpretation of the film ultimately circles back to the politics of Hollywood. Playing on a linguistic pun regarding two figurative meanings of *red*, Belton suggests that *Broken Arrow*'s depiction of "whites" and "reds" casts Jeffords as an apparent traitor to his own community, a situation that connects him to the industry's suspected Communists and "fellow travelers." Belton's discussion of *Broken Arrow* concretizes an issue treated more metaphorically in Corkin's interpretation: the Apaches' "red" skin makes them surrogates for modern "Reds" and "Pinkos," both in America and abroad.

Belton's reading of *Broken Arrow* deviates from Corkin's "containment" allegory, though, by highlighting the townspeople's suspicion of Jeffords. More specifically, Belton focuses on the scene in which Jeffords is nearly lynched as a result of his friendship with Cochise. Although Corkin's reading of *Broken Arrow* ignores this scene almost entirely, the depiction of mob violence is, for Belton, absolutely central to the film's left-wing politics. "The townspeople emerge as barely disguised Communist witch-hunters," writes Belton. "The film's sympathies clearly lie with Jeffords, who, like the blacklisted writer, is not only rejected by society but becomes the target of its violence and anger."[30] Through its emphasis on the lynch mob's violence and paranoia, Belton's analysis reminds us that although the frontier itself may be the Cold War western's most important and productive trope, the notion of frontier justice is nearly as important for what it offers to the genre's blacklist allegories.

FRONTIER INJUSTICE: THE POSSE, THE BOUNTY HUNTER, AND THE LYNCH MOB

As a consequence of its geographic isolation and physical distance from federal government protections, the frontier town of the western is socially unstable, but it retains a high degree of political autonomy. As Richard Slotkin points out, both progressive and populist ideologies treat the frontier as a cauldron for the development of desirable individual traits and grassroots democracy. Indeed, many eastern politicians valued the frontier for its regenerative power. Frontier life was thought to bring out a renewed virility within the educated ruling class and thus served to heighten those characteristics that were thought to be distinctly American: pragmatism, toughness, vigor, and self-reliance.[31]

In the western the frontier settlement's geographic isolation thus endows it with the characteristics of an open society—at least for those who were born white and male. With a highly entrepreneurial economic base, the frontier town offers few barriers to the accumulation of personal wealth. Furthermore, because of the weakness of legal structures and the relative absence of religious and moral institutions, individual behaviors are much less strictly regulated. The pursuits of wealth and vice fit hand in glove in such an open society, with saloons themselves serving as the communal meeting place for the town's citizenry. Though used primarily for lodging, entertainment, and sexual dalliances, the saloon typically also functions as a space for town meetings, city council activities, and legal proceedings.

Yet if the frontier town offers the twin prospects of social mobility and participatory democracy, its openness also carries with it the possibility of pervasive depravity. The townspeople's indulgence in vices such as whiskey and gambling sometimes serves as a symptom of a deeper corruption, one that extends even into those institutions established to secure social order. In the western, legal institutions frequently prove weak, even impotent, or, worse yet, overtly compromised by feudal landowners whose ambitions are fueled by visions of empire. As a local militia empowered to enforce the law, the posse should be a symbol of self-reliance and civic duty. More often than not, the posse functions as a blunt instrument of power dispensing justice in a manner that is swift, brutal, arbitrary, and fallacious.

Of course, this scenario is hardly ubiquitous in the western, but it is common enough to be identified as a characteristic trope. More to the point, the depiction of frontier corruption also furnishes critics with a semantic field that can map the genre's meanings in a way that creates parallels and analogies with contemporary society. In the case of 1950s westerns, the theme of frontier corruption functions as a key element of blacklist allegories. Mob violence in these films illustrates the potential abuse of power that occurs when the sanction of law and order gives rise to bloodlust and wild accusations. Thus, the theme of corruption—individual, social, or political—was an important tool for leftist filmmakers of the postwar period, who sought to use the western as a vehicle for commentary on HUAC's and McCarthy's treachery.

As I mentioned in my introduction, *High Noon* is perhaps the classic example of this type of western allegory. Basing their interpretive template on Carl Foreman's experience with HUAC, many critics read *High Noon* as a reflection of the climate of fear created by McCarthyism's "Red-baiting" tactics. What is less often acknowledged, though, is the extent to which the analogy between Hadleyville and Hollywood devolves upon the genre's thematic emphasis on social and political corruption. To be sure, *High Noon*'s treatment of the theme deviates from the norm in emphasizing inaction rather than personal vice, but its dramatization of collective cowardice proves to be the key element of its political critique. As Richard Slotkin notes, "Miller's return is a metaphorical way of identifying McCarthyism with Fascism: the same people who in an earlier and less prosperous time had risen up to defeat the enemy have now grown too comfortable or complacent to risk their lives and fortunes for the public good."[32]

Although Slotkin's comments extend the implications of Belton's brief summary, they also hint at an additional underlying parallel between Hadleyville and Hollywood. The economic opportunity generally associated with frontier settings functions in *High Noon* as a metaphor for both Hollywood's and America's postwar boom. The genre itself thus helps to delineate the implicit causes for the cowardice, conformity, and complacency found in both Hadleyville and Hollywood; the loss of some freedom and security might be compensated by the minimization of risk.

This related parallel between Hadleyville and Hollywood is elaborated in the scene that Carl Foreman singled out as the key to his own political investments in *High Noon*. The first shot of the sequence is a high-angle establishing shot that shows Kane entering the town's church in the deep background of the image. The shot is framed so that the church's minister, Dr. Mahin, addresses the congregation with his back to the camera. Director

Fred Zinnemann then cuts to a slightly low-angled medium close-up of Kane as the church suddenly falls silent. This is followed by a shot from Kane's point of view that shows Dr. Mahin and the congregation staring at him as he stands at the church's entrance. Like other point-of-view shots in the film, this one serves to emphasize Kane's sense of isolation from the townspeople of Hadleyville. Kane apologizes for interrupting the service but nonetheless receives a rebuke from Mahin, both for his absence on previous Sundays and for conducting his marriage ceremony outside the church earlier that day.

After humbly reminding Mahin that his wife has a different faith, Kane shares the news of Frank Miller's impending arrival and requests assistance from the congregation for the expected confrontation between Miller and Kane. Although several people come forward, their egress is halted when a parishioner reminds the town that Kane is no longer marshal. After this objection several other congregants chime in with questions about the townspeople's responsibilities. This ultimately leads Mayor Jonas Henderson to step to the altar to take charge of the impromptu civic debate. After allowing others to speak, Henderson finally delivers his own opinion on the matter. The mayor thanks Kane for his faithful service to Hadleyville but also reminds the congregation that northern investors are considering the town as a place for new stores and factories. Concerned about the negative publicity that would result from a gunfight on Hadleyville's main thoroughfare, Henderson recommends that Kane leave town. Henderson explains that if Kane was gone, then there is a chance that Miller and his gang would simply leave Hadleyville altogether. The mayor's speech is framed as a two-shot of Kane and Henderson, which beautifully registers the former's discomfiture regarding his boss's suggestion. After a brief series of reaction shots of Henderson and Kane, Zinnemann cuts to a wide shot showing the congregation's response to what has just transpired. Their downcast eyes tell the story; they are ashamed that the mayor has placed their interests above that of the town's faithful servant and protector.

The economic rationale that underpins Henderson's recommendation reinforces an important parallel between Hadleyville and Hollywood. Just as Henderson desires to "exile" Kane to preserve the town's prospects as a mercantile center, Hollywood studio executives collectively agreed in 1947 to fire suspected subversives in their ranks in order to (a) minimize negative publicity, (b) counter planned or existing boycotts, (c) forestall future incursions by Washington politicians, and (d) preserve future box-office revenues. Most critics emphasize Foreman and Zinnemann's depiction of the townspeople's spinelessness, but the speech by Mayor Henderson is a useful reminder that some of their concern is driven by good old-fashioned greed.

That greed functions as a secondary source of corruption in Hadleyville is, at least partly, supported by Stephen J. Whitfield's and Brenda Murphy's analyses of *High Noon,* which gesture toward an intertextual linkage between the film and Mark Twain's famed short story, "The Man That Corrupted Hadleyburg." Twain's story is about a bitter and vengeful stranger who is inadvertently offended by the citizens of Hadleyburg while passing through the town. The stranger nurses this perceived slight for a year, and eventually concocts a scheme that tests Hadleyburg's reputation as the region's most virtuous, incorruptible town. To enact his plan, the stranger travels back to Hadleyburg, where he leaves a sack of gold with the bank cashier's wife along with an anonymous note explaining that the gold is a reward for a kindness performed by one of the town's citizens a year or two ago. This unidentified citizen supposedly gave $20 to the letter's author at a time when the latter was down on his luck. Having turned that $20 into a small fortune at the gaming table, the stranger seeks to repay the citizen's kindness and asks that the town conduct a search for this unidentified Good Samaritan. "This man can be identified by the remark which he made to me," the letter states. The remark is enclosed in the sack in a sealed envelope, which can then be used to ascertain the man who uttered it. The stranger then sends nineteen identical letters to nineteen of Hadleyburg's citizens, each of which contains the phrase purportedly uttered by the town's Good Samaritan. The stranger's experiment serves its intended purpose as all of these so-called Wretched Nineteen come forward to claim the reward as their own. Having proven that the townspeople's greed would lead them to lie and cheat in order to get the gold, the stranger subsequently reveals his plan, chiding the town for its vanity: "Why, you simple creatures, the weakest of all weak things is a virtue which has not been tested in the fire."[33]

Hadleyville's trials and tribulations come about as a result of exigent circumstances rather than a deliberate experiment in ethics. Yet Whitfield's and Murphy's citation of Twain's story highlights the extent to which *High Noon* is understood, both positively and negatively, as a dramatization of a moral dilemma, one that inevitably points toward the parallels between Marshal Will Kane and HUAC's unfriendly witnesses.[34] In a simple summary of these parallels, Whitfield writes, "In Mark Twain's 'The Man That Corrupted Hadleyburg,' the sin is greed; but in Hadleyville, the problem is fear."[35] Although I find this formulation to be a bit reductive, Whitfield's analysis indicates the importance of corruption as a trope of left-wing allegories of the blacklist.

High Noon's politics, however, seem almost moderate when compared with Nicholas Ray's 1954 film, *Johnny Guitar*. As was the case with many other blacklist allegories, the "discovery" of this subtext occurred nearly two decades after *Johnny Guitar*'s release and was predicated on a retrospective matching of the film's politics to that of its makers. Ray himself stated that he chose to make *Johnny Guitar* in Spain after he was "gray-listed" by anti-Communist pressure groups following *In a Lonely Place* (1950).[36] More important, both Ray and screenwriter Philip Yordan were associated with liberal causes, the latter acting as a "front" for blacklisted writers throughout the early 1950s. Indeed, Yordan was closely affiliated with blacklisted screenwriter Ben Maddow, and some commentators have asserted that Maddow himself is the real author of *Johnny Guitar*.[37] As a western, *Johnny Guitar* adopts many of the genre's conventions but tweaks them in a way that challenges its almost automatic alignment with structures of law and society. Described as Ray's "personal" attack on McCarthyism, *Johnny Guitar* utilizes the image of a bloodthirsty lynch mob to comment on both the tactics of HUAC's investigation and the hysteria it engendered within the Hollywood community.[38]

Johnny Guitar is the story of the tumultuous romance of the title character, played by HUAC informer Sterling Hayden, and Vienna (Joan Crawford), the owner of a saloon and gambling house in the Arizona Territory. Johnny is a former gunfighter, who has sworn off violence after surviving a dangerous past in Albuquerque as "gun-crazy" Johnny Logan. Vienna was a part of that past as Johnny's lover. Although Johnny left Vienna five years ago, saying he refused to be tied down, he comes to her saloon hoping to rekindle their romance. Instead of telling Johnny to take a hike, Vienna hires him to provide music for her seemingly patronless establishment.

Despite the saloon's paucity of customers, Vienna keeps it open because it is the anticipated site of a new train depot that will be constructed for a railroad line expected to pass through her property. When the brother of Emma Small (Mercedes McCambridge) is killed in a robbery that occurs near the start of the film, the ensuing investigation enables rival landowners to cast aspersions on Vienna's character and thus attempt to forestall the railroad's encroachment on land they need for their cattle to graze. The group, led by Emma and a cattle baron named McIvers (Ward Bond), accuses Vienna of shielding the murder suspects, a small gang of outlaws led by the charismatic Dancin' Kid (Scott Brady). Vienna, however, realizes that Emma's zeal for revenge is driven less by her brother's death than by Emma's unrequited love for the Kid. By fomenting suspicion about Vienna, Emma fulfills two goals: on one hand, she hopes to protect the ranchers' economic interests in the valley; on the other hand, she also hopes to elim-inate Vienna as a rival for the Kid's affections. In an effort to pressure Vienna and the Dancin' Kid's gang to leave town, McIvers orders the saloon to close within twenty-four hours. Despite the town marshal's protesta-tions, McIvers assures his posse that he will push through an ordinance that prohibits any drinking and gambling outside the city limits. "We have a saloon in town," says McIvers. "We don't need one out here."

Knowing the gang is already suspected of murder, the Dancin' Kid and his crew rob the town's bank, believing that the additional crime will do nothing to change their status in the eyes of the law. The youngest member of the group, Turkey, is injured during the gang's getaway when his horse is rattled by an explosion. Unable to join the rest of the group at their hide-out, Turkey is taken by Tom, one of Vienna's employees, back to her saloon. Seeking shelter from the law, Turkey begs Vienna for help. Although Tom recommends turning Turkey over to the posse, both he and Vienna sympa-thize with the boy's youth, and they try to hide Turkey beneath one of the saloon's gaming tables. The posse discovers Turkey when it comes to ques-tion Vienna, but Tom intervenes when they try to take her into custody. Both Tom and the marshal are killed in the shootout that follows. With no legal authority left to curb them, the mob's violence erupts in a fury as they burn Vienna's saloon to the ground and haul her and Turkey away to be lynched.

Johnny rescues Vienna from the hangman's noose (fig. 9) and then uses the abandoned mine shafts around her saloon to escape to the Dancin' Kid's hideout. A final confrontation between the posse and the gang occurs after Turkey's skittish horse reveals the entry to the lair. Emma persuades one of the gang's members, Bart (Ernest Borgnine), to let the posse through in exchange for his freedom and half the loot from the bank job. As he makes his escape, Bart kills Cory and prepares to shoot the Kid but is prevented from doing so when Johnny leaps on Bart's back. Johnny kills Bart in a gun battle, and when the body rolls down the hill leading up to the lair, it signals the posse that Emma's plan has backfired. With most of the gang dead, Vienna and Emma face off in a showdown that ranks as one of the most unusual in the history of the genre. For his part the Dancin' Kid tries to intercede but receives a bullet in the head from Emma's gun for his trou-bles. The two women stalk each other using the porch that surrounds the cabin, and although Vienna is wounded, she kills Emma in this final show-down. Realizing the pointlessness of Emma's crusade, the mob's anger at Vienna is diffused, and she and Johnny are left to pursue their future life together.

Figure 9. In *Johnny Guitar* Vienna nearly becomes a victim of frontier justice. The image of the lynch mob is a key element in many westerns viewed by critics as anti-HUAC or anti-McCarthyist allegories.

As is true of most films covered in this study, the contemporaneous reception of *Johnny Guitar* offers little indication that reviewers were aware of its blacklist subtext. The *Hollywood Reporter* review is a case in point. Grousing that the story is filled with contradictions and inconsistencies, the reviewer also griped that *Johnny Guitar* is filled with more talk than action with "everyone threatening everyone else and nothing happening until the closing moments when practically the whole cast is wiped out by lynching, shooting, and conversation."[39]

Although contemporary critics generally steered clear of the film's political subtext, they were much more forthright in acknowledging *Johnny Guitar*'s unusual treatment of gender issues. In a rare critical rave *Cue* stated that *Johnny Guitar* "ends in a near-lynching, a spectacular fire, a frantic manhunt, and a frock-coated posse's massed assault on a mountain hide-out with two furious gun gals shooting it out with blazing carbines and spinning six-guns."[40] Notably, in a curious conflation of politics and femininity, a prerelease photo-essay accompanying the review claimed that "'Johnny Guitar' is also the film responsible for the highly publicized and apparently authentic *cold war* (no hair-pulling, that is) between Joan Crawford and Mercedes McCambridge."[41]

In 1974, critic Michael Wilmington offered the reading of *Johnny Guitar* as blacklist allegory that served as a template for many critics who followed him:

> The "outlaws" become symbolic Communists (besides living and working communally over their mine shaft, they are also the town's "whipping boys," constantly blamed for real and imagined transgressions). Johnny, the ex-gunman, is the ex-Communist (now "mere entertainers") called before HUAC. (At the time, Sterling Hayden was still famous for renouncing his past Party membership under government pressure.) Vienna—consort of the outlaws, and also the town "progressive"—is a "fellow traveler." Emma Small, driven by hysteria and jealousy suggests those vindictive witnesses and politicians who used investigations to destroy the careers of hated rivals. McIvers is big business, going along to protect threatened interests and bending the law to his will. ("I thought it was a nice inside joke to cast Ward Bond that way," Ray has said. Bond, of course, was an anti-Communist zealot in the early fifties.) The fair but powerless marshal is the good men in government, caving in under McCarthy's bluster. And the townspeople are the American middle class—the film's audience.[42]

Wilmington's analysis exemplifies the kind of cognitive framing principles that appear in more piecemeal fashion in other allegorical interpretations. In making the case for *Johnny Guitar* as blacklist allegory, Wilmington pulls together the HUAC hearings themselves, Sterling Hayden's testimony as a cooperative witness, and Ward Bond's notoriety as an MPAPAI member such that they provide a pretext for the film's allegorical meanings. Moreover, when these elements are mixed with the conventional generic trope of the posse run amok, they combine to create a rather potent critique of the way HUAC used rumor, innuendo, and unsupported accusations as political weapons.

Much more so than most critics, Wilmington maps the film's characters across the entire economic and political spectrum of American society. In his brief but provocative explanation of the film's allegorical structure, Wilmington goes considerably beyond the simple dichotomy between friendly and unfriendly witnesses seen in "informer" allegories. By broadening the scope of the allegory, Wilmington argues that *Johnny Guitar* is a devastating critique of the tacit complicity of liberal anti-Communists and bourgeois moralists that made up the so-called silent majority in the 1950s. Both before and after Wilmington's seminal article, the film's makers confirmed the broad outlines of this allegorical structure. Philip Yordan, for example, claimed, "We played a good trick on Ward Bond, who was, as you know, head of the fascist party in Hollywood. We had him play the head of the posse, an extreme fascist causing a reign of terror. And he thought the character was a hero, a sympathetic guy. He didn't understand anything."[43]

Wilmington cites the cast's political affiliations as part of the warrant for interpreting *Johnny Guitar* as blacklist allegory, but Nicholas Ray's use of genre conventions arguably plays an even more important role in that process. The scene most frequently cited to support the film's status as allegory is the one in which the lynch mob led by McIvers and Emma interrogates Turkey in Vienna's saloon. Given its legal authority, the posse is ostensibly associated with the values of civilization and social order, but it often represents a perversion of both. The lynch mob combines two particularly egregious abuses of power: a rush to judgment coupled with a penchant for swift and terrible violence. Moreover, because the lynch mob's actions circumvent the guarantee of due process, which requires proof of guilt beyond a reasonable doubt, its energies feed off an atmosphere of paranoia and suspicion. Requiring no real evidence to support its dispensation of justice, the lynch mob's actions are easily redirected at those it considers socially undesirable. As a symbol of injustice, the lynch mob is a trope particularly well-suited to critiques of the abuse of power.

The scene in which McIvers and Emma question Turkey about Vienna's involvement with the gang also illustrates the degree to which the lynch mob operates by perverting the normal procedures of the justice system. The scene begins with a medium shot of Emma as she glances at the rest of the posse. Emma turns her back to the camera as she moves through the doorway of the saloon. The camera tracks in slightly with Emma until she moves out of the frame; the camera then pans slightly to the right to reveal Vienna seated at her piano on the opposite side of the room. Ray then cuts to a long shot of the posse entering the saloon. The group is dressed in black, having begun their search for the Kid and his gang immediately after Len Small's funeral. This is followed by an additional shot of three members of the posse coming into the central space of the saloon after briefly searching the kitchen. A reverse field cut shows a slightly closer view of Vienna playing the piano, seemingly oblivious to the posse's incursion into her private domain. Vienna is clad in an elegant white dress. Her piano sits beneath a small chandelier visible in the top right part of the frame. Vienna's piano bench rests atop a black throw rug that covers a small portion of the saloon's primitive stone stage. Most striking of all, Vienna's musical performance is set against a backdrop of craggy and fissured red rock, indicating that the saloon itself has literally been carved out of a mountainside.

This composition is perhaps the film's most illuminating example of the way in which Vienna's abode is situated in a boundary space between the town and the wilderness. Vienna's dress and her piano bespeak a sense of elegance, sophistication, and cultivation—in other words, the very embodiment of the values of civilization. The exposed rock wall, however, is a cold, brute reminder of nature's inescapable presence within frontier life. Although the wall's appearance helps give the saloon the look of an "underground" space, its rugged, unrefined character serves simultaneously to connote Vienna's individualism and heighten the artificiality of her performance.

Prodded by Emma's insistence that Vienna was involved with the robbery and knows the Kid's hideout, the marshal presses Vienna to cooperate, saying that she can no longer "sit on the fence." Vienna responds by asserting that she *has* cooperated with the authorities by complying with the order to close her saloon. Emphasizing her rights as a private citizen rather than an entrepreneur, Vienna adds that she is sitting in her own house, minding her own business, and playing her own piano. Reminding the posse that they came to her establishment without any probable cause, Vienna also asserts that they can scarcely make a crime out of this simple homespun activity.

After Vienna accuses the group of hypocrisy, her self-righteousness is punctured by the discovery of Turkey, who is concealed beneath a gaming table. Although Vienna's willingness to help Turkey should not implicate her directly in the gang's crime, the fact that she is sheltering a fugitive seems to confirm her guilt in the eyes of the posse. Having been met with Vienna's resistance, McIvers and Emma now turn their attention toward Turkey to obtain the proof they need. Turkey is caught red-handed, but McIvers promises him that he will not hang and may even go free if he implicates Vienna. Turkey asks what will happen to Vienna, to which Emma coldly responds, "The law will take its course." Buffeted on all sides by the posse's incessant questions and enticements, Turkey finally turns to Vienna and asks, "What will I do? I don't want to die." Vienna responds, "Save yourself."

Despite the transparency of McIvers and Emma's efforts to suborn perjury, the marshal announces that he will take both Turkey and Vienna into custody to stand trial. Claiming that the posse pressured the young boy to lie, Tom draws down on the group, saying that he cannot allow them to take Vienna. Emma shoots Tom, who in turn shoots the marshal as a reflex. With Tom and the marshal now dead and no one left to avert the prospect of mob rule, Emma cajoles McIvers into giving the order to hang Turkey and Vienna.

The scene caps off a motif in the film in which Emma constantly pressures the other members of the town to doubt Vienna's protestations of innocence. Ray's handling of the film's narration, however, plays an extremely important role in shaping the viewer's understanding of the scene's political and allegorical implications. Consider, for example, the contrast in the narration's communicativeness regarding the two robberies depicted in the film. The first stagecoach robbery is photographed in long shot, with the camera aligned with Johnny Guitar's perspective. (Indeed, the scene treats Johnny as a "fellow traveler," perhaps an additional "inside joke" regarding actor Sterling Hayden's earlier cooperation with HUAC.) Because of the camera's distance from the action and the restriction to Johnny's point of view, the narration suppresses information about the identity of the thieves, a storytelling strategy that keeps open the question of the Dancin' Kid's guilt for the entire first half of the film.

In contrast, the style of narration used for the bank robbery is generally less restricted and more communicative. Whereas the culprits' identity and their motivations remain unknown in the first robbery, Ray includes several prior scenes that elucidate the gang's motivations and prepare us for Vienna's coincidental appearance during the commission of the crime. The unrestricted range of information in the middle sections of *Johnny Guitar* establishes a hierarchy of knowledge in which the spectator knows more about the circumstances of the robbery than do any of the film's characters. This hierarchy of knowledge enables the spectator to make judgments about Vienna's innocence and about the posse's dubious reasoning for focusing on her saloon.

Imagine, for example, if the narration restricted our knowledge to the events of Len Small's funeral, which occurs at exactly the same time as the bank robbery. This strategy would align us with Emma, McIvers, and the posse, and would suppress our knowledge of the specific events taking place inside the bank. If Ray had presented the story this way, the spectator would learn about the robbery only after the Dancin' Kid and his gang already made their getaway. In fact, if the film's narration restricted information to what is known by the posse, Vienna's presence in the bank at the time of the robbery would indeed appear rather suspicious.

Ray, though, is careful to show us Vienna's journey with Johnny to the bank and her request to withdraw her savings as a means of breaking off any business ties with Emma. We also learn in a subsequent scene that Vienna withdrew the money to pay six months wages to her employees, now out of work as a result of McIvers's order. The narration of *Johnny Guitar* communicates a great deal of information about Vienna's motivations in these scenes in order to create some cognitive dissonance between the way the posse views her actions and the way the spectator does. This regulation of information helps to build sympathy for Vienna insofar as the viewer recognizes that she was not involved in the Dancin' Kid's robbery and that Vienna's decision to harbor Turkey as a fugitive is largely the result of circumstance.[44]

If *Johnny Guitar*'s narration helps us to understand Vienna's predicament, on the one hand, then it also enables us to recognize the posse's corrupt abuse of power, on the other. At the same time that the film provides evidence of Vienna's innocence, it also primes us for Emma and McIvers's intimidation tactics with Turkey by showing us earlier instances in which the pair pressure eyewitnesses to alter their "testimony." In an early scene in the saloon McIvers tries to coerce the stagecoach driver into identifying the Kid as Len Small's killer. McIvers ignores the driver's claim that he couldn't see the culprits because the light was in his eyes and further bends the driver's statement by using the postulation that it *could* have been the Kid as a positive affirmation that it *was*, indeed, the Kid. Similarly, after the bank robbery, Emma pressures one of the tellers to identify Vienna as a member of the gang. When the teller responds by asserting that Vienna arrived separately, Emma contorts this piece of evidence by arguing that her early appearance was a ruse designed to get the employees to open the bank. The teller initially seems to resist Emma's attempt at coercion, but when she persists in her accusations, the teller gives in, saying that he did see Vienna kiss the Kid, an observation that implicates Vienna solely on the basis of her personal association.

Thus, during the crucial scene of Turkey's interrogation the viewer easily understands the subtext of the dialogue, since Ray has so carefully delineated the motivations of those involved: Emma's desire to gain evidence against Vienna, Turkey's desire to save his own neck, and Vienna's determination to keep her stake in the coming railroad. Indeed, when Turkey shrieks to Vienna, "What'll I do?" the viewer recognizes his statement as a naked plea for her sanction of his untruths. Moreover, given the highly public nature of his question, the viewer also becomes aware of the posse's eagerness to accept a lie that so conveniently serves their economic and political interests. Earlier in the film, Johnny Guitar claims that a posse is like an animal, a creature that thinks and moves. That characterization hardly seems to fit the posse shown in *Johnny Guitar*, whose behavior is governed by the all too human qualities of greed, dishonesty, and a diabolical lust for power.

All of these different traits—corruption, coerciveness, and a willingness to accept false witness—serve as the basis for *Johnny Guitar*'s analogical comparison of the posse and HUAC, the lynch mob made comparable to a witch hunt. Yet while the latter term served as a frequent appellation for HUAC's investigative techniques, it is perhaps misapplied to the situation depicted in *Johnny Guitar*. The popular belief about the witch hunts in Salem and Europe is that they resulted from a corrosive combination of fear, conformity, and religious zealotry. Although fear and conformity play their roles in *Johnny Guitar*, the film takes pains to illustrate the way in which the posse serves the interests of the valley's landowners and cattle barons, chiefly Emma and McIvers. Despite this difference, Ray's visuals nonetheless make witty allusion to the "witch hunt" in the Puritan appearance of the posse's funeral dress and in the massive fire that results from their actions. By showing the saloon being reduced to ashes, Ray reminds us that the posse may not have burned Vienna at the stake, but it most certainly torched her namesake.

Allan Dwan's *Silver Lode* (1954) is still another western that has been popularly identified as an anti-blacklist allegory. Although there is little scholarly commentary on *Silver Lode*, *Leonard Maltin's Movie & Video Guide* offers a terse but cogent explanation of the film's political subtext: "So-so melodrama is fascinating relic of its era as both a HIGH NOON variation and an obvious allegory of HUAC/McCarthyist hypocrisy. The action unfolds on July 4, and the villain is named 'McCarty'!"[45] *Silver Lode*'s status as blacklist allegory is reinforced by Martin Scorsese's reference to the film in *A Personal Journey with Martin Scorsese through American Movies* (1995), a documentary celebrating the centennial anniversary of cinema's invention.

Silver Lode tells the tale of Dan Ballard (John Payne), a rancher who came to Silver Lode two years earlier with a $20,000 stake won in a poker game. As the film begins, Dan is about to marry Rose Evans (Lizabeth Scott), the daughter of the town's wealthiest citizen, but the ceremony is interrupted by a U.S. marshal claiming to have a warrant for Dan's arrest. The marshal, named Fred McCarty (Dan Duryea), says that Ballard murdered his brother and that he plans to take Dan back to Discovery to stand trial.

Initially, the townspeople of Silver Lode rally around Dan by questioning McCarty's authority, as well as the legitimacy of the warrant. Harboring suspicions about McCarty's true motive, the sheriff swears in a posse to protect Dan while he is transported to Discovery. While the town's judge and sheriff sort out the legal issues, Dan requests two hours to try to prove that McCarty is a fraud. Initially, Dan tries to send a telegraph message to the sheriff in Discovery only to learn that the wires have been cut. Later, Dan tries to bribe Johnson (Harry Carey Jr.), one of McCarty's deputies, into coming clean, but this plan is also foiled when Johnson is silenced by a bullet from the marshal's gun.

Meanwhile, as details of Ballard's alleged crime emerge, the town begins to question Dan's innocence. Later, mere doubt turns to outright accusal when Dan is found standing over the dead bodies of Johnson and the town sheriff. The sheriff had been a friend and loyal defender of Ballard, but he is killed during Dan's failed attempt to get the deputy to come forward with the truth about McCarty. With Dan suspected of two additional murders, he becomes a fugitive in his own town, dodging the bullets not only of McCarty but also of his fellow citizens. As Dan is chased by both McCarty and the posse, he kills the marshal's two remaining deputies and injures Rose's brother, Mitch.

Desperate to clear his name, Dan finds sanctuary in the town church, hiding in its bell tower while the reverend reminds the bloodthirsty mob about God's injunction against killing. In an effort to help Dan, Rose and Dolly, the saloon's local dancehall girl, blackmail the telegraph operator into sending Dan's wires. When they do not receive a timely response, Rose and Dolly pressure the telegraph operator to forge a wire claiming that McCarty is wanted for murder and cattle rustling. Rose and Dolly's ruse persuades the townspeople that Dan was right all along. In a last-ditch effort to save himself, McCarty tries to shoot Dan while he is hiding in the bell tower but is accidentally killed when a bullet ricochets off the bell and strikes the marshal right in the heart. Feeling betrayed by the town, Dan and Rose walk away from Silver Lode in disgust. In a brief epilogue, Dolly receives a legitimate wire from the sheriff of Discovery confirming that McCarty is a wanted criminal.

The *Maltin* entry on *Silver Lode* highlights the three basic elements that account for the film's purported anti-McCarthyist slant. The first of these is the apparent similarity between *Silver Lode* and *High Noon*. Like *High Noon*, *Silver Lode* generally restricts the time period covered by the film's narration. *High Noon*, of course, became famous for its temporal compression and for the fact that the film's plot time was roughly equivalent to its screen time. *Silver Lode* is perhaps less compressed than *High Noon*, but it nonetheless covers only about four hours of plot time. Similarly, both *High Noon* and *Silver Lode* begin with their respective heroes getting married and the arrival of news that disrupts the ceremonies. Like *High Noon*, *Silver Lode* features two women who come to represent the romantic past and future of the film's hero, Dan Ballard. Rose and Dolly are not as starkly contrasted as *High Noon*'s Amy and Chihuahua—Will Kane's Quaker wife and Mexican mistress respectively—but they play similar narrative functions in *Silver*

Lode. Last, at the end of each film the hero and his wife walk away from the town and its people, leaving behind a community that is unworthy of their trust. In *High Noon* Will Kane leaves, disgusted by Hadleyville's cowardice; in *Silver Lode* Dan Ballard departs, disheartened by the town's suspicious nature, its cynicism, and its willingness to rush to judgment.

The entry in *Maltin* also indicates a second aspect of *Silver Lode* that underlines the film's political subtext. The narrative of *Silver Lode* is not set on just any day of the year. It is set on Independence Day, and this motivates several specific references to the nation's history, its values, and its core beliefs. Red, white, and blue bunting festoons several buildings in town. On a couple of occasions a drummer and fife player are shown rehearsing patriotic ditties to be performed in the Fourth of July parade. At one point Dan interrupts a young girl's recitation of the Declaration of Independence. These visual and aural references are motivated by Silver Lode's civic celebration of our nation's birth, but they also are an obvious reminder of the values of a liberal democracy and the constitutional protections that are supposedly offered to each of its citizens. This setting provides a backdrop to Dan's efforts to discredit McCarty, most of which hinge on issues related to civil liberties. Dan should be given the presumption of innocence until proven guilty, but the townspeople of Silver Lode more or less accept McCarty's accusations against Ballard without the benefit of an actual trial. Likewise, Dan is legally protected against self-incrimination, but this does not prevent the town's citizens from expecting some explanation or account of his innocence, the one thing that Dan himself seems unable to give. The film features several cutaways to town members engaged in gossip, exchanging speculations about Dan's past, his moral character, and the circumstantial evidence that seems to point to his guilt. Dan should also be afforded the opportunity to confront his accuser, but this, too, is prevented by the circumstances of the narrative. In a narrative gambit that seems like a pun on trial procedure, Dan is cut off from Discovery by the severing of Silver Lode's telegraph wires and thus is unable to gain the evidence he needs to cast reasonable doubt on McCarty's charges.

Although not a courtroom drama, *Silver Lode* dramatizes these legal issues in a way that offers oblique commentary on the tactics employed in investigations of alleged Communist subversion. Because these were congressional investigations, witnesses were not afforded the same constitutional protections that adhere during a criminal trial, a situation of which Red-baiters took full advantage politically. In this respect Dan bears a vague similarity to the archetypal HUAC witness, who struggled to find an effective legal defense and who, in the end, opted to simply challenge the authority of the investigator. Indeed, as Tony Shaw says of *Silver Lode*, "The film seemed to be criticising the very process of investigation and sneering at the public's willingness to accept 'evidence' that either suited them personally or corresponded to the temper of the times."[46]

The third, and by far the most obvious, element of *Silver Lode*'s blacklist subtext is the use of the name *McCarty* for the film's villain. In another kind of film this dimension of *Silver Lode* might function as nothing more than a simple, tongue-in-cheek topical reference to the junior senator from Wisconsin. Yet *Silver Lode* adds acuity and depth to this topical reference by linking it to the theme of corruption. Relying on the kind of naming conventions that are more commonly associated with literary allegory, "Fred McCarty" becomes a thinly veiled version of Joseph McCarthy, a man who uses the mantle of the law to foment suspicion and paranoia for his own personal gain.

Using McCarty as a surrogate for McCarthy, *Silver Lode* develops parallels between the character and his real-life counterpart in order to highlight the senator's purported dishonesty, venality, and deviousness. Like McCarthy, McCarty makes accusations for which he has no supporting evidence. The marshal comes to Silver Lode armed with a warrant alleging that Ballard murdered his brother, but McCarty's credentials and his warrant are both forged. Consequently, the paper containing the details of McCarty's arrest warrant prove to be as baseless as the lists of names that the Wisconsin senator famously brandished during press conferences. Moreover, much like his namesake, McCarty also seeks to "criminalize" legally sanctioned actions. Bent on revenge for his brother's death, the marshal seeks to redefine Ballard's act of self-defense as an act of murder and his $20,000 poker stake as stolen property. Violating the legal principles of "double jeopardy," McCarty attempts to charge Ballard with this crime despite the fact that Ballard was cleared of wrongdoing in an earlier inquiry. Last, like the junior senator, McCarty exploits the community's suspicions about Ballard's past as a means of gaining power and authority. The town initially distrusts McCarty, but he gradually gains their confidence by using anxiety and paranoia as a political weapon. By the end of *Silver Lode*, the townspeople are transformed from concerned citizens and friends into a lynch mob ready to mete out swift and harsh justice, punishment apportioned without just cause or due process.

Like *Johnny Guitar*, some of the force of *Silver Lode*'s social critique arises from director Allan Dwan and screenwriter Karen de Wolfe's approach to cinematic narration. During the early parts of the film the narration suppresses a great deal of important information about McCarty and

Ballard. During this part of the film the viewer is aligned with the towns-people in the narration's hierarchy of knowledge. We know little about Ballard's life before he came to Silver Lode and even less about the alleged crime for which he is accused. Indeed, whereas other films might provide a flashback that sketched in the details of the poker game and the shooting that ensued, the narration of *Silver Lode* is fairly parsimonious about infor-mation related to this key event. Ballard admits to Rose that he killed McCarty's brother but asserts that it was an act of self-defense rather than murder. As the film goes on, however, Dwan and de Wolfe align us increas-ingly with Dan in terms of the narration's knowledgeability. Through dia-logue exchanges between Dan and Johnson, the viewer learns that McCarty himself is suspected of cattle rustling and murder and, further, that he killed one of his deputies on the trail when that deputy displayed signs of disloy-alty. More important, the viewer also sees McCarty's naked attempts to blackmail Dan into giving up his land and assets in exchange for his free-dom. All of these exchanges take place in private, however, so the viewer is privy to information about McCarty's background and motivations that none of Silver Lode's citizenry possess.

The most decisive break between the viewer's knowledge and that of the townspeople occurs during the scene in which Johnson and the sheriff are killed in the town's livery stable. The sequence establishes a crucial plot point in the narrative by shifting to an unrestricted range of information in which the viewer learns more about the plot than any individual character. The sequence begins with a medium shot of Ballard inside the livery. Ballard's figure occupies the left-hand part of the frame. The door in the background space opens as Johnson enters the livery. Johnson quickly closes the door and moves to the foreground to fill the empty space on the right side of the frame. Ballard hands Johnson a $5,000 bribe for information about McCarty. When asked what he is buying, Johnson bluntly states that McCarty is no marshal and that he can show Ballard the place where the telegraph wires were cut.

Dwan then cuts to a shot of Zwicker, one of McCarty's deputies, telling Dolly about the shooting of McCarty's brother in Discovery. This shot returns to a previous setup in an ongoing conversation, but it also loosely matches the figure placement of the previous shot with Zwicker and Dolly occupying roughly the same positions occupied by Ballard and Johnson. Dwan then cuts to a previous setup, a high-angle long shot of the saloon's interior. The cut is motivated by the entrance of McCarty and his deputies in the background plane of the composition. Zwicker remains on the left side of the frame next to Dolly, but the right foreground of the composition shows a large table with various and sundry townsfolk crowded around it. When McCarty asks Zwicker about Johnson, Dwan cuts to a medium shot of the empty table at which Johnson had been sitting earlier. Returning to the previous setup, Zwicker tells McCarty that Johnson went to the livery stable to repair a horseshoe. McCarty then turns away from the camera and heads back to the saloon entrance. He is followed not only by his deputies but also by all of the other townspeople. The camera holds on the empty foreground as people file out of the saloon's doorway in the background.

Dwan then cuts back to the previous two-shot of Ballard and Johnson. Johnson explains that another deputy, Williams, forged McCarty's warrant and that the marshal killed him when he was no longer needed. Johnson cries, "I'm next. I know it!" while Ballard moves to the background of the composition, obviously headed for the livery's entrance. The camera then cuts to a position that shows Ballard's right shoulder as he pulls open the livery's heavy door. A shot rings out, which alerts Ballard that his confab with Johnson has been discovered.

There are several elements of this sequence that signal the shift to a less restricted, more communicative style of narration. Chief among them is the use of crosscutting to render the two lines of action taking place simultaneously: Johnson's confession of McCarty's duplicity and Zwicker's recounting of the details surrounding Ballard's shooting of McCarty's brother. Dwan's use of crosscutting also helps to underline a number of internal rhymes that develop between the two lines of action. Each line of action is structured around the use of deep staging and characters' entrances and exits in the background plane of the shot. Each line of action builds to a revelation about McCarty and Ballard's respective pasts just before they arrived in Silver Lode. And each line of action builds to a point that closes a gap between the knowledge of the viewer and the characters: McCarty and Zwicker's realization that Johnson is no longer in the saloon, on one hand, and Johnson and Ballard's recognition that their tête-à-tête has been detected, on the other.

As the sequence goes on, Dwan continues to use a less restricted style of narration in order to heighten the scene's suspense. By framing the action primarily in medium and medium long shots, Dwan breaks up the space inside and around the livery stable. This enables Dwan to cut to three contiguous spaces: the stable's ground level, where Ballard attempts to conceal himself in a corner; the stable's loft, which McCarty stealthily enters with the intent of killing Johnson to silence him; and the exterior of the stable, where Sheriff Woolley waits outside the door. Perhaps the most important shot in the sequence is the medium long shot of McCarty stepping out of the loft and announcing to the crowd that Ballard has shot Johnson, a murder that McCarty himself committed. The shot highlights the extent to which the townspeople depend on McCarty for information. Screened off from any view of the livery's occupants and hearing only the sound of the gunshot, the townspeople accept McCarty's claim while the spectator knows it to be a bald-faced lie.

Now that Johnson is dead, Dwan returns to the pattern of crosscutting we saw earlier. The same three spaces also remain active as the loci of the different lines of action. In the ground floor of the livery, McCarty holds Ballard at gunpoint and attempts to extort land and cattle, an action rendered in a long two-shot with Ballard positioned on the left half of the frame and McCarty positioned on the right. Dwan even tries to briefly ratchet up the suspense of the sequence by cutting to a shot of Johnson waiting just offscreen. In a medium shot Johnson is shown briefly raising his head and taking aim at McCarty before finally succumbing to his gunshot wound. Meanwhile, Sheriff Woolley is shown entering the space of the loft unbeknownst to either Ballard or McCarty. Woolley thus overhears McCarty's threats against Ballard and reassures Dan that he has enough information to clear Ballard's name and to take McCarty into custody. At the same time, Dwan shows exterior shots of the townspeople trying to break down the livery's door and the judge's arrival on the scene. These different plot strands finally come together on the ground floor of the livery as McCarty guns down Sheriff Woolley but is wounded in the exchange of fire. When Woolley's body falls out of the loft, Ballard enters the frame to pick up both men's guns. Thus, when the townspeople finally break into the stable, they are greeted by the sight of McCarty wounded, Woolley and Johnson dead, and Ballard holding each man's weapons as he stands over the body of the fallen lawman.

Dwan beautifully captures the townspeople's reactions in a long shot of the stable's ground floor (fig. 10). Ballard is positioned on the extreme left edge of the frame, the guns in his hands extended slightly away from his body. McCarty crouches, barely visible, in the left part of the background, a position that initially conceals him from the crowd when it bursts through the door. The bodies of Woolley and Johnson occupy the foreground of the frame, their prone figures taking up most of the bottom third of the composition. Once the doors burst open, the townspeople occupy the center background portion of the frame, a position that is highlighted by the lighting of the shot and by Dwan's aperture framing, which locates the crowd not only in the doorway but also beneath the strong horizontal axis created by the loft beams. This distant objective camera position is the logical con-

Figure 10. The hierarchy of knowledge established by the narration in *Silver Lode* places the viewer at the top, such that the audience knows more about the plot's actions and motivations than any individual character. Director Allan Dwan uses this pattern to emphasize Dan Ballard's innocence and undermine Marshal Fred McCarty's claims of authority. When the townspeople break into the stable to discover Ballard standing over the bodies of Johnson and Sheriff Woolley, the viewer quite readily recognizes the way in which McCarty has exploited their suspicion and distrust.

sequence of Dwan's crosscutting and the unrestricted range of information that it entails. Possessing more knowledge of the situation than any one of the characters, the viewer is perfectly positioned to understand the way that McCarty manipulates events to his own ends and the crowd's wrongful presumption of Dan's guilt.

As was the case with *Johnny Guitar*, the unrestricted range of information plays an important role, not only in *Silver Lode*'s narration but also in the rhetoric of its critique of McCarthyism. To dramatize the theme of political corruption, the filmmaker places the viewer at the top of the hierarchy of knowledge so that the viewer recognizes the lies, deceptions, and manipulations of certain characters and can morally judge their actions accordingly. Additionally, by establishing parallels between these duplicitous characters and contemporary historical personages, these films use the theme of "frontier justice" to comment on the Red Scare and the Hollywood blacklist, especially the tactics employed by investigators.

Still, if we accept both *Johnny Guitar* and *Silver Lode* as allegories of the blacklist, then the films seem particularly dour and cynical about the Hollywood left's ability to counter the effects of these institutions. Both Vienna and Dan Ballard are vindicated by the end of their respective films but not in ways that demonstrate or prove their protagonists' innocence. This type of narrative resolution is perhaps more typical of the courtroom drama or detective novel than the western, but it nonetheless carries certain weight in any evaluation of genre as a particular vehicle for political commentary. Vienna does little more than outlast her enemies. True, her duel to the death with Emma resolves at least one important plot strand insofar as it removes an obstacle to Vienna's future happiness with Johnny, but other potential enemies, like McIvers, simply give up their fight. Perhaps one reason that contemporary critics identified *Johnny Guitar* as a romantic melodrama is because the film's climax so strongly prioritizes Vienna and Johnny's romance over other issues raised in the course of the film's narrative. The film's last shot, a long shot of Vienna and Johnny embracing against the natural splendor of the waterfalls outside the Dancin' Kid's lair, seems to promise hope, renewal, and emotional security but only as it applies to the formation of the couple. At film's end Vienna is penniless, with her business destroyed and with little hope that her railroad enterprise will ever pay off.

Silver Lode is perhaps even starker in its treatment of the tactics used to thwart McCarty and in the questions that linger regarding Ballard's character. At two separate points in the film Dolly and Rose blackmail the telegraph operator in order to assist Dan's efforts to clear his name. In the first instance, Dolly and Rose pressure the operator to do something he should do anyway, namely to send Ballard's wire to the sheriff in Discovery. In the second instance, though, Dolly and Rose coerce the telegraph operator into fabricating a message that discredits McCarty's credentials and proclaims Dan's innocence. Although the film's epilogue shows the telegraph operator receiving a genuine message from Discovery that clears Dan's name, the veridical status of these messages is less important than how they were procured. Both messages are received as the result of interrogative intimidation, more specifically Dolly's threat to go to the telegraph operator's wife with false claims about the dance-hall girl's relationship with her husband. When the telegraph operator protests that Dolly's claims aren't true, she responds by asking which claims will have more credibility with the operator's wife: her accusations of infidelity or his denials. Viewed in this way, Dolly and Rose's tactics seem little different from those of McCarty (or those of McCarthy, for that matter). For Dolly, McCarty, and McCarthy the truth of an accusation is less important than the power gained from making it.

While the tactics used by Dolly and Rose to clear Dan's name are undoubtedly dubious, even more troubling are the lingering questions about Ballard's involvement in several of the killings that are depicted or implied during the course of the film. As I have emphasized throughout, the overriding narrative goal in *Silver Lode* is the aim to discredit McCarty by revealing his dishonesty and by showing that his appearance of lawful authority masks an underlying desire for vigilante justice. Yet it simply does not follow that the proof of McCarty's fraudulence is concomitant proof of Ballard's innocence. Ballard himself provides the only evidence that he is not guilty of the murder of McCarty's brother, and that evidence is a terse assertion of self-defense in response to a query from Rose. In letting Ballard and Rose walk away from Silver Lode at film's end, the townspeople seem to forget that Dan himself was discovered in the livery standing over two lifeless bodies and holding the weapons responsible for each man's death. Does the exposure of McCarty's dishonesty in any way exculpate Ballard's apparent involvement in these two deaths? Likewise, what about the two deputies that are gunned down during the course of Ballard's escape? Is Dan's armed resistance to arrest legally justified as a form of self-defense? In the end the viewer's moral sympathy for Ballard might well be misplaced. The viewer sympathizes with Dan largely as a result of McCarty's duplicitous manipulation of the law. Yet Ballard's ready-made status as victim obscures more fundamental questions about the gentleman farmer's past as a gambler and a gunfighter.

In the end the cynicism evident in *High Noon, Johnny Guitar,* and *Silver Lode* seems to limit their effectiveness as anti-HUAC allegories. Perhaps some of this desaturation stems from each film's "blame-the-victim" narrative strategies, which imply that the protagonist of each film bears some responsibility for the predicament in which they find themselves. Will Kane might be said to suffer from a misplaced sense of civic duty and authority and from a willingness to put ordinary citizens in harm's way. Vienna suffers from a suspect sexual history, and Dan Ballard suffers from a shady past prior to arriving in Silver Lode. In all three films the protagonists each leave their respective communities at film's end. Considering the bitterness and fatalism expressed in the endings of these anti-HUAC allegories, it is easy to see them as metaphorical articulations of the voluntary and involuntary exile experienced by many of the blacklist's victims.

Perhaps the problem in using corruption as the basis for an analogy between Old West justice and Red-baiting politics is that corruption has a way of fouling everything it touches. Paradoxically, these anti-HUAC allegories not only reveal the questionable ethics that underpin a politics of suspicion and accusation, but they also confirm its effectiveness. Like contemporary political campaigns, the Red-baiting strategies of HUAC and McCarthy render the entire field toxic by making all parties seem unworthy of the power they desire to wield. *Johnny Guitar*'s Turkey might serve as the best symbol of the notion that a corrupted society taints everyone within it. A fictional surrogate for HUAC's "friendly" witnesses, Turkey talks but he gets hanged anyway.

THREAT OR SAVIOR: THE OUTSIDER IN EDWARD DMYTRYK'S *WARLOCK*

As was true of the frontier as a generic trope, the notion of the western hero as outsider is a concept so familiar to film scholars it is almost scarcely worth mentioning. One of the most widely understood narrative conventions of the western, its place within scholarly analyses of the genre was secured early on by such trailblazing critics as Robert Warshow and Will Wright. The trope of the outsider, however, has had a somewhat parallel history as a narrative convention of blacklist allegories. Because the cowboy hero is so commonly represented as a figure caught between civilization and the wilderness, the western provides a convenient textual overlay for directors and screenwriters who explore the dynamics of American Cold War politics. Through the dovetailing of character and historical situation, the cowboy hero frequently acts as a metaphorical catalyst of the suspicion and xenophobia commonly associated with the era.

Yet as any good deconstructionist or linguistic philosopher knows, the meaning of *outside* must be defined relationally, depending as it does on some prior concept of *inside*. Because of such contextual determinations, the notion of the western hero as "outsider" proves to be a highly flexible and unstable concept, especially in its metaphorical figuration within allegories of the blacklist. As a trope whose meaning shifts quite radically within specific interpretive contexts, the cowboy hero's outsider status can render him either as a hapless victim of a corrupt, unjust society or as a patriotic defender of American freedoms and values. Because of the outsider's semiotic instability, a substantial number of 1950s westerns might be characterized as double allegories of the blacklist, whose meanings are more or less incommensurable. In this way the 1950s western serves simultaneously as both a critique and a defense of HUAC and McCarthyism, depending on how the reader frames the topical reference points that support her or his allegorical interpretation.

Edward Dmytryk's *Warlock* (1959) furnishes an especially incisive treatment of the outsider as a theme of blacklist allegories. Along with Elia Kazan, Dmytryk was widely perceived as a traitor to the Hollywood left. One of the original Hollywood Ten, Dmytryk received a prison sentence for Contempt of Congress but experienced a change of heart while serving his time in a Federal Correctional facility in Mill Point, West Virginia. On September 9, 1950, Dmytryk signed a statement, witnessed by his prison warden, attesting that he was not a Communist or Communist sympathizer and had not been one at the time of the 1947 HUAC hearings. Dmytryk defended his cooperation with authorities by suggesting that martyrdom on behalf of the Communist Party's right to exist and function freely was "possibly a laudable cause, but I believed that every martyr has a right to choose his own reason for martyrdom. Protecting the Communist Party, which I had grown to detest, was not going to be mine."[47]

Because of this change of heart, some critics have analyzed Dmytryk's films of the 1950s, especially *The Caine Mutiny* (1956) and *Warlock*, as a fictive defense of his decision to cooperate. The latter film takes its name from the town in which it is set. The people of Warlock are beset by a band of "regulators" who have been hired by Abe McQuown (Tom Drake), the owner of the San Pablo Ranch, to thwart rustlers. The "regulators" frequently ride into town to drink and carouse. The cowboys' activities often get out of hand as they brawl drunkenly, shoot up the town, and even kill people. Since every deputy sheriff in Warlock is either killed or driven out of town, its Citizen's Committee hires a notorious gunfighter, Clay Blaisedell (Henry Fonda), to stop the gang's rampages. Upon arriving, though, Blaisedell demands more money and the ability to handle the town as he sees fit. The Citizen's Committee agrees to his terms but only after Blaisedell vouches for his partner, Tom Morgan (Anthony Quinn), who just purchased one of the town's saloons.

The next Saturday night McQuown and his gang come into Morgan's saloon, renamed the French Palace. Blaisedell warns McQuown that he will kill anyone who starts a shooting scrape. McQuown stalks out of the saloon in response to Blaisedell's threat. All but one of McQuown's regulators go with him. Johnny Gannon (Richard Widmark) stays behind in the saloon, saying he doesn't want to go back to San Pablo. Thanks to Blaisedell's notoriety, an uneasy peace comes to Warlock. The surrounding areas, though, remain victims of McQuown's gang as cattle continue to be rustled and stagecoaches continue to get held up.

Meanwhile, Morgan prepares for the arrival of Bob Nicholson, who seeks to avenge the death of his brother, Ben. Blaisedell shot Ben as the latter was preparing to marry Morgan's old flame, Lily Dollar (Dorothy Malone). Morgan rides to a ridge to head off Nicholson and inadvertently witnesses two of McQuown's hired guns—Billy Gannon and Pony Benner—robbing the stage. Morgan kills Nicholson, but it looks as if Billy is the one responsible. Blaisedell leads a posse to capture Billy and Pony. The pair are acquitted at trial, but the Citizen's Committee insists that they and two other members of McQuown's gang be posted out of town. Johnny Gannon takes the job of the town's deputy sheriff, even though Blaisedell remains the official enforcer in Warlock.

Billy Gannon and two other of McQuown's gang call out Blaisedell, who sits with Jessie Marlow (Dolores Michaels) in Warlock's boardinghouse. With Gannon waiting for Blaisedell, Morgan pleads with him to move on to a new boomtown, Porphery City. Blaisedell responds that he is not leaving, that he wants to settle down in Warlock with Jessie. Blaisedell faces Gannon and the other cowboys and initially tries to talk them into leaving. Gannon orders the others to fire, and although Blaisedell is injured in the exchange, he kills Billy and Benner. Blaisedell spares the life of the remaining cowboy, though, allowing him to get on his horse and ride out of town. As Jessie tends to Clay's wound, he announces that he has been Warlock's marshal too long. Clay gives up his job but decides to remain in town to be near Jessie.

The last part of *Warlock* builds toward a pair of final showdowns. Johnny rides to San Pablo and warns McQuown and his boys to stay away from Warlock. McQuown's gang gives Johnny a rough going-over, and the old man himself runs a knife through Johnny's gun hand. Johnny lies unconscious as his horse takes him back to Warlock. Curley Burne, one of McQuown's cowboys, comes to Johnny the next day to alert him that the San Pablo crew will ride into Warlock at sundown. Lily Dollar, Johnny's new girlfriend, urges him to leave. But Johnny vows to stay, saying he is proud to be Warlock's deputy. Later, Blaisedell and Morgan watch as McQuown and his gang ride into town. Sensing that Blaisedell might attempt to intervene, Morgan pulls a gun on him, saying he won't leave the saloon until Johnny has been killed. Once that happens, Clay can reclaim his former position as the hero of Warlock. When Johnny walks out to meet the San Pablo gang, though, he is backed by Warlock's townsfolk. In the gunfight that follows, McQuown is killed, and the rest of the gang is subdued. Johnny deputizes the men of Warlock, and they take their prisoners to nearby Bright City to stand trial.

Feeling betrayed by Clay, Morgan gets drunk and shoots up the town, just as McQuown's gang did. Morgan calls out Johnny, but Clay takes away Johnny's guns and locks him in a jail cell, saying that Morgan is his responsibility. Clay orders Morgan out of town. Morgan begins to leave, but when the town mocks and jeers him, he turns and fires on Clay. Clay kills Morgan and then carries his body into the saloon. Clay denounces the people of Warlock, telling them that Morgan was the only real man among them. As a token of respect for the dead, Clay lights candles and demands that the crowd sing "Rock of Ages." Johnny asks Clay to leave Warlock, saying that if he isn't gone by morning, he'll come after him. Jessie begs Clay to stay, but he decides to take the job in Porphery City that Morgan had mentioned previously. Clay asks Jessie if she will go with him, but she says that she can't leave Warlock. Clay walks down Warlock's main street, still undecided about what to do. Johnny comes toward him, prepared to draw down on Clay if it comes to that. Clay spies Johnny's girlfriend, Lily, in mourning attire in front of Morgan's saloon. Perhaps Lily reminds Clay of Morgan's death, or perhaps he sees her as Johnny's future bride and the source of his future happiness. Or perhaps Clay knows he is outgunned as Lily holds a concealed Derringer in her glove. Whatever the reason, Clay walks past Johnny, climbs onto his horse, and rides out of town. Jessie runs after Clay, who turns back to look at her but then continues to ride off into the distance.

In his autobiography, Dmytryk offered his own take on the politics of *Warlock*, describing the Oakley Hall book upon which the film was based:

> Our novel had enough material for two good films—a Western and a story of labor conflict. For our purposes, the Western aspect was dominant and we decided to concentrate on the civilizing of a frontier area through the gradual and painful imposition of law. Not an original theme, but what made it more interesting in *Warlock* was that the process continued through several steps. First came the willful dominance of a lawless mob; then the rule of the mob legitimatized (comparable to baronial rule in feudal times or that of a Chinese war lord prior to World War II); third, the rule of the gunslinging marshal (comparable to that of a dictator); and finally, the accession of a popularly elected sheriff. It was the development of a society in microcosm.[48]

Although Dmytryk does not explicitly draw this conclusion, it is not hard to imagine his description of the "gunslinging marshal" as a "dictator" as a reference to political extremism on both sides. If this is the case, then

Dmytryk's *Warlock* is a critique of Communism as much as it is a critique of fascism. Indeed, the references to feudalism and a Chinese war lord seem to hint at the rise of Mao rather than Mussolini, Stalin rather than Hitler.

The notion that *Warlock* is a centrist critique is developed more fully by critic Michael Coyne. Calling *Warlock* "as comprehensive an engagement with the anti-communist witch-hunts of the 1940s and 1950s as are *Johnny Guitar* and *High Noon*," Coyne argues that Richard Widmark's rehabilitated outlaw, Gannon, functions as "Dmytryk's neo-centrist, neo-conformist spokesman." Coyne supports this reading of the film by citing Dmytryk's eventual capitulation to HUAC and by noting certain subtle parallels between Dmytryk and Gannon: "Against the opening credits of *Warlock*, we see nine cowboys riding toward town. Eight ride in a fairly close grouping, while the last (Widmark) hangs back, his heart clearly not in their venture. Widmark is alone in the frame as Dmytryk's screen credit appears. Thus, even before one word of dialogue is uttered, producer-director Dmytryk has established Gannon as a man of conscience, accompanying but *apart* from his confrères—literally, a reluctant fellow traveler." Note here how Coyne employs a punning heuristic—the fellow traveler—to add a political valence to the iconic image of men riding together on horseback. Coyne doesn't stop there, though: "Gannon breaks with McQuown's gang just as Dmytryk broke with the rest of the Ten. He allies himself with the established political-legal structure (by becoming deputy) as Dmytryk did (by cooperating with HUAC). As *Warlock*'s deputy Gannon earns the respect of decent citizens, just as Dmytryk's full reinstatement within the Hollywood community restored him to directorial prominence."[49]

Besides the biographical and textual similarities, Coyne also adds an intertextual dimension to his analysis by directly comparing *Warlock* to *On the Waterfront*, Elia Kazan's own apologia for cooperating with HUAC. The two directors and their films are, thus, situated within a chain of analogical comparisons; Kazan is like Dmytryk, who is like Gannon, who is like Terry Malloy: "Significantly, the one San Pablo cowboy who survives the O.K. Corral–type shoot-out with Blaisedell is called Friendly (as is the tyrannical union boss in Kazan's film). Gannon's progress in *Warlock* is identical to Marlon Brando's in *On the Waterfront*: at first tied to his old companions through his brother, he must ultimately oppose his former mentor. Brando is beaten to a pulp, Widmark's Gannon is stabbed in the hand, yet both remain resolute."[50] Like Kazan, Dmytryk epitomizes the liberal anti-Communist politics that sit in the "vital center" of the political spectrum. Citing a line of dialogue from *Warlock* that describes Blaisedell and the regulators as "two mirrors put face to face," Coyne writes, "In effect, this subtly asserts that the far right (Blaisedell) and the far left (Abe McQuown) are at heart alike, equidistant from a consensual law-abiding society."[51]

Interestingly, though, Coyne's interpretation of *Warlock* resists the temptation to treat Blaisedell as an allegorical stand-in for McCarthy. Coyne bases this conclusion both on the character's basic decency and on the righteousness and power that Henry Fonda brings to his portrayal. Because of the dignity and integrity associated with Fonda's larger screen persona, Coyne sees Blaisedell as more like Douglas MacArthur than Joseph McCarthy. Yet, somewhat bizarrely, Coyne nonetheless treats Blaisedell's sidekick, Tom Morgan, as a surrogate for Roy Cohn, McCarthy's right-hand man. The grounds for this appear to have nothing to do with Morgan's politics. Rather, Coyne bases his conclusion on *Warlock*'s insinuation that Morgan, like Cohn, is homosexual.[52] Coyne's rhetorical maneuvers here exemplify the kinds of allegorical reading strategies that we've seen throughout this book. Coyne gathers together a rather wide variety of topical reference points—Dmytryk's HUAC testimony, Kazan's HUAC testimony, McCarthy's "Red-baiting" tactics, Cohn's sexual orientation—to frame *Warlock* in a way that invests the characters and events of the film with political significance.

Although Coyne centers his interpretation on the Blaisedell, Gannon, and McQuown triangle, other critics focus on Warlock's corrupt political environment, an atmosphere of cowardice and conformity that enables Blaisedell's and McQuown's dictatorial exercise of power. John Lenihan, for example, sees *Warlock* as but one of several westerns in the 1950s that show the citizens of a town abandoning their civic duties when confronted by an external threat. According to Lenihan, the image of a weak society enabled certain filmmakers to depict the dangers associated with the rise of an unprincipled demagogue: "Although the vision of a spineless society could appeal to either left or right, the prospect of a false prophet misleading a blind society seems most appropriate as an allegorical attack on McCarthyism."[53]

Although Lenihan does not state it in these terms, his analysis of a "weak society" in these westerns seems to undercut the basic thesis of Coyne's reading of *Warlock*. Far from being a defense of Dmytryk's actions, *Warlock* seems to be the director's cinematic admission of guilt for betraying his comrades. Instead of treating cooperative witnesses' actions as principled opposition to Communism, Lenihan "frames" Kazan's and Dmytryk's co-optation by HUAC as concessions to dominant power structures rooted in fear and self-protection. If Lenihan is right, then *Warlock* is self-loathing rather than self-affirming.

A more recent reading of *Warlock* blends elements of both of these previous interpretations. Matthew Costello praises Coyne's reading of *Warlock* as an allegory of Dmytryk's break with the Hollywood Ten but argues that this construal of the film ignores *Warlock*'s complex treatment of the timeworn western theme of "law and order." Like Coyne, Costello sees Gannon defending Warlock from political extremists, but like Lenihan, he wonders whether Warlock is a community truly worth saving: "The center does hold in *Warlock*, as Coyne suggests, but what holds it together has no intrinsic meaning. Rules may keep us orderly, but they do not provide moral clarity."[54]

Because Warlock lacks a moral center, the film's depiction of its townspeople ultimately undermines the centrist political position that the film tries to advance. Lacking any redemptive power, *Warlock* does not defend the "vital center" so much as it dramatizes its fragmentation: "In the wake of red scares, threats of missile gaps, growing disaffection with an increasingly powerful and interventionist state, and the increasing voice of potential dissidents, the consensus lauded earlier in the decade is harder to find. Where it is found, it seems to lack any inherent meaning other than preventing its own dissolution. The moral vacuity and role confusion of *Warlock* mirror this changing cultural environment, revealing growing anxiety and a loss of faith in the consensus of the vital center."[55]

While the rhetoric of Costello's reading has "a pox on both houses" quality, it perhaps resonates more strongly with left-wing critiques of the blacklist than it does with right-wing defenses of domestic security policy. After all, for an outside force like HUAC to be perceived as a savior, there must be something in the community worth saving in the first place. By caving in so easily to outside pressures, Hollywood revealed itself to be an institution that could salvage its fortunes but couldn't save its soul.

CONCLUSION

The frontier, corrupt officials, the lynch mob, the stranger from another town—all of these common elements of the western provide the ground on which different semantic fields are mapped in allegorical readings of postwar westerns. Yet, because some of these different genre elements are inherently vague with respect to their politics, they come to mean very different things in particular readings of these films, depending on the rhetorical aims of the critics involved in such interpretations. The frontier in the western is the mythical divide between civilization and the wilderness, but its meaning depends on how the critic "frames" it in relation to specific topical reference points that function as its allegorical pretext. These topical reference points range across a wide variety of then-current events and policy initiatives, including the HUAC hearings themselves, the threat of Soviet expansionism, the concomitant development of the Truman Doctrine as a response to that threat, and the outbreak of the Korean War. Critics also try to bolster their particular "framing" of these genre terms by appealing to the offscreen political lives of the people involved in making these films, sometimes citing the role of "friendly" and "unfriendly" witnesses called to testify before HUAC.

Because of the constitutive ambiguity of these genre elements, critics have spun wildly different interpretations of particular titles. Some critics, for example, see *High Noon* as blacklisted screenwriter Carl Foreman's critique of Hollywood's failure to stand up to HUAC. Others see the film as a disguised representation of U.S. containment policy, with Marshal Will Kane enacting America's role as "policeman" of the world. One commonality of these double allegories, though, is the extent to which they rely on spatial metaphor as a way of mapping domestic and geopolitical tensions. The frontier towns of these westerns stand in for the nation in readings of them as expressions of containment policy or U.S. imperialism. These same towns function, though, as surrogates for Hollywood in anti-HUAC readings, emphasizing the more localized politics of the industry itself.

As John Lenihan notes, *High Noon* seems to be a particularly salient example of a film whose meanings shift according to the political perspective that is represented within the interpretation. Noting that Foreman structured his analogy in a way that bears "an unmistakable similarity to the anticommunist arguments of those he was attacking," Lenihan asks, "Could not Joseph McCarthy himself be identified with the strong individualist who refuses to compromise with that which threatens the community?"[56]

Leo Charney offers a similar analysis in his discussion of another film discussed in this chapter, *Johnny Guitar*. Charney elaborates this dualistic quality of *Johnny Guitar* by highlighting the shifting ideological position of Joan Crawford's Vienna within each of two seemingly opposed allegorical scenarios. As an allegory of Soviet containment, Vienna is figured as a psychic location more than as a flesh-and-blood character. Representing the potential for Communist expansion, Vienna, like Russia, evokes a threat that is both spatial and ideological in nature. For Charney, though, this allegory of containment overlays a second more specific, and perhaps more pertinent, drama figured around the issue of blacklisting. Charney locates this allegory of the blacklist in Emma's pivotal role in the film's drama of gender roles, in Mercedes McCambridge's performance of radical fervor and neurotic femininity, and in the historically specific allusions to the blacklist entailed in the casting of Ward Bond and Sterling Hayden that I discussed earlier. Charney's treatment of *Johnny Guitar* as double allegory is bolstered by a conflict in the conceptual scale of allegorical interpretation. Charney juxtaposes a global interpretation of the American political context with a more localized interpretation of industry politics within Hollywood.[57]

These double allegories also offer a unique illustration of a phenomenon that cognitive scientists refer to as frame switching. The ease with which we can see *High Noon* or *Johnny Guitar* as being either a blacklist allegory or containment allegory is akin to the ease with which we can see either a duck or rabbit in Jastrow's famous perceptual illusion. Frame switching in interpretations is merely a higher order version of our basic ability to find patterns in perceptual data. As several studies of frame switching have shown, such shifts in meaning depend on the particular context created by the speaker. In double allegories of the blacklist, this context is established by the critic, who mines the film for evidence that it expresses both foreign and domestic policy simultaneously.

Still, although both of these types of interpretations employ spatial metaphor, they remain on terra firma. As we will see in the next chapter, this need not be the case because spatial metaphor can also be enlarged to encompass other planets and other galaxies. Space—the "final frontier," in the famous words of James Tiberius Kirk—offers filmmakers yet another way to map the semantic fields associated with the Cold War and the Hollywood blacklist. Within the world of the science fiction film, the western's iconic "stranger from another town" gets made over as the equally iconic "stranger from another world."

7 Loving the Alien

Science Fiction Cinema as Cold War Allegory

On July 23, 1953, David Platt of the *Daily Worker* reported on a dispute between Hollywood studio bosses and J. Cheever Cowdin, new chief of the U.S. government's overseas film program. Cowdin urged the studios to include more anti-Communist content in their work, but, according to Platt, the executives pushed back, warning that such a policy risked ruining the reputations of American films abroad. "We can see their point," said Platt:

> Suppose, for example, Alan Ladd were to follow up the shooting of the sinister gunman Jack Palance in "Shane" by turning to the audience with: "We got rid of him. Now let's go after Malenkov."
>
> Or suppose the prehistoric monster in "The Beast from 20,000 Fathoms" were to stop in the midst of his crushing attack on Wall Street to announce that the Communists ordered him to do it.[1]

Platt's facetious comments underscore the sheer absurdity of inserting explicit anti-Communist messages into Hollywood genre films. Yet the notion that monsters and aliens implicitly represented the Communist menace is now a critical commonplace. Many film critics and historians argue that the science fiction films of the 1950s function as cultural documents of collective unease and social anxiety. Victoria O'Donnell, for example, says, "Whether realistic or fantasy-oriented, these films revolve around fears of nuclear weapons and Communist domination."[2] John Belton echoes these sentiments, but further characterizes the cycle as one that historically parallels the anti-Communist films made after 1947: "Even more successful than these overtly anti-Communist works were the covert 'war' films—science fiction films. These works captured the decade's greatest fears—fear of the bomb and fear of a Communist takeover—but did so without the crude tactics of the more flagrantly political films that merely restaged the HUAC hearings in a somewhat more dramatic form or simply reworked events that had taken place in Korea."[3]

Such comments indicate the degree to which this view of 1950s science fiction has taken on the force of critical dogma. Indeed, this perspective is so widespread that one is hard-pressed to find discussions of the genre that don't broach these subjects in one way or another. Where one finds the phrase "science fiction films of the 1950s," one is almost sure to find the phrases "Cold War anxieties," "nuclear terror," and "McCarthyist fears" trailing close behind.

Still this view of mid-twentieth-century science fiction cinema, like the model of zeitgeist criticism itself, has been accepted uncritically by most modern film scholars. Critics may dispute the particular ways in which films and society relate to one another, but no one doubts that some type of relation surely exists. With this in mind, it seems clear that scholarship on postwar science fiction cinema begs the same types of questions that have been posed throughout this study:

- How have film critics constructed interpretive frames around these texts?

- What semantic fields associated with this genre have critics activated in seeking to explain the films' relation to contemporary politics?

- In what ways do 1950s science fiction films offer covert commentary on Hollywood's institution of the blacklist?

The latter question is less obvious than it might appear at first blush. Because these films are commonly associated with fears of Communism, it hardly seems surprising that at least some of them either endorse or criticize the practice of blacklisting. That said, the Hollywood blacklist is hardly synonymous with McCarthyism and is even less evidently connected to American foreign policy initiatives. Consequently, the challenge posed by the metacritical analysis of 1950s science fiction films is the need to remain sensitive to the differences between these critical contexts, as well as their points of overlap.

At the outset, it is worth noting that this particular reading formation developed in a manner consistent with the larger patterns of interpretive practice outlined elsewhere in this book. The notion that 1950s science fiction films functioned as anti-Communist allegories first appeared in the 1960s with Susan Sontag's "The Imagination of Disaster" emerging as a particularly influential exemplar of zeitgeist criticism. From there, additional readings and interviews with filmmakers conducted in the 1970s and 1980s confirmed the basic assumptions of the genre's relation to its social and political contexts. Jack Arnold, the director of such science fiction classics as *Tarantula* (1955) and *The Incredible Shrinking Man* (1957), recalled, "I think science fiction films are a marvelous medium for telling a story, creating a mood, and delivering whatever kind of social message should be delivered."[4] Arnold's comments appear to activate the "representativeness heuristic." After all, if a B-movie director like Arnold admits to using the genre as a vehicle for social messages, then it seems reasonable to assume that many other directors did as well.

Some directors and screenwriters go further, though, suggesting that their films were implicitly about the Cold War and the politics that surrounded it. Kate Phillips, for example, reveals that her collaboration with director Irvin Yeaworth on *The Blob* (1958) occurred after the two met at a prayer breakfast sponsored by fundamentalist Christians. According to Jeff Sharlet, Phillips and Yeaworth conceived of *The Blob* as a response to Cold War politics, one that served as the era's "most ridiculous metaphor for communism."[5] Additionally, Jack Arnold describes *It Came from Outer Space* (1953) as a response to contemporary Red-baiting practices:

> This was the height of the McCarthy era when we were scared of everything and you didn't have to be a Communist to be suspect. It may have been the worst period this country has ever gone through. The whole political climate was one of a witchhunt. And if there were important things to be said about our society and its mores, they certainly weren't being said in the film-fare at the time. So that was the kind of thing I wanted to express, especially in those political times we were living in. We could do it, and get away with it, because it was fantasy. On the face of it, they wouldn't relate it to the problems of the day—those who weren't keen enough intellectually and especially those who were running the studio.[6]

Once paradigm examples like *The Blob* and *It Came From Outer Space* are established, modern-day critics, like the Red-hunters they analyze, find allegorists lurking everywhere. Reasoning that such social criticism is likely present in more than just the few cases at hand, film analysts find it in virtually all science fiction films made during the period. Such reliance on the representativeness heuristic occurs whether or not such meanings can be documented as part of the production process. Rather, following the line of argument later advanced by Susan Sontag, Carlos Clarens, and others, modern scholars see the allegorical possibilities of science fiction as a trait endemic to the genre itself.

Victoria O'Donnell summarizes four major themes that she discerns in this particular corpus of films: (1) extraterrestrial travel; (2) alien invasion and infiltration; (3) mutants, metamorphosis, and resurrection of extinct species; and (4) near annihilation or the end of Earth.[7] Each of these themes bears on the interpretation of 1950s science fiction films as blacklist allegories in different ways and to different degrees. Whereas readings of historical films as blacklist allegories devolve on the interplay between past and present, readings of science fiction films mobilize any number of particular textual features to offer commentary on the politics of Hollywood. The prevailing doctrine that these films are replete with images of Cold War anxiety comes in part from the sheer number of "symptoms" available for "diagnosis."

In this chapter I highlight the constitutive elements of blacklist allegory that are found in science fiction films of the 1950s. In examining this corpus, I identify several frequent "ingredients" of the genre that take on particular significance in their relation to specific events, governmental policies, discursive structures, and representational strategies from the period. Not surprisingly, these elements are often explicitly or implicitly cited as textual evidence in support of the allegorical meanings critics locate in 1950s science fiction. Through this analysis I show how particular features of the genre have come to define the zeitgeist of 1950s science fiction as one of Cold War anxieties, including those that are specifically associated with the Hollywood blacklist.

ALIENS: FEAR OF A "RED" PLANET

As I have suggested, the notion that aliens in science fiction films of the 1950s symbolize Communist aggression and subversion is so widely accepted it is almost trite. Indeed, in several essays and monographs on 1950s science fiction, critics uncritically accept the formulation that aliens function as allegorical representations of the Communist menace before moving on to the "real work" of their analysis. Patrick Luciano's *Them or Us* is a textbook example of this pattern. After initially arguing that 1950s alien invasion films are generic hybrids that combine science fiction and horror elements, Luciano offers a Proppian overview of the cycle's typical plot functions. Within this discussion, Luciano notes that alien invasion films usually show society rallying in common cause after the scientist hero explains his plans for repelling the invaders. For Luciano the combination of communal solidarity and militarism in these films has given rise to the common perception "that the aliens and monsters of the alien invasion film were surrogates for the Sino-Soviet menace."[8] Having made this observation, Luciano eventually moves on to his central argument, namely that science fiction films illustrate aspects of Jungian psychology as an artistic counterpart to Jung's own analysis of UFO sightings.[9]

Luciano's use of a Jungian approach to 1950s science fiction films is somewhat unusual in academic film studies, but his equation of aliens with the Sino-Soviet threat is not. Besides the previously cited work of Belton, O'Donnell, Sontag, and Katrina Mann, one finds countless other examples of this analytical trope, including works by Vivian Sobchack, Andrew Dowdy, David Seed, and Stuart Samuels.[10] Because the equation of Communists with aliens in science fiction films has achieved the status of canonized belief, perhaps we should step back to examine the underlying basis of the analogy.

This aspect of science fiction films rests on two imputed similarities between aliens and Communists: they are different and they are threatening. While this is a ham-fisted summary of the analogy's functions, one can nonetheless tease out more subtle dimensions to the comparison. The genre's emphasis on alien difference, for example, might be seen as an expression of coalitional thinking as a more common cultural phenomenon. In film studies science fiction's treatment of otherness is usually viewed as a kind of discursive construct. But in the social sciences the development of "us vs. them" thinking has much more fundamental roots in evolutionary biology. Pascal Boyer, for example, describes a human propensity for group solidarity that underpins the institution of tribal and religious practices. Such coalitional intuitions are themselves the outcome of strategic alliances that were common among the earliest social groupings and were necessary to preserve kinship networks against invaders from rival villages.[11] For Boyer the evolutionary roots of group identity help explain why experiments involving conflicts between in-groups and out-groups among arbitrarily chosen members are among the most easily reproduced laboratory results in social psychology. Indeed, in a particularly notorious experiment conducted in 1954, psychologist Muzafer Sherif was able to manufacture in-group/out-group conflicts simply by taking twenty-two Oklahoma City fifth-graders attending summer camp and dividing them into two teams: the Rattlers and the Eagles.[12]

The accounts by Boyer and other social scientists make a convincing case for the tendency to identify difference as a threat to group identity. Given its basis in evolutionary psychology, it should seem obvious that such definitions of otherness are expressed both in nationalist discourses of the 1950s and in the ways that filmmakers dramatize conflict. The more pertinent question is how the nationalist discourses and policies of the United States in the 1950s were yoked to representational strategies in science fiction films. The answer to this question lies in the way that shared associations of difference and threat function across the respective contexts provided by historical events and generic conventions respectively.

Much as we saw with the western, the analogy between aliens and Communists is partly supported by notions of outsider status that are derived from particular geographical claims. Whereas the western employed a shift in levels of analysis from the local to the national or global (i.e., the frontier town = the New Frontier), the science fiction film moves in the opposite direction, making conflicts that are astronomical in their scale function as surrogates for conflict between nation-states. As predicted by the model of coalitional intuitions, battles between earthlings and extraterrestrials express essential differences between inhabitants and invaders. These differences are then taken by film critics to be symptomatic representations of Cold War tensions between the United States and the Sino-Soviet alliance. In his contribution to Jürgen Müller's *Movies of the 50s* Burkhard Röwekamp offers a veritable inventory of the many ways in which the titular monster of *The Thing (From Another World)* comes to signify the otherness of the Communist threat:

> From the frozen wastelands of the Cold War, an unknown creature emerges, and it's nothing like you or me. It has the physiology of a plant and the skin of an insect, it's asexual and unfeeling. It's more than two meters tall, it can't speak, it's bloodthirsty and it has the strength of a bear. Though vaguely humanoid in appearance, The Thing is clearly very far from human; we are faced, of course, with a creature from another planet. And though its intentions are unclear, one fact is obvious: The Thing wants into that research station double quick, because it can only survive by drinking human blood. We hear about atmospheric disturbances, an explosion in the East, radioactive contamination . . . and without a doubt, we're deliberately being served up stereotypes of the Communist enemy.[13]

Yet as Peter Biskind points out, there are important limits to filmmakers' ability to imagine otherness. According to Biskind, "the anthropomorphic gravity of American films is so strong that they have difficulty dramatizing genuine otherness. Aliens, no matter how strange or exotic, end up resembling humans in one way or another."[14] Biskind's observation makes an obvious but important point. The tendency to anthropomorphize alien beings provides one of the bases for the allegorical interpretation of aliens as Communists. The critic simply extrapolates from the basic resemblance between humans and aliens to argue for even more significant, and politically pointed, similarities between the representation of aliens and the representation of Communists.

In *Running Time* Nora Sayre offers a textbook example of this rhetorical strategy. Discussing the alien-invasion cycle as a whole, Sayre writes:

> But our supernatural enemies are always endowed with an intelligence that is far superior to ours; characteristic of the fifties, intellect was suspect—in these movies, it was often evil. Martian technology outdistanced our latest inventions, as we feared that the Russians' might, especially after their first atomic explosion in 1949, and again when they launched the Sputnik in 1957. Moreover, the Martians had monitored our broadcasts for years—hence they could speak English, when we didn't know their language—and they knew how to fly to our planet when we had no idea how to visit theirs. Meanwhile, they constantly studied us and spied on us—while we remained ignorant of their very existence.[15]

Throughout this passage Sayre piles up the different ways in which "Martians" are thought to be similar to Communists, highlighting such specific traits as the Soviets' technological superiority, their advanced surveillance apparatus, and their ability to secretly infiltrate various sectors of American life.

The origin stories of alien invaders provide additional cues that sometimes strengthen the analogy between aliens and Communists. As Patrick Luciano indicates, one can discern two particular narrative tropes that serve to concretize the analogy between aliens and Communists: (1) the alien's origin in outer space and (2) the alien's metamorphosis into human form.[16] The alien's extraterrestrial origin has significance to the extent that it serves as a kind of metonym for Soviet control of airspace. Several critics, like Sayre, link this particular aspect of 1950s science fiction films to the Soviets' launching of Sputnik and to Yuri Gagarin's early foray into manned space travel. Through this connection, the "space race" becomes a source of social anxiety that is manifested in the films themselves through the figure of the alien invader.

Indeed, some critics trace this trope back to the famous closing words of Christian Nyby's *The Thing (From Another World)* (1951). The injunction "Keep watching the skies!" has itself taken on significance as a sort of synecdoche for the entire cycle of 1950s science fiction, but it plays an even more prominent role in representing the fear of Soviet military power. The warning is ostensibly intended for alien invaders, but most critics see its significance as deriving from fears about the Soviets' ability to develop extraterrestrial weapons. In making this connection, critics draw together the events of the "space race" as topical reference points to create the necessary interpretive frame for allegorical interpretation. In this way the "space race" becomes the pretext by which alien invaders function as metaphorical stand-ins for Soviet cosmonauts.

At this point, though, it becomes evident that allegorical readings of science fiction films are plagued by one of the most frequent problems of zeitgeist criticism, namely that the Soviets did not launch Sputnik until 1957, and Gagarin did not make his maiden voyage as a cosmonaut until 1961. In other words the events that function as purported sources for the alien invader trope did not occur until after many canonical films in the cycle, such as *The Thing, Invaders from Mars* (1953), and *It Came from Outer Space*, had already been produced and distributed. As was the case with *The Robe*, the implicit model of social reflectionism employed in these interpretations turns the principles of historical causation on their head. The alien invader trope as an effect of public discourse appears to precede the events that are the foundation of that discourse.

Of course, one could argue that the Sputnik launch and Soviet manned space travel were the culmination of a much larger set of policy and research initiatives. But this model of social reflectionism seems equally implausible. Declassified documents indicate that plans for Soviet space exploration were not approved until 1956. Moreover, the public announcement of the Soviet space program was not made until July of that year. Consequently, the most concrete evidence of the Soviets' research and development of space travel are still several years after the cycle of alien invader films began. Beyond that, the narrative conventions of space exploration and extraterrestrial encounters were established in science fiction literature long before their association with Sino-Soviet menace. (Jules Verne's *A Trip to the Moon* [1865] and H. G. Wells's *The War of the Worlds* [1898] are particularly notable examples.) Given these historical precedents, it seems more likely that producers and audiences responded to the alien invader trope as a literary convention—one present both in sci-fi classics and in contemporaneous pulp fiction—rather than as a signifier of current events.

If the association between cosmonauts and alien invaders proves somewhat specious, the second of these tropes—the alien's metamorphosis into human form—fares a bit better, if only because it rides the coattails of already established narrative conventions in earlier anti-Communist films. This narrative trope is featured in several canonical 1950s science fiction films, among them *It Came from Outer Space, Invasion of the Body Snatchers,* and *I Married a Monster from Outer Space* (1958). As a plot device, the "alien as human" creates a hermeneutics of suspicion by which the protagonists of these films take on roles as investigative agents. It also

WHICH ONE IS THE COMMUNIST?

Figure 11. This panel from *Two Faces of Communism,* a comic book produced by the Christian Anti-Communist Crusade, attests to widespread fears about Communists' ability to "pass" as ordinary citizens. This trope is also expressed in several science fiction films that show alien creatures disguising themselves in a humanoid form.

serves to heighten the films' uncanny and paranoiac mood insofar as the aliens blend in with the general population in a manner that makes them indistinguishable from their human counterparts.

For critics, the ability of the aliens to "pass" as ordinary beings is related to fears of Communist infiltration, subversion, and domination. As I have noted, one of the concerns about Communist Party activity was that Communists could masquerade as ordinary citizens; thus, their apparent familiarity enabled them to dupe average Joes and Janes. As late as 1961, the fear of "passing" continued to be a trope in anti-Communist propaganda. A panel from *Two Faces of Communism,* a thirty-two-page comic book published by the Christian Anti-Communist Crusade, shows a group of people seated in pews for a church service. At the top of the panel is the question, "WHICH ONE IS THE COMMUNIST?" (fig. 11).[17]

Jack Arnold underscores this point in *It Came from Outer Space* with a shot of John Putnam (Richard Carlson) and Sheriff Matt Warren (Charles Drake) looking out the latter's office window at townsfolk going about their business. The shot is framed so that Putnam and Warren have their backs to the camera, and the activities on the street make up the background plane of the shot. In frustration, Warren exclaims, "What do you mean 'See it through'? How do we know they're not taking over? They could be all around us and I wouldn't know." Although Warren occupies the seat of legal authority in the town, his visual surveillance of street activity gains him little in the way of knowledge. Warren watches the townspeople's behavior, but he cannot comprehend their underlying motivations, intentions, beliefs, or being.

This aspect of anti-Communist films has obvious resonance for science fiction allegories in that the ability to pass is thought to endow both Communists and aliens with a certain sort of subversive power. Writing about *Invasion of the Body Snatchers*, Ernesto Laura notes that "it is natural to see the pods as standing for the idea of communism, which gradually takes possession of a normal person, leaving him outwardly unchanged but transformed within."[18] As long as both are capable of hiding in plain sight, Communists' and aliens' ability to escape detection provides them with a veil of secrecy that activates fears about their potential actions. In films like *It Came from Outer Space* and *Body Snatchers* the concern is less about what aliens are actually doing than about the crisis caused by our inability to *know* what they are doing.

This loose correlation between Communists and humanoid aliens is perhaps strengthened when one compares the narrative premise of *I Married a Communist* with that of *I Married a Monster from Outer Space*. The tabloidish titles of the two films echo one another and imply a certain commutability of the central couple in each film. Each film's plot begins around the time of the couple's marriage; *I Married a Communist*'s first scene occurs during Ann and Brad's honeymoon while *I Married a Monster* is initially set on the eve of Marge and Bill's wedding. Both Brad and Bill appear outwardly normal—Brad as the manager of a shipping company in San Francisco, Bill as an insurance salesman. Each film's plot also hinges on secrets that the husbands keep from their wives but that are communicated to audiences by their very titles.

The potential threat of humanoid aliens "passing" as ordinary citizens encompasses even sympathetic portraits of alien encounters. In *The Day the Earth Stood Still* (1951) the protagonist, Klaatu (Michael Rennie), escapes from his room at Walter Reed General Hospital in Washington in an attempt to learn more about Earth's inhabitants. After the "man from the spaceship" is reported missing, director Robert Wise shows a montage of news coverage and public reaction. The sequence shows an elderly couple listening closely to a news broadcast, a mother quieting her children so that the family can hear the radio as they sit down to dinner in their humble kitchen, and a mother glancing suspiciously after ushering her two children

Figure 12. Because radio news reports describe Klaatu as eight feet tall with tentacles, he easily "passes" as Mr. Carpenter among the people at the boardinghouse. None of them realize that he is the mysterious alien ambassador to Earth.

through her front door. This is followed by a tracking shot of Klaatu walking down a quiet city street. A radio report refutes rumors that the spaceman is eight feet tall and has tentacles, but it nonetheless characterizes him as a "monster at large." The split between sound and image in this shot indicates the double valence that the "humanoid alien" embodies. On one hand, the shot of Klaatu, dressed in an ordinary business suit and carrying a small suitcase, undermines the dire warnings issued by the news media. On the other hand, the fact that Klaatu is not visibly and recognizably monstrous suggests that he potentially poses a special threat as an alien being walking among us (fig. 12).

The next morning, Klaatu joins the other lodgers at the breakfast table of his boardinghouse. They sit quietly, listening to a radio broadcast of the latest news, which again provides a pointed contrast between the fevered media hype and Klaatu's rather ordinary appearance and behavior. The radio announcer speculates that the spaceman may retreat to the north woods or hide in the sewers beneath the city, descriptions that evoke other roughly contemporary science fiction/horror hybrids like *The Thing (From Another World)* or *The Beast from 20,000 Fathoms* (1953). After Mrs. Barley (Frances Bavier) sees a newspaper cartoon depicting earthly panic at an alien invasion, she sternly requests that the radio be turned off. Unfortunately for Mrs. Barley, this does not stop the discussion as Helen Benson (Patricia Neal) asks whether it is right for the media to automatically conclude that the spaceman is a menace. Voicing suspicion of both the government and the media, Mrs. Barley opines that the spaceship is probably of earthly rather than extraterrestrial origin, offhandedly remarking, with eyebrows raised, "And you know where I mean." In her knowing reference to the Soviets, Mrs. Barley momentarily collapses the literal and metaphorical dimensions of *The Day the Earth Stood Still* by openly speculating that the entire spaceman story is a media fiction and a Communist plot. Wise's belated cut to Klaatu's bemused reaction prompts us to see Mrs. Barley's paranoia as benignly comic. This is reinforced by the film's narration, which aligns us with Klaatu and allows us to understand his peaceful mission long before any of the other characters do. Thus, *The Day the Earth Stood Still*'s brief, elliptical reference to the Soviets might seem silly, except for the fact that countless critics interpret the film as a thinly veiled allegory about the dangers of U.S. and Soviet nuclear proliferation. M. Keith Booker claims that "the most important message of the film concerns its plea for international cooperation rather than nationalist competition, accompanied by its rejection of the kind of xenophobic hysteria that informed contemporary American anti-communism."[19]

As all these films suggest, the metaphor of "passing" has special pertinence to the interpretation of 1950s science fiction films in that they evoke earlier scenarios of Communist infiltration, especially industry concerns about the potential subversion of both craft guilds and screen content. Writing about John Putnam, the hero of *It Came from Outer Space*, Peter Biskind highlights this parallel between alien invasion films and HUAC's investigations:

> John underlines his resemblance to the aliens when he jokingly tells Matt, "Wouldn't it be a fine thing if I was something from another world here to give you a lot of false leads." Ha ha! John *is* like them; they *are* like him: metaphors for difference, dissent, resistance to the community. Like Communists, the aliens hide behind false fronts because Americans destroy what they don't understand. But *It Came from Outer Space* uses the conceit of visitors from another world to imagine a much more mundane but nevertheless prickly problem: the "egghead," the person who is liable to be investigated because he thinks differently, because he is sympathetic to alien systems of thought.[20]

The blacklist subtext associated with the trope of alien metamorphosis also helps explain why a film like *Invasion of the Body Snatchers* is read both as an anti-Communist *and* an anti-HUAC film in a way that some other 1950s science fiction films are not. The fact that critics like Danny Peary, J Hoberman, Tony Shaw, Drew Casper, Philipp Bühler, and Michael Rogin recognize *Body Snatchers* as this type of double allegory attests to the ease with which we are able to flip back and forth between two conflicting cognitive frames.[21] As Casper asks of *Body Snatchers,* "Allegory certainly, but did the aliens stand for the communist takeover of the US or the dehumanizing influence of conformity, or both?"[22] The self-awareness attributed to Siegel's film extends to the critics themselves, who explicitly demonstrate the ways in which different framings of topical reference points give rise to mutually exclusive, but still viable, interpretations.

MONSTERS: EMBODYING COMMUNIST PREDATION

Although alien invaders provide one pattern of metaphoric substitution common in allegory, monsters in science fiction films offer another. Aliens themselves sometimes appear monstrous in their inhuman form, and their grotesque appearance certainly renders them objects of disgust and phobia in a manner common to the horror film. Yet the category of monsters here applies more directly to creatures of terrestrial origin. The sea monster of *The Beast from 20,000 Fathoms,* the gargantuan octopus of *It Came from Beneath the Sea* (1955), the giant ants of *Them!* (1954), and the colossal spider of *Tarantula* are archetypal examples of horrific creatures whose genesis results from the scientific activities of humans.

Because the monsters of 1950s science fiction films present obvious overlap with the horror genre, Noël Carroll's pioneering work on horror films offers insights into the way these figures function in the interpretive strategies of zeitgeist critics.[23] As Carroll points out, most movie monsters derive their horrific nature from their fantastic biologies, which violate normal classification systems as categorical contradictions. These categorical contradictions are evident in two types of monsters found in horror fictions: fusion figures and fission figures. In fusion figures, according to Carroll, "categorically contradictory elements are fused or condensed or superimposed in one spatio-temporal being whose identity is homogeneous."[24] In contrast, fission figures involve categorical contradictions that are distributed over different beings. These contradictions may be temporally distributed in the case of a horrific creature that transmutes from one being to another, or they may be spatially distributed through the creation of fantastic doubles.

Alien beings, of course, fit both types of monsters identified by Carroll. Some function as fusion figures in ways more or less consistent with monsters in the horror genre. Carroll himself summarizes the monstrous qualities of the eponymous figure in *The Thing* by describing the alien being as "an intelligent, two-legged bloodsucking carrot. Now that's interstitial."[25] An archetypal fusion figure, the creature in *The Thing* is an almost complete categorical contradiction: a carnivorous, humanoid vegetable. Other alien beings, though, are composed as fission figures. The aliens in *Invasion of the Body Snatchers* begin as seedpods that metamorphose into a humanoid form of the people that they replace. Like the alien in *The Thing*, the pod people of *Body Snatchers* combine plant and animal characteristics, but unlike the alien in *The Thing*, their vegetative and human states occur sequentially.

Still other alien beings combine elements from both of Carroll's categories. *It Came from Outer Space* and *I Married a Monster from Outer Space* each involve spatial modes of fission to the extent that aliens take on the appearance of the humans that they abduct. At the same time, though, special effects photography in each film offers sporadic reminders that the creatures themselves are fusion figures with a human form superimposed over their alien being. In *I Married a Monster*, lightning flashes within the diegesis reveal fusions of alien and human facial features. In *It Came from Outer Space*, the superimposition of a vibrating, globulous eye over human figures is a device that signals either the presence of aliens in human form or the optical perspective of alien beings.

Besides fission and fusion figures, Carroll also identifies the magnification of entities as a common symbolic structure in horror fictions. Carroll himself observes that the phobia about enlargement was quite popular in mid-twentieth-century science fiction films, and was likely suggested by the "first radiation experiments on seeds."[26] Carroll identifies a long list of examples of size magnification, including *The Deadly Mantis* (1957), *Attack of the Giant Leeches* (1959), *Mothra* (1961), and *The Night of the Lepus* (1972), a roster transnational in its scope and covering a fairly sizable period of film history. Although less common, the symbolic structure of size diminution was featured in Jack Arnold's *The Incredible Shrinking Man*, a canonical 1950s science fiction film that works as a corollary of the magnification phobia. In this instance exposure to radiation shrinks the human body such that household objects and ordinary creatures seem magnified in their relation to the ever-diminishing mass of the protagonist.

To function as allegories of the Communist threat, these films were thought to, in Carroll's words, "significantly interact with the way many

Americans came to think of communists."[27] But what, more precisely, was the basis for these analogical comparisons? What particular phobias associated with the Communist threat were embodied or instantiated by the monsters of 1950s science fiction films?

The most obvious answer is that the terrestrial monsters in these films are metaphors and metonyms of the Soviets' development of atomic weaponry.[28] As many critics note, the creatures themselves are more or less created through some exposure to atomic material. The ants in *Them!* grow to mammoth proportions as a result of their exposure to atomic radiation. The giant spider in *Tarantula* grows after being injected with atomic material. The sea monster in *The Beast from 20,000 Fathoms* is freed when the heat from a nuclear test thaws a sheet of ice in which the creature was frozen. The hero of *The Incredible Shrinking Man* passes through a radioactive cloud.

Yet, although atomic testing serves as a narrative catalyst for the fantastic changes that occur, critics are more concerned with the metaphorical implications of size magnification and diminution as symbolic structures. The growth of ants and spiders serves as the embodiment of the Soviets' increased power as a result of successfully implementing atomic weapons. Similarly, the sea monster in *20,000 Fathoms* is an objective correlative of the devastation and power of Soviet nuclear weapons if they are unleashed. And the diminishing stature of *The Incredible Shrinking Man* suggests the United States' diminished stature in world affairs as a result of Soviet development of the Bomb.

The trope of "literalizing the metaphorical" is a common thread in these readings, but the specific association of the Bomb with the Communist threat is an interpretive move film critics and historians make by extrapolating from these films' basic premises. The production history of *Them!* is a case in point. During script development, Warner Bros.' research department dug up information regarding the nine atomic explosions that followed the Alamogordo Exposition on July 16, 1945. While the research department takes note of Soviet tests, its list places as much or more emphasis on the United States' development of nuclear weapons. In fact, the list begins with the U.S. bombs dropped on Hiroshima and Nagasaki. By contrast, only two of the nine items on the list refer to atomic tests by the USSR.[29] Warner Bros. clearly did not view atomic weaponry as the sole province of the Soviets, so it is not entirely clear why so many critics and scholars do.

Warner Bros.' interest in the effects of atomic radiation also figured in the studio's promotional plans for the film. Here again, the concentration seems to be on atomic testing per se, not its role in geopolitical affairs. In a memo to the film's producers, Steve Trilling proposed that the studio develop an exploitation campaign for *Them!* around a series of magazine articles that would feature statements from "Einstein, Milliken, Huxley, and other noted physicists, scientists and entomologists." These scientists could then comment on issues like atomic radiation, genetic mutation, and the social organization of insect colonies to "lend semi-official recognition to the 'could-be' aspects of this film."[30]

The closest that Warner Bros. came to associating the Sino-Soviet threat with the giant ants of *Them!* was in the film's pressbook, which suggests that a civil defense reminder might be a good exploitation angle for the film: "Since civil defense in the face of an emergency figures in the picture, make the most of it by inviting local agency to set up a recruiting booth in lobby." Suggested copy for tie-in with the film read: *"What would you do if (name of city) were attacked by* THEM!*? Prepare for any danger by enlisting in Civil Defense today."*[31] The pressbook does not make any specific mention of the Communist threat, but one might infer that civil defense preparation more or less assumed the possibility of Communist invasion or attack. The pronoun THEM! is, of course, nondescript enough to apply to any potential threat, including foreign enemies like China or the Soviet Union.

Interestingly, Warner Bros.' most specific reference to the potential political symbolism of giant ants was made in a discussion of an entirely different story. The production files for *Them!* include correspondence regarding a plagiarism suit filed by Alfred Gordon Bennett, who claimed that the studio stole the film's basic premise from his novel, *The Demigods,* first published in London in 1939. Though both *Them!* and *The Demigods* are stories about colonies of giant ants, Warner Bros.' legal staff advised the studio that "apart from the general theme of giant ants hostile to mankind, there is no similarity whatsoever in the treatment and working out of this subject."[32]

Such a legal posture may have been necessary insofar as the studio's story department files contain evidence that Warner Bros. considered optioning the book back in 1939. Although there is no evidence that anyone connected with *Them!* was even aware of Bennett's novel, the studio maintained a file in Burbank that contained a plot synopsis of *The Demigods* from the May 30, 1939, issue of *World Wide Play Review.* The synopsis quite clearly references the "giant ant" theme, but more than that, it also connects Bennett's novel with contemporary political events.

At one point in the summary the author writes, "It will occur to many readers that the super-ant is unlikely, as each community has an Ogpu or Gestapo waiting to uproot the first dangerous sign of individual thought."[33] On one hand, the reference to both the Nazis and the Soviets in this context indicates the possibility that readers made analogical connections between the book's fantastic narrative and its contemporary historical context. On the other hand, this reference to the ants' larger meaning reads them in a manner almost diametrically opposite to the interpretations of *Them!* found in histories of the science fiction film. The reviewer of *World Wide Play Review* seems to see the ants as a subaltern political group whose activities are threatened by the power of a totalitarian state. The reference to Ogpu thus identifies the giant ants as victims of Soviet Communism rather than as its symbolic incarnation. Years later, David Platt's review of *Them!* for the *Daily Worker* would echo this logic. Describing the scene where Dr. Medford (Edmund Gwenn) and his daughter search for clues in the desert, Platt notes that "they hear the amazing news that the country is in mortal danger of destruction by the Formica Prepostera (not to be confused with the deadlier Formica Prepostera McCarthyismus)."[34]

DEHUMANIZATION: FROM YELLOW HORDES TO RED BLOBS

The notion that extraterrestrial and terrestrial monsters symbolize the threat of dehumanization can be traced back at least as far as Susan Sontag's landmark essay "The Imagination of Disaster," first published in 1965. Although Sontag focuses on films that involve spectacles of apocalyptic disaster, she also notes a secondary cycle that seems to offer its opposite: the unseen catastrophe of dehumanization. Sontag cites films like *Invasion of the Body Snatchers* as specific examples of this phenomenon:

> The other-world creatures which seek to take "us" over, are an "it," not a "they." The planetary invaders are usually zombie-like. Their movements are usually either cool, mechanical, or lumbering, blobby. But it amounts to the same thing. If they are nonhuman in form, they proceed with an absolutely regular, unalterable movement (unalterable save by destruction). If they are in human form—dressed in space suits, etc.—then they obey the most rigid military discipline and display no personal characteristics whatsoever. And it is this regime of emotionlessness, of impersonality, and of regimentation, which they will impose on the earth if they are successful.[35]

Such an interpretive strategy depends, of course, on a juxtaposition of the literal and the metaphorical. The literally "inhuman" status of aliens and terrestrial monsters, especially those that are simply enlarged animals, connotes an endangerment of the very things that make us human. Moreover, the notion of dehumanization takes on significance through an implicit conflation of "human" with "humanism." In science fiction films of the 1950s, the crucial qualities that are identified with dehumanization involve the loss of things that are associated with humanistic values and philosophies: emotion, love, freedom, rationality.

To draw the comparison between the inhuman and the dehumanized, though, one first must make a pair of metaphorical substitutions that themselves involve analogical comparisons: (1) critics must show that the monsters are like human beings in significant ways, and (2) they must show that humans' and monsters' similarities are characteristic traits of foreign and domestic Communists. The predatory nature of animals, for example, is often interpreted as a metaphor for Communist desire for conquest. The sea monster in *The Beast from 20,000 Fathoms* is a killing machine, leaving a path of destruction wherever it goes. In *The Thing* the creature hunts humans for food and, like a vampire, drains their blood for its own sustenance. This trope even extends to creatures of unknown biology, such as the titular entity in *The Blob*, which literally absorbs humans into its red, glutinous mass.

In contrast, the collective and social activity of the giant ants in *Them!* offers a variant of the predation metaphor that encourages some critics to compare ant attacks to Communist aggression. Peter Biskind writes, "If the ants are like humans, which humans are they like? In 1954, when *Them!* was made, those humans that America regarded as antlike, which is to say, behaved like a mass, loved war, and made slaves, were, of course, Communists, both the Yellow Hordes that had just swamped GIs with their human waves in Korea, and the Soviets, with their slave labor camps."[36] Victoria O'Donnell proposes, "The ants could also have been a symbolic enemy, the Soviet Union, for in one scene, the entomologist says that ants are 'savage, ruthless, and courageous fighters.' He also tells how ants use slave laborers in their colonies, evoking images of a totalitarian society."[37]

Like the interest in nuclear weaponry, the entomological understanding of ant colonies played an important role in the development of the screenplay for *Them!* The research staff at Warner Bros. collected several books and articles that were intended to help filmmakers understand the particular nature and characteristics of ant life. More than that, though, the story and screenplay for *Them!* also made explicit comparisons between humans and ants. George Worthing Yates's unpublished story includes a scene in which the hero and the entomologist, Dr. Meninger, board a subway: "Meninger remarked in the crowded car that we humans were social insects, like the ants in many ways, and in many ways much less efficient. But he prefers our company. I too." Screenwriter Russell Hughes incorporated this concept in his adaptation of Yates's story, which includes several speeches by Meninger's counterpart, Dr. Medford, intended to explain ant behavior. In a revised estimating script, Medford comments on the ants' warlike nature: "Ants are the *only* creatures on earth, other than man, who make war. They campaign; they are chronic aggressors; and they make slave laborers out of the captives they don't kill."[38]

Yet what is perhaps significant about these references is that they treat human beings as an individual species. In contrast to the readings offered by O'Donnell and Biskind, the comments by Medford apply to all people, including Americans. These scientists see aggression as an inherent quality of human life, not as something that is the sole province of Sino-Soviet menace. Thus, the evidence from the production files on *Them!* offers support for the first part of the two-step analogy cited earlier but not the second. Critics like O'Donnell and Biskind elaborate these dialogue references by extrapolating from the film's historical context such that the explicit comparison between man and ants in *Them!* is made to seem like an implicit comparison between insects and Communists.

Whereas animalistic qualities offer one form of inhumanity that serves as the representational basis for analogy, another is found in the robotic and mechanistic traits of some alien invaders. The absence of emotion often proves to be a telltale sign of an alien presence in 1950s science fiction films. The implied antinomy between emotion and rationality suggests that the ability to feel love, passion, anger, and sadness are essential traits of human beings. Several films use this absence of emotion as a mark of dehumanization. Of them, *Invasion of the Body Snatchers* has attracted the most critical attention, possibly because it explicitly articulates an underlying philosophical and ideological explanation for this aspect of the aliens' being.

Several critics, such as Biskind and Samuels, cite psychiatrist Dr. Dan Kauffman (Larry Gates) as the film's mouthpiece for this philosophy, which they take to be a veiled reference to Communism. Kauffman tells Dr. Miles Bennell (Kevin McCarthy) and Becky Driscoll (Dana Wynter) that pod people are "reborn into an untroubled world," adding, "There is no need for love or emotion. Love, ambition, desire, faith—without them, life is so simple." After referencing Kauffman's speech, Biskind then spells out the analogies between pod society and Communism: "This is a world in which 'everyone is the same,' a collectivist millennium to which all citizens contribute, as they do here, systematically distributing pods in a parody of political activism. But to the right, this rationalist world in which the head rules the heart and people act like robots is the dream of the 'creeping socialist' center, with its statists and planners, as well as the left."[39]

Danny Peary affirms many of Biskind's sentiments in his own analysis of the film's anti-Communist subtext: "While Siegel's villains are usually mad or emotionally unstable, the space aliens fit the mold that American schoolteachers describe as being characteristic of Russians: ice cold, outwardly peaceful but very authoritarian, emotionless. Of course, American schoolchildren of the fifties were taught that Communists had no feelings—especially concerning life and death—which is why, we were told, the Russians/Red Chinese would feel no qualms about going to war and losing much of their population. More than anything else I believe we kids were frightened of Communists because we were told they did not cry when people died."[40]

Peary adds evidentiary support for his reading by citing General William Westmoreland's comments in Peter Davis's landmark Vietnam documentary, *Hearts and Minds* (1974). Westmoreland rather notoriously claimed that Communists do not mourn death the way Americans do because they consider life cheap. Besides Kauffman's speech, several other critics also mention the scene of orderly, mechanistic distribution of pods as additional evidence to support the parallels between pod people and Communists. Peary, for example, refers to Noël Carroll's reading of *Body Snatchers*, especially his claim that the scene in the town square is "the quintessential fifties image of socialism."[41]

In all of these ways critics use the inhuman qualities of monsters and aliens to underline parallels to popular beliefs about Communists. The concepts of "human" and "monster" are the dominant semantic field in this discourse, giving rise to a series of terms that metaphorically link Americans to freedom, rationality, emotion, and individualism and the Soviets to slavery, collectivism, instinct, and animalistic social organization.

VEGETATION: UNTHINKING COMMUNISM

The fact that many of these monsters have a botanic component to their biological makeup offers additional grounds for the comparison of monsters and Communists. Because the monsters are derived from plants in *The Thing* and *Invasion of the Body Snatchers*, one might surmise that they represent an even lower form of life than human/animal hybrids. A werewolf, for example, may not exhibit rational control over its actions, but it is still driven by a kind of biological imperative, namely instinct. Vegetation, on the other hand, is not even granted this small degree of self-control. Because they lack the capacity to reason or act on instinct, plants are commonly thought to have only the most basic sorts of autonomic functions. This lack of self-direction finds metaphorical expression in the phrase "vegetative state," a term applied to individuals kept alive merely by the involuntary activity of their brain stem. As the Karen Quinlan and Terri Schiavo controversies remind us, a patient in a persistent vegetative state breathes and takes nourishment but hasn't the capacity to do much else.

Still, as Dr. Carrington (Robert Cornthwaite) points out in *The Thing*, an ambulatory vegetative being may have a strategic advantage over human beings precisely because the creature's mind cannot be swayed or clouded by emotion. Driven by biological imperatives of survival, these vegetative creatures not only disperse their "seeds" as widely or as quickly as possible, but they also sometimes display remarkable regenerative powers. After discovering a seedpod in the soft tissue of the alien's hand, Carrington says, "Yes. The neat and unconfused reproductive technique of vegetation. No pain or pleasure as we know it. No emotions, no heart. Our superior. Our superior in every way." By virtue of the fact that the creature lacks passions and emotions, its behavior is governed by a force akin to cold rationality. Because of these observations, Dr. Carrington has been targeted by some critics as a kind of Communist sympathizer. A 1951 review in *Time* magazine states, "The scientist (Robert Cornthwaite), who is suggestively costumed like a Russian, wants to appease The Thing to gain knowledge."[42]

Moreover, in readings of *Invasion of the Body Snatchers*, critics who compare Communists to "pod people" imply that the latter's willingness to surrender selfhood to a kind of collectivist Utopia functions as a symptom of totalitarian control. Because Americans believed that Communists conformed their own thoughts and behavior to the needs of the state, submerging their individual humanity within the masses that compose the collective, they were, by definition, subhuman, lacking even the instincts and passions that govern animal behavior. Danny Peary notes that *Body Snatchers'* depiction of "the pods' movement from the country into the towns may remind us that in the 1950s Russia was considered an agrarian society," a comment that hints at the film's use of botanical metaphors to allegorize Communists' disavowal of instincts and passion.[43]

The issue of self-direction and self-control may be a slim reed on which to hang the comparisons between Communists and "pod people," but in fact, it doesn't take much to develop the necessary associational links between "vegetative" metaphors and other beliefs about Communist activities. Many critics locate the source of these films' representational strategies in contemporary fears about Communist indoctrination. Indeed, as early as 1968, Carlos Clarens suggested a fairly loose alliance between science fiction's emphasis on dehumanization and "collective anxiety about the loss of individual identity, subliminal mindbending, or downright scientific/political brainwashing."[44]

Although these films use mind control as a dramatic conceit and certainly do not deal with the specific techniques employed in such "re-education," the loose association between Communist brainwashing and alien mind control is partly supported by contemporaneous accounts of such activities during the Korean War. Edward Hunter's *Brain-Washing in Red China: The Calculated Destruction of Men's Minds* introduced the term into the public lexicon in 1951. In 1955 a U.S. Army report indicated that many of the four thousand U.S. troops who had been captured and held as prisoners of war during the Korean conflict had been subject to Communist indoctrination by the Chinese. Prior to 1957, stories about the brainwashing of American prisoners appeared in mainstream publications like the *Saturday Evening Post, Life,* and the *New Yorker*.[45] Because brainwashed individuals lack self-control, they are akin to persons in a vegetative state. They cannot think for themselves, and their actions lack the passions and instinct that distinguish animal behaviors. Brainwashed persons exhibit powers of speech and action, but they lack the will, emotions, and rationality that root those behaviors within a humanistic concept of selfhood.

More important, these widely circulated stories about Chinese brainwashing of American prisoners have served as topical reference points for some critics, who use them as an allegorical pretext to interpret scenes of alien mind control. Peter Biskind's discussion of *Invasion of the Body Snatchers* makes this link explicit: "Possession by pods—mind stealing, brain eating, and body snatching—had the added advantage of being an overt metaphor for Communist brainwashing, which had just turned GIs into Reds in Korea."[46] M. Keith Booker makes a similar point: "The paranoid atmosphere of *Invasion of the Body Snatchers* also links it to films outside the science fiction genre. It is related in a particularly direct way to Cold War espionage thrillers such as John Frankenheimer's *The Manchurian Candidate* (1962), in which the takeover by individual humans by alien invaders is replaced by the takeover of individual American minds by communist brainwashing."[47]

Universal's *This Island Earth* (1955) offers one of the era's most vivid examples of this link between alien invasion and "brainwashing." The film brings together several of the semantic fields discussed in this chapter, as evidenced by the blurb that adorns its DVD release: "When atomic scientist Dr. Meacham (Rex Reason) is chosen to take part in a top-secret research experiment in a remote lab, he quickly discovers that he is really involved in an evil scheme by alien Metalunans to take over Earth."[48] After Meacham arrives at the lab, he confers secretly with two other American scientists, Ruth Adams and Steve Carlson, about their initial wariness in interacting with him. Steve replies that they couldn't trust Meacham until they were sure he hadn't been subjected to the Metalunans' "sun lamp," a reference to the "thought transformers" Metalunans use to control the scientists working for them. Ruth adds that, though these devices look like sun lamps, "instead of a sun tan, you get your brain cells rearranged." At this point Steve makes the analogy with brainwashing explicit: "Yeah, it's similar to a lobotomy. Renders useless certain areas of the brain. Those areas controlling the power of the will." Calling *This Island Earth* a "political allegory about a group of atomic scientists," Paul Buhle and Dave Wagner note of the Metalunans, "That they are organized on the model of the Communist Party becomes evident when the leaders receive secret messages over the phone ordering them to perform alchemical experiments transforming lead into uranium (rather than gold, the most ancient dream)."[49]

Some critics, though, argue that 1950s science fiction's theme of dehumanization is itself an expression of concerns about societal conformism. Conformism is a somewhat paradoxical concept in that it implies an individual's decision to adapt to the behaviors, beliefs, mores, and standards of a larger community. Indeed, there is nothing inherently wrong with mainstream thinking. Many of us are likely to find ourselves sharing the majority opinion on a host of social and political issues without fearing that we might be identified as conformists. Yet conformism is rarely conceived as the totality of individual choices. Rather, conformism is more commonly considered the result of external pressures exerted on individuals by their society or community. These pressures constrain individual autonomy instead of acting as a manifestation of conscious, willing assent to shared values. Viewed this way, conformism yields the same compliant, servile social subject as brainwashing does. The difference is that the conformist is minimally aware of his or her surrender of self-determination while the brainwashed person is not.

Although it requires a more tangled skein of associations, conformism is easily linked to the science fiction film's disguised representations of Communist threats. Consider, once again, the case of *Invasion of the Body Snatchers*. Both author Jack Finney and director Don Siegel claimed that their stories were not intended to be about McCarthyism, but instead were about growing concerns regarding mid-twentieth-century conformism.[50] Stuart Samuels's reading of the film supports the commentary of its creators. Samuels disavows the McCarthyist reading of the *Body Snatchers*, arguing instead that the film's pod people express a widespread concern with conformity that is evident in sociological studies of the period, such as David Riesman's *The Lonely Crowd* (1955).[51]

Samuels's reading is more the exception than the rule, however. For some critics the theme of conformism is simply scaffolding for a different interpretation of *Body Snatchers* that sees the film as an allegory of McCarthyism and the blacklist. The lack of self-direction and self-control that seems central to the film's vegetative metaphors here becomes an expression of the legal dilemmas faced by targets of anti-Communist investigations. Yielding to both legal and social pressures, cooperative witnesses said and did things that were, at least partly, outside their volition. Historians Paul Buhle and Dave Wagner provide a prime example of the way the link between conformism and McCarthyism is posited. They suggest that the "alien 'pods' taking over the bodies of the townspeople were metaphorically the globules of burgeoning suburban conformism that offered quiet complicity with McCarthyism."[52] Consistent with the interpretive strategies discussed elsewhere, Buhle and Wagner cite the uncredited work of "friendly witness" Richard Collins on *Body Snatchers'* screenplay to support this reading of the film.[53]

Danny Peary, however, attempts to balance the anti-Communist and anti-HUAC readings of the film. In doing so, he offers the most explicit equation between pod people and the anti-Communist purge: "In *Body Snatchers*, the pod people, who, like McCarthy and other red-baiters, look like typical, fine upstanding Americans, search out rebels like Miles who refuse to conform to what has been newly defined as the 'American Way'— just as McCarthy and HUAC destroyed the lives of those who refused to knuckle under to their directives. The mob hysteria, the sense of paranoia, the fascist police, the witch hunt atmosphere of the picture certainly mirror the ills of McCarthy America."[54]

This anti-HUAC reading of *Body Snatchers* is significant for several reasons, not the least being the way that it inverts the usual association between alien figures and outsiders. In Peary's reading, the position of the Communists is represented not by the pod people but rather by Miles and Becky, who appear to be victims of the townspeople's "witch hunt." Made at a time when dozens of actors, screenwriters, directors, and craft workers found themselves unable to work because of their political beliefs, the original ending of *Body Snatchers* speaks directly to their deepest fears. As Miles tries to warn passing cars of the threat of the pod people, Siegel cuts to an extreme close-up of Miles screaming at the camera, "You're next!" (fig. 13). Miles's warning, which is presented as a direct address, noticeably echoes the Hollywood Ten's concerns that HUAC's investigation would not stop with them.

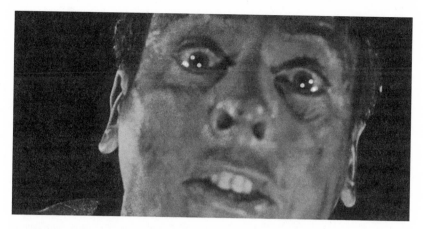

Figure 13. Many critics who describe *Invasion of the Body Snatchers* as an anti-HUAC or anti-McCarthyist allegory refer to the film's penultimate scene, in which Dr. Miles Bennell screams at passing cars, "You're next!" Bennell's warning echoes the concerns expressed by the Hollywood Ten that HUAC's investigation would not stop with them.

SLEEP: COMMUNISM AS NIGHTMARE VISION

In his terrific monograph on producer Walter Wanger, Matthew Bernstein refers to comments Wanger made in 1950 as the head of a privately funded, anti-Communist organization called the Crusade for Freedom. Said Wanger, "Communism is struggling for the minds of men while we have been sleeping." Bernstein astutely notes the parallels between Wanger's language and the scenario of *Invasion of the Body Snatchers*, which he produced. As Wanger's comments suggest, somnolence proves an important element of some science fiction films thought to function as anti-Communist allegories.

Within these films sleep is not conceived as a necessary biological process but rather as a symptom of unwariness or inattentiveness. Ordinary language, of course, reflects this kind of metaphorical dimension to sleeping. To be "caught napping" is to be caught unawares. Similarly, the term *vigilance* is derived from *vigil* and thereby refers to the practice of staying awake during normal sleep hours as part of a religious or ceremonial ritual. By incorporating sleep as a dramatic element, science fiction films cue critics to yoke these metaphorical resonances to the need to stay alert to threats to one's security. Moreover, depending on the critic's political stripes, the threat may take the form of either Communism or McCarthyism.

Invaders from Mars offers a prime example of the way in which sleep functions as a metaphor for unwariness. The invasion occurs during the early hours of night, but even more than that, most critics mention the dreamlike atmosphere created by William Cameron Menzies's direction and production design. Nora Sayre cites the "nightmarish quality" of *Invaders from Mars* while Jim Wnoroski describes it as "a nightmarish science fiction answer to *The Wizard of Oz*."[55] Indeed, this dreamlike atmosphere was so pronounced that it affected the way some reviewers described the film's plot, seemingly unconcerned about potential spoilers. The *New York Times* review, for example, divulged almost all of the film's major plot points in the span of a few sentences: "Eventually his parents are turned into slaves of the Martians, and the Army steps in with heavy ordnance. Jimmy is captured by the overgrown, bug-eyed vegetables, rescued by the militia and his parents are saved. As a matter of fact, everyone is saved, but the Martians. And then, just for a snapper at the end, the child wakes up. It was all a bad dream. Actually, it was a nightmare."[56]

The film's substitution of Martians for Communists is further strengthened by the way it yokes the semantic field of "sleep" to a scenario that dramatizes brainwashing fears. Nora Sayre concretizes the link between these two semantic elements in her reading of the film: "People keep disappearing into the quicksand where the Martians lurk underground in a buried spaceship: they take control of individual earthlings and make them commit treasonous acts, while a disembodied silver head enclosed in a plastic ball gives orders like a commissar—the Martians are 'slaves to his will.' All in all, the parallel between Martians and Communists is quite pronounced in this movie, where those who are programmed to be traitors to America are intent on perverting or suppressing the truth."[57]

The use of spatial and color metaphors in commentary on *Invaders from Mars* is evocative of certain critical tropes cited in previous chapters. The subterranean setting acts as a kind of visual pun to suggest that Martians' actions are similar to those of "underground" Communist cells. Mars itself is also known as the "red planet," a narrative conceit that evokes Communists in much the same way that *Broken Arrow*'s "red men" do. Moreover, as Vivian Sobchack reminds us, a "red crystal embedded into the base of the victim's neck accomplishes the transformation."[58] Although no critic pushes the point to its logical conclusion, it requires little to extrapolate the implied meaning of this dramatic symbol. The crystal's red color and its placement on the brain stem make the film's "gimmick" a vivid metaphor for Communist "re-education."

No film, though, does as much to associatively link the semantic fields of "sleep," "vegetation," "aliens," "brainwashing," and "dehumanization" as *Invasion of the Body Snatchers*. "Sleep" is a semantic field that is narrativized in *Body Snatchers* by virtue of the fact that the quasi-parasitic pods attack their hosts as they sleep. During the host's slumber the pod replicates his or her physical structure such that it appears externally the same but is transformed from within. Part of the reason for *Body Snatchers'* popularity as a Cold War allegory derives from the fact that it so neatly combines a dramatic conceit that parallels the "enemy within" narratives that animated anti-Communist discourse with a synecdochic structure where the individual body stands in for the body politic. As Nora Sayre further notes, "As our society is converted into a regime of totalitarian vegetables, the survivors exclaim, 'They're taking us over, *cell by cell.*'"[59]

As is true of many literary allegories, *Body Snatchers* utilizes a pun here to activate the allegorical dimensions of its Cold War subtext. The pattern of substitution hinges on the double meaning of the term *cell*. On one hand, it refers to the basic building block of all biological organisms; on the other hand, *cell* refers to the basic unit of the CPUSA's structure: a small subaltern group of party operatives. Michael Rogin spells out the associative link that connects anti-Communist propaganda films to *Body Snatchers* as Cold War allegory:

> Human beings are hosts to an alien form of life in *Body Snatchers*. Just as the Communists in *I Was a Communist* want "not just our bodies but our minds," so the body snatchers are "taking us over, cell by cell." Matt Cvetic, pretending to be taken over by a Communist cell, represents Communism's threat to personal identity. That threat is deepened in *Body Snatchers* and *Invaders from Mars* (1953). Cvetic alienated his family by masquerading as a Communist. The pods in *Body Snatchers* and the people implanted with electronic control devices in *Invaders from Mars* alienate their families by pretending still to be themselves. Reds were visibly alien in earlier Red Scares; they were the others. They moved inside our minds and bodies in the 1950s, and one could not tell them from anyone else. . . . Surveillance and inquisition exposed domestic forces that had taken possession of the nation and the self.[60]

Many other aspects of *Body Snatchers* enhance the salience of "sleep" as a semantic field. Miles's revelations of the pods' activities mostly take place under cover of darkness. The examination of Jack's double lying on his pool table takes place at night. Miles discovers Becky's double in a trunk in the Driscoll's basement at night. During an evening barbecue dinner and cocktails with Jack and Teddy, Miles comes across four pods in his greenhouse that are beginning the process of transformation. In each case Miles remains alert and watchful while the rest of the world "dozes" in blissful ignorance.

After the 1950s cycle of alien invader films was played out, Jack Webb's classic propaganda short *Red Nightmare* (1962) remapped the link between sleep and Communist threats in a manner that collapsed the distinction between the literal and metaphorical. Webb's film shows Jerry Donavan falling asleep in Everytown U.S.A. and waking up the next morning to discover that Communists have taken over the country. In a scenario similar to one of Rod Serling's *Twilight Zone* episodes, Jerry maintains his current consciousness, even though everyone around him has adapted to the strictures of Communist rule. For example, Jerry argues with his wife after she tells him that he is expected to give a speech at the Parent Teachers Association meeting that praises the new Soviet system. He chafes at the new quota system imposed on his workplace. And, echoing some of the themes discussed in earlier chapters here, Jerry offers his most vocal opposition to the notion that his family's church has been converted to a museum extolling Soviet science and technology. Later, Jerry is arrested and brought before a Soviet tribunal, where friends and family members testify against him. Just as Jerry is about to be executed as a political dissident, Webb pulls him out of his "red nightmare." Like poor little Jimmy in *Invaders from Mars*, Jerry has been having a bad dream.

PLAGUES: ILLNESS AS POLITICAL METAPHOR

To the extent that these films are seen as allegories of Communist infiltration, their narratives depict the Communist threat spreading in a manner akin to illness or contagion. Such terms, of course, were common descriptors of the Communist threat that traversed the period covered in this study. In a 1937 encyclical on "atheistic Communism," Pope Pius XI enumerated the Catholic Church's previous denunciations of the doctrine, calling particular attention to Pope Leo XIII's characterization in 1878 of socialists, communists, and nihilists as "the fatal plague which insinuates itself into the very marrow of human society only to bring about its ruin."[61] During his 1952 presidential campaign, Adlai Stevenson said that Communism was "a disease that may have killed more people in this world than cancer, tuberculosis, and heart disease combined."[62] Dr. Fred C. Schwarz, a noted anti-Communist religious leader in the Cold War period, published a pamphlet in the mid-1950s entitled *Introduction to Communism: Diagnosis and Treatment*. Comparing the spread of Communism to a kind of pathogen, Schwarz wrote,

"Communism is a disease: it is a disease of the body, of the mind, and of the spirit." And in 1975 Ronald Reagan, then the ex-governor of California, gave a radio address about Communism in which he asked, "Mankind has survived all manner of plagues and diseases, but can it survive Communism?"[63] In fact, by 1970 the frequent descriptions of Communism as a cancer within society had become so familiar, rhetoric scholar Edwin Black claimed that it should be classified as a "dead metaphor."[64]

Besides the frequent use of illness metaphors to explain the Communist threat, the representation of alien invasion as a kind of plague was presaged by earlier representational strategies in which the spread of actual disease served as either a Communist plot or as an allegory for the spread of Marxism. As I noted earlier, a subplot in *Big Jim McLain* depicts Red scientists in Hawaii working surreptitiously to create panic through the dissemination of a biological agent. In *The Whip Hand* (1951) a group of Communist scientists work in the backwoods of Wisconsin on a fatal strain of bacteria that they plan to release on an unsuspecting nation. Emblazoned on the film's poster was the phrase, "Lethal germs bred to infect water and milk supplies."[65]

Moreover, the use of plague as an allegorical term is perhaps best exemplified by Brenda Murphy's reading of Elia Kazan's film *Panic in the Streets* (1950). Describing the film as a kind of "mirror image" of *High Noon*, Murphy writes, "The use of disease and contamination imagery in this film could not be more obvious. Like the mind-disease of Communism as depicted by J. Edgar Hoover, the contamination of the plague spreads instantaneously from person to person without the knowledge or volition of its carriers or victims."[66] The threat of bubonic plague in *Panic in the Streets* adds an additional frisson by linking Communists to vermin. Says Murphy, "Again the anti-Communist imagery is unmistakable: the carriers of disease, the rats, must be destroyed if the community is to be saved from contamination."[67]

Considering that disease metaphors were already common in various kinds of anti-Communist discourse, it is not surprising that they also figure as tropes linked to scenarios of alien invasion. Indeed, in *Illness as Metaphor* Susan Sontag calls attention to the commutability of these terms: "Cancer proceeds by a science fiction scenario: an invasion of 'alien' or 'mutant' cells, stronger than normal cells (*Invasion of the Body Snatchers, The Incredible Shrinking Man, The Blob, The Thing*). One standard science-fiction plot is mutation, either mutants arriving from outer space or accidental mutations among humans. Cancer could be described as triumphant mutation and mutation is now mainly an image for cancer."[68]

The metaphor of illness contains at least four different dimensions that have made it especially apt for science fiction allegories of the Cold War. Illness is contagious, unwanted, internalized, and unseen. These four aspects of illness are so strongly linked semantically that they serve as "nested" metaphors for the potential spread of Communism. Moreover, these four aspects of illness are also rich in associations. Their meanings tentacle out from *illness* as a central term such that they also encompass some of the other semantic fields discussed earlier.

The metaphor of contagion finds parallels in the dramatic scenarios of several key science fiction titles of the 1950s. Although some science fiction films depict battles against individual creatures, others dramatize the rapid spread of monstrous beings as a kind of objective correlative of a pandemic. In *Them!* Dr. Medford warns of additional giant-ant colonies springing up around the country in quick succession. The threat of takeover is thus supported by the comparatively short reproductive cycles of ants. In *Invaders from Mars* the red planet's emissaries transform key members of the local scientific, military, and law enforcement communities in a span of a couple of hours. In *Invasion of the Body Snatchers* Dr. Bennell fields the first reports about unusual family members after returning from a conference. The town of Santa Mira is almost completely overtaken by pod people within a time span of a few days. Additionally, the potential for the rapid spread of pod people is dramatized by a late scene in which Bennell discovers truckloads of pods bound for nearby communities.

Contagion also carries an additional implication, namely that it subverts our will. A person, of course, never chooses to be sick. One is infected by contagious illness merely through exposure. This dimension of illness links up with scenarios of brainwashing. Illness causes us to change in ways that are beyond our conscious control. The same thing is true of the characters in science fiction films whose minds have been altered even though their bodies appear to be unchanged. Disease involuntarily changes the body much as brainwashing involuntarily changes the mind.

Illness and disease is also internalized within the body, which functions as the personification of the body politic. The metaphor of illness thus has obvious resonance for anti-Communist discourse, which highlighted the threat of an enemy within. Just as the agents of illness attack the body's tissues and organs from within, Communist cells operating inside our borders have the potential to subvert the systems that are necessary for a society to function. Related to this is the notion that illness and disease attack the body as an unseen enemy. The biological agents of contagion are bacteria and viruses, organisms so small that they cannot be seen by the naked eye. Yet, although these biological agents are both microscopic and internalized, they produce symptoms that enable a trained eye to detect disease as an underlying cause. This has obvious relevance for the way that some of these science fiction films employ the metaphor of passing. These films typically offer subtle cues in the mise-en-scène that enable the viewer to differentiate the humans from the humanoids on the basis of their "symptoms."

Both *It Came from Outer Space* and *Invasion of the Body Snatchers* provide good examples of the way this storytelling strategy is deployed. Despite Sheriff Warren's complaints to the contrary, the alien counterparts to Frank and George are readily discernible to viewers through two particular elements of mise-en-scène: the actors' blank expressions and their drab, utilitarian clothing. (The latter might be seen as a reference to the comparatively uniform look of Soviet and Chinese laborers.) The pod people in *Invasion of the Body Snatchers* are not as obviously different as the humanoid figures in *Outer Space,* but they are nonetheless marked by their bland expressions and slightly narcotized behavior. By using expressions and clothing as indices of alien occupation, these films draw on hierarchies of knowledge to strengthen the alignment between the spectator and each film's investigating agent. The viewer shares with John and Miles the ability to discern alien beings from the general population while the rest of society blithely goes about its business.

As with some of the other semantic fields, *Body Snatchers* proves to be the film most strongly invested in the use of plague or illness metaphors. It is telling, for example, that Miles is a medical doctor and, further, that he, rather than the police or psychiatrist Dan Kauffman, is the one to "diagnose" the problem in Santa Mira. Moreover, in an interesting scene, when Miles and Becky surreptitiously gain entrance to his office, he gives each of them injections. These are given under the pretext that they must stay awake, but the mise-en-scène suggests another implicit meaning, namely that they inoculate themselves against the spread of the pods, as though they are a deadly disease. Later, Miles uses loaded syringes as weapons against his captors. When the people guarding his office rush in as a response to his diversionary tactics, Miles injects them with sedatives that rapidly induce sleep. Although Miles's syringes do not literally contain vaccine, they prove to be his best weapon in warding off the pods' invasion and contamination of his body.

CONCLUSION

Aliens. Monsters. Vegetables. Nuclear terror. Brainwashing. Passing. Gigantism. Plagues. All these elements of science fiction plots and iconography furnish a rich set of semantic fields to film critics. Critics, in turn, combine these semantic fields in different ways to produce allegorical interpretations that read the cycle of 1950s science fiction as a symptom of McCarthyist paranoia. More important, in performing this type of analysis, critics have used both the Hollywood blacklist and the Cold War itself as reference points that create pretexts for the films' allegorical significance. While most critics conceive of these reference points quite broadly, others draw on more specific events, such as the Soviets' launch of Sputnik or the Chinese brainwashing of U.S. prisoners of war to adumbrate this basic interpretive framework. By drawing together these topical reference points, critics create a cognitive frame that enables them to read a film's characters and events in a particular way. Indeed, in some cases, like *Invasion of the Body Snatchers*, the critics themselves show how these frames can be flipped—read one way as anti-Communist tract, read another way as anti-HUAC fable.

Some films, like *Tarantula*, only activate one or two of these semantic fields. Others, like *Invasion of the Body Snatchers*, activate almost all of them. Indeed, the sheer number of semantic fields in *Body Snatchers* helps explain its centrality to discussions of 1950s science fiction as Cold War allegory. (In contrast, *Tarantula* is a peripheral example rather than a core member of the corpus.) By highlighting both the variety and multivalence of these semantic fields, the foregoing discussion goes a long way toward explaining how the link between McCarthyism and monsters quickly went from being an intriguing bit of sociocultural analysis to an outright zeitgeist cliché.

Then again, maybe not. Perhaps the real reason why *Body Snatchers* has been so central to discussions of 1950s science fiction is simply that it functions for critics as a kind of Rorschach test, a cinematic inkblot in which the pod people can stand for pretty much anything you like. In a trenchant bit of self-criticism, Jimmie L. Reeves wrote the following in the program notes for a 1981 screening of *Body Snatchers* for *Cinema Texas*:

> Near the end of the film, I looked around the room at my wide-eyed, dimly lit kinfolk, and I wondered to myself what podism meant to them. To my father, who worked twenty-five long years as a laborer for an oil company and sees retirement as the promised land, I suspected podism was somehow tied to his perception of corporate mentality; but my mother, a devout Christian fundamentalist, probably saw pods as agents of atheism. My straight-as-an-arrow sister most likely equated drug use with podhood; and I was sure her husband, a member of the National Rifle Association, thought of me as a pod. A wave of sadness flowed over me. I knew they were all wrong—that they would never recognize the true pods of our society: Republicans.[69]

Reeves's postulation of his family's response to *Body Snatchers* suggests that the film contains a kind of structural ambiguity that opens it up to a multiplicity of different meanings and a veritable treasure trove of semantic fields that can be associatively linked to them. Reeves further suggests that the pods become "all purpose bogeymen." Says Reeves, "And who among us doesn't feel oppressed or threatened by some inhuman social force? Only the pods."[70]

The multiplicity of interpretations for *Body Snatchers* and other 1950s science fiction films illustrates some of the vicissitudes of film criticism. Recall Katrina Mann's reading of *Body Snatchers*, which I mentioned in my introduction. Mann's take on *Body Snatchers* as a film expressing contemporary concerns about Mexican migrant laborers is certainly as valid as the interpretations that see the sci-fi cycle as Cold War allegory. But the longevity and frequency of the latter interpretation has rendered it banal, a cliché repeatedly uttered in capsule film reviews, on web discussion forums, and by television hosts on "classics" movie channels. By comparison, Mann's reading simply is more novel. As Mann's analysis indicates, my study of blacklist allegories may not tell us where the field of film studies is going, but it certainly tells us where we have been.

Conclusion

Old Wounds and the Texas Sharpshooter

While this manuscript was being reviewed, two things occurred that reinforce the roles of both the Hollywood blacklist and allegorical interpretation as important parts of contemporary film culture. First, on November 19, 2012, the *Hollywood Reporter* issued a public apology for its role in the blacklist, some sixty-five years after it was instituted. Written by W. R. Wilkerson III, the son of the magazine's founder, the article claims that the *Hollywood Reporter*'s virulent anti-Communist campaign had its roots in Billy Wilkerson's failed attempt to establish his own studio. Blaming the studio brass who seemingly crushed his dream, Wilkerson used the *Hollywood Reporter* as a "bully pulpit" to exact revenge. With the threat of international Communism emerging as an important political issue, Wilkerson retaliated against the studio bosses by destroying the talent essential to the industry's success. "Unfortunately," Wilkerson III writes, "they would become the collateral damage of history."[1]

Initially, the *Hollywood Reporter*'s coverage of the apology treated it as an attempt to heal a rift in the industry that has lasted for decades. In a segment on KCRW's *Which Way LA?* blacklisted actor Marsha Hunt praised Wilkerson's public gesture, saying, "For this apology to be issued now, I can't tell you how much it means."[2] Not everyone was so sanguine. On November 20 blacklisted writer Norma Barzman blasted the apology in an interview conducted with a local CBS affiliate. "The apology just gets me furious!" declared Barzman. "I think it's below comment."[3] The children of blacklisted writers also chimed in, claiming that the apology seemed like a hollow gesture, one incommensurate with the damage that Wilkerson did to people's careers.[4] Producer Howard Koch offered one of the stranger comments on the apology, limning the themes of later films made about the Hollywood blacklist: "The real victims of the Blacklist were those who had the wrong last names or went to communist meetings just to pick up girls."[5] Hecky Brown, *The Front's* tragic victim of the blacklist played by Zero Mostel, couldn't have said it better.

Whereas the controversy surrounding *The Hollywood Reporter's* apology shows an industry still coming to grips with its dark past, the second event—the 2013 release of *Room 237*—reflects continued interest in the interpretive practices associated with film criticism. Rodney Ascher's documentary yokes together five different readings of Stanley Kubrick's *The Shining* (1980). Ascher treats these interpretations as the treatises of obsessive fans, but at least three of them would not seem out of place in an academic film journal. Indeed, one of Ascher's interviewees is Professor Geoffrey Cocks of Albion College, someone whose professional livelihood depends on producing novel analyses of historical artifacts.[6]

Room 237 is an ideal addendum to my own study insofar as the interpretive strategies portrayed in the film dovetail with the ones I've discussed. Like the critics who saw postwar genre films as commentaries on the blacklist, the five armchair analysts in *Room 237* appeal time and again to Kubrick's status as *The Shining's* true author. Citing the director's reputation for meticulous preparation, they invest every aspect of *The Shining's* mise-en-scène and cinematography with latent significance. This even takes on a comical dimension when *Room 237's* interviewees treat apparent continuity errors as evidence of Kubrick's monomaniacal control.

The analysts in *Room 237* also display other similarities with the blacklist criticism described herein. As David Bordwell points out, these interpretations deploy the "punning" heuristic as a time-tested technique for developing evidentiary support: "*Snow White's* Dopey on Danny's door suggests that the boy doesn't yet realize what's going on; but when the dwarf disappears, Danny is no longer 'dopey.' A crushed Volkswagen stands for Kubrick's telling King that his artistic 'vehicle' has obliterated the novelist's original 'vehicle.'"[7] Such interpretive moves are akin to what blacklist-themed criticism did in equating "Reds" and "Redskins" in analyzing *Broken Arrow* or the "cell by cell" motif in *Invasion of the Body Snatchers*.

Room 237's interviewees also show evidence of certain mental heuristics that more generally inform the framing of interpretations. Bill Blakemore, for example, freely admits that part of the reason he fastened on the tin of Calumet baking powder in the background mise-en-scène of the Overlook Hotel's pantry is that he grew up near the Calumet River in Illinois. Blakemore uses both the product logo, which depicts an American Indian chief, and Calumet's etymology as a French Explorer word for peace pipe to support his reading of *The Shining* as a film about Native American genocide.[8] Yet part of the reason that Blakemore so easily grasped this detail is the "availability" bias. Having been raised near the Calumet, the term's original meaning was mentally available in Blakemore's recall in a way not true of most other viewers. That availability, in turn, guided attention to these baking powder tins, a background element that almost everyone else missed. Blakemore's attention to Calumet, primed by his previous experience, is similar to the way in which blacklist-themed criticism relies on well-established paradigms, such as *High Noon* and *On the Waterfront*, to expand the canon of blacklist allegories to include other films.

Writing about *Room 237*, film blogger Jim Emerson also cites Jay Weidner's reading of *The Shining* as a textbook example of "confirmation bias."[9] Weidner's "moon landing" hypothesis is perhaps the most notorious of the film's five readings, and Emerson rightly treats it as a kind of conspiracy theory. Guided by an already existing belief that Kubrick aided NASA in faking the moon landing, Weidner mines *The Shining* for evidence to support that theory, and, of course, finds it. He notes that the words on the keychain for Room 237 form an anagram for "MOON ROOM." Weidner also claims that the distance from the earth to the moon is 237,000 miles, a factoid that makes the hotel room number seem even more significant.

Weidner's rhetoric here is prima facie evidence of confirmation bias. He conveniently ignores the fact that you might just as easily read the letters on the key ring as an anagram for "MORON." Similarly, Weidner can only make the room number work by ignoring the fact that the moon has an elliptical orbit and its distance ranges from approximately 225,000 miles at its perigee to about 252,000 miles at its apogee. Of course, such a broad spectrum of distances reveals the arbitrariness that informs Weidner's claim. Kubrick might have selected any room from half of the Overlook Hotel's second floor, and its number would lead to essentially the same conclusion.

Emerson discusses confirmation bias as though it were the purview of conspiracy theorists. But, as cognitive psychologists point out, confirmation bias goes well beyond "magical thinking," informing some of our most basic reasoning processes. Although Emerson doesn't mention it, Juli Kearns's much more traditional reading of *The Shining* as a retelling of the Theseus myth displays some of the same tendencies. Primed by the film's hedge maze and the Overlook's labyrinthine hallways, Kearns reports that she was drawn to a Minotaur shape found in the upper left corner of a shot in which the mysterious twin girls appear to Danny in the hotel rec room. The shape is actually that of a skier on a poster, but because of his crouched posture, the position of the ski pole extended behind him, and the photograph's backlighting, the skier's outline does have the vague contours of a Minotaur.

Kearns builds "a bridge too far," though, by arguing the twins are bracketed by another image, that of a rodeo poster depicting a bull rider—a "bull-man" instead of a "cow-boy." Little does it matter that the animal in the picture looks more like a horse than a bull, owing to the appearance of the tail, which is shaggier and less tapered than that of a bull. A horseman doesn't work for Kearns's argument insofar as it recalls a centaur rather than a Minotaur. Minotaur imagery is what Kearns seeks and Minotaur imagery is what she finds. Kearns's example is a useful reminder that all film interpretation depends on such confirmation bias to a greater or lesser degree, including the blacklist-themed criticism profiled in this book.

The most outlandish interpretations in *Room 237* evoke a phenomenon described by psychologists as "the Texas sharpshooter" fallacy. Noting that humans tend to downplay the role of chance in their construal of specific events, psychologists suggest that such pattern-finding is akin to a cowboy, who randomly fires a shotgun at the side of a barn and then draws a bulls-eye around the resulting cluster of bullet holes. Anyone who comes across the barn will conclude that the cowboy is an amazing shot when he has, in actuality, imposed an artificial order on the random distribution of bullet holes. For David McRaney, the Texas sharpshooter fallacy underpins the gambler's belief he is on a hot streak, even though the string of wins simply balances out a string of losses that he simply ignored.[10] It also explains why religious fundamentalists see natural disasters as an expression of God's wrath. When a town is leveled by a tornado, religious leaders sometimes characterize the event as God's punishment for the state's enactment of gay marriage legislation, conveniently ignoring the fact that a dozen other states that have similar legislation remained unaffected. When the interviewees in *Room 237* highlight minutiae in *The Shining*'s mise-en-scène at the expense of thousands of other pictorial details, they commit the Texas sharpshooter fallacy, lulled by the signal and oblivious to the noise.

These two strands of my argument—the history of the Hollywood blacklist and the protocols of film criticism—are now mostly disentangled in modern film scholarship. This, though, is less a matter of the allegorical interpretations' plausibility and more a reflection that blacklist readings have lost their novelty. As I have shown, this has not always been the case. From 1955 to 2000 the interpretation of Cold War films as allegories was fertile territory for film scholars. Critics gradually enlarged a small group of paradigmatic texts to include dozens of titles, some of which encompassed major cycles of film production. This particular reading formation has now taken on the aura of critical dogma as the basic assumptions of blacklist-themed reading have filtered out to the culture at large. Of course, the popularization of such critical notions blunted the impact of new blacklist interpretations. After all, a new journal article articulating the blacklist subtext evident in, say, *The Court-Martial of Billy Mitchell* doesn't do much to burnish one's academic reputation if you can find user reviews of the film on IMDb that do more or less the same thing.[11]

Throughout my discussion of blacklist interpretations, I have keenly highlighted not only what critics have had to say but also how they derived their conclusions about what individual films mean. One cluster of factors involves the kinds of cognitive biases and heuristics just discussed in relation to *Room 237*. These mental habits, including availability bias and the representativeness heuristic, nudge scholars toward specific semantic fields that are then used to frame allegorical meanings in particular ways. Additionally, like the Texas sharpshooter, critics construct an interpretive frame around certain features of the text, which is then mapped in one-to-one correspondence with the topical elements that constitute the work's allegorical pretext. Several of these textual features involve genre conventions that, although present in earlier instances of the genre, suddenly take on new significance when placed within the Cold War's historical context. With the right framing, the reluctant witnesses of courtroom dramas seem to evoke witnesses subpoenaed by HUAC; the frontier spaces and the lynch mobs of 1950s westerns seem reflective of both the successes and excesses of U.S. domestic security policy; and the alien beings of science fiction films trigger thoughts of fifth columnists seeking to undermine American institutions from within. Although the terms of these types of interpretations have changed, their spirit lives on in every reviewer or blogger who saw *Star Wars Episode III: Revenge of the Sith* as an echo of Dick Cheney's embrace of the "dark side" or *The Dark Knight* as director Christopher Nolan's commentary on Bush-era antiterrorism measures.

The notion that many films produced between 1947 and 1960 function as blacklist or Cold War allegories tells only part of the story. The other part consists of the cycle of anti-Communist films made during the blacklist period. Displaying a different kind of didacticism, these films shaped public perceptions of Communists, who were often depicted as spies or criminals. In developing this trope, these anti-Communist films simply updated strategies used earlier in the representation of both mobsters and Nazis. Although mostly made to curry favor with HUAC, these films nonetheless hewed closely to the norms of Hollywood filmmaking, including conventions of genres that initially seem antithetical to their ostensible political message. Several anti-Communist films include femme fatales whose seductiveness comes to embody the ideological lure of the Communist Party. Others feature persons of color as party members in a manner reminiscent of Hollywood's postwar cycle of social problem films. Several scholars rightly describe these films as cinematic propaganda. Many of them undoubtedly display the kinds of "name-calling," "transfer," and "card-stacking" that was popularly associated with this type of discourse. What these scholars have overlooked, however, is the extent to which this mix of anti-Communist content with Hollywood storytelling formulas creates somewhat troubling ideological contradictions. In *The Red Menace* and *I Was a Communist for the FBI*, Communists ruthlessly exploit racial division for their own political aims. Yet in attempting to explain why people of color were attracted to the Communist Party, these films tacitly acknowledge the seriousness of racial prejudice as a destructive force in American society.

If *Film Criticism, the Cold War, and the Blacklist* has a larger lesson to impart, it is the importance of digging beneath the obvious truths of anti-Communist propaganda films and blacklist/Cold War allegories. In our hyperpartisan, post-9/11 moment the steady stream of news stories about the Patriot Act, "enhanced interrogation," Gitmo, and the Boston Marathon bombings are a constant reminder that terrorists and jihadists currently play a role in our political discourse that parallels that played by Communists for earlier generations. Every time a politician rails against the building of a mosque or the threat of Sharia law, it serves as a slightly ominous warning of how easily our political culture could revert to the paranoia and demagoguery of the HUAC/McCarthy era. In the coming years film scholars may well create a canon of "post-9/11 trauma" allegories that is as deep and wide as the canon of blacklist allegories. If so, perhaps this book can serve not only as a guide to how film interpretations contributed to such a critical enterprise but also as a useful reminder that the films themselves may contain much more than meets the eye.

Notes

INTRODUCTION

1. See Nora Sayre, *Running Time: Films of the Cold War* (New York: Dial, 1982); and J. Hoberman, *An Army of Phantoms: American Movies and the Making of the Cold War* (New York: New Press, 2011). For other examples of critical work that links films to the Hollywood blacklist and Cold War see Reynold Humphries, *Hollywood's Blacklists: A Political and Cultural History* (Edinburgh: Edinburgh University Press, 2008); Brenda Murphy, *Congressional Theatre: Dramatizing McCarthyism on Stage, Film, and Television* (New York: Cambridge University Press, 1999); Brian Neve, *Film and Politics in America: A Social Tradition* (New York: Routledge, 1992); and Stephen J. Whitfield, *The Culture of the Cold War,* 2nd ed. (Baltimore: Johns Hopkins University Press, 1996).

2. Stephen Farber, booklet for *Spartacus* (Criterion Collection, 2001), DVD.

3. "The Making of *The Robe*" featurette, *The Robe* (Fox, 2008), Blu-ray.

4. Lillian Hellman, *Scoundrel Time* (Boston: Little, Brown, 1976); Lester Cole, *Hollywood Red: The Autobiography of Lester Cole* (Palo Alto, CA: Ramparts, 1981); and Walter Bernstein, *Inside Out: A Memoir of the Blacklist* (New York: Knopf, 1996).

5. Larry Ceplair and Steven Englund, *The Inquisition in Hollywood: Politics in the Film Community, 1930–1960* (Berkeley: University of California Press, 1979); and Nancy Lynn Schwartz, *The Hollywood Writers' Wars* (New York: McGraw-Hill, 1983).

6. Thom Andersen, "Red Hollywood," in *"Un-American" Hollywood: Politics and Film in the Blacklist Era,* ed. Frank Krutnik, Steve Neale, Brian Neve, and Peter Stanfield (New Brunswick, NJ: Rutgers University Press, 2007), 225–63. Originally published in *Literature and the Visual Arts in Contemporary Society,* ed. Suzanne Ferguson and Barbara Groseclose (Columbus: Ohio State University Press, 1985), 141–96. Citations refer to the Rutgers edition.

7. See Patrick McGilligan and Paul Buhle, *Tender Comrades: A Backstory of the Blacklist* (New York: St. Martin's Griffin, 1999).

8. See Peter Biskind, *Seeing Is Believing: How Hollywood Taught Us to Stop Worrying and Love the Fifties* (New York: Pantheon, 1983).

9. For an incisive critique of the way these issues have been dramatized, see Jeanne Hall, "The Benefits of Hindsight: Re-visions of HUAC and the Film and Television Industries in *The Front* and *Guilty by Suspicion*," *Film Quarterly* 54, no. 4 (2001–2): 15–26.

10. John Joseph Gladchuk, *Hollywood and Anticommunism: HUAC and the Evolution of the Red Menace, 1935–1950* (New York: Routledge, 2007); Michael Freedland, *Hollywood on Trial: McCarthyism's War against the Movies* (London: Robson, 2007); and Humphries, *Hollywood's Blacklists*.

11. Ring Lardner Jr., *I'd Hate Myself in the Morning: A Memoir* (New York: Thunder Mouth's Press/Nation Books, 2000); Jean Rouverol, *Refugees from Hollywood: A Journal of the Blacklist Years* (Albuquerque: University of New Mexico Press, 2000); and Norma Barzman, *The Red and the Black: The Intimate Memoir of a Hollywood Expatriate* (New York: Thunder Mouth's Press/Nation Books, 2003).

12. See, e.g., Peter Hanson, *Dalton Trumbo, Hollywood Rebel: A Critical Survey and Filmography* (Jefferson, NC: McFarland, 2001); Paul Buhle and Dave Wagner, *A Very Dangerous Citizen: Abraham Polonsky and the Hollywood Left* (Berkeley: University of California Press, 2001); Gerald Horne, *The Final Victim of the Blacklist: John Howard Lawson, Dean of the Hollywood Ten* (Berkeley: University of California Press, 2006); Larry Ceplair, *The Marxist and the Movies: A Biography of Paul Jarrico* (Lexington: University Press of Kentucky, 2007); Jennifer E. Langdon, *Caught in the Crossfire: Adrian Scott and the Politics of Americanism in 1940s Hollywood* (New York: Columbia University Press, 2008); and James J. Lorence, *The Suppression of "Salt of the Earth": How Hollywood, Big Labor, and Politicians Blacklisted a Movie in Cold War America* (Albuquerque: University of New Mexico Press, 1999).

13. Jon Lewis, "'We Do Not Ask You to Condone This': How the Blacklist Saved Hollywood," *Cinema Journal* 39, no. 2 (2000): 3–30. The essay also appears in a slightly revised version in Lewis's *Hollywood v. Hard Core: How the Struggle over Censorship Saved the Modern Film Industry* (New York: New York University Press, 2000), 11–49.

14. Besides Hoberman's *Army of Phantoms* see Krutnik, Neale, Neve, and Stanfield, *"Un-American" Hollywood*; and Tony Shaw, *Hollywood's Cold War* (Amherst: University of Massachusetts Press, 2007).

15. See Paul Buhle and Dave Wagner, *Blacklisted: The Film Lover's Guide to the Hollywood Blacklist* (New York: Palgrave Macmillan, 2003); Paul Buhle and Dave Wagner, *Hide in Plain Sight: The Hollywood Blacklistees in Film and Television, 1950–2002* (New York: Palgrave Macmillan, 2003); and Paul Buhle and Dave Wagner, *Radical Hollywood: The Unheard Story behind Hollywood's Favorite Movies* (New York: New Press, 2003).

16. Thom Andersen's "Update" to "Red Hollywood" offers a thorough summary of the response to Buhle and Wagner's books. See *"Un-American" Hollywood*, 269–74.

17. See Kenneth Lloyd Billingsley, *Hollywood Party: How Communism Seduced the American Film Industry in the 1930s and 1940s* (Rocklin, CA: Forum/ Prima, 1998); and Ronald Radosh and Allis Radosh, *Red Star over Hollywood: The Film Colony's Long Romance with the Left* (New York: Encounter, 2006).

18. Joseph Litvak, *The Un-Americans: Jews, the Blacklist, and Stoolpigeon Culture* (Durham, NC: Duke University Press, 2009); Victor S. Navasky, *Naming Names* (New York: Penguin, 1980).

19. See John Lewis Gaddis, *The United States and the Origins of the Cold War, 1941–1947* (New York: Columbia University Press, 1972); John Lewis Gaddis, *The Cold War: A New History* (New York: Penguin, 2005); Martin Walker, *The Cold War: A History* (New York: Henry Holt, 1993); Irving Howe and Lewis Coser, *The American Communist Party: A Critical History* (New York: Da Capo, 1974); David Caute, *The Great Fear: The Anti-Communist Purge under Truman and Eisenhower* (New York: Simon and Schuster, 1978); Ellen Schrecker, *Many Are the Crimes: McCarthyism in America* (Princeton, NJ: Princeton University Press, 1998); Ellen Schrecker, *The Age of McCarthyism: A Brief History with Documents* (New York: Bedford/St. Martin's, 2002); and Albert Fried, *McCarthyism: The Great American Red Scare, a Documentary History* (New York: Oxford University Press, 1997).

20. See Ted Morgan, *Reds: McCarthyism in Twentieth-Century America* (New York: Random House, 2003); David M. Oshinsky, *A Conspiracy So Immense: The World of Joseph McCarthy* (New York: Oxford University Press, 2005); M. Stanton Evans, *Blacklisted by History: The Untold Story of Joseph McCarthy and His Fight against America's Enemies* (New York: Three Rivers, 2007); Harvey Klehr, John Earl Haynes, and Fridrikh Igorevich Firsov, *The Secret World of American Communism* (New Haven, CT: Yale University Press, 1995); Stéphane Courtois et al., *The Black Book of Communism: Crimes, Terror, Repression*, trans. Jonathan Murphy and Mark Kramer (Cambridge, MA: Harvard University Press, 1999).

21. James G. Ryan, *Earl Browder: The Failure of American Communism* (Tuscaloosa: University of Alabama Press, 2005); Edward P. Johanningsmeier, *Forging American Communism: The Life of William Z. Foster* (Princeton, NJ: Princeton University Press, 1994); Paul Boyer, *By the Bomb's Early Light: American Thought and Culture at the Dawn of the Atomic Age* (Chapel Hill: University of North Carolina Press, 1985); Laura A. Belmonte, *Selling the American Way: U.S. Propaganda and the Cold War* (Philadelphia: University of Pennsylvania Press, 2008); Walter L. Hixson, *Parting the Curtain: Propaganda, Culture, and the Cold War, 1945–1961* (New York: St. Martin's Griffin, 1997); Jeff Woods, *Black Struggle, Red Scare: Segregation and Anti-Communism in the South, 1948–1968* (Baton Rouge: Louisiana State University Press, 2004); and Paul C. Mishler, *Raising Reds: The Young Pioneers, Radical Summer Camps, and Communist Political Culture in the United States* (New York: Columbia University Press, 1999).

22. Whitfield, *The Culture of the Cold War;* Peter J. Kuznick and James Gilbert, eds., *Rethinking Cold War Culture* (Washington: Smithsonian

Institution, 2001); Alan Nadel, *Containment Culture: American Narratives, Postmodernism, and the Atomic Age* (Durham, NC: Duke University Press, 1995); John V. Fleming, *The Anti-Communist Manifestos: Four Books That Shaped the Cold War* (New York: Norton, 2009); Michael Barson and Steven Heller, *Red Scared! The Commie Menace in Propaganda and Popular Culture* (San Francisco: Chronicle, 2001); Thomas Doherty, *Cold War, Cool Medium: Television, McCarthyism, and American Culture* (New York: Columbia University Press, 2003); and Michael Kackman, *Citizen Spy: Television, Espionage, and Cold War Culture* (Minneapolis: University of Minnesota Press, 2005).

23. Andersen, "Red Hollywood," 225.

24. This does not mean that critics and reviewers at major newspapers and magazines did not privately ponder the implicit political meanings of *High Noon* or *The Robe*. After all, one surmises that they were professionals well aware of the effects that HUAC's investigations had on the very industry that they covered on a weekly basis. But even if this were the case, they seem to have scrubbed their columns clean of any reference to this political backdrop lest they run afoul of their editor, their publisher, their readers, or the investigative bodies determined to root out all Communists and fellow travelers from mainstream media institutions.

25. See Karel Reisz, "Hollywood's Anti-Red Boomerang: Apple Pie, Love and Endurance versus the Commies," *Sight and Sound* 22, no. 3 (1953): 132–37, 148.

26. Harry Schein, "Den Olympiske Cowboyen," *Bonniers litterära magasin*, Jan. 1954. This essay was translated and reprinted as "The Olympic Cowboy" in *American Scholar* 24, no. 3 (1955): 309–20.

27. Andre Bazin, *What Is Cinema?* edited and translated by Hugh Gray (Berkeley: University of California Press, 1971), 2:151.

28. Ernesto G. Laura, "Invasion of the Body Snatchers," *Bianco e nero* 18, no. 12 (1957): 69. Reprinted in *Focus on the Science Fiction Film*, ed. William Johnson (Englewood Cliffs, NJ: Prentice-Hall, 1972), 71–73.

29. Not surprisingly, the *Daily Worker*'s reviews reflect the broader film culture of New York in the postwar era. The staff typically reviewed not only Hollywood films but also European and Soviet art-house titles, documentaries, and even avant-garde programs. Although its reviews covered much the same territory as other New York newspapers, however, the *Daily Worker*'s staff was attuned to several issues frequently ignored by mainstream critics, such as the slander of American and Soviet Communists, "chauvinisms" directed at women or people of color, misrepresentations of American or European history, and the engagement or avoidance of frank social truths.

30. David Platt, "Ancient Rome's Ruthless and Futile Witchhunt," *Daily Worker*, Nov. 28, 1951, 7.

31. T. Jacobs, "'Salome' in Technicolor," *Daily Worker*, April 8, 1953, 7.

32. See Alvah Bessie, *Inquisition in Eden* (New York: Macmillan, 1965); and Walter Goodman, *The Committee: The Extraordinary Career of the House*

Committee on Un-American Activities (New York: Farrar, Straus and Giroux, 1968). Other key studies of the blacklist's effects on Hollywood written during the period include Robert Vaughn, *Only Victims: A Study of Show Business Blacklisting* (New York: Proscenium, 1972); and Stefan Kanfer, *A Journal of the Plague Years* (New York: Atheneum, 1973).

33. For more on the "Robert Rich" affair see my essay, "'A Good Business Proposition': Dalton Trumbo, *Spartacus*, and the End of the Hollywood Blacklist," in *Controlling Hollywood: Censorship and Regulation in the Studio Era*, ed. Matthew Bernstein (New Brunswick, NJ: Rutgers University Press, 1999), 206–37.

34. See Susan Sontag, "The Imagination of Disaster," in *Against Interpretation, and Other Essays* (New York: Farrar, Straus and Giroux, 1966), 209–25.

35. Carlos Clarens, *An Illustrated History of Horror and Science Fiction Films* (New York: G. P. Putnam's Sons, 1967), 127.

36. Michael Wilmington, "Nicholas Ray's *Johnny Guitar*," *Velvet Light Trap* 12 (Spring 1974): 19–25.

37. Andersen, "Red Hollywood," 232–43.

38. Daniel J. Leab, "How Red Was My Valley: Hollywood, the Cold War Film, and *I Married a Communist*," *Journal of American History* 19, no. 1 (1984): 59–88; Daniel Leab, "*The Iron Curtain* (1948): Hollywood's First Cold War Movie," *Historical Journal of Film, Radio, and Television* 8, no. 2 (1988): 153–88; and Thomas Doherty, "Hollywood Agit-Prop: The Anti-Communist Cycle, 1948–1954," *Journal of Film and Video* 40, no. 4 (1988): 15–27.

39. See William Rothman, *Hitchcock—The Murderous Gaze* (Cambridge, MA: Harvard University Press, 1982), 248; and Whitfield, *Culture of the Cold War*, 59–63.

40. See Sayre, *Running Time*, 191–204; Biskind, *Seeing Is Believing*, 123–36; Vivian Sobchack, *The Limits of Infinity: The American Science Fiction Film, 1950–1975* (New York: A. S. Barnes, 1980), 120–29; Michael Rogin, *Ronald Reagan, the Movie and Other Episodes in Political Demonology* (Berkeley: University of California Press, 1987), 262–67; and Noël Carroll, *The Philosophy of Horror, or Paradoxes of the Heart* (New York: Routledge, 1990), 197.

41. See John Lenihan, *Showdown: Confronting Modern America in the Western Film* (Urbana: University of Illinois Press, 1980), esp. 24–54, 117–30. See also Biskind, *Seeing Is Believing*, 230–40.

42. Edward Sorel, "Movie Classics: *High Noon*," *Esquire*, April 1981, 128.

43. Warren Spector, "The Thing from Another World," *Cinema Texas Program Notes* 15, no. 1 (1978): 11. *The Thing (From Another World)* clippings file, Margaret Herrick Library, Academy of Motion Picture Arts and Sciences (hereafter MHL).

44. Program notes for *Invasion of the Body Snatchers*, American Cinematheque, Dec. 10–12, 1993. *Invasion of the Body Snatchers* clipping file, MHL.

45. Roger Ebert, review of *The Thing*, *Chicago Sun-Times*, Jan. 1, 1982.

46. Peter Travers, review of *Body Snatchers, Rolling Stone,* Jan. 28, 1994. Travers here makes a common mistake by conflating Senator Joseph McCarthy's investigation of Communist influence in government with HUAC's investigations of Communist subversion in Hollywood.

47. Andersen, "Afterword," 264.

48. Ibid., 272.

49. Nick Madigan, "Where Credit's Due," *Variety,* March 19, 1999, www.variety.com/article/VR1117492199.

50. Obituary for Bernard Gordon, *Variety,* May 11, 2007, www.variety.com/article/VR1117964802.

51. Dave McNary, "WGA Credits Dalton Trumbo," *Variety,* Dec. 29, 2011, www.variety.com/article/VR1118047697.

52. John Belton, *American Cinema / American Culture* (New York: McGraw-Hill, 1994), 233–56.

53. Jennifer Peterson, "The Competing Tunes of *Johnny Guitar:* Liberalism, Sexuality, Masquerade," *Cinema Journal* 35, no. 3 (1996): 3.

54. Katrina Mann, "'You're Next!' Postwar Hegemony Besieged in *Invasion of the Body Snatchers,*" *Cinema Journal* 44, no. 1 (2004): 49–68.

55. Quoted in Janet Staiger, *Interpreting Films: Studies in the Historical Reception of American Cinema* (Princeton, NJ: Princeton University Press, 1992), 46.

CHAPTER 1. A BIFOCAL VIEW OF HOLLYWOOD DURING THE BLACKLIST PERIOD

1. See Dana Polan, *Scenes of Instruction: The Beginnings of U.S. Study of Film* (Berkeley: University of California Press, 2007); and Lee Grieveson and Haidee Wasson, eds., *Inventing Film Studies* (Durham, NC: Duke University Press, 2008).

2. David Bordwell, *Making Meaning: Influence and Rhetoric in the Interpretation of Cinema* (Cambridge, MA: Harvard University Press, 1989), 21.

3. *Merriam-Webster Online,* s.v. "allegory," accessed Oct. 31, 2013, www.merriam-webster.com/dictionary/allegory.

4. Bordwell, *Making Meaning,* 256.

5. Ibid., 252.

6. See Angus Fletcher, *Allegory: The Theory of a Symbolic Mode* (Ithaca, NY: Cornell University Press, 1964), 324–28.

7. J. Michael Sproule, *Propaganda and Democracy: The American Experience of Media and Mass Persuasion* (New York: Cambridge University Press, 1997), 9.

8. Ibid, 131.

9. Quoted in Sproule, *Propaganda and Democracy,* 135. Originally published as "How to Detect Propaganda," *Propaganda Analysis* 1 (Nov. 1937): 5–7.

10. See Jacques Ellul, *Propaganda: The Formation of Men's Attitudes,* trans. Konrad Kellen and Jean Lerner (New York: Alfred A. Knopf, 1965).

11. Ibid., 52–57.

12. Ibid., 64.

13. Thomas Doherty, "Hollywood Agit-Prop: The Anti-Communist Cycle, 1948–1954," *Journal of Film and Video* 40, no. 4 (1988): 16.

14. For more on Hollywood's handling of political and nationalist issues related to film content, see Ruth Vasey, *The World according to Hollywood, 1918–1939* (Madison: University of Wisconsin Press, 1997), esp. 194–224.

15. Bernice Mertes to Jack Warner, Sept. 20, 1951, *I Was a Communist for the FBI* production file, Warner Bros. Archives, School of Cinematic Arts, University of Southern California (hereafter WBA).

16. Nancy Olwine to Jack Warner, June 9, 1951, *I Was a Communist for the FBI* production file, WBA.

17. Jack D. Zeldes to Jack Warner, June 29, 1951, *I Was a Communist for the FBI* production file, WBA.

18. Julius Newman to Jack Warner, May 12, 1951, *I Was a Communist for the FBI* production file, WBA.

19. Dorothy B. Jones, "Communism and the Movies: A Study of Film Content," *Report on Blacklisting: Movies,* ed. John Cogley (New York: Fund for the Republic, 1956), 218.

20. Ibid., 220–31.

21. Quoted in Neal Gabler, *An Empire of Their Own: How the Jews Invented Hollywood* (New York: Crown, 1988), 386.

22. Harold Heffernan, "'Big Jim McLain' Hits Timely Theme," *Indianapolis Star,* Sept. 10, 1952, *Big Jim McLain* clippings file, WBA.

23. Gordon Mirams, Esq., to Warner Bros. Pictures in Auckland, Oct. 23, 1951, *I Was a Communist for the FBI* production file, WBA.

24. "Neutrals Nix Anti-Commie Pix," *Variety,* Feb. 17, 1954, 1, 20.

25. "A Bum Rap from Omaha," *Variety,* March 3, 1954, 3.

26. "The New Pictures," review of *The Iron Curtain, Time,* May 17, 1948, 104.

27. Reisz, "Hollywood's Anti-Red Boomerang," 132 (editors' preface).

28. Milton J. Shapiro, review of *Big Jim McLain,* Sept. 18, 1952, *Big Jim McLain* clippings file, Margaret Herrick Library, Academy of Motion Picture Arts and Sciences (hereafter MHL).

29. Shaw, *Hollywood's Cold War,* 52.

30. See advertising material for *Walk East on Beacon,* reproduced in Sayre, *Running Time,* 92–93.

31. Jones, "Communism and the Movies," 216.

32. Reisz, "Hollywood's Anti-Red Boomerang," 133.

33. Daniel J. Leab, "Hollywood and the Cold War, 1945–1961," in *Hollywood as Mirror: Changing Views of "Outsiders" and "Enemies" in American Movies,* ed. Robert Brent Toplin (Westport, CT: Greenwood Press, 1993), 118.

34. See, e.g., Walter Benjamin, *The Origin of German Tragic Drama,* trans. John Osborne (New York: Verso, 1998); Paul de Man, *Allegories of Reading: Figural Language in Rousseau, Nietzsche, Rilke, and Proust* (New Haven, CT:

Yale University Press, 1979); Paul de Man, *Blindness and Insight: Essays in the Rhetoric of Contemporary Criticism* (Minneapolis: University of Minnesota Press, 1983); Michelle Langford, *Allegorical Images: Tableau, Time, and Gesture in the Cinema of Werner Schroeter* (Bristol, UK: Intellect, 2006); Fredric Jameson, *Signatures of the Visible* (New York: Routledge, 1992); and Fredric Jameson, *The Geopolitical Aesthetic: Cinema and Space in the World System* (Bloomington: Indiana University Press, 1995).

35. See Fletcher, *Allegory*, 2n; Carolynn Van Dyke, *The Fiction of Truth: Structures of Meaning in Narrative and Dramatic Allegory* (Ithaca, NY: Cornell University Press, 1985), 15; Maureen Quilligan, *The Language of Allegory: Defining the Genre* (Ithaca, NY: Cornell University Press, 1979), 25–26; and Stephen A. Barney, *Allegories of History, Allegories of Love* (Hamden, CT: Archon, 1979).

36. For the best explanation of this aspect of allegory see Sayre N. Greenfield, *The Ends of Allegory* (Newark, NJ: University of Delaware Press, 1998).

37. Northrop Frye, *Anatomy of Criticism: Four Essays* (Princeton, NJ: Princeton University Press, 1957), 90.

38. See Jeremy Tambling, *Allegory* (New York: Routledge, 2010), 19–20. See also Quilligan, *Language of Allegory*, 25–28; and Van Dyke, *Fiction of Truth*, 43–45.

39. Quilligan, *Language of Allegory*, 32.

40. Ibid., 22.

41. See Van Dyke, *Fiction of Truth*, 25–61; Fletcher, *Allegory*, 157–61; and Tambling, *Allegory*, 48–49.

42. See Van Dyke, *Fiction of Truth*, 156–97; Quilligan, *Language of Allegory*, 121–31; and Tambling, *Allegory*, 69–73.

43. Quilligan, *Language of Allegory*, 42–46, 265–77.

44. Ibid., 97–98.

45. Ibid., 98–99.

46. Fletcher, *Allegory*, 365–67.

47. Angus Fletcher says bluntly, "Allegory presumably thrives on political censorship" (*Allegory*, 328). Fletcher goes on to speculate that one reason why Meyerhold was executed by the Soviets is that Meyerhold failed to be more indirect in his criticism of the new regime. See also Tambling, *Allegory*, 154–59; Gordon Teskey, *Allegory and Violence* (Ithaca, NY: Cornell University Press, 1996), 122–47; Greenfield, *The Ends of Allegory*, 111–32; Theresa M. Kelley, *Reinventing Allegory* (New York: Cambridge University Press, 1997), 85–92.

48. See Ranjit S. Dighe, ed., *The Historian's "Wizard of Oz": Reading L. Frank Baum's Classic as a Political and Monetary Allegory* (Westport, CT: Praeger, 2002); Bradley Hansen, "The Fable as Allegory: The Wizard of Oz in Economics," *Journal of Economic Education* 33, no. 3 (2002): 254–64; Henry M. Littlefield, "*The Wizard of Oz*: Parable on Populism," *American Quarterly* 16, no. 1 (1964): 47–58; and Hugh Rockoff, "The 'Wizard of Oz' as a Monetary Allegory," *Journal of Political Economy* 98, no. 4 (1990): 739–60.

49. Douglas Kellner, *Cinema Wars: Hollywood Film and Politics in the Bush-Cheney Era* (Malden, MA: Wiley-Blackwell, 2010), 120–26.

50. See Andrea Comiskey, "The Hero We Read: *The Dark Knight*, Popular Allegoresis, and Blockbuster Ideology," *Riddle Me This, Batman! Essays on the Universe of the Dark Knight*, ed. Kevin K. Durand and Mary K. Leigh (Jefferson, NC: McFarland, 2011), 124–26.

51. Justin Chang, "9/11 Lessons: A Time for Restraint," *Variety*, August 22, 2011, 30.

52. See Daniel J. Leab, *Orwell Subverted: The CIA and the Filming of "Animal Farm"* (University Park: Pennsylvania State University Press, 2007), 4–5.

53. "Vogue Spotlight by Allene Talmey," *Vogue*, Sept. 15, 1946.

54. Leab, *Orwell Subverted*, 6.

55. Murphy, *Congressional Theatre*, 133–36.

56. McAlister Coleman, "The Witches of Salem," *The Nation*, Sept. 3, 1949, 233.

57. Arthur Miller, *Timebends: A Life* (New York: Grove, 1987), 316.

58. Ibid., 333.

59. Quoted in Murphy, *Congressional Theatre*, 133.

60. Eric Bentley, "Miller's Innocence," *New Republic*, Feb. 16, 1953, 22.

61. "Witchcraft and Stagecraft," *New York Post*, Feb. 1, 1953, 9M.

62. Robert Warshow, "The Liberal Conscience of *The Crucible*," *Commentary*, March 1953. Reprinted in *The Immediate Experience: Movies, Comics, Theatre, and Other Aspects of Popular Culture* (New York: Atheneum, 1970), 196.

63. Arthur Miller, quoted in Henry Hewes, "Arthur Miller and How He Went to the Devil," *Saturday Review*, Jan. 31, 1953, 26.

64. See Murphy, *Congressional Theatre*, 158–59; and Doherty, *Cold War, Cool Medium*, 131.

65. See Buhle and Wagner, *Hide in Plain Sight*, 21.

66. Hoberman, *Army of Phantoms*, 233.

67. Bernstein, *Inside Out*, 222.

68. For a thorough inventory of these writers' contributions see Steve Neale, "Swashbuckling, Sapphire, and Salt," in *"Un-American" Hollywood: Politics and Film in the Blacklist Era*, ed. Frank Krutnik et al. (New Brunswick, NJ: Rutgers University Press, 2007), 202–4.

69. Freedland, *Hollywood on Trial*, 246.

70. James Chapman, "*The Adventures of Robin Hood* and the Origins of the Television Swashbuckler," *Media History* 17, no. 3 (2011): 281.

71. See Brian Boyd, *On the Origin of Stories: Evolution, Cognition, and Fiction* (Cambridge, MA: Belknap, 2009), 322–23.

72. Ibid., 322–69. For another critique of the conceptual weaknesses of zeitgeist criticism see David Bordwell, *On the History of Film Style* (Cambridge, MA: Harvard University Press, 1997), 43–44.

73. See Bordwell, *Making Meaning*, 29–30.

74. Ibid., 33.

75. Joseph McBride, *Searching for John Ford* (New York: St. Martin's, 2001), 498–574.

76. For a useful summary of this research see Gideon Keren, "On the Definition and Possible Underpinnings of Framing Effects: A Brief Review and Critical Evaluation," in *Perspectives on Framing*, ed. Gideon Keren (New York: Psychology Press, 2011), 3–33.

77. See Daniel Kahneman, *Thinking, Fast and Slow* (New York: Farrar, Straus and Giroux, 2011), 368–69.

78. Ibid., 119.

79. Keren, "Framing Effects," 18.

80. Ibid., 21.

81. "Witchcraft and Stagecraft," *New York Post*, Feb. 1, 1953, 9M.

82. Steven Pinker, *The Stuff of Thought: Language as a Window on Human Nature* (New York: Viking, 2007), 43–44.

83. Ibid., 4.

84. David McRaney, *You Are Not So Smart: Why You Have Too Many Friends on Facebook, Why Your Memory Is Mostly Fiction, and 46 Other Ways You're Deluding Yourself* (New York: Gotham, 2011), 69.

85. See Barry Glassner, *The Culture of Fear* (New York: Basic Books, 1999), xiii–xv.

86. Freedland, *Hollywood on Trial*, 259.

87. Kahneman, *Thinking, Fast and Slow*, 149.

88. See Daniel T. Gilbert, "How Mental Systems Believe," *American Psychologist* 46, no. 2 (1991): 107–19; Mark Snyder and Nancy Cantor, "Understanding Personality and Social Behavior: A Functionalist Strategy," *The Handbook of Social Psychology*, 4th ed., ed. Daniel Gilbert, Susan T. Fiske, and Gardner Lindzey (Boston: McGraw-Hill, 1998), 635–79; Michael J. Marks and R. Chris Fraley, "Confirmation Bias and the Sexual Double Standard," *Sex Roles* 54, no. 1–2 (2006): 19–26; and Raymond S. Nickerson, "Confirmation Bias: A Ubiquitous Phenomenon in Many Guises," *Review of General Psychology* 2, no. 2 (1998): 175–220.

89. Gilbert, "How Mental Systems Believe," 115–16.

90. See Edward Dmytryk, *It's a Hell of a Life but Not a Bad Living* (New York: New York Times Books, 1978), 233.

CHAPTER 2. I WAS A COMMUNIST FOR RKO

1. For descriptions of this anti-Communist cycle see Doherty, "Hollywood Agit-Prop," 15–18; Neve, *Film and Politics*, 187–88; Ceplair and Englund, *Inquisition in Hollywood*, 340; Belton, *American Cinema / American Culture*, 245; Navasky, *Naming Names*, 15; Jones, "Communism and the Movies," 215–18; Sayre, *Running Time*, 79–99; Whitfield, *Culture of the Cold War*, 131–44; Leab, "Hollywood and the Cold War, 1945–1961," 117–37; Ian Scott, *American Politics in Hollywood Film* (Chicago: Fitzroy Dearborn, 2000), 111–16; and

Richard A. Schwartz, *Cold War Culture: Media and the Arts* (New York: Checkmark, 1998), 100–103, 113–15.

2. Neve, *Film and Politics*, 187.

3. Quoted in Gabler, *An Empire of Their Own*, 357.

4. Ceplair and Englund, *Inquisition in Hollywood*, 340.

5. Of course, the threat of outside regulation has long been a concern of Hollywood. Although this concern was manifested in relation to a range of topics that includes antitrust legislation, labor disputes, and the ratings system, the most obvious example of how Hollywood dealt with such threats lies in the development of the Production Code. For more on self-regulation and the Production Code see Lea Jacobs, *The Wages of Sin: Censorship and the Fallen Woman Film, 1928–1942* (Madison: University of Wisconsin Press, 1991); Leonard J. Leff and Jerrold L. Simmons, *The Dame in the Kimono: Hollywood, Censorship and the Production Code from the 1920s to the 1960s* (New York: Grove Weidenfeld, 1990); and Matthew Bernstein, ed., *Controlling Hollywood: Censorship and Regulation in the Studio Era* (New Brunswick, NJ: Rutgers University Press, 1999).

6. To be fair, screenwriters have had similar difficulties in dramatizing certain political principles associated with a republican form of democratic government. Films about America's colonial period, for example, have generally failed to garner substantial box-office receipts, and consequently, films dealing with the issues surrounding the American Revolution are thought to be box-office poison. Not surprisingly, filmmakers have generally had more success dealing with political issues within biopics *(Young Mr. Lincoln, Wilson, Nixon)*, satire *(Duck Soup, Dr. Strangelove, Dick)*, and films that deal with political institutions *(Advise and Consent, The Candidate, All the President's Men)*. Here my purpose is not to offer an assessment of the relevance or importance of politics in relation to classical Hollywood cinema. Rather, I am suggesting that Hollywood has historically dealt with politics according to a certain set of strategies through which films can accommodate topical political material.

7. Richard Collins, "Confessions of a Red Screenwriter," *New Leader*, Oct. 6, 1952; repr. in Billingsley, *Hollywood Party*, 309–10 (italics in the original).

8. For more on Hollywood's attitudes about "talky" films see Sarah Kozloff, *Overhearing Film Dialogue* (Berkeley: University of California Press, 2000), 1–29.

9. "Out of the Woods," *New York Times*, June 8, 1949, *I Married a Communist* clippings file, Margaret Herrick Library, Academy of Motion Picture Arts and Sciences (hereafter MHL).

10. Arthur Jacobs, story synopsis of *The Thief*, *The Thief* clippings file, MHL.

11. For example, a review of the film in the November 1952 issue of *Films in Review* noted that "Dr. Fields has a Comintern-type contact (played by Martin Gabel)," *The Thief* clippings file, MHL.

12. Philip K. Scheuer, "'The Thief' Steals Page from Silent Era, Sounds Abound but Not a Word Is Heard," *Los Angeles Times*, June 22, 1952, D1, D3.

13. Review of *The Thief, Saturday Review*, Nov. 8, 1952, *The Thief* clippings file, MHL.

14. There has been a great deal of film criticism dealing with Capra's relation to populism. For a sampling of this work see Neve, *Film and Politics*, 28–55; Giuliana Muscio, "Roosevelt, Arnold, and Capra (or) the Federalist-Populist Paradox," in *Frank Capra: Authorship and the Studio System*, ed. Robert Sklar and Vito Zagarrio (Philadelphia: Temple University Press, 1998), 164–89; Jeffrey Richards, "Frank Capra and the Cinema of Populism," in *Movies and Methods*, ed. Bill Nichols (Berkeley: University of California Press, 1976), 1:65–78; Sam Rohdie, "Totems and Movies," in *Movies and Methods*, ed. Bill Nichols (Berkeley: University of California Press, 1976), 1:469–81.

15. See David Bordwell's chapter on historical materialist narration in *Narration in the Fiction Film* (Madison: University of Wisconsin Press, 1987), 234–73.

16. Although director Ernst Lubitsch might be guilty of simplifying Communism, William Paul argues that he does not wholly mock it. Rather, Lubitsch seems sensitive to some facets of Soviet life, such as the privations faced by Soviet citizens and the prior predations of Russia's Tsarist period. See William Paul, *Ernst Lubitsch's American Comedies* (New York: Columbia University Press, 1983), 206–7.

17. See Ceplair and Englund, *Inquisition in Hollywood*, 52; and Schrecker, *The Age of McCarthyism*, 5.

18. Schrecker, *The Age of McCarthyism*, 5.

19. Ibid., 25.

20. For more on the trial see ibid., 42–45; Michael R. Belknap, *Cold War Political Justice: The Smith Act, the Communist Party, and American Civil Liberties* (Westport, CT: Greenwood Press, 1977), 77–151; and Stanley I. Kutler, *The American Inquisition: Justice and Injustice in the Cold War* (New York: Hill and Wang, 1982), 152–82.

21. Dalton Trumbo, undated notes for a trial run of the 1947 HUAC hearings, Box 43, Folder 7, Dalton Trumbo Collection, U.S. Mss 24AN, Wisconsin Center for Film and Theater Research, State Historical Society, Madison, Wisconsin (hereafter DTC).

22. Schrecker, *Many Are the Crimes*, 194.

23. See Ceplair and Englund, *Inquisition in Hollywood*, 389; Sayre, *Running Time*, 80; and Tom Milne, ed., *Losey on Losey* (Garden City, NY: Doubleday, 1968), 75–76. It is worth noting, however, that Daniel Leab views this story as a bit of Hollywood lore that has grown out of interviews with Losey. According to Leab, RKO's production files indicate that the project was offered to only two other directors before it was finally assigned to Robert Stevenson. Says Leab, "Hughes could be mean-spirited and vindictive, and in his anti-Communist phase at RKO he did some dastardly things, but using *I Married a Communist* as a litmus test for loyalty was not among them" (Leab, "How Red Was My Valley," 79).

24. Andrew Velez, introduction to *The Woman on Pier 13* (New York: Frederick Ungar, 1976), ii.

25. See, e.g., Michael Stephens, *Film Noir: A Comprehensive Illustrated Reference to Movies, Terms, and Persons* (Jefferson, NC: McFarland, 1995); Robert Porfirio, "The Dark Age of American Film: A Study of American Film Noir, 1940–1960," 2 vols. (PhD diss., Yale University, 1979); and Arthur Lyons, *Death on the Cheap: The Lost B Movies of Film Noir* (New York: Da Capo, 2000).

26. James Naremore, *More Than Night: Film Noir in Its Contexts* (Berkeley: University of California Press, 1998), 295; Frank Krutnik, *In a Lonely Street: Film Noir, Genre, and Masculinity* (London: Routledge, 1991), 191; and Steve Neale, *Genre and Hollywood* (New York: Routledge, 2000), 159. For other books that briefly address the relationship of film noir and the Cold War see Richard Martin, *Mean Streets and Raging Bulls: The Legacy of Film Noir in Contemporary American Cinema* (Lanham, MD: Scarecrow, 1997), 40–42; and Nicholas Christopher, *Somewhere in the Night: Film Noir and the American City* (New York: Free Press, 1997), 50–52; see also Philip Kemp, "From the Nightmare Factory: HUAC and the Politics of Film Noir," *Sight and Sound* 55, no. 4 (1986): 266–70.

27. See Doherty, "Hollywood Agit-Prop," 16.

28. Krutnik, *In a Lonely Street*, 19.

29. Marc Vernet, "*Film Noir* on the Edge of Doom," in *Shades of Noir*, ed. Joan Copjec (London: Verso, 1993), 1–31.

30. Michael Renov, *Hollywood's Wartime Women: Representation and Ideology* (Ann Arbor, MI: UMI Research Press, 1988), 167–74; Elizabeth Cowie, "*Film Noir* and Women," in *Shades of Noir*, ed. Joan Copjec (London: Verso, 1993), 121–65.

31. Neale, *Genre and Hollywood*, 168.

32. See, e.g., Rick Altman, *Film/Genre* (London: British Film Institute, 1999); and Nick Browne, ed., *Refiguring American Film Genres* (Berkeley: University of California Press, 1999).

33. Naremore, *More Than Night*, 5.

34. Ibid., 103–5. See also Kemp, "From the Nightmare Factory," 266–70; and Andersen, "Red Hollywood," 183–91.

35. Paul Schrader, "Notes on Film Noir." *Film Comment* 8, no. 1 (1972): 12. See also Kemp, "From the Nightmare Factory," 266.

36. John Houseman, "What Makes American Movies So Tough," *Vogue*, Jan. 15, 1947, 125. Quoted in Richard Maltby, "Film Noir: The Politics of the Maladjusted Text," *Journal of American Studies* 18, no. 1 (1984): 56.

37. Quoted in Schwartz, *The Hollywood Writers' Wars*, 135.

38. Maltby, "Film Noir," 53.

39. See Leab, "How Red Was My Valley," 79.

40. Tom Flinn, "Daniel Mainwaring: An Interview," in *The Big Book of Noir*, ed. Ed Gorman, Lee Server, and Martin H. Greenberg (New York: Carroll and Graf, 1998), 66.

41. Naremore, *More Than Night*, 175. See also Janey Place and Lowell Peterson, "Some Visual Motifs of Film Noir," *Film Comment* 10, no.1 (1974): 30–32.

42. Patrick Keating, *Hollywood Lighting: From the Silent Era to Film Noir* (New York: Columbia University Press, 2010), 246.

43. Irwin F. Gellman, *The Contender: Richard Nixon, the Congress Years, 1946–1952* (New York: Free Press, 1999), 115–16.

44. Neve, *Film and Politics*, 188.

45. Velez, introduction, ii.

46. T.M.P., "One Man's Battle against Communism," *New York Times*, June 16, 1950, 28.

47. The New Pictures, review of *I Married a Communist*, *Time*, Oct. 17, 1949, 102.

48. *I Married a Communist* Production Code Administration file, MHL.

49. Robert Warshow, "Movie Chronicle: The Westerner," in *The Immediate Experience: Movies, Comics, Theatre, and Other Aspects of Popular Culture* (New York: Atheneum, 1970), 136.

50. This drawing is in the pressbook items for *I Married a Communist* archived at the Margaret Herrick Library. Daniel Leab notes that all of the various drafts of the script included a "sophisticated" cocktail party in "modern surroundings" at which potential draftees into the party learn about "culture" (Leab, "How Red Was My Valley," 70). The drawing was undoubtedly intended to highlight that particular "indoctrination" scene in the film.

51. T.M.P., "One Man's Battle against Communism," *New York Times*, June 16, 1950, 28.

52. Bosley Crowther, "'The Red Menace,' Dealing with Communist Party in U.S., Shown at the Mayfair," *New York Times*, June 27, 1949, 18.

53. Quoted in Leab, "How Red Was My Valley," 76.

54. Sayre, *Running Time*, 81.

55. Dana Polan, *Power and Paranoia: History, Narrative, and the American Cinema, 1910–1950* (New York: Columbia University Press, 1986), 13.

56. See, e.g., Cowie, "*Film Noir* and Women," 121–65; Mary Ann Doane, *Femmes Fatales: Feminism, Film Theory, Psychoanalysis* (New York: Routledge, 1991); Jans B. Wager, *Dangerous Dames: Women and Representation in the Weimar Street Film and Film Noir* (Athens: Ohio University Press, 1999); and several essays in E. Ann Kaplan, ed., *Women in Film Noir*, new ed. (London: British Film Institute, 1998).

57. Gordon White to S. Barret McCormick, Oct. 13, 1949, *I Married a Communist* Production Code Administration file, MHL.

58. S. Barret McCormick to Perry W. Lieber, Nov. 22, 1949, *I Married a Communist* Production Code Administration file, MHL.

59. See Kathryn S. Olmsted, *Red Spy Queen: A Biography of Elizabeth Bentley* (Chapel Hill: University of North Carolina Press, 2002), 123–26.

60. Ibid., 134.

61. Hoberman, *An Army of Phantoms*, 93.

62. Shooting script, *The Red Menace*, March 3, 1949, Republic Collection, Powell Library, UCLA.

63. Joseph Breen to Allen Wilson, Jan. 17, 1949, *The Red Menace* Production Code Administration file, MHL.

64. Janey Place's "Women in Film Noir" is still the best explanation of the ideological function of the "nurturing woman" in film noir.

65. Paul, *Ernst Lubitsch's American Comedies*, 194.

66. It is worth noting that the egalitarian and communitarian spirit in *Tender Comrade* is unusual, even within the World War II home-front film. Both *In Which We Serve* (1942) and *Since You Went Away* (1944) deal with women during wartime but preserve a social hierarchy within their narrative structures. In the case of *In Which We Serve* this is accomplished through the use of a military setting; in *Since You Went Away* it is through the power relations established within the family. The latter pushes this to the point of absurdity when the maid, played by Hattie McDaniel, offers to work as an unpaid servant in order to preserve the family's stability and thereby make her contribution to the American war effort.

CHAPTER 3. REDS AND BLACKS

1. Reisz, "Hollywood's Anti-Red Boomerang," 135.

2. See Schrecker, *Many Are the Crimes*, 389–95.

3. Quoted in Gordon Kahn, *Hollywood on Trial: The Story of the Ten Who Were Indicted* (New York: Boni and Gaer, 1948), 176–77; for more on the role of anti-Semitism in HUAC's investigations see Dalton Trumbo, *The Time of the Toad: A Study of Inquisition in America* (West Nyack, NY: Journeyman, 1949), 11.

4. Many film historians argue the liberal social problem film went into a period of decline in the postwar period, largely because of the political pressures HUAC exerted on studio executives. Much of the support for this assertion derives from Dorothy B. Jones's pioneering analysis of the blacklist's effect on motion picture content, a study that scholars have cited unstintingly since its publication in 1956. More recent research, though, shows that the relationship between the investigations and this postwar production cycle is far more complicated than first thought. Pearl Latteier argues that although there was a widespread perception in Hollywood that the hearings caused some individual projects to be canceled, the actual number of social problem films declined only modestly in 1953 and 1954. Combing the trade press of the period for titles described as "problem" stories, social dramas, and message pictures, Latteier shows that Hollywood, on average, made only about six to eight social problem films each year. Consequently, these films never constituted a large percentage of Hollywood's output, despite their prestige and topicality. The cycle peaked at about 3 percent of the total number of films released in 1949. The cycle bottomed out in 1953, when the genre accounted for less than 1 percent of the total. See Pearl Latteier, "The Hollywood Social Problem Film, 1946–1959" (PhD diss., University of Wisconsin–Madison, 2010), 66–95.

294 / NOTES TO PAGES 86-90

5. Fraser M. Ottanelli, *The Communist Party of the United States: From the Depression to World War II* (New Brunswick, NJ: Rutgers University Press, 1991), 36–37; Mark Naison, *Communists in Harlem during the Depression* (Urbana: University of Illinois Press, 1983), 18–19; William Z. Foster, *History of the Communist Party in the United States* (New York: Greenwood Press, 1968), 266–67; and Nathan Glazer, *The Social Basis of American Communism* (New York: Harcourt, Brace, 1961), 170–71.

6. Ottanelli, *Communist Party of the United States*, 38; Naison, *Communists in Harlem*, 47–49; and Glazer, *Social Basis of American Communism*, 172. Yokinen never was able to rejoin the party because he was arrested on immigration violations the day after the trial.

7. Foster, *History of the Communist Party*, 290–91; Glazer, *Social Basis of American Communism*, 172. In 1936 Ford was nominated a second time as the CPUSA's vice-presidential candidate, this time teaming with Foster's rival, Earl Browder. The ticket received about eighty thousand votes, about 20 percent fewer votes than in 1932.

8. See Ottanelli, *Communist Party of the United States*, 40–42; Naison, *Communists in Harlem*, 57–89; Foster, *History of the Communist Party*, 286–88; and Glazer, *Social Basis of American Communism*, 173–74.

9. Throughout this period the Communists' interest in racial issues filtered down to the grassroots level of the party in several ways, perhaps most notably in the outreach and educational efforts aimed at children. As historian Paul C. Mishler notes, during the 1920s Communists, socialists, and anarchists established children's camps in places like New York, Pennsylvania, and North Carolina. These radical summer camps not only provided children with opportunities for recreational activities but also sought to instill the basic values and tenets of their political philosophy. See Mishler, *Raising Reds*, 83–108.

10. I am deeply indebted to the anonymous reviewer of my earlier manuscript, who reminded me of this quite important plot detail in *Sahara*.

11. For a detailed production history of the film see Lorence, *The Suppression of "Salt of the Earth."*

12. Glazer, *Social Basis of American Communism*, 174.

13. Ibid., 173.

14. Winston Record, *The Negro and the Communist Party* (Chapel Hill: University of North Carolina Press, 1951).

15. *Motion Picture Herald*, Nov. 21, 1953, *The Red Menace* clippings file, Margaret Herrick Library, Academy of Motion Picture Arts and Sciences (hereafter MHL).

16. Republic Pictures flyer, undated, *The Red Menace* clippings file, MHL.

17. Ibid.

18. *The Red Menace* pressbook file, MHL.

19. "Resolution Urges All See 'Red Menace' Film," *Los Angeles Examiner*, June 6, 1949, *The Red Menace* clippings file, MHL.

20. See Polan, *Power and Paranoia*, 13.

21. Examples of this semidocumentary cycle include *T-Men* (1947), *The Naked City* (1948), *Call Northside 777* (1948), and *He Walked by Night* (1949). For analyses of this cycle see Naremore, *More Than Night*, 142–43; Krutnik, *In a Lonely Street*, 202–8; Neale, *Genre and Hollywood*, 176; Schrader, "Notes on Film Noir"; and J. P. Telotte, *Voices in the Dark: The Narrative Patterns of Film Noir* (Urbana: University of Illinois Press, 1989), 134–78.

22. Lowell Redelings, "New Republic Film Opens," *Citizen News*, undated, *The Red Menace* clippings file, MHL.

23. Sidney Burke, "'The Red Menace'—Stupid but Dangerous," *Daily People's World*, June 1, 1949, 5.

24. Shooting script, *The Red Menace*, March 3, 1949, Republic Pictures Corporation Records, Charles E. Young Research Library, University of California, Los Angeles (hereafter RPC).

25. Ibid.

26. Ibid.

27. Ibid.

28. Robert Joseph, "Cinema," *Arts and Architecture*, June 1949, 20, 53. In fact, Joseph's account actually garbles some of the details of the scene. He reports that the Statue of Liberty sings "God Bless America" at the end of the film.

29. Shooting script, *The Red Menace*, March 3, 1949, RPC.

30. Ibid.

31. Ibid.

32. For more on the treatment of racial issues in the western see Edward Buscombe, "The Western: A Short History," in *The BFI Companion to the Western*, ed. Edward Buscombe (London: Andre Deutsch/British Film Institute, 1988), 15–54; Michael Coyne, *The Crowded Prairie: American National Identity in the Hollywood Western* (London: I. B. Tauris, 1997); Lee Clark Mitchell, *Westerns: Making the Man in Fiction and Film* (Chicago: University of Chicago Press, 1996); Richard Slotkin, *Gunfighter Nation: The Myth of the Frontier in Twentieth-Century America* (New York: Atheneum, 1992); Jane Tompkins, *West of Everything: The Inner Life of Westerns* (New York: Oxford University Press, 1992); Virginia Wright Wexman, "The Family on the Land: Race and Nationhood in Silent Westerns," in *The Birth of Whiteness: Race and the Emergence of U.S. Cinema*, ed. Daniel Bernard (New Brunswick, NJ: Rutgers University Press, 1996), 129–69.

33. For more on Cvetic's checkered career see Daniel Leab, *I Was a Communist for the FBI: The Unhappy Life and Times of Matt Cvetic* (University Park: Pennsylvania State University Press, 2000). Leab's book is largely about Cvetic's rise and fall as anti-Communist hero, but it contains a chapter on the film. For additional discussions of *I Was a Communist for the FBI* see Whitfield, *The Culture of the Cold War*, 134–35; Belton, *American Cinema / American Culture*, 245; Rogin, *Ronald Reagan*, 246–47; and Sayre, *Running Time*, 86–91.

34. *Variety*, April 19, 1951, *I Was a Communist for the FBI* clippings file, MHL.

35. *Motion Picture Herald*, April 21, 1951, *I Was a Communist for the FBI* clippings file, MHL.

36. Richard Griffith, "'Communist for FBI' Called Formula Film," *Los Angeles Times*, May 15, 1951, *I Was a Communist for the FBI* clippings file, MHL.

37. Whitfield, *Culture of the Cold War*, 140.

38. See Lowell E. Redelings, "The Hollywood Scene," *Hollywood Citizen News*, August 9, 1950; "The New Pictures," *Time*, May 7, 1951, 104–5; "Warners Documenting 'Communist' Expose," *Variety*, April 6, 1950, *I Was a Communist for the FBI* clippings file, MHL; and production notes on *I Was a Communist for the FBI*, Production Code Administration (hereafter PCA) file, MHL.

39. Jack Warner to Blumenstock, telegram, April 7, 1951, *I Was a Communist for the FBI* production file, Warner Bros. Archives, School of Cinematic Arts, University of Southern California (hereafter WBA).

40. "Provocative Drama of Red Menace," *Hollywood Reporter*, April 19, 1951, *I Was a Communist for the FBI* clippings file, MHL.

41. Review of *I Was a Communist for the FBI*, *Cue*, May 5, 1951, *I Was a Communist for the FBI* clippings file, MHL.

42. Crane Wilbur, story outline for *I Was a Communist for the FBI*, dated Sept. 20, 1950, 4, *I Was a Communist for the FBI* production file, WBA.

43. Ibid., 21–22.

44. Crane Wilbur, screenplay draft for *I Was a Communist for the FBI*, dated Dec. 21, 1950, 4. *I Was a Communist for the FBI* production file, WBA. Although there is no explanation for it in the production file, Wilbur dropped the scene in a subsequent draft dated the very next day.

45. Crane Wilbur, screenplay draft for *I Was a Communist for the FBI*, dated Dec. 30, 1950, 17, *I Was a Communist for the FBI* production file, WBA.

46. Ibid., 18.

47. According to a front-page story in *Variety*, during the production of *I Was a Communist* the production crew had to lock up the large framed photo of Stalin at the end of each day's work. Apparently, the first prop photo that the staff created was stolen and taken home as a souvenir; see J. Hoberman, *Army of Phantoms*, 164.

48. Review of *I Was a Communist for the FBI*, *Hollywood Citizen News*, April 24, 1951, *I Was a Communist for the FBI* clippings file, MHL.

49. Bosley Crowther, "Don't Look Now, but Two Great Big Menaces Are Here in New Films," *New York Times*, May 6 1951, XI.

50. Film Content Analysis, *I Was a Communist for the FBI* PCA file, MHL.

51. Joseph Breen to Jack Warner, Jan. 10, 1951, *I Was a Communist for the FBI* PCA file, MHL.

52. Ibid.

53. For more on *Big Jim McLain* see Doherty, "Hollywood Agit-Prop," 23–26; Sayre, *Running Time*, 83; Belton, *American Cinema / American Culture*, 245; Murphy, *Congressional Theatre*, 85–96; Whitfield, *The Culture of the Cold War*, 139–40; Neve, *Film and Politics*, 187–88; and Garry Wills, *John Wayne's America* (New York: Touchstone, 1997), 200–201.

54. Wills, *John Wayne's America*, 200–227.

55. Carl Milliken Jr. to Finlay McDermid, memorandum, March 18, 1952, *Big Jim McLain* production file, WBA.

56. Carl Milliken Jr. to Roy Obringer, memorandum, March 28, 1952, *Big Jim McLain* production file, WBA.

57. Carl Milliken Jr. to Roy Obringer, memorandum, June 24, 1952, *Big Jim McLain* production file, WBA. For more on this exchange see J. Hoberman, *Army of Phantoms*, 202.

58. *Big Jim McLain* screenplay, estimating draft, May 15, 1952, *Big Jim McLain* production file, WBA.

59. Doherty, "Hollywood Agit-Prop," 23.

60. Ibid., 24.

61. Schrecker, *Many Are the Crimes*, 392–93.

62. Quoted in "How the Reds Make Martyrs," *Life*, Oct. 17, 1955, 77.

63. Schrecker, *Many Are the Crimes*, 391.

64. Ibid., 389–95.

CHAPTER 4. STOOLIES, CHEESE-EATERS, AND TIE SELLERS

1. Victor Navasky, "Mr. Kazan Goes to Washington: A Case Study of Misguided Ambivalence," in *Kazan Revisited*, ed. Lisa Dombrowski (Middletown, CT: Wesleyan University Press, 2012), 52.

2. Hoberman, *Army of Phantoms*, 107.

3. See "Ginger Rogers Given 'Storm' Role Spurned by Bacall," *Variety*, Oct. 21, 1949; Eliza Schallert, "Ginger Rogers Replaces Lauren Bacall in Film," *Los Angeles Times*, Oct. 21, 1949, *Storm Warning* clippings file, Margaret Herrick Library, Academy of Motion Picture Arts and Sciences (hereafter MHL).

4. Robert J. Corber, *Homosexuality in Cold War America: Resistance and the Crisis of Masculinity* (Durham, NC: Duke University Press, 1997), 10–13.

5. Jerry Wald to Carl Guthrie, memorandum, Dec. 12, 1949, *Storm Warning* production file, Warner Bros. Archives, School of Cinematic Arts, University of Southern California (hereafter WBA).

6. *Storm Warning*, Production Code Administration file, MHL.

7. Warner Bros. production notes, *Storm Warning* clippings file, MHL.

8. Capsule review of *Storm Warning*, *Time*, March 5, 1951, *Storm Warning* clippings file, MHL.

9. "The Klan at Work," *New Yorker*, March 10, 1951, *Storm Warning* clippings file, MHL.

10. Carl Milliken Jr. to Jerry Wald, memorandum, Oct. 11, 1949, *Storm Warning* legal file, WBA.

11. R.J. Obringer to Carl Milliken Jr., memorandum, Oct. 6, 1949, *Storm Warning* legal file, WBA.

12. Carl Milliken Jr. to Roy Obringer, memorandum, Oct. 6, 1949, *Storm Warning* legal file, WBA.

13. Jerry Wald to Irv Kupcinet, Nov. 11, 1949, *Storm Warning* legal file, WBA.

14. Quoted in Stephen Vaughn, *Ronald Reagan in Hollywood: Movies and Politics* (Cambridge: Cambridge University Press, 1994), 188.

15. For representative discussions of Kazan's early career see Navasky, *Naming Names*, 200–202; and Neve, *Film and Politics in America*, 10–12.

16. Elia Kazan, "A Statement," *New York Times*, April 12, 1952, 7. See also C. Trussell, "Elia Kazan Admits He Was Red in 30s," *New York Times*, April 12, 1952, 8.

17. See Navasky, *Naming Names*, 202.

18. Kazan, "A Statement," 7.

19. John Howard Lawson, "Celluloid Revolution," in *Film in the Battle of Ideas* (New York: Masses and Mainstream, 1953), 40.

20. Quoted in Paul J. Vanderwood, "An American Cold Warrior: *Viva Zapata!*," in *American History / American Film*, ed. John E. O'Connor and Martin A. Jackson (New York: Frederick Ungar, 1979), 189–90.

21. Quoted in Michel Ciment, *Kazan on Kazan* (New York: Viking, 1974), 110.

22. Brenda Murphy, "*Man on a Tightrope:* Kazan as Liberal Anticommunist," in *Kazan Revisited*, ed. Lisa Dombrowski (Middletown, CT: Wesleyan University Press, 2012), 69.

23. Vanderwood, "An American Cold Warrior," 188.

24. Ibid., 190–92.

25. Quoted in Leo Braudy, "'The Director, That Miserable Son of a Bitch': Kazan, *Viva Zapata!* and the Problem of Authority," in *Kazan Revisited*, ed. Lisa Dombrowski (Middletown, CT: Wesleyan University Press, 2012), 40.

26. Lawson, "Celluloid Revolution," 41–42.

27. Ibid., 36.

28. Sayre, *Running Time*, 154.

29. Navasky, *Naming Names*, 206.

30. One of the Czech policemen is played by Gert Frobe, who later would play the title role in *Goldfinger* (1963). Although Frobe was likely cast in this bit part because of his vaguely European appearance, there is some irony in the fact that both he and Joseph Wiseman would move from supporting roles in Kazan's films to iconic status as archvillains in the James Bond series.

31. Murphy, "*Man on a Tightrope*," 64. Kazan's quotes are from his notebooks for *Man on a Tightrope*, which are part of the Elia Kazan Collection at the Wesleyan Cinema Archives.

32. See, e.g., Sayre, *Running Time*, 151–63; Navasky, *Naming Names*, 199–222; Billingsley, *Hollywood Party*, 242–45; Biskind, *Seeing Is Believing*, 169–82; Whitfield, *The Culture of the Cold War*, 108–13; Joanna Rapf, ed., *On the Waterfront* (New York: Cambridge University Press, 2003); Brian Neve, "The 1950s: The Case of Elia Kazan and *On the Waterfront*," in *Cinema, Politics, and Society in America*, ed. Philip Davies and Brian Neve (New York: St. Martin's, 1981), 97–118; Murphy, *Congressional Theatre*, 208–15; and Kenneth R. Hey, "Ambivalence as a Theme in *On the Waterfront* (1954): An Interdisciplinary

Approach to Film Study," in *Hollywood as Historian: American Film in a Cultural Context*, rev. ed., ed. Peter C. Rollins (Lexington: University Press of Kentucky, 1998), 159–89.

33. Brian Neve, "The Personal and the Political: Elia Kazan and *On the Waterfront*," in *On the Waterfront*, ed. Joanna Rapf (New York: Cambridge University Press, 2003), 28.

34. Ibid., 32.

35. Ibid., 28; and Joanna E. Rapf, "Introduction: 'The Mysterious Way of Art': Making a Difference in *On the Waterfront*," in *On the Waterfront*, ed. Joanna E. Rapf (New York: Cambridge University Press, 2003), 13. Ironically, Kazan's notes indicate that he intuitively made a connection that had been abandoned as a story angle earlier in the production process. In 1950 Kazan developed a very similar waterfront project called *The Hook* with friend and playwright Arthur Miller. The project fell apart when Harry Cohn, the long-time head of Columbia Pictures, pressured Kazan and Miller to explicitly identify the longshoremen's union leaders as Communists. Miller summarily rejected this suggestion and pulled himself out of the project. For more on this incident see Elia Kazan, *Elia Kazan: A Life* (New York: Knopf, 1988), 410–15.

36. Humphries, *Hollywood's Blacklists*, 130–31.

37. Kenneth R. Hey, "Ambivalence as a Theme in *On the Waterfront* (1954): An Interdisciplinary Approach to Film Study," in *Hollywood as Historian: American Film in a Cultural Context*, ed. Peter C. Rollins, rev. ed. (Lexington: University Press of Kentucky, 1998), 159–89; the essay first appeared in *American Quarterly* 31 (1979) in a special issue devoted to film culture.

38. Budd Schulberg, foreword to Rapf, *On the Waterfront*, xxi.

39. It is worth noting that diVincenzo later sued the makers of *On the Waterfront*, claiming that the film was a thinly veiled version of his own life and that its production constituted an invasion of his privacy. See "Consultant Says He's 'Waterfront' Carbon," *Variety*, Dec. 12, 1954, *On the Waterfront* clippings file, MHL.

40. See Bordwell, *Narration in the Fiction Film*, 36; and Kristin Thompson, *Breaking the Glass Armor: Neoformalist Film Analysis* (Princeton, NJ: Princeton University Press, 1988), 15–17.

41. Rapf, "Introduction," 7.

42. Jeffrey Chown, "Visual Coding and Social Class in *On the Waterfront*," in *On the Waterfront*, ed. Joanna E. Rapf (New York: Cambridge University Press, 2003), 117.

43. Ibid. For more on the contemporary debates surrounding the issue of film authorship see Dudley Andrew, "The Unauthorized Auteur Today," in *Film Theory Goes to the Movies*, ed. Jim Collins, Ava Preacher Collins, and Hilary Radner (New York: Routledge, 1993): 77–85; James Naremore, "Authorship," in *A Companion to Film Theory*, ed. Toby Miller and Robert Stam (Malden, MA: Blackwell, 1999), 9–24; and Paisley Livingston, "Cinematic Authorship," in *Film Theory and Philosophy*, ed. Richard Allen and Murray Smith (New York: Oxford University Press, 1997), 132–48. Ironically, while Rapf and Chown share

reception studies' misgivings about authorial intentions, they also dismiss the long-term critical reception of *On the Waterfront* since it is largely within this latter context that one finds the reading of the film as blacklist allegory.

44. See A.H. Weiler, "The Screen: Astor Offers *On the Waterfront*," *New York Times*, July 29, 1954 (repr. in Rapf, *On the Waterfront*, 151–53); Mr. Harper, "The Big Sell: A Review," *Harper's*, August 1954 (repr. in Rapf, *On the Waterfront*, 153–56); Philip T. Hartung, "Man's Hope: A Review," *Commonweal*, August 20, 1954 (repr. in Rapf, *On the Waterfront*, 157–58); and Penelope Houston, review of *On the Waterfront*, *Sight and Sound* 24, no. 2 (1954): 85–86 (repr. in Rapf, *On the Waterfront*, 158–61).

45. Quoted in Jack Karr's review of *On the Waterfront*, *Toronto Star Weekly*, Oct. 2, 1954, *On the Waterfront* clippings file, MHL.

46. Ed Sullivan, "Little Old New York," *New York Daily News*, March 30, 1955, C14.

47. Edwin Schallert, "'Waterfront' Big in Drama, Emotion," *Los Angeles Times*, August 7, 1954, *On the Waterfront* clippings file, MHL.

48. Philip K. Scheuer, "'Waterfront' Called Dark Horse of '54," undated article, *On the Waterfront* clippings file, MHL.

49. See ibid., as well as the film reviews in *Variety*, July 14, 1954 and *Hollywood Reporter*, July 14, 1954, both in *On the Waterfront* clippings file, MHL.

50. Of course, J. Parnell Thomas (R, NJ) was the HUAC chair at the time of the 1947 hearings on Communist influence in Hollywood. He was later convicted on graft charges and found himself imprisoned alongside some of the Hollywood lefties that he persecuted. Velde took over as HUAC chair in 1953 and remained in that position for a good portion of *On the Waterfront*'s run.

51. Arthur M. Schlesinger Jr., *The Vital Center: The Politics of Freedom* (New York: Riverside, 1949).

52. Litvak, *The Un-Americans*, 123–24.

53. Capsule review of *Pickup on South Street*, *Village Voice*, July 14, 1992, *Pickup on South Street* clippings file, MHL.

54. Lee Server, *Sam Fuller: Film Is a Battleground* (Jefferson, NC: McFarland, 1994), 71–72.

55. Nicholas Garnham, *Samuel Fuller* (New York: Viking, 1971), 114.

56. Dwight Taylor, "Blaze of Glory," undated story, *Pickup on South Street* production file, 20th Century–Fox collection, Film & Television Archive, University of California, Los Angeles (hereafter TCF).

57. See Samuel Fuller, *A Third Face: My Tale of Writing, Fighting, and Filmmaking* (New York: Applause, 2002), 292; and Server, *Sam Fuller*, 33. For additional discussion of *Pickup on South Street*'s production history see Lisa Dombrowski, *The Films of Samuel Fuller: If You Die, I'll Kill You!* (Middletown, CT: Wesleyan University Press, 2008), 67–76.

58. Taylor, "Blaze of Glory." Unfortunately, I cannot confirm the page number for the quote. My understanding is that the Fox Collection is no longer accessible to researchers.

59. Harry Brown, "Blaze of Glory," writer's working script, Jan. 25, 1952, *Pickup on South Street* production file, TCF.

60. Ibid., 114.

61. Harry Brown, "Blaze of Glory," first draft continuity, March 13, 1952, 113, *Pickup on South Street* production file, TCF.

62. Story conference memo, March 20, 1952, *Pickup on South Street* production file, TCF.

63. Ibid., 1-A.

64. Ibid.

65. Ibid., 7.

66. Ibid., 1-C.

67. See Fuller, *A Third Face*, 292; see also Server, *Sam Fuller*, 33.

68. Fuller, *A Third Face*, 292–93.

69. Ibid., 294.

70. Conference notes on story outline of June 25, 1952, Mssrs. Blaustein and Fuller, June 27, 1952, 3, *Pickup on South Street* production file, TCF.

71. Ibid., 4.

72. Samuel Fuller, "Blaze of Glory," working script, August 6, 1952, 59–61, *Pickup on South Street* production file, TCF.

73. Conference notes on first draft continuity of August 13, 1952, Mssrs. Blaustein, Schermer, and Fuller, August 29, 1952, *Pickup on South Street* production file, TCF.

74. For Fuller's description of the title's genesis see *A Third Face*, 297–98.

75. Howard McClay, capsule review of *Pickup on South Street*, *Los Angeles Daily News*, May 30, 1953, *Pickup on South Street* clippings file, MHL.

76. "Pickup on South Street," *Variety*, May 13, 1953, *Pickup on South Street* clippings file, MHL.

77. John L. Scott, "Hard-Boiled Film Stresses Realism," *Los Angeles Times*, May 30, 1953, *Pickup on South Street* clippings file, MHL.

78. See, e.g., "Pickup on South Street," *Variety*, May 13, 1953, *Pickup on South Street* clippings file, MHL.

79. See Peter Stanfield, *Maximum Movies—Pulp Fictions: Film Culture and the Worlds of Samuel Fuller, Mickey Spillane, and Jim Thompson* (Piscataway, NJ: Rutgers University Press, 2011), 112–51.

80. Capsule review of *Pickup on South Street*, *Saturday Review*, June 20, 1953, *Pickup on South Street* clippings file, MHL.

81. Fuller, *A Third Face*, 292.

82. Jack Shadoian, *Dreams and Dead Ends: The American Gangster Film*, 2nd ed. (New York: Oxford University Press, 2003), 189.

83. Server, *Sam Fuller*, 35.

84. Fuller, *A Third Face*, 293.

85. Trumbo, *Additional Dialogue*, 570.

86. Bordwell, *Making Meaning*, 224–48.

87. Robert J. Corber, *In the Name of National Security: Hitchcock, Homophobia, and the Political Construction of Gender in Postwar America* (Durham, NC: Duke University Press, 1996).

88. It seems fair to say that Corber focuses on rather canonical Hitchcock works of the Cold War period, such as *Strangers on a Train* (1951), *Rear*

Window (1954), *Vertigo* (1958), and *Psycho* (1960). As a result, he ignores lesser known Hitchcock works, such as *I Confess* and *The Trouble with Harry*, that might challenge or problematize his central thesis. Moreover, Corber attempts to buttress his thesis by looking back to much earlier, pre–Cold War films, such as *Blackmail* (1929) and *The Man Who Knew Too Much* (1934), but does not look forward to the two films that are most explicitly about the threat of Communism, namely *Torn Curtain* (1965) and *Topaz* (1969).

89. Rothman, *Hitchcock*, 248.

90. Theodore Price, *Hitchcock and Homosexuality: His 50 Year Obsession with Jack the Ripper and the Superbitch Prostitute—A Psychoanalytic View* (Metuchen, NJ: Scarecrow, 1992), 245–47.

91. Ironically, just after *I Confess* was released, Tabori was involved with a theater production that leftist critics described as an anti-HUAC allegory. In February of 1953 Tabori debuted a new adaptation of Hans Christian Andersen's *The Emperor's New Clothes*. Tabori retold Andersen's fairy tale by setting it in 1930s Hungary and by focusing on a blacklisted university professor, who is pressured to renounce his son's characterization of him as a heroic leader of the Resistance. As the *Daily Worker* noted, the boy's friend tells his parents, the parents tell the police, and the professor is "faced with a reality he never anticipated. He has a choice: he can clear himself of charges if he characterizes his ten-year-old son's imagination as insanity, as the working of a diseased mind, or he can indeed be the hero his son believes him to be." See D.L.N. "'Emperor's Clothes' Is Powerful Drama of Anti-fascist Struggle," *Daily Worker*, Feb. 17, 1953, 7.

92. Price, *Hitchcock and Homosexuality*, 248.

93. See Eric Rohmer and Claude Chabrol, *Hitchcock: The First Forty-Four Films*, trans. Stanley Hochman (New York: Frederick Ungar, 1979), 112–19.

94. Robin Wood, *Hitchcock's Films* (New York: Paperback Library, 1970), 42–43.

95. Donald Spoto, *The Art of Alfred Hitchcock: Fifty Years of His Motion Pictures* (Garden City, NY: Dolphin, 1976), 226.

96. Fulton Brylawski to Morris Ebenstein, July 11, 1952, *I Confess* legal file, WBA.

97. Wes Haynes, studio memorandum, April 15, 1948, *I Confess* legal file, WBA.

98. Harry Mayer and Morris Ebenstein to Jack Warner, undated, *I Confess* legal file, WBA.

99. Jack Warner to Harry Mayer and Morris Ebenstein, telegram, Nov. 5, 1952, *I Confess* legal file, WBA.

100. Morris Ebenstein to S. Carlisle, undated, *I Confess* legal file, WBA.

101. George Tabori, revised screenplay for *I Confess*, July 3, 1952, WBA.

102. Barbara Keon to Alfred Hitchcock, memorandum, July 31, 1952, *I Confess* screenplay file, WBA.

103. Corber, *In the Name of National Security*, 100.

CHAPTER 5. THE CROSS AND THE SICKLE

1. Stephen King, *Stephen King's Danse Macabre* (New York: Berkley, 1983), 130.

2. Ismail Xavier, "Historical Allegory," in *A Companion to Film Theory*, ed. Toby Miller and Robert Stam (Malden, MA: Blackwell, 1999), 354.

3. For representative examples of this type of scholarship see Leger Grindon, *Shadows on the Past: Studies in the Historical Fiction Film* (Philadelphia: Temple University Press, 1994), 88–90; Belton, *American Cinema / American Culture*, 247; Maria Wyke, *Projecting the Past: Ancient Rome, Cinema, and History* (New York: Routledge, 1997), 142–46; Anthony Miller, "*Julius Caesar* in the Cold War: The Houseman-Mankiewicz Film," *Literature/Film Quarterly* 28, no. 2 (2000): 95–100; Mark Jancovich, "'The Purest Knight of All': Nation, History, and Representation in *El Cid* (1960)," *Cinema Journal* 40, no. 1 (2000): 79–103; and David Eldridge, *Hollywood's History Films* (New York: I. B. Tauris, 2006), 78–96.

4. Belton, *American Cinema / American Culture*, 247.

5. Tiberius's speech is quoted in Bruce Babington and Peter William Evans, *Biblical Epics: Sacred Narrative in the Hollywood Cinema* (New York: Manchester University Press, 1993), 211. See also Monica Silveira Cyrino, *Big Screen Rome* (Malden, MA: Blackwell, 2005), 55–56.

6. Sayre, *Running Time*, 206; see also Wyke, *Projecting the Past*, 143.

7. Xavier, "Historical Allegory," 337.

8. See Philip Dunne, *Take Two: A Life in Movies and Politics* (New York: McGraw-Hill, 1980), 253–56.

9. Just prior to his work on *The Robe*, Maltz found himself embroiled in a controversy regarding an essay he wrote for *New Masses* entitled, "What Shall We Ask of Writers?" There Maltz critiqued a great deal of leftist fiction for adopting an "art as a weapon" approach that resulted in vulgar theories of aesthetics, unconvincing characterizations, and a lot of shallow writing. Breaking with the Zhdanovist/Leninist line, Maltz proposed a more Engelsian conception of literary art that separated aesthetic values from ideological commitments. For an incisive exploration of this controversy see Colin Burnett, "The 'Albert Maltz Affair' and the Debate about Para-Marxist Formalism in *New Masses*, 1945–1946," *Journal of American Studies* (May 2013): 1–28, http://dx.doi.org/doi:10.1017/S0021875813000728.

10. For more on the political shifts in Hollywood after World War II see Ceplair and Englund, *The Inquisition in Hollywood*, 200–253.

11. Lloyd C. Douglas, *The Robe* (Boston: Houghton Mifflin, 1942), 351.

12. Darryl Zanuck to Philip Dunne and Frank Ross, conference memorandum, 20th Century–Fox collection, Film & Television Archive, University of California, Los Angeles (hereafter TCF).

13. It is worth noting, however, that Zanuck's biographer, George Custen, argues that Zanuck was personally opposed to the blacklist, even if he never publicly spoke out against it. Perhaps the best example of Zanuck's opposition

was his work behind the scenes to adapt Albert Maltz's *The Journey of Simon McKeever* after the screenwriter was blacklisted. Zanuck made an agreement with Jules Dassin to film *McKeever*, with John Huston doing the screenplay and Walter Huston starring. For his part Dassin said that he would take care of Maltz and would tell no one about the project until Zanuck had secured it with Fox. Shortly thereafter, Maltz went public with the news of the project and declared to the *Hollywood Reporter* that the film of *McKeever* was in a prime position to break the blacklist. After Maltz's gaffe Zanuck cancelled the production and denied to Fox management that he knew anything about it. See Custen's *Twentieth Century's Fox: Darryl F. Zanuck and the Culture of Hollywood* (New York: Basic Books, 1997), 312–13.

14. Quoted in Eldridge, *Hollywood's History Films*, 90.

15. Quoted in Kahn, *Hollywood on Trial*, 84. Trumbo appears to have gotten his dates mixed up. The Reichstag fire did not occur until February 27, 1933.

16. Bernard F. Dick, *Radical Innocence: A Critical Study of the Hollywood Ten* (Lexington: University Press of Kentucky, 1989), 92.

17. Albert Maltz, first draft screenplay of *The Robe*, dated August 21, 1945, Box 7, Folder 6, Albert Maltz Papers, U.S. Mss 17AN, Wisconsin Center for Film and Theater Research, State Historical Society Library, Madison, Wisconsin (hereafter AMP).

18. Ibid.

19. Ibid.

20. Ibid.

21. Ibid.

22. Philip Dunne, *The Robe*, final screenplay, August 13, 1952, TCF.

23. Philip Dunne, *The Robe*, writer's working script, June 26, 1952, TCF.

24. Quoted in Custen, *Twentieth Century's Fox*, 315.

25. Wyke, *Projecting the Past*, 28–29.

26. Philip T. Hartung, "The Screen," *Commonweal*, Oct. 9, 1953, 12–13.

27. Ben Levine, "There Were McCarthys in Ancient Rome," *Daily Worker*, Jan. 10, 1954, 9.

28. David Platt, "Ancient Rome's Ruthless and Futile Witchhunt," *Daily Worker*, Nov. 28, 1951, 7.

29. *New York Daily Worker*, July 10, 1953, 5.

30. "'Robe' an Undertaking of Many Problems," *Motion Picture Herald*, July 7, 1945, *The Robe* clippings file, Margaret Herrick Library, Academy of Motion Picture Arts and Sciences (hereafter MHL).

31. "Ross and Anderson Confer on 'Robe' Prod.," *Hollywood Reporter*, June 8, 1948; and "Ross to Produce 'Robe' in 1949," *Motion Picture Herald*, June 12, 1948, *The Robe* clippings file, MHL.

32. "Howard McClay," *Los Angeles Daily News*, August 26, 1952, *The Robe* clippings file, MHL.

33. Film notes, *The Robe*, Sept. 10, 1980, *The Robe* clippings file, MHL.

34. Albert Maltz's research notes for *The Robe*, undated, Box 7, Folder 6, AMP (emphasis in original).

35. Psychologist Jonathan Haidt argues that there is a great deal of neurobiological evidence to suggest that our moral judgments are rooted in our emotional responses to particular kinds of perceptual data. This neurobiological evidence is linked in myriad ways to the kinds of cognitive biases and heuristics I discussed in chapter 1. According to Haidt we recruit our reason to provide ex post facto justification for our emotional responses, not the other way around. If this is the case, then it seems likely that the moral intuitions of film critics and historians, particularly their view of Communism, would appear to inform the way we interpret films as blacklist allegories. See Jonathan Haidt, *The Righteous Mind: Why Good People Are Divided by Religion and Politics* (New York: Pantheon, 2012).

36. Albert Maltz, "The American Artist and the American Tradition," speech delivered at the Hotel Astor, March 16, 1948, Box 15, Folder 2, AMP.

37. Throughout this section I am greatly indebted to Maria Wyke's excellent work in *Projecting the Past* on cinematic representations of Spartacus.

38. Murray Schumach, "Trumbo to Get Credit for Script," *New York Times,* August 8, 1960, 25.

39. See my "'A Good Business Proposition.'"

40. J. Hoberman, *The Dream Life: Movies, Media, and the Mythology of the Sixties* (New York: New Press, 2003), 4–5.

41. Wyke, *Projecting the Past,* 65.

42. Kirk Douglas, audio commentary, *Spartacus* (Criterion Collection, 2001), DVD.

43. Wyke, *Projecting the Past,* 36–41.

44. Ibid., 48.

45. Ibid.

46. Quoted in ibid., 60–61.

47. Stan Marguilies to Kirk Douglas, June 24, 1960, Box 33, file 19, Kirk Douglas Papers, U.S. Mss 102AN, Wisconsin Center for Film and Theater Research, State Historical Society Library, Madison, Wisconsin (hereafter KDP).

48. Kirk Douglas to J. David Johnson, May 6, 1960, Box 33, file 16, KDP. See also Kirk Douglas to K. L. Kerins, May 6, 1960, Box 33, file 16, KDP.

49. *Spartacus* study guide, prepared by Joseph Mersand, general editor, and William Lewin, PhD, *Photoplay Studies* 25, no. 4 (August 1960), distributed by the National Council of Teachers of English, Box 37, file 14, KDP.

50. *Time,* Oct. 24, 1960, Box 79, *Spartacus* Reviews and Press, Dalton Trumbo Collection, U.S. Mss 24AN, Wisconsin Center for Film and Theater Research, State Historical Society, Madison, Wisconsin (hereafter DTC). Reviews of *Exodus* continued in the same vein. For example, the *San Diego Union* wrote, "It *[Exodus]* is a picture illustrative of the longing, the internal bickering, the selfless heroism, and sacrifices that men have paid to breathe the air of freedom." The *Cleveland Press and News* added, "Suffice it to say that this *[Exodus]* is a chapter in the history of man's yearning for and acquisition of freedom." See James Meade, "'Exodus' Is Big Exciting Picture," *San Diego*

Union, May 24, 1961; and Stan Anderson, "Stirring *Exodus* Opens Tonight," *Cleveland Press and News,* March 14, 1961, both in Box 80, *Exodus* Reviews and Press, DTC.

51. James Powers, "'Spartacus' Magnificent Picture, Should Be Smash Attraction," *Hollywood Reporter,* Oct. 7, 1960, Box 79, *Spartacus* Reviews and Press, DTC.

52. Bruce Cook, *Dalton Trumbo* (New York: Scribner, 1977), 277; Navasky, *Naming Names,* 327; "Kennedy Attends Movie in Capital," *New York Times,* Feb. 5, 1961, Box 80, *Spartacus* clippings, DTC.

53. Kirk Douglas, audio commentary, *Spartacus* (Criterion Collection, 2001), DVD.

54. See, e.g., the national Catholic magazine, *The Sign,* which says of the film, "It glamorizes the slave Spartacus, who has risen high in Marxist hagiography" (*The Sign,* Dec. 1960, 51, Box 37, file 14, KDP). Attached to the magazine is a note from Jeff Livingston to Stan Margulies that says, "An ominous 'Sign.'"

55. Radie Harris, "Broadway Ballyhoo," *Hollywood Reporter,* Dec. 20, 1960, 4, Box 80, miscellaneous blacklist clippings, DTC.

56. *New York Teachers News,* Box 80, blacklist clippings on *Exodus,* DTC.

57. For a detailed analysis of this conflict see Larry Ceplair, "Who Killed Spartacus?" *Cineaste* 18, no. 3 (1991): 18–29; and Duncan Cooper, "Dalton Trumbo vs. Stanley Kubrick: Their Debate over Arthur Koestler's *The Gladiators,*" *Cineaste* 18, no. 3 (1991): 34–37.

58. Xavier, "Historical Allegory," 338.

59. Dick, *Radical Innocence,* 208–10.

60. Dalton Trumbo to Michael Wilson, Feb. 24, 1959, Box 7, file 2, DTC; repr. in Dalton Trumbo, *Additional Dialogue: Letters of Dalton Trumbo, 1942–1962,* ed. Helen Manfull (New York: M. Evans, 1970), 480–86.

61. For more on Wilson's battle to get credit on *Friendly Persuasion* see J. Smith, "A Good Business Proposition," 214–15.

62. See Cook, *Dalton Trumbo,* 259–60; and "'Author' of Movie Deepens Mystery," *New York Times,* April 1, 1957, 18.

63. See "Dalton Trumbo Gags 'Rich' Tale," *Variety,* April 3, 1957, 1.

64. See "'Author,'" *New York Times,* 18; and "Case of the Missing Scripter," *Time,* April 15, 1957, 116.

65. See the memo written by Trumbo for the collection, Box 9, *The Brave One* file, DTC; "'Oscar' Mystery Takes New Turn," *New York Times,* April 4, 1957, 40; and Thomas Pryor, "Studios Settle Suit over Story," *New York Times,* April 9, 1957, 40.

66. Dalton Trumbo to Lewis Metzer for transmission to the Writers Guild Board, c. Jan. 1959, Box 7, file 2, DTC; and Thomas Pryor, "Trumbo Evaded Film Ban," *New York Times,* April 11, 1957, 39. See also Cook, *Dalton Trumbo,* 260.

67. Dalton Trumbo to Aubrey Finn, Nov. 19, 1957, Box 6, file 2, DTC. Trumbo later said that CBS Studio One did a bit on "Robert Rich" two days before the 1958 Academy Awards ceremony. Dalton Trumbo to Michael Wilson, March 30, 1958, Box 6, file 3, DTC; repr. in Trumbo, *Additional Dialogue,* 414–17.

68. Dalton Trumbo to Aubrey Finn, Dec. 8, 1957, Box 6, file 2, DTC; repr. in Trumbo, *Additional Dialogue,* 406–8. The story of *Mr. Adam* was about the only man left on Earth capable of fathering a child. All of the other men in the world were infertile. All of the women in the world, on the other hand, wanted to have babies. Despite its apocalyptic premise, *Mr. Adam* was a comedy.

69. Michel de Certeau, *The Practice of Everyday Life,* trans. Steven Rendall (Berkeley: University of California Press, 1984), 37.

70. Quoted in Dalton Trumbo, "Who Is Robert Rich?" *Frontier,* Box 40, Folder 6, DTC.

71. Dalton Trumbo, "Blacklist = Black Market," *The Nation,* May 4, 1957, 383–87.

72. Trumbo, "Who Is Robert Rich?"

73. Hanson, *Dalton Trumbo, Hollywood Rebel,* 145.

74. Cyrino, *Big Screen Rome,* 117.

75. Producer Edward Lewis, however, denies that screenwriter Dalton Trumbo sought to make *Spartacus* a political tract at all, claiming instead that Trumbo's chief interest was in telling a compelling story. Although this seems to counter the evidence in Trumbo's writings, Lewis's comments speak more to Trumbo's disinterest in polemics. Trumbo appeared to have no stake in overt political lessons, which is why allegory itself becomes such an important tool for communicating the film's politics. See Lewis's commentary on the *Spartacus* DVD released as part of the Criterion Collection in 2001.

CHAPTER 6. ROAMING THE PLAINS ALONG THE "NEW FRONTIER"

1. Capsule review, *Time,* June 23, 1952, *California Conquest* clippings file, Margaret Herrick Library, Academy of Motion Picture Arts and Sciences (hereafter MHL).

2. See Shaw, *Hollywood's Cold War,* 51; and Michael Strada and Harold Troper, *Friend or Foe? Russians in American Film and Foreign Policy, 1933–1991* (London: Scarecrow, 1997), 86.

3. See, e.g., Phillip Drummond, *High Noon* (London: British Film Institute, 1997); Michael Blake, *Code of Honor: The Making of America's Great Westerns* (Lanham, MD: Taylor Trade, 2003), 3–64; Biskind, *Seeing Is Believing,* 44–49; and Murphy, *Congressional Theatre,* 255–59.

4. See Lionel Chetwynd and Norman Powell's documentary *Darkness at High Noon: The Carl Foreman Documents* (Whidbey Island Films, 2002). See also Blake, *Code of Honor,* 8–10; and Drummond, *High Noon,* 37–38.

5. "Kramer Buyout of Foreman Ends 4-Year Teamup," *Variety,* Oct. 24, 1951, 4, 20; "Kramer, Foreman Sever Relations," *New York Times,* Oct. 23, 1951, 35.

6. "Carl Foreman Organizes New Film Company," *Los Angeles Times,* Oct. 25, 1951, A8. See also "Foreman Sets Up Own Film Concern," *New York Times,* Oct. 25, 1951, 36.

7. Quoted in Anthony Holden, *Behind the Oscar: The Secret History of the Academy Awards* (New York: Penguin, 1993), 202.

8. Joe Medjuck, "Carl Foreman," *Take One*, Jan.-Feb. 1972, 21.

9. Buhle and Wagner, *Radical Hollywood*, 418.

10. Belton, *American Cinema / American Culture*, 247.

11. See Whitfield, *Culture of the Cold War*, 146–49; Murphy, *Congressional Theatre*, 255–59; Slotkin, *Gunfighter Nation*, 391–96; Drummond, *High Noon*, 10, 69–73; and Biskind, *Seeing Is Believing*, 44–48.

12. Philip French, *Westerns: Aspects of a Movie Genre* (London: British Film Institute, 1973), 41.

13. In addition to Slotkin's *Gunfighter Nation*, see his *Regeneration through Violence: The Mythology of the American Frontier, 1600–1860* (Middletown, CT: Wesleyan University Press, 1973); and his *The Fatal Environment: The Myth of the Frontier in the Age of Industrialization* (New York: Atheneum, 1985).

14. Jim Kitses, *Horizons West: Directing the Western from John Ford to Clint Eastwood* (London: British Film Institute, 2004), 12–13.

15. Besides Kitses's work see John Cawelti, *The Six Gun Mystique* (Bowling Green, OH: Bowling Green University Popular Press, 1970); and Will Wright, *Six Guns and Society: The Structural Study of the Western* (Berkeley: University of California Press, 1975).

16. See, e.g., Edward Buscombe and Roberta Pearson, eds., *Back in the Saddle: New Essays on the Western* (London: British Film Institute, 1998); Matthew Bernstein and Gaylyn Studlar, eds., *John Ford Made Westerns: Filming the Legend in the Sound Era* (Bloomington: Indiana University Press, 2001); and Peter C. Rollins and John E. O'Connor, eds., *Hollywood's West: The American Frontier in Film, Television, and History* (Lexington: University Press of Kentucky, 2005).

17. Quoted in Stanley Corkin, *Cowboys as Cold Warriors: The Western and U.S. History* (Philadelphia: Temple University Press, 2004), 131–32.

18. Ibid., 154.

19. At one point in his discussion Corkin articulates this link between security and economic prosperity by citing suburban homebuilder William Levitt's claim that "no homeowner can be a Communist. He has too much to do" (Corkin, *Cowboys as Cold Warriors*, 158–59).

20. Ibid., 96.

21. Belton, though, mistakenly ascribes the authorship of *Broken Arrow*'s screenplay to Alvah Bessie, a member of the Hollywood Ten. In fact, the screenplay was written by Albert Maltz, who, as we have seen, had also written the early drafts of the screenplay for *The Robe*. Maltz finally received belated credit for his work on *Broken Arrow* in 1991. For more on Maltz's relationship with Blankfort see Terry Pristin, "Mending 'Broken Arrow': Writers Guild Considers Award for Blacklisted Writer of 1950 Film," *Los Angeles Times*, June 29, 1991, F1, F16.

22. Synopsis of *Broken Arrow*, Harry Brand, Director of Publicity, 20th Century–Fox, *Broken Arrow* clippings file, MHL.

23. Philip K. Scheuer, "Indian's Culture Captured on Film," *Los Angeles Times*, May 21, 1950, *Broken Arrow* clippings file, MHL.

24. "'Broken Arrow' Cited," June 14, 1950, *Broken Arrow* clippings file, MHL.

25. Scheuer, "Indian's Culture," *Broken Arrow* clippings file, MHL.

26. Review of *Broken Arrow, Boxoffice*, June 7, 1950, *Broken Arrow* clippings file, MHL.

27. Angela Aleiss, "Hollywood Addresses Postwar Assimilation: Indian/White Attitudes in *Broken Arrow*," *American Indian Culture and Research Journal* 11, no. 1 (1987): 72.

28. Aleiss seems to be strategically conflating McCarthy's suspicion of Communists within government with HUAC's investigation of Communist subversion in the private sector. McCarthy himself was never a member of the House Committee on Un-American Activities.

29. Corkin, *Cowboys as Cold Warriors*, 106.

30. Belton, *American Cinema / American Culture*, 248.

31. See Slotkin, *Gunfighter Nation*, esp. 29–62.

32. Ibid., 395.

33. Mark Twain, "The Man That Corrupted Hadleyburg," in *Great Short Works of Mark Twain*, ed. Justin Kaplan (New York: Perennial, 1967), 266.

34. Not everyone, however, sympathized with Will Kane's plight in *High Noon*. Some observers, like Howard Hawks, criticized the film because it seemed disgraceful for a law enforcement official to seek help from the public. Others, like John Wayne, despised the absence of any volunteer spirit in Hadleyville. Indeed, both men made films, *Rio Bravo* (1959) and *The Alamo* (1960) respectively, that were intended to counter the image of Kane's solicitude and the townspeople's cowardice. Moreover, even the *Daily Worker* expressed a degree of indifference toward Kane in its review: "This spectator must admit to a certain sympathy with those the sheriff failed to convince that they were duty bound to take part in repulsing a personal vendetta." See E. R. "'High Noon' Exciting but Cynical," *Daily Worker*, August 26, 1952, 7. If Communists of the period were at all aware of *High Noon*'s blacklist subtexts, they seem to have eluded the staff there.

35. Whitfield, *Culture of the Cold War*, 148.

36. John Francis Kreidl, *Nicholas Ray* (Boston: Twayne, 1977), 43–45.

37. See Bernard Eisenschitz, *Nicholas Ray: An American Journey* (London: Faber and Faber, 1990), 200.

38. Ibid.

39. Milton Luban, "Inept Yarn Matched by Mugging, Acting," *Hollywood Reporter*, May 5, 1954, *Johnny Guitar* clippings file, MHL.

40. "Joan Crawford Hits Them Wide Open Spaces," *Cue*, June 5, 1954, *Johnny Guitar* clippings file, MHL.

41. Ibid. (my emphasis).

42. Wilmington, "Nicholas Ray's *Johnny Guitar*," 23.

43. Bertrand Tavernier, "Interview with Philip Yordan," *Cahiers du cinéma* 128 (Feb. 1962): 18. Note that while Yordan's comments were published long

before Wilmington's *Velvet Light Trap* article, they did not really become an important part of *Johnny Guitar*'s American reception until the publication of Kreidl's biography of Nicholas Ray in 1977.

44. For more on the concept of a structure of sympathy and the role of moral judgments regarding character actions see Murray Smith, *Engaging Characters: Fiction, Emotion, and the Cinema* (New York: Oxford University Press, 1995).

45. *Leonard Maltin's Movie & Video Guide* (New York: Signet, 1998), 1240.

46. Shaw, *Hollywood's Cold War*, 145.

47. Dmytryk, *It's a Hell of a Life*, 141.

48. Ibid., 233.

49. Coyne, *The Crowded Prairie*, 99–101.

50. Ibid., 100.

51. Ibid.

52. Ibid., 101.

53. Lenihan, *Showdown*, 127.

54. Matthew Costello, "Rewriting *High Noon*: Transformations in American Popular Political Culture during the Cold War," *Film & History* 33, no. 1 (2003): 35.

55. Ibid., 36.

56. Lenihan, *Showdown*, 120.

57. Leo Charney, "Historical Excess: *Johnny Guitar*'s Containment," *Cinema Journal* 29, no. 4 (1990): 27.

CHAPTER 7. LOVING THE ALIEN

1. David Platt, "Government Propaganda Proposal Too Crude for Movie Magnates," *Daily Worker*, July 20, 1953, 7.

2. Victoria O'Donnell, "Science Fiction Films and Cold War Anxiety," in *The Fifties: Transforming the Screen, 1950–1959*, ed. Peter Lev (Berkeley: University of California Press, 2003), 196. For an alternative view of postwar science fiction cinema, one that situates this cycle within the context of Hollywood's business strategies, see Brad Schauer, "Science Fiction Film and the Exploitation Tradition in Hollywood, 1956–1986" (PhD diss., University of Wisconsin–Madison, 2010).

3. Belton, *American Cinema / American Culture*, 246.

4. Quoted in Terry Christensen, *Reel Politics: American Political Movies from "Birth of a Nation" to "Platoon"* (Boston: Basil Blackwell, 1987), 101.

5. Jeff Sharlet, *The Family: The Secret Fundamentalism at the Heart of American Power* (New York: Harper Perennial, 2008), 182. See also Tom Weaver, *Sci-Fi Confidential* (Jefferson, NC: McFarland, 2002), 234–46.

6. Quoted in Dana M. Reemes, *Directed by Jack Arnold* (Jefferson, NC: McFarland, 1988), 24.

7. O'Donnell, "Science Fiction Films," 173.

8. Patrick Luciano, *Them or Us: Archetypal Interpretations of Fifties Alien Invasion Films* (Bloomington: Indiana University Press, 1987), 42.

9. Ibid., 82–130.

10. See Vivian Sobchack, *Screening Space: The American Science Fiction Film* (New Brunswick, NJ: Rutgers University Press, 1987), 121–25; Andrew Dowdy, *The Films of the Fifties: The American State of Mind* (New York: Morrow, 1975); David Seed, *American Science Fiction and the Cold War: Literature and Film* (Edinburgh: Edinburgh University Press, 1999), 133–34; Stuart Samuels, "The Age of Conspiracy and Conformity: *Invasion of the Body Snatchers* (1956)," in *American History / American Film*, ed. John E. O'Connor and Martin A. Jackson (New York: Frederick Ungar, 1979), 203–17.

11. Pascal Boyer, *Religion Explained: The Evolutionary Origins of Religious Thought* (New York: Basic Books, 2001), 287–90.

12. For more on Sherif's experiment and an overview of his career see David Berreby, *Us & Them: The Science of Identity* (Chicago: University of Chicago Press, 2005), 157–81.

13. Burkhard Röwekamp, "The Thing from Another World," *Movies of the 50s*, ed. Jürgen Müller (New York: Barnes & Noble, 2006), 10.

14. Biskind, *Seeing Is Believing*, 132.

15. Sayre, *Running Time*, 193–96.

16. Luciano, *Them or Us*, 17–18.

17. *Two Faces of Communism*, *Comics with Problems*, no. 27 (Houston: Christian Anti-Communist Crusade, 1961), 24 (repr. available at www.ep.tc/problems/27/24.html).

18. Laura, "Invasion of the Body Snatchers," 71.

19. M. Keith Booker, *Alternate Americas: Science Fiction Film and American Culture* (Westport, CT: Praeger, 2006), 36.

20. Biskind, *Seeing Is Believing*, 150.

21. See Danny Peary, *Cult Movies: The Classics, the Sleepers, the Weird, and the Wonderful* (New York: Delta, 1981), 154–57; Hoberman, *An Army of Phantoms*, 308–13; Shaw, *Hollywood's Cold War*, 50; Drew Casper, *Postwar Hollywood: 1946–1962* (Malden, MA: Blackwell, 2007); Philipp Bühler, "Invasion of the Body Snatchers," in *Movies of the 50s*, ed. Jürgen Müller (New York: Barnes & Noble, 2006), 194–96; and Rogin, *Ronald Reagan*, 262–67.

22. Casper, *Postwar Hollywood*, 206.

23. Carroll, *The Philosophy of Horror*, 42–58.

24. Ibid., 46.

25. Ibid., 32.

26. Ibid., 49.

27. Ibid., 197.

28. For a discussion of the atomic bomb's impact on literary science fiction of the early Cold War period see Boyer, *By the Bomb's Early Light*, 243–74.

29. Research Dept. to Mr. Yates, memorandum, Nov. 10, 1952, *Them!* production files, Warner Bros. Archives, School of Cinematic Arts, University of Southern California (hereafter WBA).

30. Steve Trilling re THEM, undated memorandum, *Them!* production files, WBA.

31. Pressbook for *Them!*, *Them!* production files, WBA.

32. Denton Hall & Burgin to Messrs. Rubinstein, Nash, & Co., Oct. 1, 1954, *Them!* production files, WBA.

33. Excerpt from *World Wide Play Review* 9, no. 42 (May 1939), ed. Irving Deaken, Warner Bros. story department, *Them!* production files, WBA. Note that Ogpu refers to a security and police force that operated in the Soviet Union until 1934. As a secret police force, Ogpu is usually seen as a forerunner to the KGB and a counterpart to the Nazi security force, the Gestapo.

34. David Platt, "'Them,' Well Done Movie Thriller," *Daily Worker*, July 16, 1954, 7.

35. Sontag, "Imagination of Disaster," 47.

36. Biskind, *Seeing Is Believing*, 132.

37. O'Donnell, "Science Fiction Films," 186.

38. Revised estimating script by Ted Sherdeman, June 18, 1953, 63, *Them!* production files, WBA.

39. Biskind, *Seeing Is Believing*, 141.

40. Peary, *Cult Movies*, 157.

41. Ibid.

42. Review of *The Thing*, *Time*, May 14, 1951, *The Thing (From Another World)* clippings file, Margaret Herrick Library, Academy of Motion Picture Arts and Sciences (hereafter MHL).

43. Peary, *Cult Movies*, 157.

44. Clarens, *An Illustrated History*, 134.

45. For more on the public's interest in the phenomenon of brainwashing see Louis Menand's introduction to Richard Condon's *The Manchurian Candidate* (New York: Four Walls Eight Windows, 2001), x–xii.

46. Biskind, *Seeing Is Believing*, 140.

47. Booker, *Alternate Americas*, 72–73.

48. Copy from the DVD case for *This Island Earth* (Universal Pictures, 2006).

49. Buhle and Wagner, *Hide in Plain Sight*, 78.

50. David Seed, for example, cites a letter from Finney written in 1993 in which the author claimed, "When I wrote this book *[Invasion of the Body Snatchers]* I was not thinking of McCarthy, Communism, fascism" (Seed, *American Science Fiction*, 143). See also Guy Braucourt, "Interview with Don Siegel," *Focus on the Science Fiction Film*, ed. William Johnson (Englewood, NJ: Prentice-Hall, 1972), 74–76.

51. Samuels, "Age of Conspiracy and Conformity," 204–8.

52. Buhle and Wagner, *Hide in Plain Sight*, 73.

53. Ibid. It is worth noting that even the participation of blacklisted person-nel is also open to multiple interpretations. J. Hoberman also mentions Collins's involvement in *Body Snatchers* but treats it as evidence that the film possibly was intended as a cautionary tale about Communist takeover. Hoberman cites Collins's testimony before HUAC, where he says that "the thousands of hours of work for the Communist Party during World War II turned him into a 'trained zombie'" (Hoberman, *An Army of Phantoms*, 309–10).

54. Peary, *Cult Movies*, 157–58.

55. Sayre, *Running Time*, 199; and Jim Wnoroski, review of *Invaders from Mars, Photon*, no. 21 (1971), *Invaders from Mars* clippings file, MHL.

56. O.A.G., "Here Come Those Flying Saucers Again," *New York Times*, May 30, 1953, 7.

57. Sayre, *Running Time*, 199.

58. Sobchack, *Screening Space*, 121.

59. Sayre, *Running Time*, 201 (emphasis in original).

60. Rogin, *Ronald Reagan*, 267.

61. See Encyclical 219, *Divini Redemptoris*, March 19, 1937; repr. in *The Papal Encyclicals, 1903–1939*, ed. and trans. Claudia Carlen (Raleigh, NC: Consortium, 1981), 537–54. For Pope Leo XIII's original comment see Encyclical 79, *Quod Apostolici Muneris*, Dec. 28, 1878; repr. in *The Papal Encyclicals, 1878–1903*, ed. and trans. Claudia Carlen (Raleigh, NC: Consortium, 1981), 11–16.

62. Quoted in Sayre, *Running Time*, 201.

63. Kiron K. Skinner, Annelise Anderson, and Martin Anderson, eds., *Reagan, in His Own Hand: The Writings of Ronald Reagan That Reveal His Revolutionary Vision for America* (New York: Touchstone, 2002), 10.

64. Edwin Black, "The Second Persona," *Quarterly Journal of Speech* 56, no. 2 (1970): 109–19.

65. The poster for *The Whip Hand* is reproduced in Barson and Heller's *Red Scared!* (79).

66. Murphy, *Congressional Theatre*, 262.

67. Ibid., 264.

68. Susan Sontag, *Illness as Metaphor* (New York: Farrar, Straus and Giroux, 1977), 68.

69. Jimmie L. Reeves, *Cinema Texas Program Notes* 21, no. 1 (Oct. 1, 1981): 49, *Invasion of the Body Snatchers* clippings file, MHL.

70. Ibid.

CONCLUSION

1. W.R. Wilkerson III, "An Apology: The Son of THR Founder Billy Wilkerson on the Publication's Dark Past," *Hollywood Reporter*, Nov. 19, 2012, www.hollywoodreporter.com/news/blacklist-billy-wilkersons-son-apolo-gizes-391977.

2. Aaron Couch, "Blacklist Victim Thanks THR Founder's Son for Apology," *Hollywood Reporter*, Nov. 19, 2012, www.hollywoodreporter.com/news/black-list-victim-thanks-hollywood-reporter-393679.

3. "Hollywood Blacklist Victim Responds to Trade Paper's Apology for Fueling Witch Hunt," CBS Los Angeles, http://losangeles.cbslocal.com/2012/11/20/hollywood-blacklist-victim-responds-to-the-hollywood-reporters-apology-for-role-in-witch-hunt/.

4. Gary Baum, "Blacklist Victims' Children Blast Apology from THR Founder's Son," *Hollywood Reporter*, Dec. 12, 2012, www.hollywoodreporter.com/news/hollywood-blacklist-victims-children-blast-401168.

5. Quoted in Wilkerson, "An Apology."

6. For a more detailed analysis of *The Shining* see Geoffrey Cocks, *The Wolf at the Door: Stanley Kubrick, History, and the Holocaust* (New York: Peter Lang, 2004).

7. David Bordwell, "All Play and No Work? ROOM 237," *Observations on Film Art*, April 7, 2013, www.davidbordwell.net/blog/2013/04/07/all-play-and-no-work-room-237/.

8. William Blakemore, "'Room 237' Subject Bill Blakemore Writes about His 'The Shining' Theories," *Daily Beast*, March 29, 2013, www.thedailybeast.com/articles/2013/03/29/room-237-subject-bill-blakemore-writes-about-his-the-shining-conspiracy-theories.html.

9. Jim Emerson, "To the Moon, Stanley!" *Scanners*, April 27, 2013, www.rogerebert.com/scanners/to-the-moon-stanley.

10. McRaney, *You Are Not So Smart*, 36–43.

11. See, e.g., Alice Liddel's user review of *The Court-Martial of Billy Mitchell* at www.imdb.com/title/tt0047956/reviews?start=10.

Bibliography

Aleiss, Angela. "Hollywood Addresses Postwar Assimilation: Indian/White Attitudes in *Broken Arrow.*" *American Indian Culture and Research Journal* 11, no. 1 (1987): 67–79.

Altman, Rick. *Film/Genre*. London: British Film Institute, 1999.

Andersen, Thom. "Afterword." In Krutnik et al., *"Un-American" Hollywood*, 264–75.

———. "Red Hollywood." In Krutnik et al., *"Un-American" Hollywood*, 225–63.

Andrew, Dudley. "The Unauthorized Auteur Today." In *Film Theory Goes to the Movies*, edited by Jim Collins, Hilary Radner, and Ava Preacher Collins. 77–85. New York: Routledge, 1993.

Babington, Bruce, and Peter William Evans. *Biblical Epics: Sacred Narrative in the Hollywood Cinema*. New York: Manchester University Press, 1993.

Barney, Stephen A. *Allegories of History, Allegories of Love*. Hamden, CT: Archon, 1979.

Barson, Michael, and Steven Heller. *Red Scared! The Commie Menace in Propaganda and Popular Culture*. San Francisco: Chronicle, 2001.

Barzman, Norma. *The Red and the Black: The Intimate Memoir of a Hollywood Expatriate*. New York: Thunder Mouth's Press/Nation Books, 2003.

Bazin, Andre. *What Is Cinema?* 2 vols. Edited and translated by Hugh Gray. Berkeley: University of California Press, 1967–71.

Belknap, Michael R. *Cold War Political Justice: The Smith Act, the Communist Party, and American Civil Liberties*. Westport, CT: Greenwood Press, 1977.

Belmonte, Laura A. *Selling the American Way: U.S. Propaganda and the Cold War*. Philadelphia: University of Pennsylvania Press, 2004.

Belton, John. *American Cinema / American Culture*. New York: McGraw-Hill, 1994.

Benjamin, Walter. *The Origin of German Tragic Drama*. Translated by John Osborne. New York: Verso, 1998.

Bernstein, Matthew, ed. *Controlling Hollywood: Censorship and Regulation in the Studio Era*. New Brunswick, NJ: Rutgers University Press, 1999.

Bernstein, Matthew, and Gaylyn Studlar, eds. *John Ford Made Westerns: Filming the Legend in the Sound Era.* Bloomington: Indiana University Press, 2001.

Bernstein, Walter. *Inside Out: A Memoir of the Blacklist.* New York: Knopf, 1996.

Berreby, David. *Us & Them: The Science of Identity.* Chicago: University of Chicago Press, 2005.

Bessie, Alvah. *Inquisition in Eden.* New York: Macmillan, 1965.

Billingsley, Kenneth Lloyd. *Hollywood Party: How Communism Seduced the American Film Industry in the 1930s and 1940s.* Rocklin, CA: Forum/Prima, 1998.

Biskind, Peter. *Seeing Is Believing: How Hollywood Taught Us to Stop Worrying and Love the Fifties.* New York: Pantheon, 1983.

Black, Edwin. "The Second Persona." *Quarterly Journal of Speech* 56, no. 2 (1970): 109–19.

Blake, Michael. *Code of Honor: The Making of America's Great Westerns.* Lanham, MD: Taylor Trade, 2003.

Booker, M. Keith. *Alternate Americas: Science Fiction Film and American Culture.* Westport, CT: Praeger, 2006.

Bordwell, David. *Making Meaning: Influence and Rhetoric in the Interpretation of Cinema.* Cambridge, MA: Harvard University Press, 1989.

———. *Narration in the Fiction Film.* Madison: University of Wisconsin Press, 1987.

———. *On the History of Film Style.* Cambridge, MA: Harvard University Press, 1997.

Boyd, Brian. *On the Origin of Stories: Evolution, Cognition, and Fiction.* Cambridge, MA: Belknap, 2009.

Boyer, Pascal. *Religion Explained: The Evolutionary Origins of Religious Thought.* New York: Basic Books, 2001.

Boyer, Paul. *By the Bomb's Early Light: American Thought and Culture at the Dawn of the Atomic Age.* Chapel Hill: University of North Carolina Press, 1985.

Braucourt, Guy. "Interview with Don Siegel." In Johnson, *Focus on the Science Fiction Film*, 74–76.

Braudy, Leo. "'The Director, That Miserable Son of a Bitch': Kazan, *Viva Zapata!* and the Problem of Authority." In Dombrowski, *Kazan Revisited*, 37–45.

Browne, Nick, ed. *Refiguring American Film Genres.* Berkeley: University of California Press, 1999.

Buhle, Paul, and Dave Wagner. *Blacklisted: The Film Lover's Guide to the Hollywood Blacklist.* New York: Palgrave Macmillan, 2003.

———. *Hide in Plain Sight: The Hollywood Blacklistees in Film and Television, 1950–2002.* New York: Palgrave Macmillan, 2003.

———. *Radical Hollywood: The Unheard Story behind America's Favorite Movies.* New York: New Press, 2003.

———. *A Very Dangerous Citizen: Abraham Polonsky and the Hollywood Left*. Berkeley: University of California Press, 2001.

Bühler, Philipp. "*Invasion of the Body Snatchers*." In Müller, *Movies of the 50s*, 194–96.

Burnett, Colin. "The 'Albert Maltz Affair' and the Debate about Para-Marxist Formalism in *New Masses*, 1945–1946." *Journal of American Studies* (May 2013): 1–28, http://dx.doi.org/doi:10.1017/S0021875813000728.

Buscombe, Edward. "The Western: A Short History." In *The BFI Companion to the Western*, edited by Edward Buscombe, 15–54. London: Andre Deutsch/British Film Institute, 1988.

Buscombe, Edward, and Roberta Pearson, eds. *Back in the Saddle: New Essays on the Western*. London: British Film Institute, 1998.

Carroll, Noël. *The Philosophy of Horror, or Paradoxes of the Heart*. New York: Routledge, 1990.

Casper, Drew. *Postwar Hollywood: 1946–1962*. Malden, MA: Blackwell, 2007.

Caute, David. *The Great Fear: The Anti-Communist Purge under Truman and Eisenhower*. New York: Simon and Schuster, 1978.

Cawelti, John. *The Six Gun Mystique*. Bowling Green, OH: Bowling Green University Popular Press, 1970.

Ceplair, Larry. *The Marxist and the Movies: A Biography of Paul Jarrico*. Lexington: University Press of Kentucky, 2007.

———. "Who Killed Spartacus?" *Cineaste* 18, no. 3 (1991): 18–29.

Ceplair, Larry, and Steven Englund. *The Inquisition in Hollywood: Politics in the Film Community, 1930–1960*. Berkeley: University of California Press, 1979.

Certeau, Michel de. *The Practice of Everyday Life*. Translated by Steven Rendall. Berkeley: University of California Press, 1984.

Chapman, James. "*The Adventures of Robin Hood* and the Origins of the Television Swashbuckler." *Media History* 17, no. 3 (2011): 273–87.

Charney, Leo. "Historical Excess: *Johnny Guitar*'s Containment." *Cinema Journal* 29, no. 4 (1990): 23–34.

Chown, Jeffrey. "Visual Coding and Social Class in *On the Waterfront*." In Rapf, *On the Waterfront*, 106–23.

Christensen, Terry. *Reel Politics: American Political Movies from "Birth of a Nation" to "Platoon."* Boston: Basil Blackwell, 1987.

Christopher, Nicholas. *Somewhere in the Night: Film Noir and the American City*. New York: Free Press, 1997.

Ciment, Michel. *Kazan on Kazan*. New York: Viking, 1974.

Clarens, Carlos. *An Illustrated History of Horror and Science Fiction Films*. New York: G. P. Putnam's Sons, 1967.

Cocks, Geoffrey. *The Wolf at the Door: Stanley Kubrick, History, and the Holocaust*. New York: Peter Lang, 2004.

Cole, Lester. *Hollywood Red: The Autobiography of Lester Cole*. Palo Alto, CA: Ramparts, 1981.

Comiskey, Andrea. "The Hero We Read: *The Dark Knight*, Popular Allegoresis, and Blockbuster Ideology." In *Riddle Me This, Batman! Essays on the*

Universe of the Dark Knight, edited by Kevin K. Durand and Mary K. Leigh, 124–46. Jefferson, NC: McFarland, 2011.

Cook, Bruce. *Dalton Trumbo.* New York: Scribner, 1977.

Cooper, Duncan. "Dalton Trumbo vs. Stanley Kubrick: Their Debate over Arthur Koestler's *The Gladiators.*" *Cineaste* 18, no. 3 (1991): 34–37.

Copjec, Joan, ed. *Shades of Noir: A Reader.* London: Verso, 1993.

Corber, Robert J. *Homosexuality in Cold War America: Resistance and the Crisis of Masculinity.* Durham, NC: Duke University Press, 1997.

———. *In the Name of National Security: Hitchcock, Homophobia, and the Political Construction of Gender in Postwar America.* Durham, NC: Duke University Press, 1996.

Corkin, Stanley. *Cowboys as Cold Warriors: The Western and U.S. History.* Philadelphia: Temple University Press, 2004.

Costello, Matthew. "Rewriting *High Noon:* Transformations in American Popular Political Culture during the Cold War." *Film & History* 33, no. 1 (2003): 30–40.

Courtois, Stéphane, Nicolas Werth, Jean-Louis Panné, Andrzej Paczkowski, Karel Bartošek, and Jean-Louis Margolin. *The Black Book of Communism: Crimes, Terror, Repression.* Translated by Jonathan Murphy and Mark Kramer. Cambridge, MA: Harvard University Press, 1999.

Cowie, Elizabeth. "*Film Noir* and Women." In Copjec, *Shades of Noir,* 121–65.

Coyne, Michael. *The Crowded Prairie: American National Identity in the Hollywood Western.* London: I.B. Tauris, 1997.

Custen, George. *Twentieth Century's Fox: Darryl F. Zanuck and the Culture of Hollywood.* New York: Basic Books, 1997.

Cyrino, Monica Silveira. *Big Screen Rome.* Malden, MA: Blackwell, 2005.

De Man, Paul. *Allegories of Reading: Figural Language in Rousseau, Nietzsche, Rilke, and Proust.* New Haven, CT: Yale University Press, 1979.

———. *Blindness and Insight: Essays in the Rhetoric of Contemporary Criticism.* Minneapolis: University of Minnesota Press, 1983.

Dick, Bernard F. *Radical Innocence: A Critical Study of the Hollywood Ten.* Lexington: University Press of Kentucky, 1988.

Dighe, Ranjit S., ed. *The Historian's "Wizard of Oz": Reading L. Frank Baum's Classic as a Political and Monetary Allegory.* Westport, CT: Praeger, 2002.

Dmytryk, Edward. *It's a Hell of a Life but Not a Bad Living.* New York: New York Times Books, 1978.

Doane, Mary Ann. *Femmes Fatales: Feminism, Film Theory, Psychoanalysis.* New York: Routledge, 1991.

Doherty, Thomas. *Cold War, Cool Medium: Television, McCarthyism, and American Culture.* New York: Columbia University Press, 2003.

———. "Hollywood Agit-Prop: The Anti-Communist Cycle, 1948–1954." *Journal of Film and Video* 40, no. 4 (1988): 15–27.

Dombrowski, Lisa. *The Films of Samuel Fuller: If You Die, I'll Kill You!* Middletown, CT: Wesleyan University Press, 2008.

———, ed. *Kazan Revisited.* Middletown, CT: Wesleyan University Press, 2012.

Douglas, Lloyd C. *The Robe.* Boston: Houghton Mifflin, 1942.

Dowdy, Andrew. *The Films of the Fifties: The American State of Mind.* New York: Morrow, 1975.

Drummond, Phillip. *High Noon.* London: British Film Institute, 1997.

Dunne, Philip. *Take Two: A Life in Movies and Politics.* New York: McGraw-Hill, 1980.

Eisenschitz, Bernard. *Nicholas Ray: An American Journey.* London: Faber and Faber, 1990.

Eldridge, David. *Hollywood's History Films.* New York: I. B. Tauris, 2006.

Ellul, Jacques. *Propaganda: The Formation of Men's Attitudes.* Translated by Konrad Kellen and Jean Lerner. New York: Alfred A. Knopf, 1965.

Evans, M. Stanton. *Blacklisted by History: The Untold Story of Joseph McCarthy and His Fight against America's Enemies.* New York: Three Rivers, 2007.

Fleming, John V. *The Anti-Communist Manifestos: Four Books That Shaped the Cold War.* New York: Norton, 2009.

Fletcher, Angus. *Allegory: The Theory of a Symbolic Mode.* Ithaca, NY: Cornell University Press, 1964.

Flinn, Tom. "Daniel Mainwaring: An Interview." In *The Big Book of Noir,* edited by Ed Gorman, Lee Server, and Martin H. Greenberg, 65–68. New York: Carroll and Graf, 1998.

Foster, William Z. *History of the Communist Party in the United States.* New York: Greenwood Press, 1968.

Freedland, Michael. *Hollywood on Trial: McCarthyism's War against the Movies.* London: Robson, 2007.

French, Philip. *Westerns: Aspects of a Movie Genre.* London: British Film Institute, 1973.

Fried, Albert. *McCarthyism: The Great American Red Scare, a Documentary History.* New York: Oxford University Press, 1997.

Frye, Northrop. *Anatomy of Criticism: Four Essays.* Princeton, NJ: Princeton University Press, 1957.

Fuller, Samuel. *A Third Face: My Tale of Writing, Fighting, and Filmmaking.* New York: Applause, 2002.

Gabler, Neal. *An Empire of Their Own: How the Jews Invented Hollywood.* New York: Crown, 1988.

Gaddis, John Lewis. *The Cold War: A New History.* New York: Penguin, 2005.

———. *The United States and the Origins of the Cold War, 1941–1947.* New York: Columbia University Press, 1972.

Garnham, Nicholas. *Samuel Fuller.* New York: Viking, 1971.

Gellman, Irwin F. *The Contender: Richard Nixon, the Congress Years, 1946–1952.* New York: Free Press, 1999.

Gilbert, Daniel T. "How Mental Systems Believe." *American Psychologist* 46, no. 2 (1991): 107–19.

Gladchuk, John Joseph. *Hollywood and Anticommunism: HUAC and the Evolution of the Red Menace, 1935–1950.* New York: Routledge, 2007.

Glassner, Barry. *The Culture of Fear.* New York: Basic Books, 1999.

Glazer, Nathan. *The Social Basis of American Communism.* New York: Harcourt, Brace, 1961.

Goodman, Walter. *The Committee: The Extraordinary Career of the House Committee on Un-American Activities.* New York: Farrar, Straus and Giroux, 1968.

Greenfield, Sayre N. *The Ends of Allegory.* Newark, NJ: University of Delaware Press, 1998.

Grieveson, Lee, and Haidee Wasson, eds. *Inventing Film Studies.* Durham, NC: Duke University Press, 2008.

Grindon, Leger. *Shadows on the Past: Studies in the Historical Fiction Film.* Philadelphia: Temple University Press, 1994.

Haidt, Jonathan. *The Righteous Mind: Why Good People Are Divided by Religion and Politics.* New York: Pantheon, 2012.

Hall, Jeanne. "The Benefits of Hindsight: Re-visions of HUAC and the Film and Television Industries in *The Front* and *Guilty by Suspicion*." *Film Quarterly* 54, no. 4 (2001–2): 15–26.

Hansen, Bradley. "The Fable as Allegory: *The Wizard of Oz* in Economics." *Journal of Economic Education* 33, no. 3 (2002): 254–64.

Hanson, Peter. *Dalton Trumbo, Hollywood Rebel: A Critical Survey and Filmography.* Jefferson, NC: McFarland, 2001.

Harper, Mr. "The Big Sell: A Review." *Harper's,* August 1954. Reprinted in Rapf, *On the Waterfront,* 153–56.

Hartung, Philip T. "Man's Hope: A Review." *Commonweal,* August 20, 1954. Reprinted in Rapf, *On the Waterfront,* 157–58.

Hellman, Lillian. *Scoundrel Time.* Boston: Little, Brown, 1976.

Hey, Kenneth R. "Ambivalence as a Theme in *On the Waterfront* (1954): An Interdisciplinary Approach to Film Study." In *Hollywood as Historian: American Film in a Cultural Context,* edited by Peter C. Rollins, 159–89. Rev. ed. Lexington: University Press of Kentucky, 1998.

Hixson, Walter L. *Parting the Curtain: Propaganda, Culture, and the Cold War, 1945–1961.* New York: St. Martin's Griffin, 1997.

Hoberman, J. *An Army of Phantoms: American Movies and the Making of the Cold War.* New York: New Press, 2011.

———. *The Dream Life: Movies, Media, and the Mythology of the Sixties.* New York: New Press, 2003.

Horne, Gerald. *The Final Victim of the Blacklist: John Howard Lawson, Dean of the Hollywood Ten.* Berkeley: University of California Press, 2006.

Houston, Penelope. Review of *On the Waterfront. Sight and Sound* 24, no. 2 (1954): 85–86. Reprinted in Rapf, *On the Waterfront,* 158–61.

Howe, Irving, and Lewis Coser. *The American Communist Party: A Critical History.* New York: Da Capo, 1974.

Humphries, Reynold. *Hollywood's Blacklists: A Political and Cultural History.* Edinburgh: Edinburgh University Press, 2008.

Jacobs, Lea. *The Wages of Sin: Censorship and the Fallen Woman Film, 1928–1942.* Madison: University of Wisconsin Press, 1991.

Jameson, Fredric. *The Geopolitical Aesthetic: Cinema and Space in the World System.* Bloomington: Indiana University Press, 1995.

———. *Signatures of the Visible.* New York: Routledge, 1992.

Jancovich, Mark. "'The Purest Knight of All': Nation, History, and Representation in *El Cid* (1960)." *Cinema Journal* 40, no. 1 (2000): 79–103.

Johanningsmeier, Edward P. *Forging American Communism: The Life of William Z. Foster.* Princeton, NJ: Princeton University Press, 1994.

Johnson, William, ed. *Focus on the Science Fiction Film.* Englewood, NJ: Prentice-Hall, 1972.

Jones, Dorothy B. "Communism and the Movies: A Study of Film Content." In *Report on Blacklisting: Movies,* edited by John Cogley, 196–233. New York: Fund of the Republic, 1956.

Kackman, Michael. *Citizen Spy: Television, Espionage, and Cold War Culture.* Minneapolis: University of Minnesota Press, 2005.

Kahn, Gordon. *Hollywood on Trial: The Story of the Ten Who Were Indicted.* New York: Boni and Gaer, 1948.

Kahneman, Daniel. *Thinking, Fast and Slow.* New York: Farrar, Straus and Giroux, 2011.

Kanfer, Stefan. *A Journal of the Plague Years.* New York: Atheneum, 1973.

Kaplan, E. Ann, ed. *Women in Film Noir.* New ed. London: British Film Institute, 1998.

Kazan, Elia. *Elia Kazan: A Life.* New York: Knopf, 1988.

Keating, Patrick. *Hollywood Lighting: From the Silent Era to Film Noir.* New York: Columbia University Press, 2010.

Kelley, Theresa M. *Reinventing Allegory.* New York: Cambridge University Press, 1997.

Kellner, Douglas. *Cinema Wars: Hollywood Film and Politics in the Bush-Cheney Era.* Malden, MA: Wiley-Blackwell, 2010.

Kemp, Philip. "From the Nightmare Factory: HUAC and the Politics of Film Noir." *Sight and Sound* 55, no. 4 (1986): 266–70.

Keren, Gideon. "On the Definition and Possible Underpinnings of Framing Effects: A Brief Review and Critical Evaluation." In *Perspectives on Framing,* edited by Gideon Keren, 3–33. New York: Psychology Press, 2001.

King, Stephen. *Stephen King's Danse Macabre.* New York: Berkley, 1983.

Kitses, Jim. *Horizons West: Directing the Western from John Ford to Clint Eastwood.* London: British Film Institute, 2004.

Klehr, Harvey, John Earl Haynes, and Fridrikh Igorevich Firsov. *The Secret World of American Communism.* New Haven, CT: Yale University Press, 1995.

Kozloff, Sarah. *Overhearing Film Dialogue.* Berkeley: University of California Press, 2000.

Kreidl, John Francis. *Nicholas Ray.* Boston: Twayne, 1977.

Krutnik, Frank. *In a Lonely Street: Film Noir, Genre, and Masculinity.* London: Routledge, 1991.

Krutnik, Frank, Steve Neale, Brian Neve, and Peter Stanfield, eds. *"Un-'American" Hollywood: Politics and Film in the Blacklist Era.* New Brunswick, NJ: Rutgers University Press, 2007.

Kutler, Stanley I. *The American Inquisition: Justice and Injustice in the Cold War.* New York: Hill and Wang, 1982.

Kuznick, Peter J., and James Gilbert, eds. *Rethinking Cold War Culture.* Washington: Smithsonian Institution, 2001.

Langdon, Jennifer E. *Caught in the Crossfire: Adrian Scott and the Politics of Americanism in 1940s Hollywood.* New York: Columbia University Press, 2008.

Langford, Michelle. *Allegorical Images: Tableau, Time, and Gesture in the Cinema of Werner Schroeter.* Bristol, UK: Intellect, 2006.

Lardner, Ring, Jr. *I'd Hate Myself in the Morning: A Memoir.* New York: Thunder Mouth's Press/Nation Books, 2000.

Latteier, Pearl. "The Hollywood Social Problem Film, 1946–1959." PhD diss., University of Wisconsin–Madison, 2010.

Laura, Ernesto G. "Invasion of the Body Snatchers," *Bianco e nero* 18, no. 2 (1957): 69. Reprinted in Johnson, *Focus on the Science Fiction Film,* 71–73.

Lawson, John Howard. *Film in the Battle of Ideas.* New York: Masses and Mainstream, 1953.

Leab, Daniel J. "Hollywood and the Cold War, 1945–1961." In *Hollywood as Mirror: Changing Views of "Outsiders" and "Enemies" in American Movies,* edited by Robert Brent Toplin, 117–37. Westport, CT: Greenwood Press, 1993.

———. "How Red Was My Valley: Hollywood, the Cold War Film, and *I Married a Communist." Journal of American History* 19, no. 1 (1984): 59–88.

———. "*The Iron Curtain* (1948): Hollywood's First Cold War Movie." *Historical Journal of Film, Radio, and Television* 8, no. 2 (1988): 153–88.

———. *I Was a Communist for the FBI: The Unhappy Life and Times of Matt Cvetic.* University Park: Pennsylvania State University Press, 2000.

———. *Orwell Subverted: The CIA and the Filming of "Animal Farm."* University Park: Pennsylvania State University Press, 2007.

Leff, Leonard J., and Jerrold L. Simmons. *The Dame in the Kimono: Hollywood, Censorship and the Production Code from the 1920s to the 1960s.* New York: Grove Weidenfeld, 1990.

Lenihan, John. *Showdown: Confronting Modern America in the Western Film.* Urbana: University of Illinois Press, 1980.

Lewis, Jon. *Hollywood v. Hard Core: How the Struggle over Censorship Saved the Modern Film Industry.* New York: New York University Press, 2000.

———. "'We Do Not Ask You to Condone This': How the Blacklist Saved Hollywood." *Cinema Journal* 39, no. 2 (2000): 3–30.

Littlefield, Henry M. "*The Wizard of Oz:* Parable on Populism." *American Quarterly* 16, no. 1 (1964): 47–58.

Litvak, Joseph. *The Un-Americans: Jews, the Blacklist, and Stoolpigeon Culture.* Durham, NC: Duke University Press, 2009.

Livingston, Paisley. "Cinematic Authorship." In *Film Theory and Philosophy,* edited by Richard Allen and Murray Smith, 132–48. New York: Oxford University Press, 1997.

Lorence, James J. *The Suppression of "Salt of the Earth": How Hollywood, Big Labor, and Politicians Blacklisted a Movie in Cold War America.* Albuquerque: University of New Mexico Press, 1999.

Luciano, Patrick. *Them or Us: Archetypal Interpretations of Fifties Alien Invasion Films.* Bloomington: Indiana University Press, 1987.

Lyons, Arthur. *Death on the Cheap: The Lost B Movies of Film Noir.* New York: Da Capo, 2000.

Maltby, Richard. "Film Noir: The Politics of the Maladjusted Text." *Journal of American Studies* 18, no. 1 (1984): 49–71.

Maltin, Leonard. *Leonard Maltin's Movie & Video Guide.* New York: Signet, 1998.

Mann, Katrina. "'You're Next!' Postwar Hegemony Besieged in *Invasion of the Body Snatchers.*" *Cinema Journal* 44, no. 1 (2004): 49–68.

Marks, Michael J., and R. Chris Fraley. "Confirmation Bias and the Sexual Double Standard." *Sex Roles* 54, no. 1–2 (2006): 19–26.

Martin, Richard. *Mean Streets and Raging Bulls: The Legacy of Film Noir in Contemporary American Cinema.* Lanham, MD: Scarecrow, 1997.

McBride, Joseph. *Searching for John Ford.* New York: St. Martin's, 2001.

McGilligan, Patrick, and Paul Buhle. *Tender Comrades: A Backstory of the Blacklist.* New York: St. Martin's Griffin, 1999.

McRaney, David. *You Are Not So Smart: Why You Have Too Many Friends on Facebook, Why Your Memory Is Mostly Fiction and 46 Other Ways You're Deluding Yourself.* New York: Gotham, 2011.

Menand, Louis. Introduction to *The Manchurian Candidate,* by Richard Condon, vii–xiii. New York: Four Walls Eight Windows, 2001.

Miller, Anthony. "*Julius Caesar* in the Cold War: The Houseman-Mankiewicz Film." *Literature/Film Quarterly* 28, no. 2 (2000): 95–100.

Miller, Arthur. *Timebends: A Life.* New York: Grove, 1987.

Miller, Toby, and Robert Stam, eds. *A Companion to Film Theory.* Malden, MA: Blackwell, 1999.

Milne, Tom, ed. *Losey on Losey.* Garden City: Doubleday, 1968.

Mishler, Paul C. *Raising Reds: The Young Pioneers, Radical Summer Camps, and Communist Political Culture in the United States.* New York: Columbia University Press, 1999.

Mitchell, Lee Clark. *Westerns: Making the Man in Fiction and Film.* Chicago: University of Chicago Press, 1996.

Morgan, Ted. *Reds: McCarthyism in Twentieth-Century America.* New York: Random House, 2003.

Müller, Jürgen, ed. *Movies of the 50s.* New York: Barnes & Noble, 2006.

Murphy, Brenda. *Congressional Theatre: Dramatizing McCarthyism on Stage, Film, and Television.* New York: Cambridge University Press, 1999.

———. "Man on a Tightrope: Kazan as Liberal Anticommunist." In Dombrowski, *Kazan Revisited,* 56–71.

Muscio, Giuliana. "Roosevelt, Arnold, and Capra, (or) the Federalist-Populist Paradox." In *Frank Capra: Authorship and the Studio System*, edited by Robert Sklar and Vito Zagarrio, 164–89. Philadelphia: Temple University Press, 1998.

Nadel, Alan. *Containment Culture: American Narratives, Postmodernism, and the Atomic Age*. Durham, NC: Duke University Press, 1995.

Naison, Mark. *Communists in Harlem during the Depression*. Urbana: University of Illinois Press, 1983.

Naremore, James. "Authorship." In Miller and Stam, *A Companion to Film Theory*, 9–24.

———. *More Than Night: Film Noir in Its Contexts*. Berkeley: University of California Press, 1998.

Navasky, Victor S. "Mr. Kazan Goes to Washington: A Case Study of Misguided Ambivalence." In Dombrowski, *Kazan Revisited*, 49–55.

———. *Naming Names*. New York: Penguin, 1980.

Neale, Steve. *Genre and Hollywood*. New York: Routledge, 2000.

———. "Swashbuckling, Sapphire, and Salt." In Krutnik et al., *"Un-American" Hollywood*, 198–209.

Neve, Brian. *Film and Politics in America: A Social Tradition*. New York: Routledge, 1992.

———. "The 1950s: The Case of Elia Kazan and *On the Waterfront*." In *Cinema, Politics, and Society in America*, edited by Philip Davies and Brian Neve, 97–118. New York: St. Martin's, 1981.

———. "The Personal and the Political: Elia Kazan and *On the Waterfront*." In Rapf, *On the Waterfront*, 20–39.

Nichols, Bill, ed. *Movies and Methods: An Anthology*. 2 vols. Berkeley: University of California Press, 1976–85.

Nickerson, Raymond S. "Confirmation Bias: A Ubiquitous Phenomenon in Many Guises." *Review of General Psychology* 2, no. 2 (1998): 175–220.

O'Connor, John E., and Martin A. Jackson, eds. *American History / American Film*. New York: Frederick Ungar, 1979.

O'Donnell, Victoria. "Science Fiction Films and Cold War Anxiety." In *The Fifties: Transforming the Screen, 1950–1959*, edited by Peter Lev, 169–96. Berkeley: University of California Press, 2003.

Olmsted, Kathryn S. *Red Spy Queen: A Biography of Elizabeth Bentley*. Chapel Hill: University of North Carolina Press, 2002.

Oshinsky, David M. *A Conspiracy So Immense: The World of Joseph McCarthy*. New York: Oxford University Press, 2005.

Ottanelli, Fraser. *The Communist Party of the United States: From the Depression to World War II*. New Brunswick, NJ: Rutgers University Press, 1991.

Paul, William. *Ernst Lubitsch's American Comedies*. New York: Columbia University Press, 1983.

Peary, Danny. *Cult Movies: The Classics, the Sleepers, the Weird, and the Wonderful*. New York: Delta, 1981.

Peterson, Jennifer. "The Competing Tunes of *Johnny Guitar*: Liberalism, Sexuality, Masquerade." *Cinema Journal* 35, no. 3 (1996): 3–18.

Pinker, Steven. *The Stuff of Thought: Language as a Window on Human Nature*. New York: Viking, 2007.

Place, Janey. "Women in Film Noir." In *Women in Film Noir*, edited by E. Ann Kaplan, 35–67. London: British Film Institute, 1978.

Place, Janey, and Lowell Peterson. "Some Visual Motifs of Film Noir." *Film Comment* 10, no. 1 (1974): 30–32.

Polan, Dana. *Power and Paranoia: History, Narrative, and the American Cinema, 1940–1950*. New York: Columbia University Press, 1986.

———. *Scenes of Instruction: The Beginning of the U.S. Study of Film*. Berkeley: University of California Press, 2007.

Porfirio, Robert. "The Dark Age of American Film: A Study of American Film Noir, 1940–1960." 2 vols. PhD diss., Yale University, 1979.

Price, Theodore. *Hitchcock and Homosexuality: His 50 Year Obsession with Jack the Ripper and the Superbitch Prostitute—A Psychoanalytic View*. Metuchen, NJ: Scarecrow, 1992.

Quilligan, Maureen. *The Language of Allegory: Defining the Genre*. Ithaca, NY: Cornell University Press, 1979.

Radosh, Ronald, and Allis Radosh. *Red Star over Hollywood: The Film Colony's Long Romance with the Left*. New York: Encounter, 2006.

Rapf, Joanna E. "Introduction: 'The Mysterious Way of Art': Making a Difference in *On the Waterfront*." In Rapf, *On the Waterfront*, 1–19.

———, ed. *On the Waterfront*. New York: Cambridge University Press, 2003.

Record, Winston. *The Negro and the Communist Party*. Chapel Hill: University of North Carolina Press, 1951.

Reemes, Dana M. *Directed by Jack Arnold*. Jefferson, NC: McFarland, 1988.

Reisz, Karel. "Hollywood's Anti-Red Boomerang: Apple Pie, Love, and Endurance versus the Commies." *Sight and Sound* 22, no. 3 (1953): 132–37, 148.

Renov, Michael. *Hollywood's Wartime Women: Representation and Ideology*. Ann Arbor, MI: UMI Research Press, 1988.

Richards, Jeffrey. "Frank Capra and the Cinema of Populism." In Nichols, *Movies and Methods*, 1:65–78.

Rockoff, Hugh. "The 'Wizard of Oz' as a Monetary Allegory." *Journal of Political Economy* 98, no. 4 (1990): 739–60.

Rogin, Michael. *Ronald Reagan, the Movie and Other Episodes in Political Demonology*. Berkeley: University of California Press, 1987.

Rohdie, Sam. "Totems and Movies." In Nichols, *Movies and Methods*, 1:469–81.

Rohmer, Eric, and Claude Chabrol. *Hitchcock: The First Forty-Four Films*. Translated by Stanley Hochman. New York: Frederick Ungar, 1979.

Rollins, Peter C., and John E. O'Connor, eds. *Hollywood's West: The American Frontier in Film, Television, and History*. Lexington: University Press of Kentucky, 2005.

Rothman, William. *Hitchcock—The Murderous Gaze*. Cambridge, MA: Harvard University Press, 1982.

Rouverol, Jean. *Refugees from Hollywood: A Journal of the Blacklist Years.* Albuquerque: University of New Mexico Press, 2000.

Röwekamp, Burkhard. "The Thing from Another World." In Müller, *Movies of the 50s,* 6–11.

Ryan, James G. *Earl Browder: The Failure of American Communism.* Tuscaloosa: University of Alabama Press, 2005.

Samuels, Stuart. "The Age of Conspiracy and Conformity: *Invasion of the Body Snatchers* (1956)." In O'Connor and Jackson, *American History / American Film,* 203–17.

Sayre, Nora. *Running Time: Films of the Cold War.* New York: Dial, 1982.

Schauer, Brad. "Science Fiction Film and the Exploitation Tradition in Hollywood, 1956–1986." PhD diss., University of Wisconsin–Madison, 2010.

Schein, Harry. "Den Olympiske Cowboyen." *Bonniers litterära magasin,* Jan. 1954. Translated and reprinted as "The Olympic Cowboy," *American Scholar* 24, no. 3 (1955): 309–20.

Schlesinger, Arthur M., Jr. *The Vital Center: The Politics of Freedom.* New York: Riverside, 1949.

Schrader, Paul. "Notes on Film Noir." *Film Comment* 8, no. 1 (1972): 8–13.

Schrecker, Ellen. *The Age of McCarthyism: A Brief History with Documents.* New York: Bedford/St. Martin's, 2002.

———. *Many Are the Crimes: McCarthyism in America.* Princeton, NJ: Princeton University Press, 1998.

Schulberg, Budd. Foreword to Rapf, *On the Waterfront,* xv–xxii.

Schwartz, Nancy Lynn. *The Hollywood Writers' Wars.* New York: McGraw-Hill, 1983.

Schwartz, Richard A. *Cold War Culture: Media and the Arts.* New York: Checkmark, 1998.

Scott, Ian. *American Politics in Hollywood Film.* Chicago: Fitzroy Dearborn, 2000.

Seed, David. *American Science Fiction and the Cold War: Literature and Film.* Edinburgh: Edinburgh University Press, 1999.

Server, Lee. *Sam Fuller: Film Is a Battleground.* Jefferson, NC: McFarland, 1994.

Shadoian, Jack. *Dreams and Dead Ends: The American Gangster Film.* 2nd ed. New York: Oxford University Press, 2003.

Sharlet, Jeff. *The Family: The Secret Fundamentalism at the Heart of American Power.* New York: Harper Perennial, 2008.

Shaw, Tony. *Hollywood's Cold War.* Amherst: University of Massachusetts Press, 2007.

Skinner, Kiron K., Annelise Anderson, and Martin Anderson, eds. *Reagan, in His Own Hand: The Writings of Ronald Reagan That Reveal His Revolutionary Vision for America.* New York: Touchstone, 2002.

Slotkin, Richard. *The Fatal Environment: The Myth of the Frontier in the Age of Industrialization.* New York: Atheneum, 1985.

———. *Gunfighter Nation: The Myth of the Frontier in Twentieth-Century America.* New York: Atheneum, 1992.

————. *Regeneration through Violence: The Mythology of the American Frontier, 1600–1860*. Middletown, CT: Wesleyan University Press, 1973.

Smith, Jeff. "'A Good Business Proposition': Dalton Trumbo, *Spartacus*, and the End of the Hollywood Blacklist." In M. Bernstein, *Controlling Hollywood*, 206–37.

Smith, Murray. *Engaging Characters: Fiction, Emotion, and the Cinema*. New York: Oxford University Press, 1995.

Snyder, Mark, and Nancy Cantor. "Understanding Personality and Social Behavior: A Functionalist Strategy." In *The Handbook of Social Psychology*, ed. Daniel Gilbert, Susan T. Fiske, and Gardner Lindzey, 635–79. 4th ed. Boston: McGraw-Hill, 1998.

Sobchack, Vivian. *The Limits of Infinity: The American Science Fiction Film, 1950–1975*. New York: A. S. Barnes, 1980.

————. *Screening Space: The American Science Fiction Film*. New Brunswick, NJ: Rutgers University Press, 1987.

Sontag, Susan. *Illness as Metaphor*. New York: Farrar, Straus and Giroux, 1977.

————. "The Imagination of Disaster." In *Against Interpretation, and Other Essays*, 209–25. New York: Farrar, Straus and Giroux, 1966.

Spoto, Donald. *The Art of Alfred Hitchcock: Fifty Years of His Motion Pictures*. Garden City, NY: Dolphin, 1976.

Sproule, J. Michael. *Propaganda and Democracy: The American Experience of Media and Mass Persuasion*. New York: Cambridge University Press, 1997.

Staiger, Janet. *Interpreting Films: Studies in the Historical Reception of American Cinema*. Princeton, NJ: Princeton University Press, 1992.

Stanfield, Peter. *Maximum Movies—Pulp Fictions: Film Culture and the Worlds of Samuel Fuller, Mickey Spillane, and Jim Thompson*. Piscataway, NJ: Rutgers University Press, 2011.

Stephens, Michael. *Film Noir: A Comprehensive Illustrated Reference to Movies, Terms, and Persons*. Jefferson, NC: McFarland, 1995.

Strada, Michael, and Harold Troper. *Friend or Foe? Russians in American Film and Foreign Policy, 1933–1991*. London: Scarecrow, 1997.

Tambling, Jeremy. *Allegory*. New York: Routledge, 2010.

Telotte, J. P. "The Doubles of Fantasy and the Space of Desire." *Film Criticism* 6, no. 1 (1982): 56–68.

————. *Voices in the Dark: The Narrative Patterns of Film Noir*. Urbana: University of Illinois Press, 1989.

Teskey, Gordon. *Allegory and Violence*. Ithaca, NY: Cornell University Press, 1996.

Thompson, Kristin. *Breaking the Glass Armor: Neoformalist Film Analysis*. Princeton, NJ: Princeton University Press, 1988.

Tompkins, Jane. *West of Everything: The Inner Life of Westerns*. New York: Oxford University Press, 1992.

Trumbo, Dalton. *Additional Dialogue: Letters of Dalton Trumbo, 1942–1962*. Edited by Helen Manfull. New York: M. Evans, 1970.

————. *The Time of the Toad: A Study of Inquisition in America*. West Nyack, NY: Journeyman, 1949.

Twain, Mark. "The Man That Corrupted Hadleyburg." In *Great Short Works of Mark Twain*, edited by Justin Kaplan, 231–77. New York: Perennial, 1967.

Vanderwood, Paul J. "An American Cold Warrior: *Viva Zapata!*" In O'Connor and Jackson, *American History / American Film*, 183–201.

Van Dyke, Carolynn. *The Fiction of Truth: Structures of Meaning in Narrative and Dramatic Allegory*. Ithaca, NY: Cornell University Press, 1985.

Vasey, Ruth. *The World according to Hollywood, 1918–1939*. Madison: University of Wisconsin Press, 1997.

Vaughn, Robert. *Only Victims: A Study of Show Business Blacklisting*. New York: Proscenium, 1972.

Vaughn, Stephen. *Ronald Reagan in Hollywood: Movies and Politics*. Cambridge: Cambridge University Press, 1994.

Velez, Andrew. "Introduction." *The Woman on Pier 13: Screenplay*. New York: Frederick Ungar, 1976.

Vernet, Marc. "*Film Noir* on the Edge of Doom." In Copjec, *Shades of Noir*, 1–31.

Wager, Jans B. *Dangerous Dames: Women and Representation in the Weimar Street Film and Film Noir*. Athens: Ohio University Press, 1999.

Walker, Martin. *The Cold War: A History*. New York: Henry Holt, 1993.

Warshow, Robert. *The Immediate Experience: Movies, Comics, Theatre, and Other Aspects of Popular Culture*. New York: Atheneum, 1970.

Weaver, Tom. *Sci-Fi Confidential*. Jefferson, NC: McFarland, 2002.

Weiler, A. H. "The Screen: Astor Offers *On the Waterfront*." *New York Times*, July 29, 1954. Reprinted in Rapf, *On the Waterfront*, 151–53.

Wexman, Virginia Wright. "The Family on the Land: Race and Nationhood in Silent Westerns." In *The Birth of Whiteness: Race and the Emergence of U.S. Cinema*, edited by Daniel Bernard, 129–69. New Brunswick, NJ: Rutgers University Press, 1996.

Whitfield, Stephen J. *The Culture of the Cold War*. 2nd ed. Baltimore: Johns Hopkins University Press, 1996.

Wills, Garry. *John Wayne's America*. New York: Touchstone, 1997.

Wilmington, Michael. "Nicholas Ray's *Johnny Guitar*." *Velvet Light Trap* 12 (Spring 1974): 19–25.

Wood, Robin. *Hitchcock's Films*. New York: Paperback Library, 1970.

Woods, Jeff. *Black Struggle, Red Scare: Segregation and Anti-Communism in the South, 1948–1968*. Baton Rouge: Louisiana State University Press, 2004.

Wright, Will. *Six Guns and Society: The Structural Study of the Western*. Berkeley: University of California Press, 1975.

Wyke, Maria. *Projecting the Past: Ancient Rome, Cinema, and History*. New York: Routledge, 1997.

Xavier, Ismail. "Historical Allegory." In Miller and Stam, *A Companion to Film Theory*, 333–62.

Index

Academy Awards. *See* Oscars (Academy Awards)

Academy of Motion Picture Arts and Sciences, 8

actors, 3, 15, 137, 273

Actors Studio, 139–40

adventure films, 11

Adventures of Robin Hood, The (television series), 36

Advertising Code Administration, 71

Aesop, fables of, 21

Aesopian language, 21, 57, 200–201

African Americans, 14, 83, 84, 124, 126; *Broken Arrow* as parable of postwar assimilation of, 206; Communist Party policies appealing to, 86–88; as disenfranchised group, 161; in *I Was a Communist for the FBI*, 100, 104–8, 117; as party members, 83, 84, 87, 105; in *The Red Menace*, 91, 94, 99–100, 108, 117; southern blacks as "oppressed nation," 86

Agar, John, 62

agit-prop, 24

Al Qaeda, 32

Alamo, The (1960), 110, 309n34

Aleiss, Angela, 206, 207, 309n28

alien invasion, 32, 245–46, 251, 266; absence of emotion as sign of, 257; brainwashing and, 260; as hybrid of science fiction and horror, 242, 250;

as plague, 267. *See also* science fiction films

allegoresis, 30

allegories, 7, 9, 11, 14, 15, 120, 136; anti-Communist, 180; blacklist cinema and political allegory, 28–37; censorship evaded by, 137; Christianity in premodern allegories, 30, 39; cognitive psychology and, 37–41; corruption as trope of, 211; critics' use of, 171; definition of *allegory*, 16, 18, 29; didactic function of, 20–21; frames and reference points in interpretation of, 41–48, 120; "hide and seek" duality of blacklist allegories, 127; intention-utterance-interpretation framework and, 174; interpretation and, 20; in Kazan's films, 129, 139–40, 141–42, 146; literary, 30–36, 223; moral dimension of, 13; pragmatic allegories, 171–72; as rhetorical mode, 18; *The Robe* as, 173–84; science fiction films as, 15–16, 240, 242, 263, 268; in variety of film genres, 119; westerns as, 196, 197. *See also* double allegories

Allied Artists, 185

allusion, 30

amendments, constitutional: First Amendment, 40, 56, 84; Fifth Amendment, 56, 112, 121, 155–56, 165, 166

Communist Party, American
(CPUSA), 3, 5, 54, 231; as agents of
the Kremlin, 20; appeals to racial
minorities, 13, 14–15, 93; appeals to
women, 13, 77, 78, 82; in *Big Jim
McLain*, 114; cell as basic structural
unit of, 265; criminalization of
membership in, 61; electoral candi-
dates of, 86, 294n7; film noir criticized by, 60; Gitlow's exposé of, 163;
growth in 1930s, 54; in *I Married a
Communist*, 61–62; Kazan as member, 128; Ku Klux Klan compared to,
123–24, 126, 127, 169; left-wing
influences in Hollywood and, 40;
racial issues and, 83–88, 294n9; in
The Red Menace, 69, 91–100; sex
and criminal violence associated
with, 28; Smith Act prosecutions of
leaders, 4, 21, 55, 56, 178; witnesses'
past membership in, 155, 165
Communist threat, 9, 20, 89, 160; allegories from other historical periods,
172; atomic weapons associated
with, 253; disease metaphors and,
115; dramaturgical problems posed
by, 51; reference points in interpretation of, 43; in science fiction films,
252–53, 261; sleep and, 263–66
compositional imbalance, 59
Confessions of a Nazi Spy (1939),
103
Confidence Man, The (Melville), 31
confirmation bias, 46, 47, 275
conformity, 261–62
Constitution, U.S., 140
consumerism, 171
container-locative constructions, 44
content-locative constructions, 44
context-activated reception, 12–13
Cooper, Gary, 3, 52–53, 198, 204
Copland, Judith, 110
Corber, Robert J., 123, 161–62, 166,
301–2n88
Corkin, Stanley, 202–4, 207, 308n19
Cornthwaite, Robert, 259
Costello, Matthew, 236

Court Martial of Billy Mitchell, The
(1955), 172
courtroom dramas (legal thrillers), 28,
54, 119, 121, 169, 277
Cowboys as Cold Warriors (Corkin),
202
Cowdin, J. Cheever, 239
Cowie, Elizabeth, 59
Coyne, Michael, 234
Crawford, Joan, 212, *214*, 215
credits, restored, 10
crime melodramas, 28, 59, 60
criminal violence, Communism associ-
ated with, 28
Criss Cross (1949), 68
Cromwell, John, 57
crosscutting, 225, 226, 227
Crossfire (1947), 85, 87, 99
Crowther, Bosley, 6, 69, 107
Crucible, The (Miller), 33, 34–35, 43,
44, 146
Crusade for Freedom, 263
Crying of Lot 49, The (Pynchon), 30
Curtis, Tony, 193
Custen, George, 180, 303n13
Cvetic, Matt, 103, 104, 105, 106; as
anti-Communist icon, 101; ethnic
background of, 108; "true story" of,
107
Cyrino, Monica Silveira, 194

D'Agostino, Albert, 61
Daily Worker (Communist Party
newspaper), 7, 73–74, 282n29,
302n91; *The Red Menace* critiqued
in, 89, 90; *The Robe* reviewed in,
181–82; on science fiction films, 239,
255
Danse Macabre (King), 171
Dark Knight, The (2008), 32, 277
Darkness at High Noon (documentary
film, 2002), 198
Dassin, Jules, 138, 304n13
Daves, Delmer, 204, 207
David and Bathsheba (1951), 176
Davies, Joseph, 79–80
Davies, Lloyd G., 94

Wise, Robert, 248, 250
Wiseman, Joseph, 298n30
Wittgenstein, Ludwig, 59
Wizard of Oz, The (Baum), 32, 35
Wnoroski, Jim, 264
Woltman, Frederick, 72
Woman on Pier 17, The. See *I Married a Communist* (1949)
women: "bad girl," 76, 77; Communism's perceived appeal to, 13, 77, 78, 82; contrast of roles for Russian and American women, 79–80; as disenfranchised group, 161; female voice-over narrator, 92; norms of femininity and domesticity, 14, 76; "nurturing woman" archetype, 76, 77; wartime participation in U.S. workforce, 80–81, 293n66
Wood, Rep. John, 51
Wood, Robin, 163
wordplay, 30, 31, 44
Wordsworth, William, 21
World War I, 21
World War II, 55, 80–81, 177, 200, 293n66
World Wide Play Review, 254, 255, 312n33
Wright, Richard, 87–88
Wright, Will, 230
writers, blacklisted, 3, 8, 207; belated recognition of, 10; memoirs of, 17;

pseudonyms used by, 191. *See also* screenwriters
Writers Guild of America (WGA), 8, 185
Wrong Man, The (1957), 166
Wyke, Maria, 173, 180, 181, 185–86
Wyler, William, 10, 185
Wynter, Dana, 257

Xavier, Ismail, 171–72, 174, 189
xenophobia, 111, 137, 204, 250

Yates, George Worthing, 256
Yates, Herbert, 89
Yeaworth, Irvin, 241
yellow peril/yellow hordes, 111, 256
Yokinen, August, 86, 294n6
Yordan, Philip, 212, 215–16, 309–10n43
You Are Not So Smart (McRaney), 45
You Are There (television series), 35–36, 41, 172
Young, Art, 182

Zanuck, Darryl, 130, 148, 150–52, 153, 154, 170; private opposition to blacklist, 303–4n13; *The Robe* and, 176–77, 183
Zapata, Emiliano, 131–34
Zeldes, Jack D., 25
Zhdanovism, 303n9
Zinnemann, Fred, 197, 198, 210